VOLUME 609 JANUARY 2007

THE ANNALS

of The American Academy of Political
and Social Science

PHYLLIS KANISS, *Executive Editor*

*Race, Ethnicity, and Inequality
in the U.S. Labor Market:
Critical Issues in the New Millenium*

Special Editor of this Volume
GEORGE WILSON
University of Miami

SAGE Publications Thousand Oaks • London • New Delhi
Weeks-Townsend Memorial Library
Union College
Barbourville, KY 40906

The American Academy of Political and Social Science

3814 Walnut Street, Fels Institute of Government, University of Pennsylvania,
Philadelphia, PA 19104-6197; (215) 746-6500; (215) 573-3003 (fax); www.aapss.org

Board of Directors
DOUGLAS S. MASSEY, *President*
STEPHEN B. BURBANK, *Chair*

JULIA ADAMS	SARA MILLER McCUNE
ELIJAH ANDERSON	MARY ANN MEYERS
HARRY DeVERTER	KLAUS NAUDÉ
HEIDI HARTMANN	NORMAN H. NIE
DONALD F. KETTL	LOUIS H. POLLAK
JERRY LEE	ERIC WANNER
JANICE FANNING MADDEN	

Editors, THE ANNALS

PHYLLIS KANISS, *Executive Editor*   RICHARD D. LAMBERT, *Editor Emeritus*
JULIE ODLAND, *Managing Editor*

Origin and Purpose. The Academy was organized December 14, 1889, to promote the progress of political and social science, especially through publications and meetings. The Academy does not take sides in controverted questions, but seeks to gather and present reliable information to assist the public in forming an intelligent and accurate judgment.

Meetings. The Academy occasionally holds a meeting in the spring extending over two days.

Publications. THE ANNALS of The American Academy of Political and Social Science is the bimonthly publication of the Academy. Each issue contains articles on some prominent social or political problem, written at the invitation of the editors. Also, monographs are published from time to time, numbers of which are distributed to pertinent professional organizations. These volumes constitute important reference works on the topics with which they deal, and they are extensively cited by authorities throughout the United States and abroad. The papers presented at the meetings of the Academy are included in THE ANNALS.

Membership. Each member of the Academy receives THE ANNALS and may attend the meetings of the Academy. Membership is open only to individuals. Annual dues: $84.00 for the regular paperbound edition (clothbound, $121.00). Members may also purchase single issues of THE ANNALS for $17.00 each (clothbound, $26.00). Student memberships are available for $53.00.

Subscriptions. THE ANNALS of The American Academy of Political and Social Science (ISSN 0002-7162) (J295) is published six times annually—in January, March, May, July, September, and November—by Sage Publications, 2455 Teller Road, Thousand Oaks, CA 91320. Telephone: (800) 818-SAGE (7243) and (805) 499-9774; Fax/Order line: (805) 499-0871; e-mail: journals@sagepub.com. Copyright © 2007 by The American Academy of Political and Social Science. Institutions may subscribe to THE ANNALS at the annual rate: $612.00 (clothbound, $692.00). Single issues of THE ANNALS may be obtained by individuals who are not members of the Academy for $34.00 each (clothbound, $47.00). Single issues of THE ANNALS have proven to be excellent supplementary texts for classroom use. Direct inquiries regarding adoptions to THE ANNALS c/o Sage Publications (address below). Periodicals postage paid at Thousand Oaks, California, and at additional mailing offices.

All correspondence concerning membership in the Academy, dues renewals, inquiries about membership status, and/or purchase of single issues of THE ANNALS should be sent to THE ANNALS c/o Sage Publications, 2455 Teller Road, Thousand Oaks, CA 91320.Telephone: (800) 818-SAGE (7243) and (805) 499-9774; Fax/Order line: (805) 499-0871; e-mail: journals@sagepub.com. *Please note that orders under $30 must be prepaid.* Sage affiliates in London and India will assist institutional subscribers abroad with regard to orders, claims, and inquiries for both subscriptions and single issues.

Printed on acid-free paper

THE ANNALS
© 2007 by The American Academy of Political and Social Science

All rights reserved. No part of this volume may be reproduced or utilized in any form or by any means, electronic or mechanical, including photocopying, recording, or by any information storage and retrieval system, without permission in writing from the publisher. All inquiries for reproduction or permission should be sent to Sage Publications, 2455 Teller Road, Thousand Oaks, CA 91320.

Editorial Office: 3814 Walnut Street, Fels Institute for Government, University of Pennsylvania, Philadelphia, PA 19104-6197.
For information about membership* (individuals only) and subscriptions (institutions), address:
Sage Publications
2455 Teller Road
Thousand Oaks, CA 91320

For Sage Publications: Joseph Riser and Esmeralda Hernandez

From India and South Asia, write to:
SAGE PUBLICATIONS INDIA Pvt Ltd
B-42 Panchsheel Enclave, P.O. Box 4109
New Delhi 110 017
INDIA

From Europe, the Middle East, and Africa, write to:
SAGE PUBLICATIONS LTD
1 Oliver's Yard, 55 City Road
London EC1Y 1SP
UNITED KINGDOM

*Please note that members of the Academy receive THE ANNALS with their membership.
International Standard Serial Number ISSN 0002-7162
International Standard Book Number ISBN 978-1-4129-5503-4 (Vol. 609, 2007 paper)
International Standard Book Number ISBN 978-1-4129-5502-7 (Vol. 609, 2007 cloth)
Manufactured in the United States of America. First printing, January 2007.

The articles appearing in *The Annals* are abstracted or indexed in Academic Abstracts, Academic Search, America: History and Life, Asia Pacific Database, Book Review Index, CABAbstracts Database, Central Asia: Abstracts &Index, Communication Abstracts, Corporate ResourceNET, Criminal Justice Abstracts, Current Citations Express, Current Contents: Social & Behavioral Sciences, Documentation in Public Administration, e-JEL, EconLit, Expanded Academic Index, Guide to Social Science & Religion in Periodical Literature, Health Business FullTEXT, HealthSTAR FullTEXT, Historical Abstracts, International Bibliography of the Social Sciences, International Political Science Abstracts, ISI Basic Social Sciences Index, Journal of Economic Literature on CD, LEXIS-NEXIS, MasterFILE FullTEXT, Middle East: Abstracts&Index, North Africa: Abstracts&Index, PAIS International, Periodical Abstracts, Political Science Abstracts, Psychological Abstracts, PsycINFO, Sage Public Administration Abstracts, Scopus, Social Science Source, Social Sciences Citation Index, Social Sciences Index Full Text, Social Services Abstracts, SocialWork Abstracts, Sociological Abstracts, Southeast Asia: Abstracts& Index, Standard Periodical Directory (SPD), TOPICsearch, Wilson OmniFileV, and Wilson Social Sciences Index/Abstracts, and are available on microfilm from ProQuest, Ann Arbor, Michigan.

Information about membership rates, institutional subscriptions, and back issue prices may be found on the facing page.

Advertising. Current rates and specifications may be obtained by writing to The Annals Advertising and Promotion Manager at the Thousand Oaks office (address above).

Claims. Claims for undelivered copies must be made no later than six months following month of publication. The publisher will supply missing copies when losses have been sustained in transit and when the reserve stock will permit.

Change of Address. Six weeks' advance notice must be given when notifying of change of address to ensure proper identification. Please specify name of journal. POSTMASTER: Send address changes to The Annals of The American Academy of Political and Social Science, c/o Sage Publications, 2455 Teller Road, Thousand Oaks, CA 91320.

THE ANNALS

OF THE AMERICAN ACADEMY OF
POLITICAL AND SOCIAL SCIENCE

Volume 609   January 2007

IN THIS ISSUE:

*Race, Ethnicity, and Inequality
in the U.S. Labor Market:
Critical Issues in the New Millenium*

Special Editor: GEORGE WILSON

Introduction . . . . *George Wilson*	6
Social Closure and Processes of Race/Sex Employment Discrimination . . . . *Vincent J. Roscigno, Lisette M. Garcia, and Donna Bobbitt-Zeher*	16
Discrimination and Desegregation: Equal Opportunity Progress in U.S. Private Sector Workplaces since the Civil Rights Act . . . . *Donald Tomaskovic-Devey and Kevin Stainback*	49
Racial Composition of Workgroups and Job Satisfaction among Whites . . . . *David J. Maume and Rachel Sebastian*	85
The Use of Field Experiments for Studies of Employment Discrimination: Contributions, Critiques, and Directions for the Future . . . . *Devah Pager*	104
Family Background, Race, and Labor Market Inequality . . . . *Dalton Conley and Rebecca Glauber*	134

What Happens to Potential Discouraged?
   Masculinity Norms and the Contrasting
   Institutional and Labor Market Experiences
   of Less Affluent Black and White Men . . . . *Deirdre A. Royster*   153

Black Underrepresentation in Management
   across U.S. Labor Markets . . . . *Philip N. Cohen*
                                                    and Matt L. Huffman   181

Demobilization of the Individualistic Bias:
   Housing Market Discrimination
   as a Contributor to Labor Market
   and Economic Inequality . . . . *Gregory D. Squires*   200

Racialized Life-Chance Opportunities
   across the Class Structure:
   The Case of African Americans. . . . . *George Wilson*   215

Quick Read Synopsis

Race, Ethnicity, and Inequality in the U.S. Labor Market:
   Critical Issues in the New Millennium.   233

FORTHCOMING

NAFTA and Beyond:
Alternative Disciplinary Perspectives in
the Study of Global Trade and Development
Special Editors: PATRICIA FERNÁNDEZ-KELLY
and JON SHEFNER
Volume 610, March 2007

The Politics of Consumption/
The Consumption of Politics
Special Editors: DHAVAN V. SHAH, LEWIS FRIEDLAND,
DOUGLAS McLEOD, and MICHELLE NELSON
Volume 611, May 2007

Social Entrepreneurship for Women and Minorities
Special Editors: JIM JOHNSON, TIM BATES, and WILLIAM JACKSON
Volume 612, July 2007

Introduction

By
GEORGE WILSON

Studies of racial/ethnic inequality in the American labor market at the dawn of the new millennium are, arguably, of unprecedented importance. First, from a sheer numbers standpoint, forms of inequality have the potential to have more widespread consequences than in the past: in recent decades, racial/ethnic minorities (both males and females) have experienced growing representation in the American labor market. In this vein, their proportion of the full-time labor force has nearly doubled since 1970 (Foner and Frederickson 2004), and it is projected that this trend will accelerate in the next few decades (Farley 1996). In addition, along this same line, the number of minority groups in the labor force in the United States has increased: the growing number of groups who have a more visible presence than in the past is a product of the "new immigration" in the post-1965 period, which has included Latino and sub-Latino groups; Asian populations from virtually all parts of that continent; as well as a growing number of groups from the Middle East, the continent of Africa, and the small island countries in the Caribbean (Farley 1996; Bean and Bell-Rose 1999). Second, a range of emerging trends within racial and ethnic minority populations pose fundamental new research challenges for sociologists. Especially noteworthy, in this regard, is the growing socioeconomic differentiation experienced by minority groups in recent decades (Farley 1996; Anderson and Massey 2000). In particular, minorities have become increasingly represented across the hierarchical occupational structure from low-end, entry-level positions in the rapidly expanding service sector, to traditional manual labor occupations associated with the "working class" to management, executive, and professional positions that constitute the basis for the new minority "middle class" (Landry 1987). Accordingly, researchers continue to focus principally on issues of exclusion on

DOI: 10.1177/0002716206297017

the basis of race/ethnicity from coveted slots across the occupational structure. A critical new focus of research is the equivalency of material and symbolic "returns" among racial/ethnic majority and minority incumbents who are similarly situated and who have similar profiles regarding, for example, human capital endowments (Tomaskovic-Devey 1993; Niemonen 2002; Wilson 1997).

[A] range of emerging trends within racial and ethnic minority populations pose fundamental new research challenges for sociologists.

With these trends serving as a backdrop, a large and continuously growing body of sociological research in recent decades has examined issues surrounding the extent to which race and ethnicity serve as a source of socioeconomic inequality in the American labor market. While the sheer volume of this research output precludes providing an in-depth summary of findings, it does not seem contentious or controversial to offer a general conclusion: race and ethnicity continue to matter as salient factors in the American labor market. Accordingly, findings from this voluminous literature have helped to assess the merits of prominent theoretical perspectives that most directly address the nature and extent of racial/ethnic stratification in the American workplace. Two examples of this will suffice: findings render fundamentally incorrect the predictions from what is now a relatively distant generation of sociologists, who, operating through the lens of a structural functional theory, maintained that the use of ascriptive criteria such as race and ethnicity were deemed fundamentally incompatible with the logical imperatives dictated by advanced capitalist societies that put a premium on meritocratic criteria and principles of efficiency in determining access to socioeconomic rewards in the American labor market (Glazer and Moynihan 1975; Stone 1985). Furthermore, findings from contemporary studies have demonstrated that facile and sweeping conclusions regarding the accuracy of the more recently enunciated thesis about the "declining significance of race" (Wilson 1978), at least, as it applies to dynamics within the civil rights era, are unwarranted. For example, it appears to vary across discrete labor market outcomes (e.g., more support for the thesis = race/class determinants of intragenerational and intergenerational occupational mobility [Hout 1984; Featherman and Hauser 1978]; less support for the thesis = returns in the form of earnings to individuals across racial/ethnic groups who occupy similar positions in the occupational/job structure [Niemonen 2002; Tomaskovic-Devey 1993; Wilson 1997]).

Overall, in contemporary studies, a series of overarching analytic approaches that posit how race/ethnicity operate to structure inequality in the American labor market can be identified. Two such prominent approaches are offered as illustrations. The first maintains that race/ethnicity operates under the umbrella of broader causal statements about the distribution of rewards in the labor market. Illustrative of this are attempts to analyze race/ethnicity in the workplace in the context of theories of class conflict (Bonacich and Modell 1980; Rosenfeld 1980; Wright 1985) as well as within the framework of tools adopted from neoclassical economics—such as "monopolistic" practices that have been used to maintain that strategically placed groups that have incentives to maintain racial/ethnic inequality (Williams 1982). A second line of research is noteworthy because it assesses the salience of race/ethnicity in the workplace on a basis that is independent of, and not reducible to, other causal, supposedly more fundamental determinants such as class relations and the logic of supply and demand dynamics in the labor market (Omi and Winant 1994; Pettigrew and Martin 1987). In particular, the thrust of the approach derives from causal statements about the immediacy of race/ethnicity as a "meaning system" (Omi and Winant 1994) that permeates a range of institutional spheres—such as the workplace—in daily life, so that inequality is related to historically contingent, shifting ideologies of race/ethnicity (Bobo, Kluegel, and Smith 1997; Omi and Winant 1994; Bonilla-Silva and Forman 2000).

Race and ethnicity continue to matter as salient factors in the American labor market.

These overarching analytic approaches are reflected in contributions to this volume of *The Annals*. Nevertheless, the pieces contained in the volume may, perhaps, best be thought of as constituting a representative sample of the most important substantive and methodological issues sociologists are addressing as they tackle the complex relationship between racial/ethnic status and patterns of labor market inequality as the new millennium unfolds. The piece by Roscigno, Garcia, and Bobbitt-Zeher is an important call for the integration of a mature conceptualization of social closure into analyses of the processes that drive racial/ethnic and gender inequality in the American labor market. The authors do an exemplary job of detailing this mature conceptualization and also take a step toward demonstrating its viability in empirical analysis. For the authors, processes of social closure are predicated on analyzing across bases of exclusion (e.g., firing, failure to promote, harassment, etc.) how discriminatory practices operate within the context of firm structure and goals, which, in turn, help to account for structure varying degrees of opportunity for, and constraint upon, employers to resort to discriminatory practices. This dynamic conceptualization, which injects structure-agency dynamics between employers and firms (as well as among the victims of discrimination who react to and make efforts to ameliorate their plight and, ultimately, reinforce or contest it on a daily basis) is best captured by a multimethod approach based on complementary qualitative and quantitative strategies in which narrative can fill out the interpretation of findings from regression analyses. In fact, the kind of closure analysis Roscigno, Garcia, and Bobbitt-Zeher advocate has been difficult to carry out in prior research because of a variety of substantive and methodological limitations, including (1) the tendency to rely upon one method, usually the analysis of representative survey data, in which case discriminatory processes are inferred from patterns of significant and nonsignificant regression coefficients; (2) the tendency to use nationally or locally representative data rather than firm or establishment-level data, which produces a de-contextualized analysis in which discriminatory processes sought to be identified and explained are not related to firm/organizational behavior; and (3) the tendency to restrict the scope of study to one basis of exclusion. Empirically, the authors move in the direction of the kind of closure analysis they advocate through an examination of unique data, namely, documented "serious" equal employment opportunity (EEO) cases from Ohio, which are used in a complementary quantitative and qualitative fashion to assess processes of race and gender inequality. The results from analyses are contextually sensitive and nuanced with expulsion and harassment emerging as the principle bases of closure, which, in turn, are a product of dynamics as diverse as "differing policing," and particularly in the context of race, "particularistic" employment practices. Finally, not to be overlooked, and consistent with theoretical concerns, the authors place underlying causal dynamics in the context of firm-driven opportunities for employers to practice discrimination.

The important piece by Tomaskovic-Devey and Stainback examines the impact of EEO law on patterns of racial/ethnic (i.e., African Americans, whites, Latinos, Asians) inequality across the post-1965 civil rights era. Specifically, the authors use establishment-level EEO data to examine changing access to coveted working-class (craftsmen) and middle-class (professional/managerial) slots (indexed by segregation levels) as well as search for sources of variation in access, primarily, in organizational dynamics. The sample analyzed is uniquely broad, and the analysis of developments over the course of an era that has too often been treated as monolithic is a vital contribution (see Wilson 2005; Stainback, Robinson, and Tomaskovic-Devey 2005) but, perhaps, what is most important is making organization/firm dynamics causal centerpieces in their study. Conspicuously absent in the formal analysis of organizational structure, goals, and concerns is how they are related to issues of inequality. The authors posit that firms are critical entities that interact with legal mandates in a dynamic fashion to structure levels of inequality. In the context of EEO law, its interpretation and application by firms is not straightforward. Consistent with tendencies toward inertia, conservatism, and interest in maintaining existing stratification hierarchies, firms are noninnovative and proceed along lines toward equality only as far as they have to. Accordingly, at various times, firm interpretation and application of EEO law will range from resistance to symbolic compliance to more meaningful compliance so that the force of discriminatory mechanisms including statistical discrimination, homosocial reproduction, and forms of cognitive bias, all of which constitute proximate causes of exclusion and closure, will wax and wane temporally. The authors project that the greatest inroads by minorities in access to coveted slots are made in (1) periods of organizational uncertainty regarding how to accommodate EEO law (typically, at an early stage after legal enactments); and (2) in situations when "stakes" for firms are low, that is, they will make greatest accommodations in contexts where they have the least to lose (increased access to lower-level positions across a relatively broad time span of the post-1965 period). In fact, the authors' empirical analyses support their theoretical discussion. Specifically, among the majority of groups considered, most ground in access to upper-tier position occurred in the first decade of the civil rights era, but they have stagnated or suffered retrenchment in access thereafter, and minorities have gradually become more integrated into lower-levels slots throughout the same period. Overall, Tomaskovic-Devey and Stainback's article constitutes a call to reform how sociologists conduct analyses of the effects of workplace-based policies—such as EEO legal mandates—that are directed at social change: we need to consider how their impact is mediated by dynamic agents, namely, the very firms that are entrusted to accommodate social change.

Maume and Sebastian address the relationship between racial/ethnic status and job satisfaction, an experiential domain in the workplace that is of importance because, for example, it has a demonstrated relationship to material attainments such as earnings and mobility trajectories (Tuch and Martin 1991). Findings from previous studies across racial/ethnic groups have found overwhelming support for "structural" determinants; that is, levels of satisfaction are rooted in intrinsic characteristics of jobs, such as amount of task repetitiveness and creativity, rather than "dispositional" factors encompassing values and orientations brought to the workplace that mediate the impact of structural characteristics of jobs on levels of satisfaction. Maume and Sebastian's focus on whites enhances our understanding of the durability of the structural explanation for job satisfaction. Specifically, their analyses of data from the National Studies of the Workforce reveal that the racial/ethnic composition of the workplace, a potential causal explanation not considered in prior research, is not as statistically significant a determinant of whites' satisfaction as the nature of the jobs themselves. Accordingly, negative racial affect or feelings of ill will toward minorities that often accompanies increasing diversity in the workplace is more than compensated for by the job tasks and/or material rewards associated with job tasks in determining levels of job satisfaction.

The piece by Pager is both an important discussion of audit studies as an approach to identify discrimination in the labor market and a timely analysis of how audit studies are related to other methodological approaches to accomplish the same end. A hallmark of Pager's article is her synthetic and integrative analysis: whether of the "correspondence test" (Bertrand and Mullainathan 2004) or "in-person" (Pager 2003) variety, audit studies represent one of the most rigorous ways to identify discrimination, though they appear to be most suited to analyzing dynamics at the hiring stage. Other approaches—such as survey analyses of representative samples—appear to shed light on discriminatory dynamics at other phases (such as promotion and material compensation) of the employment process (Tomaskovic-Devey 2005; Wilson 1997). Accordingly, squabbles about methodological propriety, which are rooted in divergent findings regarding level of discrimination across methodological approaches, are misplaced and can be reconciled on at least one fundamental ground—different methods have been used to assess discrimination at different stages of the employment process, where varying levels of discrimination would be expected. Pager is cognizant that in an era in which overt discrimination is not pronounced and assumes a more benign, subtle, and even ostensibly nonracial form than in the Jim Crow era (Bobo, Kluegel, and Smith 1997; Wilson 1997), divergent substantive findings should be expected, and this can be the basis of descending into attacks about methods. The author urges sociologists to take steps to stave off this often nonproductive form of discourse by paying heed to the nuanced and complex subject matter, namely, discrimination.

Conley and Glauber's piece also breaks new ground. In the context of race, studies of intergenerational occupational mobility, which have been conducted primarily in the status attainment (Featherman and Hauser 1978; Sewell, Haller, and Portes 1969) and race/class (Hout 1984; Pomer 1986) substantive contexts, have found that class effects exert a weaker influence in the transmission process for African Americans than whites. Significantly, the weaker effects have been interpreted as a reflection of a more haphazard and discrimination-laden mobility process, which severs the class link in transmission for African Americans. The point of departure for Conley and Glauber are two conceptual limitations in existing studies: first, they tend to focus on only one socioeconomic outcome, with the majority of studies focusing on either occupation or a composite measure of socioeconomic status. Second, studies tend to use only one time point across the adult life span. The authors use a life-course perspective to assess the degree of similarity/difference in family income, individual earnings, and occupational prestige among siblings, which serves as a proxy for the effect of background status. Their findings with Panel Study of Income Dynamics (PSID) data across the early stages of the adult life span are similar to those from previous research. However, past the age of forty—a later stage of the life span—data for African American siblings converge rapidly. Based on these findings and on an impressive knowledge of speculative causal statements made in prior research, the authors maintain that at least two scenarios emerge, each of which depicts vastly differing stratification dynamics. On one hand, "intervening events," that is, discriminatory behaviors that early in the adult life span set African Americans back relative to whites, as well as separate the attainments of African American siblings, may be overcome as the work-career proceeds. Thus, similar to whites,

African Americans in the civil rights era increasingly transmit status across generations. On the other hand, the effects of "resource constraint" that cause African American parents to invest in only one sibling, thus creating differences at an early career stage, is negated by discrimination in employment that cause siblings to converge as they regress to a low mean level in socioeconomic attainments. These are fundamentally differing processes that have completely different stratification trajectories. Thanks to the authors, we now know we need to conduct additional research to determine which set of dynamics are at work.

Royster's article is a statement about the irreducibility of race/ethnic differences in socioeconomic attainments to class stratification in the American labor market. Her impressive synthesis of relevant literatures, which she brings to bear on her analysis of her Baltimore sample, identifies the sources of divergent labor market trajectories among less affluent African American youth, relative to white youth who have similar norms, aspirations, and labor market potential. In this vein, Royster documents the cumulative relative disadvantage experienced by African American youth in the schooling process and how it leads to a drastically inferior transition to the American labor market. For example, during school years, school officials respond differently to students' masculine behavior (African Americans = conform to invidious stereotypes about fitness for and commitment to work that are permanent characteristics of adults; Whites = seen as temporary aberrations so that "boys will be boys"). This discrimination creates differential access to meaningful job-related networks that, in significant part, are structured by school officials. A side effect is seemingly mundane differential acceptance by schools of youth rebellion styles of comportment and dress (African American = certain jean brands and sweat suits, banned; Whites = "satanic" looking t-shirts, not banned) produce race-based perceptions of belonging and alienation from school, and set in motion racial differences in early career dynamics. Furthermore, add to this scenario, as Royster skillfully does, the differential impact by way of stigma and legal proscriptions on certain types of work that result from relatively higher rates of incarceration and felony arrest among African American youth (which may also be discriminatorily induced—see Pager 2003), and you have a formula for labor market disadvantage among black youth as they enter the "starting gate" in the labor market and that presumably carries over to disadvantage in medium- and long-term career trajectories relative to white youth. Finally, Royster's passionate call for "institutional accountability" in producing these inequities among African Americans, who bring relatively few skills by way of social/cultural capital and other resources to resist the inequities, particularly, in the education system is timely and resonates with considerable force.

Cohen and Huffman's ambitious article focuses on the causes and consequences of restricted minority access to managerial slots. Rooted theoretically in competition theory (Olzak and Nagel 1986; Burr, Galle, and Fossett 1991), the authors use EEO establishment-level data from 2002 to empirically assess the extent to which restricted minority access is a product of the racial composition of local labor markets. Significantly, in this vein, the authors—in a very conscious manner—build on previous research that has found that increasing minority composition in local labor markets is related to other outcomes, including most notably wages inequality (Cohen 1998; Huffman and Cohen 2004). The authors find considerable support for the notion that increases in minority concentration in labor markets (but not firms) induces whites to engage in dynamics of exclusion from minority access to managerial slots. Accordingly, this finding, in conjunction with those from previous research, serve as the foundation for the authors' critical and insightful conclusion: black exclusion from management creates the basis for whites to engage in discriminatory practices in other aspects of the employment experience—such as firing, hiring, promotion, and wages. In other words, the authors conclude that discrimination across a wide range of labor market outcomes is traceable back to minority exclusion from managerial and, presumably, other key decision-making positions. The article by Cohen and Huffman enhances our understanding of the breadth of competition theory: competitively driven lack of access of minorities to key decision-making roles, which, in turn, are rooted in labor market composition, triggers socioeconomic disadvantage across a wide range of outcomes in the American labor market.

The piece by Squires is unique in focusing on issues regarding the ideological lens used to diagnose patterns of racial/ethnic stratification. In particular, Squires is concerned with identifying impediments to constructing a "structural" level (i.e., extraindividual causal explanations focusing on institutions, discriminatory policies, etc.) diagnosis of the sources of racial/ethnic inequality in the residential and employment spheres as well as establishing causal links between the two institutional spheres. The culprit, for Squires, is the "individualistic bias," which is an aspect of the "dominant American stratification ideology" (Huber and Form 1973) and is deeply embedded in our cultural fabric: blaming the personal characteristics of the victim is a hallmark of the individualistic causal analysis, and adherence to it, according to Squires, precludes using research that has documented how forms of socioeconomic disadvantage and unequal treatment in the labor market are directly a product of finite opportunities in the residential market. For example, well-documented residential segregation in the residential market experienced in the most pronounced fashion by African Americans, and to a lesser extent by Latinos and Asians (Massey and Denton 1987, 1993) at all levels of the class structure inhibits life-chance opportunities through limited access to important informal networks that generate knowledge of market opportunities and offer opportunities to demonstrate informal, job-relevant, personal characteristics that overcome invidious stereotypes (Royster 2003; Massey and Denton 1993), as well as restricting individuals to disadvantaged local/neighborhood opportunity structures (Wilson 1996). For Squires, who is deeply concerned with policy implications of social science analyses, the "bottom line" is the failure to engage in a structural level analysis of racial/ethnic stratification across major institutional spheres, which precludes obtaining the fundamental analytic tools necessary to generate a meaningful solution to fundamental inequities that can be ameliorated.

Finally, the piece by Wilson is also concerned with the stratification-relevance of the residential and employment spheres. In particular, Wilson examines how the two institutional spheres account for racialized life-chance opportunities at the impoverished and middle-class levels. Based on an integration of sociological research, he documents that, at both class levels, segregation in the employment and residential spheres constitutes analytically separable but interlocking sources of economic prospects for African Americans that are inferior to those of white class peers. However, at the impoverished level, segregation in the residential sphere, and at the middle-class level, segregation in the employment sphere, are particularly critical underpinnings of African Americans' inferior life-chance opportunities. Finally, these findings are the basis of the author's argument that, in the context of race/ethnicity, classic Marxian and Weberian modes of class analysis may have questionable utility: politically induced dynamics as the basis of class position and inferior socioeconomic rewards at discrete class levels for African Americans vis-à-vis white class peers is not consonant with either classic conceptualization, both of which maintain that class position is based on a defined set of socioeconomic rewards that derive from laboring in the private labor market.

In sum, the well-crafted and thoughtful pieces contained in this volume represent significant and timely contributions that enhance our understanding of the dynamics of racial/ethnic inequality in the contemporary American labor market. The brevity of any overview of their contents is bound to constitute an injustice. Hopefully, however, the overview will serve to spur the reader to consult the pieces in the original. They deserve that attention as sociologists strive to further understand the dynamics of a crucial cleavage that continues to account for inequality in the new millennium.

References

Anderson, Elijah, and Douglas Massey, eds. 2000. *Problem of the century: Racial stratification in the United States*. New York: Russell Sage Foundation.
Bean, Frank, and Stephanie Bell-Rose. 1999. *Immigration and opportunity*. New York: Russell Sage Foundation.
Bertrand, Marianne, and Sendhil Mullainathan. 2004. Are Emily and Greg more employable than Lakisha and Jamal? A field experiment on labor market discrimination. *American Economic Review* 94:991-1013.
Bobo, Lawrence, James Kluegel, and Ryan Smith. 1997. Laissez-faire racism: The crystallization of a kinder, gentler, antiblack ideology. In *Racial attitudes in the 1990's*, ed. Steven Tuch and Jack Martin, 15-44. Westport, CT: Praeger.
Bonacich, Edna, and John Modell. 1980. *The economic basis of ethnic solidarity*. Berkeley: University of California Press.
Bonilla-Silva, Eduardo, and Tyrone Forman. 2000. I am not a racist but . . . Mapping white college students' racial ideology in the USA. *Discourse and Society* 13:50-85.
Burr, Jeffrey, Omer Galle, and Mark Fossett. 1991. Racial occupational inequality in southern metropolitan areas: 1940-1980: Revising the visibility-discrimination hypothesis. *Social Forces* 69:831-51.
Cohen, Philip. 1998. Black concentration effects on black-white and gender inequality: Multilevel analyses for U.S. metropolitan areas. *Social Forces* 77:207-29.
Farley, Reynolds. 1996. *The new American reality*. New York: Russell Sage Foundation.
Featherman, David, and Robert Hauser. 1978. *Opportunity and change*. New York: Academic Press.

Foner, Nancy, and George Frederickson, eds. 2004. *Not just black and white.* New York: Russell Sage Foundation.
Glazer, Nathan, and Daniel Moynihan, eds. 1975. *Ethnicity: Theory and experience.* Cambridge, MA: Harvard University Press.
Hout, Michael. 1984. Occupational mobility of black men: 1962-1973. *American Sociological Review* 49:308-23.
Huber, Joan, and William Form. 1973. *Income and ideology: An analysis of the American political formula.* Glencoe, IL: Free Press.
Huffman, Matt, and Philip Cohen. 2004. Racial wage inequality: Job segregation and devaluation across U.S. labor markets. *American Journal of Sociology* 109:902-36.
Landry, Bart. 1987. *The new black middle class.* Berkeley: University of California Press.
Massey, Douglas, and Nancy Denton. 1987. Residential segregation among blacks, Hispanics, and Asians by age and socioeconomic status. *Social Science Quarterly* 43:296-310.
———. 1993. *American apartheid.* Chicago: University of Chicago Press.
Niemonen, Jack. 2002. *Race, class and the state in contemporary sociology.* Boulder, CO: Lynne Riener.
Olzak, Susan, and Joane Nagel. 1986. *Competitive ethnic relations.* New York: Academic Press.
Omi, Michael, and Howard Winant. 1994. *Racial formation in the United States.* New York: Routledge.
Pager, Devah. 2003. The mark of a criminal record. *American Journal of Sociology* 108:937-75.
Pettigrew, Thomas, and Joanne Martin. 1987. Shaping the organizational context for African American inclusion. *Journal of Social Issues* 43:41-78.
Pomer, Marshall. 1986. Labor market structure, intragenerational mobility, and discrimination. *American Sociological Review* 51:650-59.
Rosenfeld, R. 1980. Race and sex differences in career dynamics. *American Sociological Review* 45:583-609.
Royster, Deirdre. 2003. *Race and the invisible hand.* Berkeley: University of California Press.
Sewell, William, Archibald Haller, and Ajejandro Portes. 1969. The educational and early occupational attainment process. *American Sociological Review* 34:575-613.
Stainback, Kevin, Corrie L. Robinson, and Donald Tomaskovic-Devey. 2005. Race and workplace integration: A politically mediated process? *American Behavioral Scientist* 48:1200-28.
Stone, John. 1985. *Racial conflict in contemporary society.* Cambridge, MA: Harvard University Press.
Tomaskovic-Devey, Donald. 1993. *Gender and racial inequality at work.* Ithaca, NY: ILR Press.
———. 2005. Race and the accumulation of human capital across the career: A theoretical model and fixed-effects application. *American Journal of Sociology* 111:58-89.
Tuch, Steven, and Jack Martin. 1991. Race in the workplace: Black-white differences in the sources of job satisfaction. *Sociological Quarterly* 32:103-16.
Williams, James. 1982. *The state against blacks.* New York: McGraw-Hill.
Wilson, George. 1997. Payoffs to power among the middle class: Has race declined in its significance? *Sociological Quarterly* 38:607-22.
———. 2005. Race, ethnicity and inequality in the American workplace: Evolving issues. *American Behavioral Scientist* 48:1151-56.
Wilson, William Julius. 1978. *The declining significance of race.* Chicago: University of Chicago Press.
———. 1996. *When work disappears.* Cambridge, MA: Harvard University Press.
Wright, Eric Olin. 1985. *Classes.* London: Verso.

Social Closure and Processes of Race/Sex Employment Discrimination

By
VINCENT J. ROSCIGNO,
LISETTE M. GARCIA,
and
DONNA BOBBITT-ZEHER

Research on race and gender inequalities in employment typically infers discrimination as an important causal mechanism. The authors' systematic explication of social closure as a discriminatory mechanism reveals that traditional analyses of structural effects and process are not competing, but rather complementary. Analyzing race and sex discrimination cases filed in Ohio from 1988 to 2003, the authors highlight dominant processes of social closure that impact discriminatory exclusion, expulsion, mobility, and harassment on the job. Rather than employing the typical cause and effect modeling centering on outcomes, qualitative analyses serve to clarify discriminatory processes at play. Commonalities between race and sex (e.g., particularistic criteria in evaluation) emerge, as do specific racialized and gendered processes. The authors discuss similarities and differences in process; tie qualitative insights to the existing literature; and discuss the implications of their results for theoretical formulations of structure, agency, and inequality within institutional/ organizational environments and society at large.

Keywords: discrimination; race and gender inequality; social closure; harassment; mobility; hiring

Race and gender inequalities in the labor market have received considerable attention by researchers over the past twenty years. Most concede that human capital deficits may account for some outcome differences. Yet income and wage deficits (e.g., Cotter, Hermsen, and Vanneman 1999; Marini and Fan 1997; Tomaskovic-Devey 1993; Tomaskovic-Devey and Skaggs 2002), employment disparities (Cohn and Fossett 1995; Wilson, Tienda, and Wu 1995), and inequalities in promotion and authority (McBrier and Wilson 2004; Smith 2002; Wilson 1997; Wilson, Sakura-Lemessy, and West 1999) remain even in face of human capital controls. But why?

Some correctly note how labor market sectoral differences contribute to persistent disparities (e.g., Cohen 1998; Huffman 2004). More proximately meaningful, however, may be the firms in which minorities and women work and the extent to which they are segregated. Men earn more than women even when they are in the same general occupation (U.S. Census Bureau 2003), yet occupational sex segregation remains a significant source of wage disparities (England 1992; Padavic and Reskin 2002). Kaufman (1986, 2002) recently found similar segregation of African Americans into lower-skilled, race-typed jobs involving menial tasks and poor working conditions. Tomaskovic-Devey (1993), who examined levels of both race and gender segregation for a sample of firms in North Carolina, concurs, while also noting that some of the inequality he found is likely due to *social closure* processes wherein women and minorities are sorted into jobs that require fewer educational credentials and that offer less job training.

Such analyses, including some of the articles in this particular issue, are incredibly useful for specifying the prevalence and consequences of labor market opportunities and workplace segregation for race and gender groups, the general devaluation of female and minority work, and corresponding wage and mobility inequalities. Discrimination, often inferred as a contributing mechanism, however, has received considerably less attention, owing, in part, to data limitations (for some exceptions, see Feagin 1991; Feagin and McKinney 2003; Pager 2003; and Pager and Quillian 2005). Theoretical clarity on the topic of stratification and how it manifests, however, is also partially to blame. Indeed, while analyses of organizational or geographic variations in levels of inequality provide understanding of macro-level sociological outcomes and relations with, for instance, racial competition across neighborhoods or gender segregation at work, they tend to offer less insight into micro-interactional processes that most assuredly play a role in social closure (Feagin and Eckberg 1980). Our conceptualization of inequality as a dynamic, interactive process occurring within real workplaces reflects an effort to address this gap. It is also a commensurable extension of prior

---

Vincent J. Roscigno is a professor of sociology at Ohio State University and editor of the American Sociological Review. *His main interests revolve around stratification, work, education, social movements, and labor. He is currently involved in several studies, including a large quantitative/qualitative project on processes of race/sex discrimination in employment and housing, drawing from archived Civil Rights Commission files. He is the author of* The Face of Discrimination: How Race and Sex Impact Work and Residential Lives *(Rowman & Littlefield, forthcoming) and (with W. Danaher)* The Voice of Southern Labor *(University of Minnesota Press, 2004).*

Lisette M. Garcia is currently a doctoral student in the Department of Sociology at Ohio State University. Her current research interests are in stratification and inequality and, more specifically, how race shapes interactions at work. She is currently an ASA minority fellow funded by the National Institute of Mental Health. She received this award for her dissertation work focusing on the mental health consequences of discrimination at work.

Donna Bobbitt-Zeher is a PhD candidate in the Department of Sociology at Ohio State University. Her research focuses on gender and racial inequality, with particular emphasis on workplace discrimination, educational stratification, and violence against women. Her dissertation examines changing gendered patterns of educational success and their implications for gender stratification in later life.

work and an explicit effort to address the call for "mechanism-oriented" analyses of stratification and its origins (Reskin 2000, 2003).

Drawing from a unique data set of 60,743 workplace race and sex discrimination cases filed in the state of Ohio from 1988 to 2003, we analyze processes of race and sex-based social closure in employment. We limit our analyses to "serious" cases, wherein a probable cause finding was reached by a third-party investigator following state and federal (Equal Employment Opportunity Commission [EEOC]) guidelines or a settlement was reached in the charging party's favor. This strategy bolsters confidence in our ability to describe *processes of discrimination* rather than just perceptions of it, possibly laden with subjective biases. We draw from the quantitative data to highlight the form of injury that occurred in serious sex ($n = 6,162$) and race ($n = 9,013$) cases but remain centered on our main analytic goal—explicating how such discrimination occurs, whether there are commonalities by sex and race, and the ways processes of closure by race and sex may be unique. This is undertaken through qualitative immersion into a random subsample of case files ($n = 740$). Qualitative immersion itself does not have the aim of prediction. Nor does it concern itself strictly with outcomes, as is the case with more quantitative work in the field. Rather, the intent is to reveal and highlight processes that have either only been inferred in the dominant literature or that warrant theoretical explication and clarification.

Racial and gender stratification in employment

Extensive research over the past several decades has examined workplace racial and gender inequalities, and sociological work on the topic is clear. Gaps in wages, organizational power, and employment opportunities have narrowed somewhat, but disparities remain. Traditionally, neoeconomic theorizing and status attainment research identify differences in human capital as the principal cause of labor market disadvantages. The assumption here is that individual investments, such as education, can increase productive capability and, thus, worth and compensation (Kingston et al. 2003). Kaufman (2002) referred to this as the "skills deficit" argument, noting how some workers have differing (i.e., lower) levels of human capital that will result in differential labor market opportunities. If one accepts this premise, it might historically make sense that women or African Americans, for instance, will earn lower wages, have less organizational power, and have fewer overall economic opportunities.

Most problematic with the aforementioned explanation, however, is its "methodological individualist" orientation, wherein societal outcomes are seen as rooted largely in individual behaviors (Blaug 1976). A solitary focus on human capital simply overlooks the role of inequality in institutional processes generally, and closure enacted by institutional and dominant group actors that reifies existing stratification hierarchies—factors beyond the control of any given individual. Moreover, human capital investments are seen as relatively fixed across all segments of the labor market. This assumption is problematic because research has documented both how the social organization of labor varies across industrial sectors and workplaces, as well as the ways in which economic and social rewards correspondingly follow (Beck, Horan, and Tolbert 1978; England 1992; Kaufman, Hodson, and Fligstein 1981; Tomaskovic-Devey 1993).

Labor market sectoral differences and levels of workplace segregation seem more paramount for understanding employment inequality. Indeed, an abundance of the work and stratification literature has highlighted the structure of the labor market, workplace contexts, and their relations to race and gender disparities (e.g., Huffman and Cohen 2004; McCall 2001; Beggs 1995; Mason 2000). Cohen (1998), for instance, in his multilevel analyses of race and gender inequalities across labor markets of the United States, found that income disparities vary rather systematically as a function of local economic conditions. A similar point has been made by William J. Wilson (1978) in his historical overview of African American secondary sector employment in large, inner-city areas of the United States. Even more recently, Huffman (2004) found sectoral variations in employment for men and women and empirically denoted the consequences for wage inequalities holding constant human capital differences.

Sex and race segregation at occupational and workplace levels may be even more influential (England 1992; Padavic and Reskin 2002; Kaufman 1986, 2002). Tomaskovic-Devey (1993) agreed but suggested that more systematic processes of social closure may be at play in statistical associations between structure and group economic well-being. More recent scholarship, noted below, concurs on this point. In particular, researchers have suggested that social closure, and unmeasured discrimination specifically, are likely an important part of the process.

> The large residual raises the possibility that unmeasured discrimination accounts for differential rates of employment exit and, again, intra-firm processes would shed light on the issue. (Reid and Padavic 2005, 1257)

> Data should be collected in specific organizations, where the potential exists to observe first-hand the extent to which the practices of employers structure layoffs . . . our understanding of the dynamics will be vastly improved. (Wilson and McBrier 2005, 316)

> Discrimination against workers—especially exclusion from better-paying jobs—is an important mechanism for the effect of black population size on the racial wage gap. (Huffman and Cohen 2004, 902)

Discrimination is thus often inferred as a mediating process between structural attributes of labor markets/workplaces and group inequalities. Alternatively, social closure via discrimination against women or minorities is conceived of as a more direct cause—a cause of workplace disparities captured in statistical residuals once other factors have been accounted for.

The possibility of discrimination

Sorting mechanisms, including discretionary decision making and, thus, discrimination by employers and coworkers, may be partially responsible for the persistent disparities we find. And there is good reason to suspect that such foci will contribute to our understanding of social closure and stratification in employment. Research pertaining to downward race and gender mobility by McBrier and Wilson (2004) and employment exits by Reid and Padavic (2005) suggest that arbitrary and subjective decision making within firms may be key. Huffman and Cohen's (2004) and Peterson and Saporta's (2004) recent analyses of race and gender wage disparities, respectively, although they did not measure or analyze discrimination directly, similarly came to the conclusion that discrimination in worker allocation and exclusion are likely playing a part in the inequalities that they found.

The possibility of discrimination as an important, although seldom directly studied, mechanism is bolstered further by recent analyses of employer attitudes by Moss and Tilly (2001). These researchers demonstrated that, like subjective biases and stereotypes in the more general population, employers too may hold biased views and consequently make skewed hiring, promotion, and firing decisions (see also Kirschenman and Neckerman 1991). Experimental and audit designs, not the least of which is Pager's (2003) recent analysis of hiring decisions, highlight more directly the centrality of employer preconceptions and especially the ways in which subjective biases translate into discriminatory behaviors (see also Laband and Lentz 1998; Neumark, Bank, and Van Nort 1996).

For African Americans, detrimental employer biases might include, for instance, the view that they are more inclined toward criminality or less dependable, each of which may influence hiring and promotion decisions (Moss and Tilly 2001; Pager 2003). For women, employer biases may include the match between a prospective or current employer and gender-typed work, or an expectation that a prospective or existing employee may become pregnant or be less committed to their job due to motherhood. This may lead to exclusion, stagnation in mobility, or sexual harassment—particularly when gender expectations are violated and males attempt to reify gender hierarchies (e.g., Gruber 1998; Gutek and Cohen 1987; Padavic and Orcutt 1997). Providing in-depth analyses of how such processes unfold in concrete work settings would inform more structural research and its interpretations of employment inequality. It would also contribute to our theoretical understanding of workplace relations and the social processes implicated in the reproduction of race/gender boundaries and inequalities (Vallas 2003).

Stratification, Social Closure, and Processes of Discrimination

A sound understanding of stratification, including that pertaining to gender, race, and work, brings together awareness of structure and action and their potentially reinforcing and/or conditional nature (Bruce, Roscigno, and McCall 1998; Lawler, Ridgeway, and Markovsky 1993; Roscigno and Hodson 2004). For the purposes of this article, this entails not only consideration of prior research on disparities in employment, but also serious consideration and theoretical development pertaining to the very social processes that create and reinforce those disparities. Without doing so, conceptions of inequality remain overly structural, with little room for, or acknowledgment of, agency—agency on the part of gatekeeping actors within institutional and organizational contexts, as well as that often exercised by those victimized by inequality.

Contemporary research has been relatively weak in the aforementioned regards, perhaps owing to data limitations, noted previously. Yet theoretical orientations that guide much contemporary research, knowingly or not, are also to blame. This very point was made recently by Tomaskovic-Devey, Thomas, and Johnson (2005).

> Within a status-attainment or human capital framework, we cannot observe discrimination. These are essentially theoretical models that assume a more or less meritocratic labor market allocation process. They have encouraged social scientists to collect data on individuals' characteristics and labor market attainment. Thus, discrimination is not observed, but must be inferred as a residual significant effect, once presumably meritocratic factors have been statistically accounted for. It seems unlikely that we will ever advance knowledge of discrimination mechanisms with data collected in a human capital or status-attainment framework. (p. 85)

It is for this reason that we draw, instead, from perspectives pertaining to social closure given their emphases on how inequality is created and maintained, rather than merely its extent or individual foundations. For Weber (1978), social closure reflects the process by which collectivities seek to maximize advantage by restricting access and privileges to others. This often occurs through institutional exclusion and dominant group positioning. It also comes about, however, within the context of everyday interaction—interaction that, through language, symbolic acts, and/or physical control or force, has as its aim status-hierarchy preservation and the various advantages/disadvantages that such hierarchy affords (Blau 1977; Feagin 1991; West and Zimmerman 1987). Parkin (1974, 1979) elaborated further by stressing the two-pronged, dynamic nature of stratification, wherein dominant group members undertake actions (closure) to preserve privilege while subordinate groups hold some capacity to resist and change prevailing stratification arrangements (usurpation) (see also Murphy 1988). Reskin (2003) has reinvigorated such themes more recently by pushing stratification scholars to not only examine the extent or forms of inequality, but perhaps more important, pertinent processes and mechanisms (see also Feagin and Eckberg 1980). Rather than merely delineating the extent of inequality, then, social closure as a sociological construct directs us toward an in-depth understanding of the processes through which stratification hierarchies are both defined and maintained.

Figure 1 provides a general conceptual model of social closure and its dimensions relative to group inequality as applied to any given institutional realm. The innermost circle reflects organizational structure, including but not limited to workplace composition and mandated procedures and practices. The outer circle

FIGURE 1
STRUCTURAL AND INTERACTIONAL DIMENSIONS OF SOCIAL CLOSURE

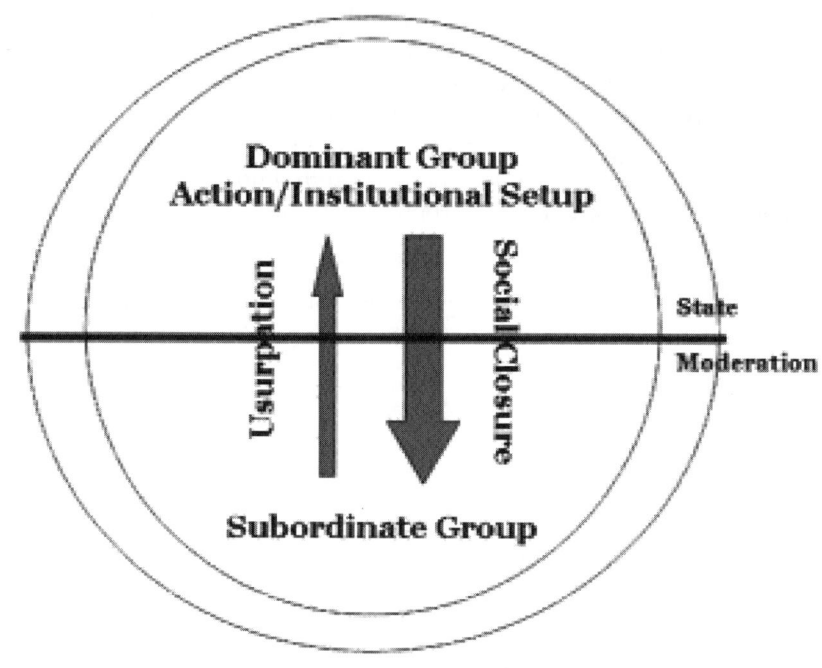

represents, generally, extraorganizational structures (e.g., labor markets, spatial demographics, and competition patterns) that may influence the more proximate patterning of organizational and institutional practices and the inequality that they may produce. Of course, the state (federal or local, captured by the horizontal line) may intrude, and certainly has historically, in a manner that shapes organizational and extraorganizational dynamics pertaining to race and gender access and treatment.

The preponderance of research pertaining to race and gender employment-related inequality has focused on relations between each of the two rings and, to some extent in the historical, political, and social movements literature, the role of the state in relation to racial minorities and women's economic well-being. This includes research pertaining to workplace race/sex composition, labor market processes, organizational practices, and racially competitive processes across geographic space. While useful in documenting aggregate relations between structure and group outcomes, such empirical literature remains significantly underdeveloped on the interactions represented in the center of the figure: how do superordinate and subordinate actors play a role within this process and engage in inequality production, reduction, and/or maintenance within the constraints of preexistent workplace, labor market, and/or spatial and political structures? To address this question, we examine the multidimensional nature of discriminatory forms themselves and, arguably more important, how they are enacted.

While exclusion from employment, wage differentials, or uneven mobility patterns—the principal outcome foci in the literature—are important and more easily captured empirically, social closure via discrimination involves much more both sociologically and legally. It also entails various forms of differential treatment and harassment once employed. These forms of closure are less easily captured in an objective empirical sense but nevertheless reflect inequality and status hierarchy maintenance. It is on this point that research has been largely limited to but a small handful of experiential and retrospective analyses. Feagin and McKinney (2003), for instance, elaborated on the significant physical, psychological, familial, and community costs of discrimination, including that encountered in workplaces, drawing from detailed interviews. What is notable in their account is that respondents often reflect negatively on supervisor and coworker behavior that is mundane and very much day-to-day in character, yet race-specific in its targeting.

> *There is a disjuncture . . . between the types of discrimination highlighted or inferred in quantitative analyses . . . and that which is more effectively captured using case or in-depth, interviewing techniques.*

There is a disjuncture, to some extent, between the types of discrimination highlighted or inferred in quantitative analyses, which tends to focus on objective workplace rewards, and that which is more effectively captured using case, or in-depth, interviewing techniques. Retrospective and experiential accounts of sexual harassment at work and more general differential treatment of women within particular occupations and workplace contexts similarly seem to suggest that, alongside possible efforts to exclude women from certain forms of employment or from promotion ladders, discriminatory actions are often aimed toward reifying gender hierarchies among those already employed. Although such studies can be critiqued for relying on perceptions of discrimination and small samples, not to mention retrospective biases, they nevertheless add a much needed social and interactional dimension to our understanding of inequality. Moreover, they direct attention toward discrimination beyond its purely material consequences. Rather than relying simply on perceptions, the data described shortly focus on thousands of verified incidences (i.e., cases) of discrimination wherein the complaint received investigative validation by a neutral, third-party, governmental agency. Importantly, our analyses of processes include (1) exclusionary forms of workplace discrimination, (2) forms that impact mobility and expulsion from the workplace, and (3) more informal manifestations that appear to have as their goal hierarchy maintenance.

These distinctions are important. Indeed, particular discriminatory forms shape the target's objective employment status and often require complicit behavior or neglect on the part of more powerful institutional actors. More informal manifestations (e.g., harassment, intimidation, sexual harassment), in contrast, may be carried out by actors with or without institutional authority (i.e., coworkers). Although one's objective status in employment may not be impacted, such discrimination is nevertheless quite consequential for victims, and often in an ongoing manner. The ability to distinguish between types of discrimination and address its multiple consequences is thus essential.

Data and Analytic Strategy

Our main sampling frame includes all cases of racial and sex discrimination in employment filed with the Civil Rights Commission of the state of Ohio (OCRC) between 1988 and 2003. Since 1988, the base data for each case has been input into a database file—a copy of which was made available to the authors. These data include a case ID number, the charging party's race and sex, the respondent (e.g., employer name) and his or her location, the basis of the charge (e.g., race, gender, religion, etc.), the harm or injury that occurred (e.g., exclusion, promotion, firing, sexual harassment, etc.), the industry, the outcome of the investigation, and a host of geographic identifiers (zip codes, metropolitan statistical area [MSA] codes, and county federal information processing [FIPS] codes). Cases that are filed with the OCRC are typically doubly filed with the EEOC, although this federal agency often relies on OCRC findings unless the case falls into an already existent EEOC investigation, litigation, or national initiative. Thus, the data provide a rich body of discrimination suits from a state that, given both the heterogeneity in its industrial structure and significant minority composition in quite large urban areas (i.e., Cincinnati, Akron, Cleveland, Toledo, Dayton, and Columbus), is a reasonably generalizable case in point.

Since our aim is to contribute to stratification literature in general, but specifically to that pertaining to race and gender, analyses are limited to cases in which the self-reported basis of the charge itself is race/ethnicity and/or sex. This equates to approximately 61,000 employment cases of race and/or sex discrimination. Since it would be erroneous to assume that a discrimination *claim* necessarily implies that discrimination occurred, OCRC's case determination (and a probable cause finding in particular) helps distinguish cases with little supporting evidence from those with significant and supporting evidence in favor of the charging party's claim. Along with probable cause cases, we also select those wherein a settlement was reached in the charging party's favor (prior to litigation). Settlement is often deemed as supporting evidence from the point of view of legal scholars who both study and testify in discrimination suits. Thus, we limit analyses to the 14,091 "serious" cases wherein probable cause determinations were reached or favorable settlements for the charging party were brokered by a neutral third party (OCRC or district attorney's office)—a neutral third party whose job it is to collect evidence, eyewitness accounts, and case histories and to weigh the preponderance of all evidence following EEOC guidelines.

Admittedly, significant levels of sex and race discrimination are never reported or realized. Moreover, many of the nonprobable cause cases may reflect instances of actual discrimination but with a lack of supporting evidence. We thus recognize that these data do not capture all discrimination in the arena of work and, in fact, are a significant underestimate. Yet significant advantages are worth highlighting. First, and relative to prior work that attempts to capture discrimination by relying on retrospective interviews or experimental techniques (e.g., audit testing in hiring), the cases we focus on reflect concrete acts of discrimination, confirmed by a neutral, third-party, investigation following state and federal civil rights guidelines. Second, the qualitative materials in particular provide rare insight into the processes involved—our principal aim and something that existing quantitative work has seldom been able to capture. Finally, our sample of cases includes significant labor market representation and occupational status (Roscigno forthcoming).

Our focus on "serious" cases will certainly have the effect of underestimating discrimination by excluding cases where there simply was not enough evidence, or those many cases that never go reported. Nevertheless, it bolsters confidence and the ability to conclude that the *processes* uncovered pertain directly to discrimination (rather than alleged or perceived discrimination). Indeed, seldom if ever has research been able to qualitatively document discriminatory processes within workplaces, and with the confidence afforded by neutral, third-party civil rights investigative reports and conclusions. Figure 2 offers a visual representation of these more serious employment ($n = 14,091$) cases, broken down by the race and gender attributes of the charging party (note: "other" represents combined categories of Asian, Hispanic, and other race/ethnic minorities). Given limited representation of "other" racial/ethnic minorities, our race analyses focus largely on African Americans.

We begin the analyses by reporting the forms of injury for race and sex discrimination cases, respectively. Figure 3 offers further breakdowns by forms of discrimination. Given the overwhelming representation of African Americans among race-based cases, and women among sex-based discrimination cases, our qualitative analyses focus on these groups.

Central to our analytic aims, we were granted permission to analyze qualitative materials from the case files themselves. These files, ranging from 20 to

FIGURE 2
DISTRIBUTION OF SERIOUS RACE/SEX EMPLOYMENT DISCRIMINATION
CASES BY RACE AND SEX OF THE CHARGING PARTY

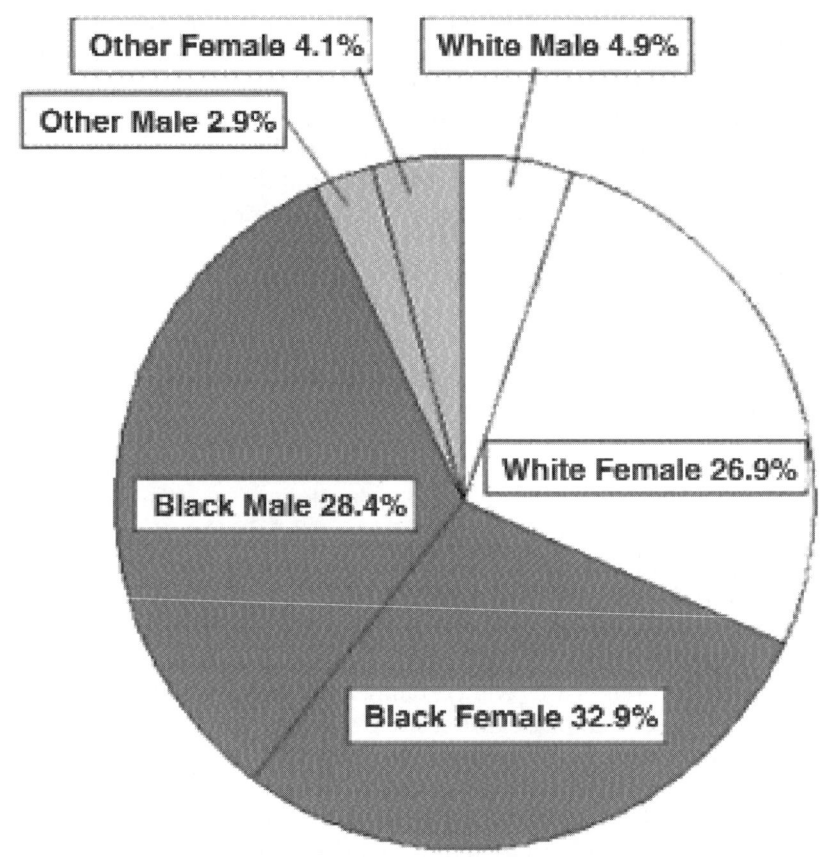

120 pages each, include important information including, but not limited to the following:
- firsthand accounts of what occurred from the charging party's viewpoint, often in his or her own words;
- a response and/or explanation from the respondent as to what happened;
- witness statements as to what occurred;
- who carried out the discrimination (i.e., supervisor, owner, coworkers, etc.);
- a deposition of testimony, taken by the attorney general's office, if the case reached that point; and
- the occupation of the charging party, or occupation in question.

The qualitative case material denotes processes of race and sex discrimination, rather than simply the outcome of that discrimination. Moreover, the ways in

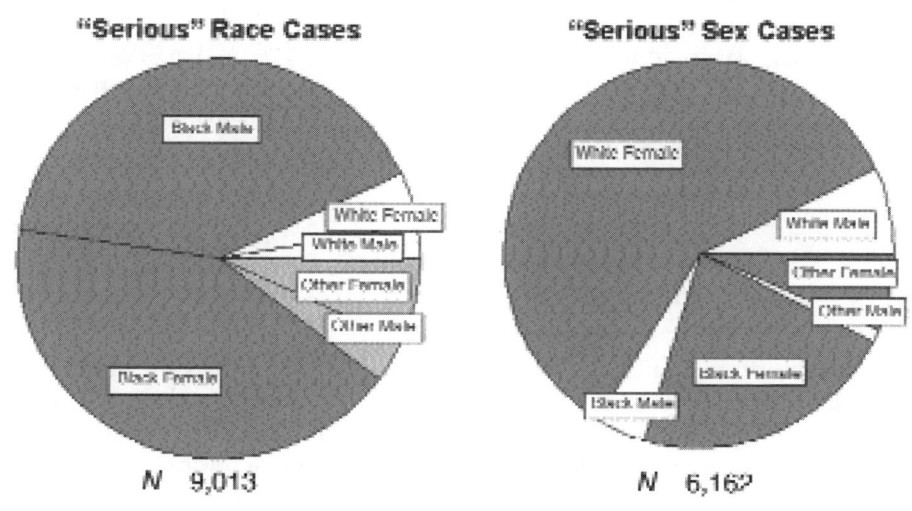

FIGURE 3
ATTRIBUTES OF VICTIMS FOR SERIOUS RACE (LEFT)
AND SEX (RIGHT) DISCRIMINATION CASES

which discriminatory actors justify their actions and organizations mitigate, encourage, or turn a blind eye to what is occurring becomes quite clear. A random subsample of approximately 740 cases (372 race-based, 364 sex-based) was chosen from microfiche reels of cases.

This subsample parallels the broader body of serious cases nearly identically with regard to discrimination type (race and sex) and the charging party's race and sex. We immersed ourselves in these cases, read through them for patterns and emergent themes, and also used a preestablished coding device to record information on many issues, including some of those noted above. Given that our principal goal in this particular article is the explication of process, we highlight emergent themes in our reading of the preponderance of the material. All individual and business names have been changed.

This more inductive strategy leaves open the possibility that undertheorized or inadequately theorized processes will be uncovered. Although some may take issue with such a strategy, it is in our view that it is quite commensurable with literature whose aims are more predictive in nature. Indeed, our findings speak to several processes either inferred or speculated about in more quantitative work, while also highlighting several dimensions of social closure that have received scant attention at best.

Twenty-seven potential discriminatory injuries recorded by civil rights investigators are collapsed into five primary ones here, for summary purposes: exclusion, expulsion, promotion, demotion, and harassment. Expulsion captures being pushed out or fired from employment, while exclusion relates instances of hiring discrimination. Discrimination in promotion and demotion are relatively self-explanatory. Harassment—an empirical focus seldom dealt with in the employment inequality literature—includes forms of outright harassment and differential treatment while on the job that do not directly pertain to the more objectively measurable forms already noted (i.e., exclusion, expulsion, promotion, and demotion). As our analyses of both race and sex discrimination reveal, harassment is a predominant form of discrimination in its own right. It is also woven within many discriminatory accounts that culminated in firing, promotion, and demotion.

Race, Social Closure, and Discrimination in Employment

Racial discrimination and closure processes as they unfold in the arena of employment are hardly singular in terms of outcome. Rather, and as noted in the vast body of prior work, the costs may be multiple and can include exclusion (i.e., from jobs, from networks, etc.), inequalities in material rewards, or potential blocks to mobility. The data employed for our analyses touch upon these, as well as costs of discrimination not adequately dealt with in the current body of literature. Figure 4 reports the distribution of injuries across the entire sample of serious race discrimination cases.

Most notable is the prevalence of both expulsion (firing) and racial harassment on the job. Our designation of harassment includes wage inequality, yet these make up only a very small fraction of harassment claims (117 out of 2,758 cases, or 4 percent). Instead, most harassment charges entail outright antagonism, neglect, or differential treatment on the job. The high rate of expulsion, or firings and layoffs, for employment is consistent with recent analyses of employment exits and race and gender inequalities (e.g., Reid and Padavic 2005; see also Wilson and McBrier 2005). Racial harassment, in contrast, is seldom addressed in the workplace stratification literature, perhaps owing to difficulties in capturing it within quantitative measurement.

What processes are at play with regard to racial discrimination and the injuries reported above? Our case immersion suggests three elements of racial closure and discrimination that shape and indeed transcend the particular outcomes reported above. These include, most notably, the disparate policing of minority workers on the job, the managerial use of particularistic or "soft skill" criteria in employee or prospective employee evaluation, and ongoing racial hierarchy maintenance in the course of everyday workplace interactions.

Disparate policing of minority employees

Many workplaces are governed by formalized procedures that are meant to standardize the labor process but that also ideally constrain arbitrary decision

FIGURE 4
DISCRIMINATORY INJURIES FOR RACE-BASED
DISCRIMINATION CASES

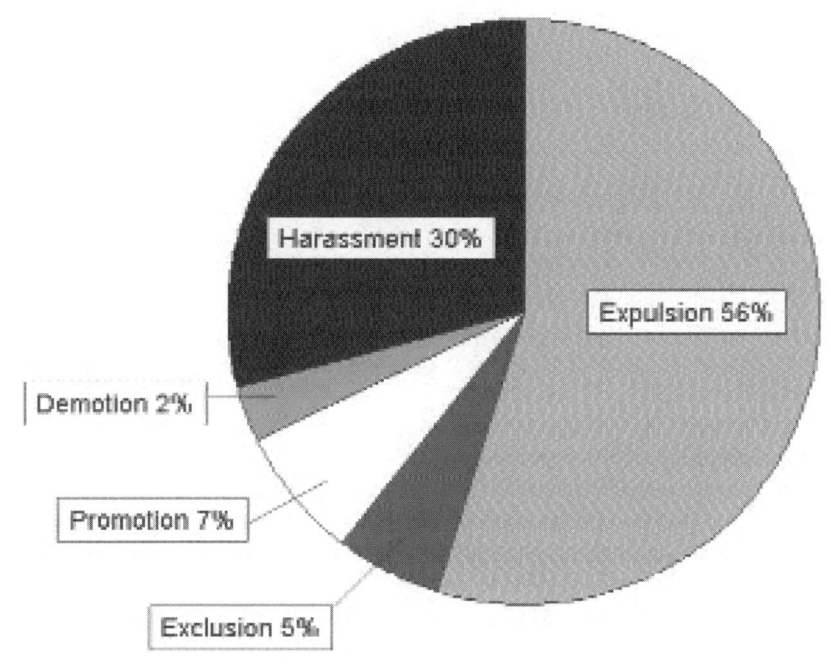

making on the part of gatekeeping actors. A consistent theme throughout case materials is that such seemingly neutral procedures are differentially targeted or applied, depending on race. Procedures and policies may indeed be neutral, in and of themselves; yet managerial discretion in their application clearly results in race-targeted bullying.

Consider the case of James Adams, an operator at a large metal manufacturing facility. Like any employee of this facility, Mr. Adams's performance was subject to "review." His supervisor indeed followed through on this and consistently rated Adams's performance as poor. Although reasonable at face value, and within the realm of managerial discretion, it turns out that this supervisory prerogative was initiated quite arbitrarily and negatively for this single employee. His performance was deemed as "lacking," and he was held responsible for broken cutters. Notably, reports of Mr. Adams by other supervisors noted good performance, and investigative findings revealed that similarly situated whites were not held accountable for breaking cutters themselves.

Ben Goodwell, an operator in a manufacturing business, was fired by his supervisor for "improper conduct" when he failed to properly "report off" when leaving his equipment, and for taking a break in a restricted area. Civil rights investigators, however, found that employees routinely took breaks in this area and that the supervisor was using this excuse to fire Mr. Goodwell. Here, selective application of policy and targeted policing of violations of that policy are key, resulting in workplace sanctions, demotion, expulsion, and day-to-day harassment.

The case of Alvin Collins is another good illustration of disparate policing. Collins was a high-level manager employed by a large manufacturer, who was demoted to shift supervisor after allegedly violating company policy. As he notes,

> John Davies, assistant personnel manager, and Denny Oden, plant manager, told me my demotion was the result of my unauthorized use of a company vehicle. In my twenty years with the respondent, with the exception of myself, I know of no one else to be demoted for a disciplinary infraction. I followed the same procedure for signing out a vehicle as did all other salaried employees, yet I was the only employee disciplined. To this day, Caucasians sign out vehicles in an identical manner, without being disciplined. . . . I believe that the vehicle issue was merely a ruse to humiliate me into resigning my position, because respondent was uncomfortable with a black in its highest salaried classification.

This final statement is quite poignant. That discrimination, by default or design, creates and preserves advantage is clearly demonstrated in Mr. Collins's concluding thoughts. In this case, as in many more, differential policing of legitimate and arguably neutral organizational policy and procedure is at the core of much discrimination, and with a host of consequences pertaining especially to demotion, harassment, and expulsion from the workplace.

Managerial use of particularistic criteria

The centrality of managerial discretion in the discrimination process does not simply revolve around targeted applications of policy or sanctions. It is also influential and arguably pivotal in the evaluation process—evaluation of whom to hire or whom to promote into higher status positions. Here, the issue is not so much targeted use of formalized rules and sanctions, but rather significant subjective flexibility in supervisory decision making—decision making that often works to the disadvantage of minorities. Consider the example of Rose Gold, an employee of a large retail department store. Rose was employed for more than seven years and had never been promoted, despite often undertaking managerial duties.

> In the past six months, I have been denied promotions to the positions of Jewelry Department Manager, Ladies Department Manager, and Drug Department Manager. Caucasians, Lisa Mann, Linda Belli, and Nicole Lewis, were hired for the department manager positions. I have more experience and seniority than the Caucasians who were hired.

During their investigation, civil rights investigators found that the employer had no formal application process for promotions, but rather relied on the current store manager, a white male, to select "management material." Such discretionary power, in this particular case, resulted in an all Caucasian managerial staff.

Mike Haywood's experience is another excellent case in point. Mike was not promoted, nor were any African Americans in the company. Rather, there was a history of African Americans being passed over for promotion in favor of less senior white employees. Mike recounts confronting his manager about being denied promotion.

> I asked him about the criteria . . . and, how did he get the position over me or any other blacks in the company who had been there much longer than him. His comment was, in effect was, that remark about laying his wallet down and it being there when he get back and . . . I said "do you know what you're saying? . . . like you're laying your wallet down, say like, like blacks are going to steal from you or something," I said, "do you know what you're saying?" He said it was his prerogative or at his discretion to make what promotions that he wanted to and the way he see fit, it was best for the department or something to that effect.

As in much of the qualitative material analyzed, managers exercise considerable discretion when it comes to hiring and promotion. Assumptions regarding dependability, presentability, communication skills, and work ethic are widespread and are used as rationales in many cases, including that of Delia Jordan. Ms. Jordan, who worked for an insurance company, was the person primarily responsible for training new hires—new hires eventually promoted over her. Notably, she received many awards and commendations for her work, a testament to her ability to succeed at higher levels, yet was continually bypassed for promotion. Investigative materials pertaining to the case suggest that management felt she did not "present herself as well as the other candidates." In particular, management asserts that she was "too 'negative,' did not focus enough on the 'positive' aspects of her work history, and did not make enough 'eye contact' with the interviewer." In contrast, the white candidates presented themselves "clearly," "positively," and "concisely." In Ms. Jordan's case, even objective evidence of exemplary performance were outweighed by soft skill considerations.

> It is now obvious that there was no intent to seriously consider me for this position. I am aware that the decision to hire the other applicant was made prior to my second interview and the interview only served as a formality to appease me. Lisa Davenport was given the position despite the fact that she was trained by me and that she has only been employed with the company for 15 months; I for seven years. In the seven years I have been employed, I have trained 15 assistants and have taken on many managerial duties. [You have] no legitimate reason to deny me this promotion. . . . Throughout this whole ordeal, my education, experience, and knowledge all seemed to have been of no consequence to the individuals in charge.

Managerial abuse and particularistic criteria fuel inequality in the workplace, most notably in the case of mobility. Extra information on the criteria being used, as well as experiencing its differential application, helps prompt challenge on the part of the victim. Otis Phillips, for instance, was a security guard seeking employment as a police officer. He completed the necessary paperwork and was awaiting the results of his background investigation (common practice for civil servants) when he was told that his name had been removed from the police recruit eligibility list due to a poor credit history. Mr. Phillips was "aware of a younger white applicant, Chris Childs, who also had a poor credit history, yet he has not been removed from the Police Recruit Eligibility list." In fact, the officer conducting the background on the white applicant had this to say:

> After completing this applicant's background investigation there are several areas of concern:
> 1. This applicant has a very poor credit rating, he has 9 accounts up for collection. He has many civil judgments rendered against him. He attempted to file bankruptcy. It appears that he will not pay his bills at all.
> 2. This applicant has worked 13 different jobs. He doesn't seem to last too long at any job.
> 3. The oral board should take a very close look at this applicant to determine if he should be accepted for the position of police recruit.

In contrast, the officer who conducted Mr. Phillip's background check made these comments:

> The only negative thing found is the fact that the applicant is currently under a Chapter 13 judgment as a result of two divorces. He is currently meeting his financial obligations which should be completed in 2 1/2 years. Despite his advanced age for an applicant, he appears to possess the necessary physical and mental skills for the position.

Notable in the face of distinct recommendations above is that the black applicant, Phillips, was removed from the list while the white applicant remained in contention for a job. Obviously, differential standards were being employed. And although not explicitly racial, the effect was nevertheless the exclusion of an African American man from the police force.

Racial hierarchy maintenance in employment

Interactional processes are important to consider in studies of stratification at work. Inequality that may result from workplace interactions is not, strictly speaking, only tied to objective workplace outcomes (e.g., hiring, firing, mobility, promotion, or pay). This is quite evident in our data, which includes a significant number of cases (21 percent) pertaining to racial harassment and differential treatment on the job. Sometimes such harassment can be explicitly racist in nature, as in the case of David Smith. He notes that his supervisor "called me 'boy' and after I asked him to refrain it was done again." Evidence collected by investigators substantiates that he was called derogatory names by his supervisor and that the supervisor in question used such derogatory terms commonly. Ben Goodwell, discussed earlier, experienced racial slurs at the hands of his supervisor who joked with other employees in Goodwell's absence that Goodwell was "probably selling watermelons."

The case of Paul Jensen, an accountant with a large parts distributor, offers a compelling account of explicitly racial harassment and in a quite hostile environment.

> For the past year a six-page letter with 114 racial jokes has been circulating throughout the Respondent's facility. A picture of various types of monkeys has been posted on the bulletin board, which included a picture of myself. It was posted in plain sight for all employees to view.

Also posted in his work areas was a "nigger application" for employment and a picture of black female giving birth to a baby who is listening to a radio. The clear and explicit intent in such cases is racial hierarchy maintenance.

Although one may conceive of higher-status African Americans as somehow protected from such explicitly racialized treatment, this is by no means the case. When Andre Ross, an upper-level manager with a large education firm, questioned a hiring decision, he was met with racially insensitive backlash and retaliation. He makes this clear in his note to his employer and supervisor.

> I was subjected to an interrogation on issues which you [Joe Mack, supervisor] chose to characterize as related or unrelated to the affirmative action concerns that I raised, with your only apparent criteria being, what was convenient to the argument you wanted to make, in a thinly veiled attempt to divert focus and shift responsibility. The baseness of your derogatory and racially insensitive and offensive name calling as well as your profane antics does not merit that I should diminish my own professionalism to stoop so low as to respond in-kind. Rest assured however, that I am not only willing, but very well prepared to address your unwarranted and unjustifiable behavior in a more appropriate forum. Your attacks both professional as well as personal that I, as a successful long term employee and senior manager have had to endure for raising legitimate policy and legal concerns are by any measure harassment. . . . Your reaction as well as those of your subordinate serves only to provide further evidence of the continuing and unrelenting hostile environment that exists within this organization toward African-American as well as other ethnic minority staff.

His words pinpoint what victims of discrimination and harassment at work must deal with on a somewhat regular basis, namely unwarranted attacks and an overall hostile environment. Notably, he is not a low-status employee.

Harassment is replete throughout case files, although is less commonly racially explicit in tone. Indeed, in the preponderance of cases, harassment is more subtle yet clearly racial in who is being affected. Paul Ferguson, a custodial worker, explains the sorts of mundane yet race-targeted harassment he endures.

> In order to get to the dumpster, I am required to go the long way around, even though there is a shorter route through the gate. . . . The Caucasian Coordinator and Caucasian Supervisor have refused to unlock the gate in order to allow me to dump trash. They have, however, unlocked the gate for Caucasian employees when they required access to complete their job duties.

His remarks highlight that harassment does not have to be blatant to have a disparaging impact. We find similar examples for African Americans, such as Brad Dover, whose effectiveness as manager of a retail franchise was continually undermined.

> On several occasions, I was made to travel to Corporate Headquarters . . . just to find out the meeting was canceled. *Everyone* (charging party's emphasis) else was notified.

Upon my hiring I was told I could hire and fire. I was told I would have my own (new) store. I was not allowed to hire *anyone* (charging party's emphasis) and was told by (the District Manager) that I didn't need to hire anyone. I began with a staff of three, when one quit, I couldn't hire anyone. Immediately after I received the old store they changed the hours of operating. About two week(s) later, Stan (an employee) quit. This forced me to work a 7-day work schedule. . . . I was finally allowed to take applications, I was not allowed to hire however. I had to call Corporate Headquarters set up an appointment for them to come down and interview. . . . No other manager was told that they could not hire! The general manager before me was afforded a staff of three. Not I!

Such acts are not overtly racist, yet are clearly targeted and discriminatory. Indeed, regardless of the explicitness with which acts of harassment are racist, harassment in and of itself matters in important ways for those on the receiving end. It isolates minority employees in their workplaces, undermines their capacity to perform their jobs properly, and impacts their sense of dignity in quite meaningful ways. Moreover, it reifies racial hierarchy on a daily basis, and in ways seldom captured by standard analyses of racial inequalities at work.

Sex Discrimination and Social Closure in Employment

The distribution of injuries pertaining to sex discrimination is reported in Figure 5. As in the case of racial discrimination in employment, serious cases of sex discrimination disproportionately involve job expulsion and harassment on the job. Indeed, more than half involve job loss and another third concern some form of harassment or antagonism. Notable among charges of harassment is that over a quarter of them—the single largest subcategory—pertain directly to sexual harassment followed by general gender antagonism, maternity/pregnancy-related harassment, and differential discipline on the job. Wage inequality constitutes only 2 percent of harassment cases.

Similar to racial patterns, qualitative immersion into case materials reveals some noteworthy processes, regardless of outcome—processes that speak to the question of how and why women are not hired, are disparately fired, stagnate in terms of mobility, and harassed. Three pronounced, interrelated, and reinforcing themes include (1) gender appropriateness; (2) dependability, often tied to pregnancy and maternity; and (3) harassment, including that which is explicitly sexual in character.

Gender appropriateness

Gender scholars have suggested for some time that essentialist notions about women and men have negative consequences for women in the workplace. For example, Yoder (1991, 182) discussed how "occupational gender typing establishes norms about what is and what is not appropriate work for women and men. Deviations from normative expectations evoke negative consequences." Moreover, Acker (1990) theorized that gendered assumptions built into the organization of

FIGURE 5
DISCRIMINATORY INJURIES FOR SERIOUS
SEX-BASED DISCRIMINATION CASES

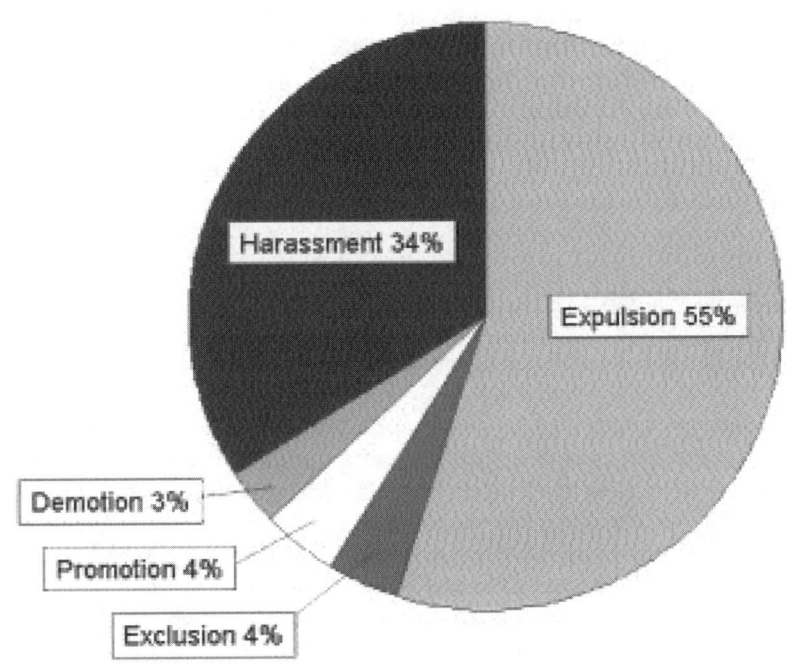

work contribute to women's marginalization as well as sex segregation. We find significant evidence of such gendered assumptions and their link to discrimination, with women being variously described as less intelligent, hormonal, and sensitive. Take, for instance, the following examples from three distinct cases:

> Bob [the editor] made sexist comments openly in front of everyone. He attributed any conflict between females to PMS. The men were held in higher esteem. In discussing with Bob a disagreement with another female employee, the witness was told "now you girls need to get along." The witness stated that Bob made it sound like a cat-fight instead of a professional disagreement, which it was. Additionally, Bob also stated that women didn't deserve equal pay because they had husbands. . . . He wanted her terminated because he has a thing against women who are smarter than him, women with ideas. He frequently yelled and screamed if she challenged him with an idea that was better than his own.

> He told me that I could not read a ruler when I was at the interview, but if anything came up he would let me know. . . . I informed him that I could read a ruler. However, that I thought this was supposed to be an on-the-job training position and any lack of experience, I would learn from being taught. His response was, "I guess that is true, we do have to train you women that come through here."

> [The director of affirmative action] more or less made it sound like some people are just sensitive to that kind of stuff, and maybe some workers should watch it, because some people are overly sensitive.

Such assumptions about women, when combined with gender typing of jobs, lead to blocked opportunities. In this vein, we repeatedly find cases wherein witnesses support allegations that supervisors, owners, or others in positions of authority simply do not want to work with women. Consider the case of Kate Young, who applied for a job as a shoe repairperson.

> Kate asked if they had hired anyone for the job that was in the paper, the owner then replied, "No, I haven't hired anyone yet, but I don't hire women." Kate then replied that the newspaper stated that someone [was needed] to learn shoe repair, no experience necessary, then the owner said he didn't care what the paper said; he was the owner of the shop and he didn't hire women. Then she asked for an application for employment. He said, "No, just write your name and address down on paper," but he said it wouldn't do any good because he still wasn't going to hire any women.

Although she was denied a formal job application, as Kate left her information, she noticed a stack of completed employment applications on the counter. In his correspondence with the civil rights investigators, the store owner noted that he did hire women as "counter girls" and that as the owner, he would hire whomever he wanted. For him, women belonged behind the counter, not in the shop. Such gender typing no doubt leads to more hiring discrimination than our data reveal given that many decision makers are not as blatant as this store owner.

Assumptions of gender appropriateness are evident not only in hiring, but in harassment of women on the job as well. Rebecca Frisco, for instance, who was promoted to a line supervisor position, was consistently disrespected on the job and subjected to hostile behavior by male line workers on an ongoing basis. She was told on numerous occasions:

> If I wanted a man's job, I should buy tools and work on machines like a man does. When equipment broke down or lines needed changing, I was forced to do the work myself while men who had similar positions were given assistance.

While owners or supervisors may do the dirty work of discrimination themselves, as in the case of the shoe repair shop above, those in positions of authority often abuse their managerial powers to block assistance to women workers, as in Rebecca's case. In another example, a male sheriff denied a female officer access to various areas of the department, including restrooms, elevators, interrogation rooms, and booking areas, and male deputies were to enforce these restrictions. Similarly, a male district manager "would not allow the witness to train or assist" a female manager of a service station. In other instances women were denied basic equipment, such as female law enforcement officers being deprived of functioning radios and bulletproof vests. By denying women training, assistance, and equipment, employers make evident their disdain for women and translate their ideas about gender appropriateness into gender disadvantage.

In addition to excluding women from certain opportunities, gender typing in employment plays out through the assignment of gender stereotyped responsibilities. While witness statements suggest that the employer "didn't feel she could do the job [coordinating freight deliveries] because she was a female," the supervisor assigned her clerical responsibilities in addition to those associated with the job. Men in similar positions were not expected to fulfill a clerical role.

Women and dependability

In addition to "gender appropriateness" generally, much of the case data examined reveal clear assumptions about the dependability of women relative to men—dependability often tied pregnancy and maternity, or the potential for pregnancy and maternity. Going beyond general gender stereotyping or sex typing of jobs, preconceptions about pregnant women and "mommy typing" are visible in a variety of workplace settings. In particular, women who become pregnant are often assumed to no longer be dependable. Katrina Mitchell's case illustrates this point well.

> I had a doctor's appointment on April 1, at which time it was confirmed that I was pregnant. On April 2, I went to work and told everyone in the office that I was pregnant. The Owner's wife, Sue McGill, was visiting the office when I was telling everyone of my news. Ms. McGill asked me if it was a planned pregnancy. She told me I should deal with Sam about it. On April 3, my supervisor, Sam Jennison and Sue McGill . . . were in a meeting for the majority of the morning. At approximately 5:15 p.m. that same day, Sam told me that I was let go because I was no longer dependable. . . . My doctor did not place any restrictions on me and I am able to perform my job as Credit Manager. . . . I know of another, Kate Fitcher, who was discharged while out on leave after giving birth.

Although she had only just learned of her pregnancy and had not requested any type of accommodation, this worker was labeled as unreliable and subsequently fired.

Employer concerns over dependability are sometimes explicit. At other times, the assumption may not be vocalized, but it is evident in the employer's actions. Such was the case with Mary Rossi, who recounts what occurred following disclosure of her pregnancy.

> I began being treated less favorably than my non-pregnant co-workers and [my employer] attempted to force me to sign a warning letter/agreement regarding my attendance. Since I notified Mr. Savier of my pregnancy he has required me to do the work of two people. On the attendance warning/agreement Mr. Savier wants me to sign, it is stated that if I miss one day, I'm suspended and at three days missed, I am terminated. The warning/agreement also states that I will have a designated break and lunchtime. No one else has these stipulations nor were they required to sign such an agreement.

Plainly, the supervisor's sudden actions reflect a belief that his now pregnant employee will become an unreliable worker.

Sometimes this issue of dependability is broached in terms of attendance, as in Mary's case. On other occasions, the assumption is that pregnant women will not work as long or hard as others. In the case of a jewelry store manager who was demoted, her replacement's assessment of the situation raises the issue of reliability.

> The company's concern was the fear that business would suffer if she had been allowed to remain in the manager's position. Their feeling was that due to her "high risk" pregnancy, she would be unable to fulfill her duties for the duration of her pregnancy.

This witness goes on the say that by demoting the pregnant manager, she would work fewer hours and be under less stress, which company representatives contended would be of benefit to the pregnant employee.

While cases such as these reveal employer assumptions about dependability during pregnancy, such biases do not end with birth. Indeed, as revealed in many cases, motherhood status itself may be used by employers as a marker of unreliability. In the aforementioned case of the jewelry store manager, the witness continues,

> It was implied that they [company management] were unsure that she would return after the birth of her baby and therefore they wanted to implement a change of management before this would transpire. However, no one ever asked her what she planned for the future.

In a parallel case, the discriminator clearly articulated this sentiment to the employee who was told she would not be returned to her job as an admissions representative following maternity leave.

> When I asked Janet if my position would be there when I came back, she asked me if I could realistically see coming back after having a baby. She told me that I was not going to have the energy and I'm not going to want to work.

Most notably in such cases is the fact that workers are seldom given a chance to challenge preconceptions, as decisions concerning their employment are made without their consultation. For those who are not immediately forced out, assumptions taint how supervisors view workers and lead to an environment of distrust and disdain. Furthermore, these notions of dependability also play out in how some employers treat all women, not just pregnant ones. As they assume that women will put family before work, institutional actors close off job opportunities leading to a variety of discrimination outcomes, including job loss and demotion. Such patterns fly in the face of neoclassic economic assumptions regarding women's preferences or proclivities toward work in the face of family obligations and goals. Instead, we find large numbers of women who want to work but who are being pushed out.

Gender hierarchy maintenance and harassment

Essentialist notions and assumptions about dependability have very real consequences for how gender discrimination is enacted in workplaces. Another way of hierarchy is maintained is through harassment, generally, and sexual harassment in particular. As examples in the previous sections illustrate, various forms of general antagonism and intimidation toward women are present within most sex discrimination claims, including those pertaining to firing, promotion, or demotion. Harassment nevertheless stands out in its own right in these data, constituting more than a third of all serious sex discrimination charges. Sexual harassment is particularly notable not only in terms of its statistical representation, but also in women's narratives of what occurred and its consequences. Our case immersion denotes how women are indeed often sexualized and subjected to quid pro quo demands and, at times, physically assaultive behavior. For example,

> Mark asked me to come over and he rolled his desk chair over towards me, grabbed me by my hips and pushed me towards him. He put his legs around me and put his head on my breasts. He then said "I can make your job easy for you here." I became very upset and left the room. . . . Mark became abusive towards me. He would call me "Goddamn mother fucker" and yelled at me. He constantly used foul language when talking to me.

Such actions make it clear that women workers are first and foremost women, women who are to be subordinate. Sometimes this is an individual effort, as this witness notes: "Andy was upset because she would not go out with him, and after she kept turning him down, he would punish her by giving her all of the dirty job assignments." Often, though, sexual harassment permeates the work environment. A civil rights investigator recounts such a situation in a case involving Rebecca Downs, a female line supervisor:

> Former employees Lisa Smith and Mark Kline paint a much different picture of Charging Party's work environment, however. Both witnesses informed Staff that Charging Party was an excellent supervisor who was forced to endure an almost endless barrage of abuse from her male counterparts. For them it appeared that these actions were taken to make Charging Party's life miserable while at work and contrary to their denials, both [Supervisors] Kevin Stevens and Patrick Jones were aware of the situation but did nothing to stop it. Ms. Smith confirmed that she too had been sexually harassed by Supervisor Reynolds, as were initially all of the female employees he came in contact with. According to former Supervisor Kline, it was common knowledge that Supervisor Reynolds was sexually harassing female employees as they talked among themselves about what a pervert he was.

As this case suggests, key personnel may contribute to the legitimation and perpetuation of such behavior by failing to follow institutional policies against sexual harassment. In the case of this female line supervisor, human resource representatives refused to investigate when offensive articles were posted in the company bulletin board or when pornographic drawings were found in a public work space. Rather than looking into these matters, the director of affirmative action suggested that male employees "watch it, because some people are overly sensitive." In a similar case, management went so far as to document meetings concerning the harassment, although evidence collected by investigators suggests that such meetings never took place.

Although we have discussed themes of gender appropriateness, dependability, and harassment separately, these themes are, in fact, intertwined and reinforcing.

By defining women as inferior and articulating their subordination, institutional actors create and reinforce gender dominance in the workplace, often through job expulsion and hostile work environments. The case of a female electrician, Kay Reinhold, illustrates one way these issues tie together. She endured a hostile and sexually charged work environment as well as unwelcome sexual advances, including being approached "seductively about a light bulb and [saw] a male co-worker have it between his legs." She found a clay penis left on her work bench, and had her face "pushed toward a male co-worker's crotch."

> One [coworker] told me that in other countries the women know their place and that I was taking a good paying job away from a man and that I should be at home taking care of my kids. . . . He said maybe I should move to another "cunt'ry."

On a daily basis, Kay's coworkers set her apart as deviant and reminded her of her inferior position though a variety of sexualized actions. There is clear disdain here for a woman working in a male-typed job, as she violates both expectations for women's work and women's role as mother.

Discussion

By conceiving of social closure broadly from the outset, we leave open the possibility that undertheorized or inadequately theorized processes of discrimination and closure may be captured. The data we have employed are especially notable in this regard, given their richness on the question of injury, not to mention the significant detail afforded on precisely what happened and its consequences. For both race and sex, discrimination impacts employment access. It also influences treatment once employment has been obtained. And finally, as revealed by the prevalence of harassment in both race and sex discrimination cases, status hierarchy maintenance is clearly an important part of the social closure story.

While harassment makes up a significant portion of both race and gender discrimination cases, it is also woven throughout other discrimination claims—claims pertaining to differential mobility in employment, and especially expulsion from one's job. This seems to suggest that, even in the contemporary era, some workplaces are highly charged, in a race and gender sense, and in ways that stratification research has not been able to empirically capture. In fact, it may be the case that by prioritizing individual background attributes in our modeling of objective and material workplace outcomes, researchers have missed important, albeit sometimes informal, group dynamics that have very significant consequences for well-being—consequences that are perhaps even more significant to the victim, according to our qualitative accounts, than the objectively measurable inequalities on which social scientists have tended to focus.

Beyond experiencing harassment, African Americans and women also witness the application of differential criteria by gatekeepers—gatekeepers with significant discretion in workplace contexts. The invoking of "soft skill" criteria works to the disadvantage of women and minorities, who are often seen as less dependable albeit for distinct reasons. Indeed, two key insights emerged on the issue of managerial discretion. First, and quite consistent with what more quantitative scholars have inferred for some time, the use of "soft skill" criteria impacts women and minorities in job mobility. Wilson and McBrier (2005) referred to this as the particularistic mobility thesis. Others employing quantitative modeling, such as Huffman and Cohen (2004) and Prokos and Padavic (2005), have concurred that differential treatment by race and sex must be playing a role in high-status job attainment. As much of our qualitative materials attest, gatekeeping actors exercise considerable agency when making promotion and hiring decisions, and invoke a relatively flexible set of filters for "who fits the job best" and "who might be best for the promotion." Given specific stereotypical assumptions about woman and minorities, such subjectivity hardly tends to work in their favor.

> *The invoking of "soft skill" criteria works to the disadvantage of women and minorities, who are often seen as less dependable albeit for distinct reasons.*

Second, discretion is activated not only in the course of hiring or mobility decisions but in the day-to-day monitoring of employees. This, according to our results, seems to have serious implications for women and minority employees. They are policed more closely and sanctioned more often and severely. In a very real sense, this is targeted workplace bullying, often carried out under the guise of following organizational procedures and rules. The problem, of course, as many of our cases revealed, is when organizational procedures, policies, and penalties are followed only when convenient and when disparately applied to particular individuals and status groups. Disparate policing, characteristic especially of the race discrimination cases we examined, no doubt explains why discriminatory firing is so prevalent in these data.

Despite similarities, our findings also denote a racialized and gendered character to what we are describing. For women, several patterns stand out. First, much of the discrimination women face is gendered. Stereotypical assumptions about women are employed by gatekeeping actors, women are often sexualized, and issues of dependability linger in the minds of employers. In the aforementioned regards, we have seen that soft skill criteria and gatekeeper evaluation often work to the disadvantage of women over men in hiring and mobility processes, sometimes subtly and sometimes quite explicitly. Several of the employment examples indeed denote how powerful actors periodically feel that women "just don't belong" in certain work environments, or are "just not dependable."

Maternity and pregnancy, in the case of employment, likewise stand out as pivotal discriminatory issues. Frankly, we were surprised at the extent to which this was the case. Clearly, maternity and pregnancy (or even potential future maternity or pregnancy) are considerations that some employers consider during hiring, when making promotion decisions, and in arbitrary firing. Such is the case here, despite the intent and goals of female targets to remain employed. These are, in essence, stories of exclusion, forced demotion, and *being pushed out* of the labor market. Such realities, evidenced in countless case files, fly in the face of the neoclassic economic assumption that women merely choose, via socialization or life-course decisions, to opt out of productive work or mobility contests.

> *Clearly, maternity and pregnancy (or even potential future maternity or pregnancy) are considerations that some employers consider during hiring, when making promotion decisions, and in arbitrary firing.*

It is also clear that women are often sexualized and degraded in employment contexts, either through general harassment or more obviously through explicit sexual harassment. Approximately one-fourth of sex discrimination cases entailed some degree of sexual harassment on the job. Admittedly, some workplaces (not represented in our data) have little tolerance for such conduct and apply the brunt of organizational sanctions against perpetrators. Female efforts to resolve the harassment themselves, the significant psychological and job-related consequences of such harassment, and the virtual lack or organizational response in our data are nevertheless noteworthy, not to mention troubling.

Racial minorities, or in the case of our study in particular, African Americans, experience significant levels of discretionary sanctioning and policing while on their jobs. While some of this is tied to harassment on the job, such policing is no doubt playing a large part in the levels of expulsion (or firing) of African American employees. Both African American men and women, as our examples demonstrated, seem to be systematically targeted for oversight by supervisors—something one female victim referred to as "just watching." In some cases this targeted attention appears to be part of a plan to terminate the employee in question from the outset. In others, disparate oversight and then harsher sanctions when policy is violated appear to be shaped by assumptions regarding black employees, including the view that they are more aggressive or inclined toward laziness while on the job.

In either scenario, the issue is disparate enforcement and policing relative to organizationally defined, "legitimate" policies and procedures. Indeed, it is not the policy itself that is in question, rather the extent to which it is followed and by whom. Here, again, discretion and arbitrary decision making by immediate supervisors is particularly key. The consequences, beyond the most obvious ones pertaining to demotion or job loss, are numerous and often devastating psychologically. Victims within our data become paranoid, perhaps with good reason, that they are being watched by several employees. Absenteeism goes up as a result of stress, and in many cases, workers relate ways in which their overall sense of dignity has been assaulted. They also recognize quite clearly the race-based nature of such treatment given observations that other employees routinely undertake the behavior in question yet are never penalized.

Quite notable throughout is the contemporary persistence of race-based discriminatory harassment. Overt racist acts by coworkers and managers continue to occur and obviously have profound consequences for the targets, including fear, insult, and a sense of indignity.

Particularistic mobility processes and the invocation of "soft skill" criteria in job access and promotions are also important. Here we see those in more powerful positions defining desirable job qualities informally or "on the spot," and in a manner that undermines minority hiring and promotion. Whether such soft skills, such as communicative ability, confidence, ability to work with others, and so on are important for a given job is a matter of debate. What is not in question, however, is the problematic nature of using such criteria arbitrarily to exclude some at the cost of others, particularly where there is either racist intent from the outset or subjective interpretation invoked on the spot.

Quite notable throughout is the contemporary persistence of race-based discriminatory harassment. Overt racist acts by coworkers and managers continue to occur and obviously have profound consequences for the targets, including fear, insult, and a sense of indignity. Yet such harassment does not have to be explicitly racist in tone. Rather, it may take the form of general taunting, systematic isolation on the job, or neglect of employee needs. This breeds frustration, no doubt, as well as overall stress. It is notable, throughout cases of harassment, that the harassment is often carried out over a significant time frame and that victims often attempt to rectify the situation themselves. It is often only after other options are exhausted, and a desperation point is reached, that an external discrimination charge is filed.

We temper our conclusions pertaining to race-based patterns, of course, with the recognition that our case data are largely limited to African Americans given the state from which they are drawn. There is, however, little reason to believe that the patterns highlighted would not play out similarly in contexts that are largely white and Latino, for instance. In fact, we believe that many of the discriminatory processes revealed in our analyses—particularistic criteria, disparate policing of racial/ethnic minorities, and harassment on the job—likely prevail and shape minority employment and housing status in most U.S. contexts. The flavor of particularistic criteria may take on distinct forms, especially for language minorities. Yet the role of discretionary decision making among gatekeepers will, in all likelihood, remain central. We hope that scholars will be able to access similar data in the future, but from state contexts with varying racial and ethnic compositions, to see whether this is the case.

Conclusions

Social stratification is more than simply a remnant of historical exclusion played out through slowly declining intergenerational disadvantages in, for instance, education, skills, job experience, or wealth. It is also much more than the culmination of individual proclivities toward work, residence, or education patterned by cultural lag and socialization processes. While individual pathways, attributes, and preferences are unquestionably relevant, they are only influential within the bounds and constraints of social closure dynamics, including but not limited to contemporary discrimination.

Sociologists, at least in their theorizing, have largely concurred about the importance of social closure generally, and the rigidity of social statuses in particular. Yet scholarship on persistent inequalities has analytically prioritized not processes of closure but, instead, the ways in which subordinate group attributes (e.g., education, preferences, etc.) matter for contemporary status and well-being. As noted by Tomaskovic-Devey, Thomas, and Johnson (2005), this tendency is driven by the adoption of human capital and status attainment assumptions pertaining to stratification—assumptions that, explicitly or by default, treat institutional and organizational processes as relatively neutral. The social scientist is correspondingly left with a theoretical orientation wherein individuals are conceived of as competing in a largely meritocratic environment. Race or gender disadvantages, to the extent they exist, are merely residues. Racist and sexist structures, ideologies, differential organizational and institutional treatment, and discrimination by gatekeeping actors fall out of theoretical and empirical sight.

Important exceptions certainly pertain to the influence of queuing, job networks, segregation, and constraints on workplace mobility. Such work—work that indeed takes closure seriously in its theoretical orientation—nevertheless remains hard-pressed to explicitly capture social closure processes including, most fundamentally, discrimination. It is perhaps for this reason that recent multimethodological and qualitative, attitudinal work has generated excitement in the field by providing a momentary window into the very discriminatory processes that scholars have only been able to speculate about. Our analyses reflect an effort to contribute in this regard by highlighting both forms and processes of social closure impacting women and minorities in contemporary workplaces.

By virtue of the data that have been employed in the preceding pages and what they communicate, it is obvious that human action and agency are part and parcel of social closure and stratification maintenance, creation, and challenge (see also Roscigno forthcoming). As the qualitative materials so poignantly suggest, human beings actively engage in reifying inequality within organizational environments, and victims of inequality are much more than mere recipients of differential treatment. Victims, instead, often go through a series of steps to try to counter the inequality they are experiencing, including negotiation, avoidance, confrontation, and, in the case of filing a discrimination suit, politically and legally fighting what is unjust.

Although these points may seem all too obvious, it should be noted that the acknowledgment of such agency within sociological scholarship is relatively rare. Indeed, the distinctly human behavioral component is seldom woven into analyses of stratification aside from, perhaps, ethnographic analyses or research pertaining to collective behavior and social movements. This is unfortunate. Introducing some dimension of agency into our theoretical models provides leverage for talking about processes of inequality (rather then just relations and associations) and helps highlight ways in which individuals and groups play a part in producing (or reproducing) the structures within which they exist. Moreover, and perhaps more directly, introducing agency and interaction into overly structural accounts of inequality tempers relatively deterministic sociological claims. The construct of social closure pushes scholars to do just this.

As theoretically important as it is, the introduction of agency and action/interaction into our conceptions of stratification can render sociological theorizing relatively useless unless the framing, discussion, and analyses of relevant processes are placed within context. Indeed, without doing so, we resort simply to individual, unique stories with little in the way of generalizable lessons, theoretical growth, and predictive power. It is for this very reason that we embed our own conclusions regarding agency and discretion within broader research traditions emphasizing the influence of labor markets, compositional contexts, and workplace structures. Interactions and expressions of agency are fundamentally bounded and conditioned by the structures within which they exist. Workplace supervisors, for instance, activate discretion and potentially discriminatory criteria, but only to the extent that organizational structures, procedures, and rules give them the flexibility to do so. By default, this implicates organizations and institutions themselves in the inequalities that we have described. Conversely, there are organizations and businesses not represented in our data that mandate and formalize procedures that constrain actors—actors perhaps with a proclivity to do so—from discriminating.

Obviously there is an interplay between expressions of human agency/discretion and the environments within which they are embedded. And it is at the crux of this interplay where the most interesting sociological questions lie. How does the structure of workplaces, for instance, alter the nature of individual and group interactions in a manner that reifies or mitigates prevailing stratification arrangements and social status hierarchies? Or, how might processes of social closure and related micro-level interactions reinforce or alter structural arrangements themselves? Whether one builds one's research question from micro to macro or from macro to micro, or defines the question itself in terms of agency to structure or structure to agency, does not really matter. What is more paramount is that theorists and researchers alike make explicit the ways in which human action, conditioned and constrained to some degree by structure, is responsible for the patterns they describe.

The patterns, processes, and forms of inequality and discrimination that we have described are far-reaching and beyond specific considerations pertaining to employment. There is no reason to believe that the differential treatment we have uncovered does not apply equally to other institutional domains including, for instance, education, politics, medical care, housing, and legal-judicial processes. We know through prior research that race and gender inequalities exist within these arenas. Would it thus not make sense that gatekeeping discretion and differential evaluative processes might be contributing to these disparities? We believe so, and leave it to other scholars to distinguish precisely how.

Many of the lessons garnered from our empirical analyses of employment discrimination also hold implications for everyday encounters and interactions—encounters and interactions that may not be explicitly shaped or constrained by formalized rules, but that are no less influenced by broader societal and cultural views regarding women and racial ethnic minorities. Our findings suggest that actors within organization environments oftentimes filter evaluations of others and their interactions with others through preset cultural views and stereotypes. Such beliefs are by no means the creation of a given workplace, but rather of societal culture and history. The implication of this is that all social interaction—formal and informal, context-specific or not—has the potential to recreate status hierarchies whether or not the parties involved are aware of it. Remaining cognizant of any such preconceptions, particularly in the discretion we all use on a daily basis, may go a long way in ensuring that our own behaviors are not contributing to the sorts of inequalities that shape the everyday work lives of women and minorities.

References

Acker, Joan R. 1990. Hierarchies, jobs, bodies: A theory of gendered organizations. *Gender & Society* 4:139-58.
Beck, E. M., P. Horan, and Charles Tolbert. 1978. Stratification in a dual economy. *American Sociological Review* 43 (5): 704-20.
Beggs, John J. 1995. The institutional environment: Implications for race and gender inequality in the U.S. labor market. *American Sociological Review* 60:612-33.
Blau, Peter. 1977. *Inequality and heterogeneity: A primitive theory of social structure*. New York: Free Press.
Blaug, Mark. 1976. The empirical status of human capital theory: A slightly jaundiced survey. *Journal of Economic Literature* 14 (3): 827-55.
Bruce, Marino, Vincent J. Roscigno, and Patricia McCall. 1998. Structure, context and agency in the reproduction of black-on-black violence. *Theoretical Criminology* 2:29-55.
Cohen, Philip N. 1998. Black concentration effects on black-white and gender inequality: Multilevel analysis for U.S. metropolitan areas. *Social Forces* 77 (1): 207-29.
Cohn, S., and M. Fossett. 1995. Why racial employment inequality is greater in northern labor markets: Regional differences in white-black employment differentials. *Social Forces* 74:511-42.
Cotter D. A., J. M. Hermsen, and R. Vanneman. 1999. The effects of occupational gender segregation across race. *Sociological Quarterly* 44:17-36.
England, Paula. 1992. *Comparable worth: Theories and evidence*. New York: Aldine de Gruyter.
Feagin, Joe R. 1991. The continuing significance of race: Antiblack discrimination in public places. *American Sociological Review* 56:101-16.
Feagin, Joe R., and Douglas Lee Eckberg. 1980. Discrimination: Motivation, action, effects, and context. *Annual Review of Sociology* 6:1-20.
Feagin, Joe R., and Karyn D. McKinney. 2003. *The many costs of racism*. Lanham, MD: Rowman & Littlefield.
Gruber, James E. 1998. The impact of male work environments and organizational policies on women's experiences of sexual harassment. *Gender & Society* 12:301-20.
Gutek, B. A., and A. G. Cohen. 1987. Sex ratios, sex role spillover and sex at work: A comparison of men's and women's experiences. *Human Relations* 40:97-115.
Huffman, Matthew L. 2004. Gender inequality across local wage hierarchies. *Work & Occupations* 31:323-44.
Huffman, Matthew L., and Philip N. Cohen. 2004. Racial wage inequality: Job segregation and devaluation across U.S. labor markets. *American Journal of Sociology* 109:902–36.
Kaufman, Robert L. 1986. The impact of industrial and occupational structure on black-white employment allocation. *American Sociological Review* 51:310-23.
———. 2002. Assessing alternative perspectives on race and sex employment segregation. *American Sociological Review* 67:547-72.
Kaufman, Robert L., Randy Hodson, and Neil D. Fligstein. 1981. Defrocking dualism: A new approach to defining industrial sectors. *Social Science Research* 10:1-31.
Kingston, Paul W., Ryan Hubbard, Brent Lapp, Paul Schroeder, and Julia Wilson. 2003. Why education matters. *Sociology of Education* 76:53-70.
Kirschenman, Joleen, and Kathryn M. Neckerman. 1991. "We'd love to hire them, but . . .": The meaning of race for employers. In *The urban underclass*, ed. C. Jencks and P. E. Peterson, 203-32. Washington, DC: Brookings Institution.
Laband, David N., and Bernard F. Lentz. 1998. The effects of sexual harassment on job satisfaction, earnings, and turnover among female lawyers. *Industrial and Labor Relations Review* 51 (4): 594-607.
Lawler, Edward, Cecilia Ridgeway, and Barry Markovsky. 1993. Structural social psychology and the micro-macro problem. *Sociological Theory* 11:268-90.
Marini, M. M., and P. L. Fan. 1997. The gender gap in earnings at career entry. *American Sociological Review* 62:588-604.
Mason, Patrick. 2000. Understanding recent empirical evidence on race and labor market outcomes in the USA. *Review of Social Economy* 58 (3): 319-38.
McBrier, Debra Branch, and George Wilson. 2004. Going down? Race and downward occupational mobility for white-collar workers in the 1990s. *Work & Occupations* 31 (3): 283-322.
McCall, Leslie. 2001. Sources of racial wage inequality in metropolitan labor markets: Racial, ethnic, and gender differences. *American Sociological Review* 66 (4): 520-41.

Moss, Philip, and Chris Tilly. 2001. *Stories employers tell: Race, skill, and hiring in America*. New York: Russell Sage Foundation.
Murphy, R. 1988. *Social closure: The theory of monopolization and exclusion*. Oxford, UK: Clarendon.
Neumark, David, Roy J. Bank, and Kyle D. Van Nort. 1996. Sex discrimination in restaurant hiring: An audit study. *Quarterly Journal of Economics* 111 (3): 915-41.
Padavic, Irene, and David Orcutt. 1997. Perceptions of sexual harassment in the Florida legal system: A comparison of dominance and spillover explanations. *Gender & Society* 11:682-98.
Padavic, Irene, and Barbara Reskin. 2002. *Women and men at work*. Thousand Oaks, CA: Pine Forge Press.
Pager, Devah. 2003. The mark of a criminal record. *American Journal of Sociology* 108:937-75.
Pager, Devah, and Lincoln Quillian. 2005. Walking the talk? What employers say versus what they do. *American Sociological Review* 70:355-80.
Parkin, Frank. 1974. Strategies of social closure in class formation. In *The social analysis of class structure*, ed. F. Parkin. London: Tavistock.
———. 1979. Social closure and class formation. In *Classes, power, and conflict*, ed. Anthony Giddens and David Held. Los Angeles: University of California Press.
Peterson, Trond, and Ishak Saporta. 2004. The opportunity structure for discrimination. *American Journal of Sociology* 109:852-901.
Prokos, Anastasia, and Irene Padavic. 2005. An examination of competing explanations for the pay gap among scientists and engineers. *Gender & Society* 19:523-43.
Reid, Lori L., and Irene Padavic. 2005. Employment exits and the race gap in young women's employment. *Social Science Quarterly* 86:1242-60.
Reskin, Barbara F. 2000. The proximate causes of discrimination. *Contemporary Sociology* 29:319-29.
———. 2003. Including mechanisms in our models of ascriptive inequality. *American Sociological Review* 68:1-21.
Roscigno, Vincent J. Forthcoming. *The face of discrimination: How race and gender impact work and residential lives*. Lanham, MD: Rowman & Littlefield.
Roscigno, Vincent J., and Randy Hodson. 2004. The organizational and social foundations of worker resistance. *American Sociological Review* 69:14-39.
Smith, Ryan A. 2002. Race, gender, and authority in the workplace: Theory and research. *Annual Review of Sociology* 28:509-42.
Tomaskovic-Devey, Donald. 1993. *Gender and racial inequality at work: The sources and consequences of job segregation*. Ithaca, NY: ILR Press.
Tomaskovic-Devey, Donald, and Sheryl Skaggs. 2002. Sex segregation, labor process organization, and gender earnings inequality. *American Journal of Sociology* 108:102-28.
Tomaskovic-Devey, Donald, Melvin Thomas, and Kecia Johnson. 2005. Race and the accumulation of human capital across the career: A theoretical model and fixed-effects application. *American Journal of Sociology* 111:58-89.
U.S. Census Bureau. 2003. *Occupations: 2000, Census 2000 brief*. Written by Peter Fronczek and Patricia Johnson. http://www.census.gov/prod/2003pubs/c2kbr-25.pdf.
Vallas, Steven P. 2003. Rediscovering the color line within work organizations: The "knitting of racial groups" revisited. *Work & Occupations* 30:379-400.
Weber, Max. 1978. *Economy and society. An outline of interpretive sociology*. Edited by G. Roth and C. Wittich. Berkeley: University of California Press.
West, Candace, and Don H. Zimmerman. 1987. Doing gender. *Gender & Society* 1:125-51.
Wilson, F. D., M. Tienda, and L. Wu. 1995. Race and unemployment: Labor market experiences of black and white men, 1968-1988. *Work & Occupations* 22:245-70.
Wilson, George. 1997. Pathways to power: Racial differences in determinants of job authority. *Social Problems* 44:38-54.
Wilson, George, and Debra B. McBrier. 2005. Race and loss of privilege: African American/white differences in the determinants of layoffs from upper-tier occupations. *Sociological Forum* 20:301-21.
Wilson, George, I. Sakura-Lemessy, and J. P. West. 1999. Reaching the top: Racial differences in mobility paths to upper-tier occupations. *Work & Occupations* 26:165-86.
Wilson, William J. 1978. *The declining significance of race: Blacks and changing American institutions*. Chicago: University of Chicago Press.
Yoder, Janice D. 1991. Rethinking tokenism: Looking beyond numbers. *Gender & Society* 5:178-92.

Discrimination and Desegregation: Equal Opportunity Progress in U.S. Private Sector Workplaces since the Civil Rights Act

By
DONALD TOMASKOVIC-DEVEY
and
KEVIN STAINBACK

Numerous commentators have concluded that the Civil Rights Act was effective in promoting increased access to quality jobs for racial minorities. Many have worried as well that the pace of change has been too slow or stalled, particularly after 1980. Few have directly discussed under what conditions we might expect equal employment opportunity (EEO) to flourish. Explanations of status inequalities in the workplace have primarily relied on theories of social conflict and discrimination. Organizational perspectives on stratification, while not completely absent from previous research, remain a road less traveled. In this paper we present trends in race-sex inequality in U.S. workplaces since the Civil Rights Act of 1964 and describe the organizational practices and discrimination processes that are likely to maintain status inequalities in the workplace and those which might be catalysts of change.

Keywords: race; sex; workplace; segregation; inequality

In 1964 the U.S. Congress enacted and President Johnson signed the Civil Rights Act. Although it was not the first or the last legislative moment in the struggle for civil rights, it was a particularly powerful one. As outlined in the preamble to the Act, it was designed:

> to enforce the constitutional right to vote, to confer jurisdiction upon the district courts of the United States to provide injunctive relief against discrimination in public accommodations, to authorize the attorney General to institute suits to protect constitutional rights in public facilities and public education, to extend the Commission on Civil Rights, to prevent discrimination in federally assisted programs, to establish a Commission on Equal Employment Opportunity, and for other purposes. (Civil Rights Act of 1964)

The Civil Rights Act went on to outlaw segregation and discrimination by race, ethnicity, and religion in public education; public accommodations; voting; and federal assistance. Title VII of the Act also extended the equal opportunity principle to employment and for the first time explicitly mentioned sex as a protected category. Title VII of the Civil Rights Act of 1964 made it illegal for an employer to

> (1) fail or refuse to hire or to discharge any individual, or otherwise to discriminate against any individual with respect to his compensation, terms, conditions, or privileges of employment, because of such individual's race, color, religion, sex, or national origin; or (2) limit, segregate, or classify his employees or applicants for employment in any way which would deprive or tend to deprive any individual of employment opportunities or otherwise adversely affect his status as an employee, because of such individual's race, color, religion, sex, or national origin. (SEC. 2000e2. [Section 703a])

The Act also created the Equal Employment Opportunity Commission (EEOC) to monitor Title VII of the Act concerning employment discrimination. Initially the commission was not granted the power to impose sanctions, or even file suit against employers in violation of Title VII, but was authorized to monitor progress and issue guidelines for Title VII compliance. The Equal Employment Opportunity Act of 1972 amended Title VII such that the EEOC was able to file lawsuits. Private sector firms with more than fifty employees, twenty-five if federal contractors, were required to submit yearly reports on the race/ethnic and sex composition of their workforce in each establishment with twenty-five or more employees.[1]

In 1965, less than a year after the passage of the Civil Rights Act, the Office of Federal Contract Compliance (OFCC) was established under Executive Order 11246 to advance the hiring of people of color in firms engaged in contractual relations with the federal government. Federal contractors or first-tier subcontractors with more that fifty employees or contracts amounting to $50,000 were subject to oversight by the OFCC. These contractors were required to maintain a plan of affirmative action detailing how equity goals would be reached. If a firm was audited by the OFCC and affirmative action plans were not on file or over longer periods progress toward goals was not apparent, firms could potentially be subject to severe sanctions such as exclusion from federal contract bidding or less

---

Donald Tomaskovic-Devey is a professor and chair of Sociology at the University of Massachusetts, Amherst. He is interested in processes of organizational inequality and change, particularly with regard to equal employment opportunity. He also is exploring interorganizational market relationships, contrasting market, hierarchy, and embeddedness approaches. His recent publications have appeared in the American Sociological Review, Social Forces and the American Journal of Sociology.

Kevin Stainback is a post doctoral/visiting assistant professor at the University of Massachusetts. His previous research examines changes in race and sex employment opportunity through an organizational perspective paying particular attention to the historical record and the role of political and legislative uncertainty in bringing about change. His current research agenda is centered on the development of sampling and estimation techniques to perform dynamic models of organizational change with EEO-1 data.

NOTE: This research is being supported, in part, by a grant from the Russell Sage Foundation. Direct correspondence to Don Tomaskovic-Devey at the Department of Sociology, University of Massachusetts, 200 Hicks Way, Amherst, MA 01003; e-mail: Tomaskovic-Devey@soc.umass.edu.

harsh penalties including fines, back payment, and affirmative relief. In 1978 the Office of Federal Contract Compliance Programs (OFCCP) was created, which subsumed the OFCC and eleven other federal compliance agencies.

Evaluating the impact of this extension of rights to equal opportunity in employment is the central goal of this article. The article accomplishes two linked tasks. First, we explain why the simple enactment of equal employment opportunity (EEO) law should not be expected to automatically produce EEO progress by design. We then empirically chart what progress has been made and for whom in private sector employment since 1966. Strong theoretical expectations at the level of individuals as well as organizations suggest that EEO progress requires much more than simple changes in law to be achieved. We examine trends in race/ethnic segregation and access to quality employment to illustrate the unevenness of progress toward equal opportunity in U.S. workplaces.

Numerous commentators have concluded that the Civil Rights Act was effective in promoting increased access to good-quality jobs for minorities. Many have worried as well that the pace of change has been too slow or stalled, particularly after 1980. Few have directly discussed under what conditions we might expect EEO to flourish. A naive view might be that after equal opportunity laws were enacted, organizations responded and EEO became widespread. A political struggle continues, however, over the enforcement, interpretation, and managerial commitment to those laws. In the next section of this article, we describe the organizational practices and processes that are likely to maintain status inequalities in the workplace and those that might be catalysts of change.

The Inertial Tendencies of All Organizations

Organizational research and theory reveals the stability of organizational structure and practice. Organizations are "action generators." Successful organizations reproduce behavior regardless of the individuals who populate them. Organizations produce jobs defined in terms of tasks that need to be accomplished and specify the responsibilities, authority, reporting and career linkages, and rewards associated with these positions. Typically people are hired to fill positions; more rarely are positions created to employ a specific person. Organizations also develop informal cultures that script expected behaviors for people in different jobs. Such cultures may in some circumstances discourage following formal rules and procedures.

The combination of the formal structure of positions and the informal culture of practice ensures that behaviors are relatively stable in organizations, even as individual employees come and go. Thus, organizational theory predicts that change is the exception rather than the rule. This is the case because of the strong weight of inertia created by existing divisions of labor and cultural expectations (Stinchcombe 1965; Hannan and Freeman 1984). In addition, when innovation is required, perhaps because of the founding of a new firm or uncertainty in the environment introduced by equal opportunity law, the typical behavioral strategy of organizations is the copying of organizational practices from existing firms in the same organizational field (DiMaggio and Powell 1983). The implications of this line of reasoning is that eliminating discrimination or reaching EEO goals will not simply follow from legal change. Organizations are inherently conservative in the sense that they tend to reproduce past behaviors irrespective of the personalities or preferences of their employees.

This is not to say that organizations never change and EEO progress is impossible. Rather, the point is that change in employment practices are far from mechanical responses to law. At the most general level, we see three generic forces influencing organizational change. The first is inertia, the tendency of organizations to resist change. Inertia is probably the most powerful force and tends to reproduce organizational practices over time.

The second force is pressure from the environment to adopt new organizational routines and practices (Pfeffer and Salancik 1978; DiMaggio and Powell 1983). In the case of employment discrimination this pressure can be coercive (e.g., government regulation or discrimination lawsuits) or normative (e.g., expectations for appropriate human resource practices or in the culture more generally). The Civil Rights Act of 1964 is certainly such an, albeit diffuse, environmental pressure, which may have encouraged expanded minority access to desirable positions. EEOC reporting and OFCCP monitoring are unquestionably more direct pressures than the simple passage of legislation. Lawsuits might be a much more direct pressure from the environment. Moreover, the firm, industry, and community context of workplaces may also encourage or discourage equal opportunity behaviors and practices.

The third force is internal pressures for organization change. This pressure might come from organizational leadership (Baron 1991), human resource professionals with an EEO agenda (Cockburn 1991), or female and minority workforces demanding increased access to good jobs or fair treatment from management (Smith and Elliott 2002). Internal pressures, of course, may also have the effect of retarding progress toward EEO goals.

Pressures to Preserve and Expand Racial Status Inequalities

The inertial tendencies of organizations are typically recognized to emerge from the routine scripting of behavior within specific organizations, as well as the isomorphic tendencies in the selection of expected divisions of labor, managerial orientations, recruitment and promotion practices, and other behavioral routines from the environment. Routine practices assume cognitive legitimacy in the sense that they are culturally appropriate repertoires of action, which are deemed successful and reasonable methods to achieve organizational goals.

For EEO practice we see inertia as built around the institutional and interactional processes that create and reinforce status distinctions and expectations (Ridgeway 1997). Status groups become associated with certain types of work, in certain industries, and within specific firms (Tomaskovic-Devey 1993). Prior to the Civil Rights movement, racial segregation in employment was required under Jim Crow in some southern states and normatively legitimate in most American workplaces. Although we do not have any workplace-level estimates of black-white employment segregation prior to 1964, we can assume it was high but had already been declining since World War II, based on occupational desegregation trends after 1950 documented by previous scholars (Carlson 1992) and the enactment of both federal and local Fair Employment Practice (FEP) laws prior to the 1964 Civil Rights Act (Stainback, Robinson, and Tomaskovic-Devey 2005).

Employment segregation is the product of a series of well-recognized micro-level mechanisms—prejudice, cognitive bias, statistical discrimination, social closure around desirable employment opportunities, and network-based recruitment. These mechanisms tend to be mutually reinforcing and lead to status expectations about the appropriateness of different types of people for different jobs as well as to the value of those jobs to the organization (Ridgeway 1997). It is important to note that the negative impact that these micro-mechanisms have on reproducing workplace inequality are likely to be reduced by formal rules and procedures (Bielby 2000; Reskin 2000); however, these are also the same social processes that are deployed to circumvent the interference of formal rules and procedures. We outline these mechanisms to make explicit that the relation between legal shifts in equal opportunity law and the production of intended social change is not path dependent; instead, there are also considerable countervailing pressures in the society and in workplaces that encourage continued and even expanded discrimination.

Prejudice and cognitive bias

Normative explanations for discrimination are widespread in popular treatments of civil rights change. In these explanations, discrimination reflects the prejudiced behavior of individuals. A great deal of evidence shows that the endorsement of racist statements declined dramatically during and after the civil rights movement (Schuman et al. 1997). Some scholars have asserted that racial discrimination has withered because of these general normative changes (Thernstrom and Thernstrom 1997). Other scholars have concluded that the historical mutation of racial prejudice into cultural rather than naturalistic explanations of difference suggests that the civil rights movement may have defeated only the most obvious expressions of status prejudice (Sears, Henry and Kosterman 2000).

When most people think of discrimination they think of some active bigot, deliberately excluding certain groups because of their stereotyped or even hostile evaluation of all members of a status group. It is clear that this kind of active bigotry is less socially acceptable than it was prior to the civil rights movements for racial equality. It is likely that active self-conscious racial animus has declined because of these more general social prohibitions. On the other hand, the use of cultural stereotypes to justify exclusionary decisions clearly remains prevalent in U.S. society.

We can think of employment discrimination as resulting from a series of decisions to include or exclude job candidates that are linked to the status characteristics of job or promotion candidates. While some decisions may be explicitly bigoted in justification, many are the result of more subtle social psychological processes of cognitive bias, stereotyping, and in-group preferences (Bielby 2000; Reskin 2000). Bigoted decision making relies on active status-linked animus or dislike by powerful decision makers. Bigots with no decision-making power are merely rude, but cannot discriminate, although they can, if not properly supervised, create a hostile work environment. Cognitive bias, on the other hand, refers to how information is routinely processed and distorted in decision making. The human brain tends to process information in terms of preexisting cognitive categories, such as race, gender, or age (Fiske 1998). These cognitive shortcuts can lead to misperception and bias in the evaluation of information. New information is most easily assimilated when it is distorted to fit preexisting categories. Three aspects to cognitive bias processes are typically relevant to discussions of employment bias—stereotyping, attribution errors, and in-group bias.

Stereotyping refers to the attribution of traits associated culturally with a group to all members of the group (Hamilton and Sherman 1994; Hilton and Von Hipple 1996). Stereotypes are culturally flexible and can be adapted to explain almost any exclusionary decision. For example, in the United States today, common stereotypes about African Americans include that they as a group are lazy, intellectually slow, and aggressive; women are often stereotyped as more concerned with family than work or as indecisive leaders; and Asians as studious but weak.

In practice, stereotypes are used to describe all members of a group. This is more likely when individuals are not well known to decision makers, and so they use stereotypes to "fill in the blanks." Stereotypes, in addition to being culturally flexible, can be deployed selectively. Perhaps an African American worker has a series of positive employee evaluations suggesting that he or she is not slow or lazy. Decision makers may downplay the positive evaluations and attribute the stereotype of being too aggressive to the candidate, thus justifying a negative employment decision. Importantly, individuals attend to and remember more clearly information that is consistent with a stereotype and miss or ignore information that is inconsistent with it. This does not suggest ill will, but is simply a function of how we process information. Information that is consistent with prior categorizations and cultural content is simply easier to make sense of and remember.

People are often unaware of how stereotypes affect their perceptions and behavior, and individuals whose personal beliefs are relatively free of prejudice or animus are susceptible to stereotypes in the same ways as people who hold a personal animosity toward a minority group (Devine 1989; Bodenhausen and MacCrae 1996). The practice of crossing the street or locking car doors in the presence of African American or Hispanic males is an example of stereotyping. Assuming that all black women are single mothers is another example. Assuming Asians are great technical workers but poor managers is a third.

Attribution errors tend to focus on the successes of in-group members, attributing them to skill or talent, while ignoring or downplaying mistakes, attributing them to bad luck or situational factors. For out-group members attribution errors tend to be reversed; mistakes are taken as evidence of lack of skill or potential; and successes may be overlooked or treated as situational, luck, or even the work of others (Hewstone 1990; Brewer and Kramer 1985). Attribution errors tend to reinforce the success of high-status groups and the failures of low-status groups; thus they will tend to lead to bias in evaluation contexts, such as hiring or promotion decisions. Ignoring positive evidence in favor of a minority candidate is an attribution error. Assuming aggressive tendencies in the absence of the observation of aggression is the application of a stereotype.

In-group bias refers to social preferences for people similar to the observer (Perdue et al. 1990; Fiske 1998). Substantial evidence indicates that most whites prefer whites to nonwhites in social encounters and that much of this preference is precognitive; that is, it is largely automatic and emotional in character. A long history of workplace studies on this phenomenon holds that people are more comfortable working with members of their own group. One of the earliest scholarly examples of in-group bias was Rosabeth Moss Kanter's 1977 study *Men and Women of the Corporation*. She studied a 1970s workplace and termed the strong preference of the white male top management to reproduce themselves with other white males "homosocial reproduction."

In-group bias influences not only hiring and promotion decisions but also the sharing of information about potential new employees and among informal work groups and the creation of bonds of friendship and mentoring within organizations (Braddock and McPartland 1987; Ibarra 1993, 1995). Many organizations rely on their current employees to find new employees. Sometimes these systems of network-based recruitment are even formalized through incentive systems that pay employees for recruiting new workers. Historically, some union hiring halls required new candidates to be nominated by existing employees. Some estimates suggest that in the United States about 50 percent of hiring is done through various types of network-based referrals. Since networks tend to be ethnically homogeneous, informal recruitment will tend to reproduce the current ethnic composition of a workforce (Stainback 2006b).

Friendship, influence, and information tend to travel through networks of socially similar others. While the motivations for these informal ties are likely to be social similarity and comfort, they can also lead to the marginalization of people who do not share the dominant status characteristics. These informal manifestations of in-group bias lead to increased positive information and visibility of majority members to decision makers higher in the chain of command. Cognitive bias processes often require minorities to demonstrate superior credentials to comparable majorities to be competitive for hiring and promotion (Wilson, Sakura-Lemessy, and West 1999; Wilson 1997a, 1997b).

Although there is evidence of secular decline in classic racial bigotry in the United States since the civil rights era, it is clear that cultural prejudice as well as the more subtle processes of cognitive bias against minority group members and in favor of whites remain culturally widespread and active at the societal level. Thus, at the level of individual perception and preferences, discriminatory tendencies remain widespread in U.S. society.

Statistical discrimination

The theory of statistical discrimination explains why employers in particular might *consciously* use stereotypes to exclude minority job candidates or to demand higher credentials before hiring them. Statistical discrimination refers to employers using known average differences in competencies between groups to discriminate against all members of the subordinate group. When statistical discrimination is happening, the employer relies on stereotypes about status group productivity to justify making discriminatory hiring decisions against individuals. Although in some accounts this behavior is described as economically rational, it is clearly discrimination under the law, since individuals are denied employment because of their status group membership. We really have no idea how widespread this type of direct self-conscious discrimination by employers is, but evidence from studies of employer hiring decisions demonstrates that it continues to operate in workplaces (Neckerman and Kirschenman 1991; Holzer 1996; Moss and Tilly 2001).

The key distinction between statistical discrimination and prejudice as discriminatory mechanisms is that employers are expected to be able to justify their actions in terms of business goals. Statistical discrimination is different from a cognitive bias discrimination mechanism in that the deployment of stereotypes is used as a self-conscious justification of discriminatory behavior. In both cases, stereotypes are treated as accurate. When cognitive processes reacting to preexisting categories of people arouse stereotypes, these stereotypes are seen as self-evident truths in their own right. When stereotypes are deployed in a statistical discrimination framework, an employer may be aware that they are unfair but justify his or her actions in terms of some presumed added financial risk or cost associated with employing the stereotyped group.

Social closure

Of course, discrimination is not just about individual psychology or even simply a misguided profit motive. It is also clearly the case that individuals have identities tied to group membership, and these identities influence how we interact with members of our own group and of others. Shared ethnicity, nationality, race, and even gender can be the basis for pride and a sense of mutual obligation (Tilly 1998; Tomaskovic-Devey 1993). In-group bias and network-based referrals are forms of discrimination that can be justified in terms of being amicable to socially similar others. Helping people you like and know is expected of friends and even acquaintances. When opportunities are closed to outsiders and reserved only for members of our own group, we refer to that process as social closure.

Social closure processes are widespread in social life generally; because they are tied to identities they are prominent mechanisms for both creating discrimination and justifying it. A manager who hires his friend's or current employee's son rather than a minority applicant may not be discriminating against the minority candidate as much as discriminating in favor of his friend's son. He may also know that if he had hired the minority candidate he would have to justify to his friend or employees why the son was not hired. Thus, social-closure-based discrimination is both about protecting opportunities for the dominant group but also acts to preserve the status distinctions between in-group and out-group.

Social closure processes are consistent with any of the discriminatory mechanisms we have already outlined—prejudice, cognitive bias, and statistical discrimination—but are not merely conditioned by individual psychology or the profit motive but by both social accountability to one's status group and the elaboration of cultural stories that explain and justify status based inequalities.

Social closure processes are also contextual in a way that processes of cognitive bias or prejudice often are not. Since social closure is about the exclusion of out-groups from opportunities, a social closure analysis of discrimination always assumes that social boundaries and segregation are less clearly demarcated where the cost to dominant groups is low or nonexistent. Thus, we would expect workplaces to integrate in the face of the various pressures arising from the civil rights movement before desirable jobs within those workplaces would. Under a social closure model, we would expect desirable jobs to integrate more slowly, if at all, as dominant groups attempt to continue to maintain their monopoly over the most desirable jobs, even as they lose the ability to control all jobs.

Given organizational tendencies toward inertia, equal opportunity employment change is likely to arise not simply because of the enactment of law but when there are significant coercive or normative pressures for change in workplaces or their environments.

But of course, social closure can fail (Parkin 1979). Dominant groups can be forced to give up their control over valuable positions and resources. The desegregation of hotels and restaurants in the United States since the Civil Rights Act of 1964 is a clear example. The expulsion of colonial powers from many non-European countries after World War II is another. The end of apartheid in South Africa is another. In all of these cases, subordinate groups struggled continually to usurp the power of dominant groups and gain access to opportunities previously hoarded for the dominant nationality, ethnicity, or race. At this point in U.S. history, the desegregation of public accommodations stands in stark contrast to the continued race segregation of neighborhoods and workplaces. Of course, from a social closure perspective, integrated restaurants and hotels may have generated less threat and less resistance than leveling the economic benefits of segregated housing and employment.

Consistent with a social closure account, strong evidence demonstrates that when women or minorities have gained access to managerial jobs, it has often been supervising other women or minorities. Elliott and Smith (2001) discussed this as a process of bottom-up ascription in which the integration of workplaces leads eventually to demands for access to more desirable jobs in those workplaces. This usurpation of the managerial jobs traditionally controlled by white male managers is, however, typically only partially successful as women and minorities gain access to lower-level supervisory jobs but continue to be excluded from higher-level managerial ones.

Organizational Innovation

Prejudice, cognitive bias, statistical discrimination, and social closure are all potential sources of racial discrimination in employment decision making. They operate through the flows of information and influence they produce about applicants and jobs, as well as how that information is evaluated by decision makers. The implication is that EEO law faces a powerful set of countervailing forces that both reinforce existing employment segregation and set the stage for new rounds of discrimination. Given organizational tendencies toward inertia, equal opportunity employment change is likely to arise not simply because of the enactment of law, but when there are significant coercive or normative pressures for change in workplaces or their environments. Progress can be expected to be most rapid when the costs to dominants are small and environmental pressures for change are strong.

Progress can be expected to be most rapid when the costs to dominants are small and environmental pressures for change are strong.

Burstein (1985) and others have suggested that general societal normative change has driven EEO progress. This explanation is inconsistent with most organizational theory, which sees institutional norms as emanating from much more proximate organizational environments. Mimetic isomorphism—the copying of organizational practices—is typically conceptualized to happen within an organizational field (DiMaggio and Powell 1983). Normative pressures for change inhere in social relationships and legitimate practices within an organizational field. Organizational practices are not compulsory as much as obvious and proper. For this reason, we expect that organizational change tracks change in organizational fields rather than societal norms. Practically, this suggests that when prominent firms in an industry begin to employ more African Americans or perhaps move women into management, we should see the behavior generalizing across the industry. Some industries will change for one dimension (say, race) but not for another (sex), some may never change at all. Some very recent research suggests that equal opportunity workplace change is more strongly tied to federal regulation or lawsuits in an industry than to the regulation or lawsuits targeted at specific firms (Hirsch 2005; McTague, Stainback, and Tomaskovic-Devey 2006). The interpretation is that the coercive regulation or legal action changes behavior in an industry rather than in the target firm. Thus, equal opportunity gains happen through the diffusion of new less discriminatory practices through the industry.

When there is greater uncertainty in dynamic environments, organizations are particularly likely to seek out field-specific legitimate practices. We think that the early years after the Civil Rights Act, when firms were unsure of the demands or sanctions they would face from the EEOC, OFCC, or other actors, probably qualifies as such a period of uncertainty in EEO practice. When organizations are uncertain about normatively appropriate behavior, experimentation in practices may arise, leading to higher variance in observed organizational practices. As behaviors become legitimate, institutionalized variance drops. We have observed such a phenomenon for black-white segregation trends, suggesting to us that racial EEO practice has become institutionalized even as EEO progress has stalled (McTague, Stainback, and Tomaskovic-Devey 2006).

Another model of organizational change is that powerful actors in the environment *coerce* organizational change. This may be because certain organizational forms or practices are viewed as legitimate and so become required by powerful actors, such as the EEOC. On the other hand, actors that are relatively powerful in their environments are more able to resist coercive pressures emanating from the environment. Organizations comply or resist influence based on their relative power in resource exchange relationships (Pfeffer and Salancik 1978). New institutional theory recognizes this process with the concept of *coercive isomorphism*, in which a position of exchange or regulatory dependence leads to isomorphic change at the demand of the more powerful actor (DiMaggio and Powell 1983).

These power relations become particularly evident when interdependency is paired with uncertainty in the ability to predict the actions of the more powerful organization. To ensure its viability, the weaker organization will adapt to or even anticipate demands from the more powerful organization through strategic action. Asymmetrical interdependence not only allows more powerful organizations to effectively influence weaker organizations within the resource exchange relationship, but it also allows powerful organizations to resist the influence of weaker organizations (Salancik 1979).

Past research has shown that job opportunities for minorities, and women to a lesser extent, have improved in firms and industries that depend on government support and are subjected to the most extensive regulatory pressure (Baron, Mittman, and Newman 1991; Leonard 1984a, 1984b, 1990; Salancik 1979). Sutton et al. (1994) found that close proximity to the state sector increases the adoption of policies and practices associated with due process (i.e., grievance procedures). On the other hand, Dobbin et al. (1993) did not find that federal contractors were more likely to adopt internal labor market practices, which are often associated with EEO plans. We suspect that the inconsistent findings in this literature reflect real historical changes in federal regulatory activity.

Change can also be driven by *internal constituencies*, particularly the dominant coalition in the organization, but other groups may produce pressure for change as well. Status-based processes of exclusion and usurpation over scarce or valuable opportunities are central to the production of workplace inequality (Reskin 1988; Tomaskovic-Devey 1993). Although the specific mechanisms producing exclusion and inclusion will vary as a function of human inventiveness and historical context, status groups dynamically attempt to preserve their advantages by limiting access to others outside of the status group (Tilly 1998). Excluded groups will tend to devise means to usurp status monopolies, either by directly challenging superordinate's advantages or monopolizing other resources (Parkin 1979).

When the dominant coalition, typically top management and professional staff, are committed to EEO goals, we would expect stronger pressures for EEO change. Baron (1991) cited considerable anecdotal evidence that leadership commitment is required to advance EEO agendas. Cockburn (1991) found that EEO initiatives are most likely to be successful when supported by top management. Hultin and Szulkin (1999) in a study of Swedish workplaces found that women's wages are higher in firms with more women managers. Two studies have found that gender segregation is lower in organizations with more women in managerial roles (Baron, Mittman, and Newman 1991; Cohen, Broschak, and Haveman 1998).

Equal opportunity goals may have more support when minority or female constituencies become large enough to pressure for access to better jobs within the organization. Kanter (1977) argued that when a minority group rises to above 15 percent of employees, stereotyping will be reduced by the availability of individual-level variation among employees. Another model predicts that women and minorities are most likely to attain supervisory roles in workplaces where they are large proportions of the nonmanagerial workforce. Some authors have argued that this is a basic mechanisms of political appeasement through which dominant status groups diffuse political pressure and maintain control of both the labor force and the top jobs (Elliott and Smith 2001; Smith and Elliott 2002). The process of bottom-up ascription can be interpreted as a limited reaction to demands for inclusion by women and ethnic minorities. When female or minority access to supervisory or managerial positions is achieved, it is often in the segregated sphere of supervising others within the subordinate status group.

Phillip Selznick (1949) referred to this process in a slightly different way. According to his early institutional perspective, cooptation is "the process of absorbing new elements into the leadership or policy determining structure of an organization as a means of averting threats to its stability or existence" (p. 249). While Selznick's original notion of cooptation refers to the management of interorganizational power relations, we see cooptation functioning within organizations as well. He further discussed formal and informal cooptation. Formal cooptation was for the purpose of gaining external legitimacy, although those in power remained in power. On the other hand, informal cooptation refers to a similar process where some power sharing occurs.

Because this is a dynamic political struggle, we can also expect that advantaged groups will tend to monopolize the best positions, rather than all positions. Thus, we expect women and minorities to gain access to managerial jobs in lower-wage industries or in large firms with internal, often segregated, managerial hierarchies. Social closure theory leads to the expectation that there will be historical changes in status hierarchies, but these changes are most likely where subordinate groups are strong, superordinate groups weak, and the costs of relinquishing privilege small. Social closure pressures are weaker when dominant status coalitions have less incentive to exclude (i.e., low wage levels, declining opportunities; see Reskin and Roos 1990).

It is fairly clear that EEO law has encouraged the adoption of formalized human resource practices to demonstrate compliance with those laws. This has been primarily interpreted as a legitimating device under a new institutional interpretation—it is merely symbolic adoption to forestall regulatory or legal action. Some evidence, however, indicates that inequality is lower in organizations with more formalized personnel practices. Formalization has been hypothesized to reduce inequality precisely because it reduces the influence of the basic micro-level mechanisms that produce status segregation and inequality (Szafran 1982). That is, formalization tends to moderate particularism (Anderson and Tomaskovic-Devey 1995). For example, Reskin and McBrier (2000), using data from around 1990, showed that women's access to managerial jobs increases with formalized recruitment strategies. Formalization may encourage employers to search for candidates qualified for specific jobs, rather than select candidates because they are simply socially comfortable or familiar. When the jobs themselves have clear skill requirements, we might expect to see more progress for minority workers. Professions have exactly this character. Since professions typically require specific educational credentials, they have a strong formal criteria that will trump race (or sex) in the selection of most applicants. Desirable jobs with more diffuse criteria, such as managerial roles, are more likely to resist equal opportunity integration.

Summary of expectations

EEO progress is not likely to be a simple result of legal change. Rather, organizational theory leads us to expect that change will happen as experimental changes in human resource practices become legitimate and diffuse. This experimentation is likely to happen during periods of regulatory uncertainty, when law and enforcement criteria are still in flux. Some of these new human resource practices will become legitimate and diffuse more rapidly because of coercive and mimetic isomorphic pressures from the firm's environment. At the same time, resistance to equal opportunity progress should be expected. Resistance will be generated by both the bias processes that operate at the individual and group level and by the basic tendency toward inertia in organizational practices.

In the next section of this article, we examine actual changes in black-white-Hispanic-Asian private sector employment opportunity since the Civil Rights Act. Although we have some expectations based on the preceding discussion, we also treat this analysis as exploratory. This article is the first to produce long-time trends on workplace equal employment outcomes. It is also unique in that we compare the fates of black, white, Hispanic, and Asian men and women over the entire period. Most equal opportunity law and practice were developed in response to African American's and later white women's claims for nondiscriminatory workplaces. Much less is known about the Latino or Asian experience and virtually nothing at the level of workplace trends. Before we proceed, it is useful to summarize our expectations:

- EEO progress will be most rapid early in the post–Civil Rights Act period as corporations face an uncertain regulatory environment.
- EEO progress will stall when political pressure for further progress recedes after 1980.
- EEO progress will happen faster when whites' privilege is less threatened; that is, minorities will make faster access in employment than they will in good working-class jobs and faster progress in both of these than in access to management positions.
- EEO managerial progress will happen faster in low-wage industries.
- EEO managerial progress will happen faster in workplaces with large minority nonmanagerial workforces.
- EEO progress will be stronger and more sustained in professional occupations than in managerial occupations.

Documenting Desegregation

The trends we present are derived from workplace-level data authorized to be collected from private sector employers by the Civil Rights Act. Title VII created the EEOC and granted it limited powers of investigation and enforcement of the employment provisions of the Civil Rights Act. The Act also required employers to submit annual reports to the EEOC on their employment distributions. Since 1966 the EEOC has been collecting data on sex by race/ethnic employment and occupational segregation from U.S. employers. These data were to be used to monitor progress both at the workplace and societal level.

Remarkably, we have very poor descriptive knowledge as to the effectiveness of this defining legislation of the civil rights era. This is at first surprising, but with the exception of the EEO-1 reports collected as a result of the Civil Rights Act, no systematic time series data on workplace segregation have been available. The

EEO-1 data have only recently become available to the research community and are sure to become an important resource for studies of workplace inequality and dynamic organizational change.

All of our previous systematic knowledge of change in the employment opportunities of women and race/ethnic minorities comes from surveys of individuals that describe employment in terms of occupations detached from their workplace context, the presumed site of discrimination. This occupation-based literature suggests that since 1964 minorities have had increased access to better occupations and that there have been declines in occupational segregation. A comparison of the various time series available on black-white and Hispanic-white occupational segregation shows strong declines across the 1970s and little or none across the 1980s. Various scholars have interpreted this stalling of EEO progress in the 1980s as reflecting the relaxation of federal regulatory activity (Bergmann 1996; Stainback 2006a).

We report basic trends in access to private sector employment since the 1964 Civil Rights Act. At this point we are not yet ready to explain why things have turned out as they have but want to make clear that progress has been far from uniform. What we have learned from documenting these basic trends is that while almost all workplaces have incorporated women and racial/ethnic minorities as employees, status segregation within workplaces remains very high, white males continue to have advantaged access to the best quality jobs, most racial progress in EEO stalled after 1980, and white women seem to have benefited the most from the struggles for EEO. We begin by documenting trends in workplace employment diversity.

Status homogeneity in private sector workplaces since 1966

Figure 1 reports time trends in the percentage of EEO-1 establishments that totally exclude various status groups from their labor forces. In 1966, more than 50 percent of EEOC reporting workplaces had no black male employees. In the mid-1960s, more than 70 percent of workplaces contained no Hispanic male or black female employees. Hispanic females were absent from about 85 percent of EEOC reporting workplaces in 1966. And Asian males and Asian females were almost entirely absent from EEOC reporting firms, with 90 and 93 percent of establishments reporting no Asian males and females, respectively, at the beginning of the EEO regulatory period. Thus, the large- to midsize-firm private sector began the post–Civil Rights Act period with very low levels of minority representation. White men and women, in contrast, were employed in almost all EEOC reporting workplaces in 1966. For the majority of workplaces, the implication of the Title VII of the Civil Rights Act and associated enforcement was that they had to begin to hire minority workers for the first time.

The complete exclusion of minority workers declined steeply in EEO reporting workplaces in the late 1960s. This early period preceded most enforcement efforts, but was the period of maximum regulatory uncertainty in which organizations

FIGURE 1
TRAJECTORY OF EQUAL EMPLOYMENT OPPORTUNITY (EEO) REPORTING
WORKPLACES WITH NO GROUP REPRESENTATION

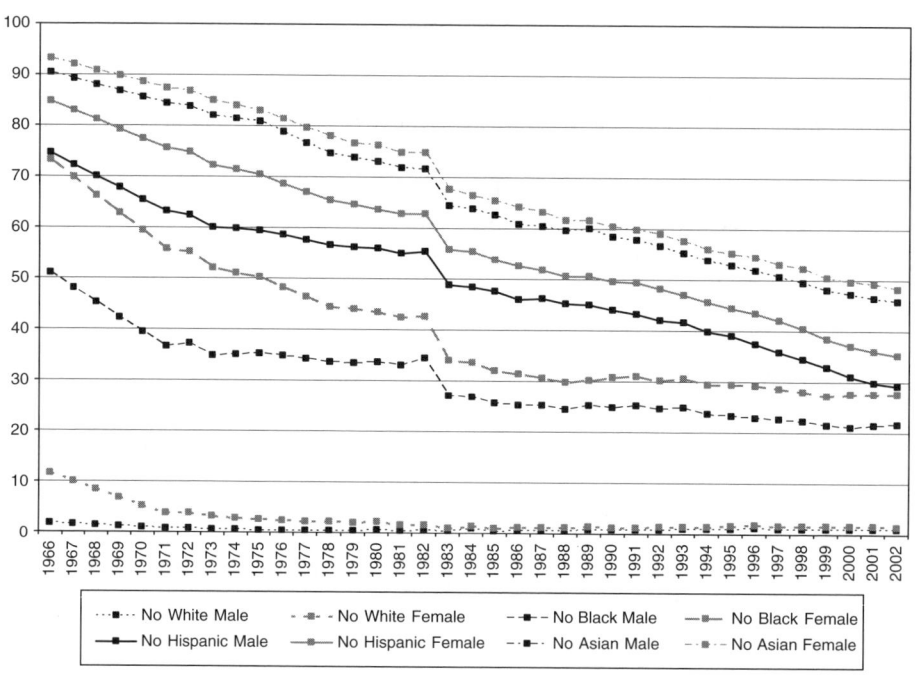

experimented with demonstrating compliance with the new law in the absence of clear regulatory expectations (Edelman 1992). The initial declines in ethnic exclusion from 1966 to 1971 were larger for black men (15 percent) and black women (17 percent) than they were for Hispanic men (12 percent), Hispanic women (9 percent), and Asian males (6 percent) and Asian females (6 percent).

Across the 1970s, the complete employment exclusion of black, Hispanic, and Asian women showed continued declines. During this same period of maximum regulatory attention black men made no further gains in desegregating, while Hispanic and Asian males continued to enter EEOC workplaces, although at a reduced rate compared to the late 1960s. After 1980, there was almost no increase in the representation of African American men or women in EEOC reporting firms, although the absence of Hispanic and Asian men and women declined and continued through to the end of the century. By the year 2002, 21 percent of EEOC workplaces still employed no African American men and 28 percent no African American women. Hispanic males were absent from 28 percent of regulated workplaces, while Latinas were not employed in 35 percent of private sector workplaces. Finally, more than 45 percent of EEOC reporting firms employed no Asian males or females. Interestingly, among this same sample of EEOC reporting workplaces only 5.4 percent of workplaces end the period with no minority workers at all. Among private sector EEO-1 reporting establishments, sex and ethnically homogeneous workplaces have almost disappeared since the Civil Rights Act of 1964. Thus, while many workplaces lack representation from among all six groups most employers can point to at least one black, Hispanic, or Asian employee.

Figure 1 makes clear that minority employment has made strong gains in the regulated private sector but that most of those gains came in the period immediately after the 1964 Civil Rights Act. This is particularly true for black men who see few, if any, gains after 1973. Hispanic and Asian men and women continue to integrate new workplaces over the entire period, primarily reflecting their continued growth as a proportion of the U.S. labor force overall.

Most striking is that white men and white women are found in virtually all workplaces. In 1966, 11 percent of workplaces had no white women employed in them, but this had fallen to 3 percent by the early 1970s and about 1 percent currently. These patterns mean that even today when white men and women go to work they will often be employed in workplaces where there is not a single black male, black female, Hispanic male, Hispanic female, Asian male, or Asian female coworker. One of these groups will almost always be represented among their coworkers, but one or more groups may be entirely absent. While there has been clear progress in the desegregation of American private sector workplaces, substantial racial homogeneity remains common in many workplaces.

Relative to our expectations, we find that the most rapid integration into homogeneous workplaces for all groups happened in the earliest period, during the period of maximum regulatory and human resource uncertainty. Progress stalls during the 1970s, perhaps because few firms were left with no women or minority employees at all. Fewer workplaces were truly diverse, containing representatives from all six sex-race groups.

Workplace segregation trends

We have just seen the rapid but incomplete declines in between-firm segregation implied by racially homogeneous workplaces. Some of this homogeneity, including the substantial proportion of workplaces that continue to lack specific minority employment, represents the spatial distribution of African Americans, Hispanics, and Asians across the country. Some places employ so few non-Anglo whites that we would expect many workplaces might have no African American, Latino, or Asian employees. In this section we turn to employment segregation within workplace divisions of labor.

The Civil Rights Act specifically prohibited employment segregation. The end of slavery led to a short period of legal equality between whites and blacks, which ended with the imposition of Jim Crow laws in the South and segregated employment and housing practices across the country. Segregation was one of the central tactics used by whites to reinstitute their social advantages over African Americans

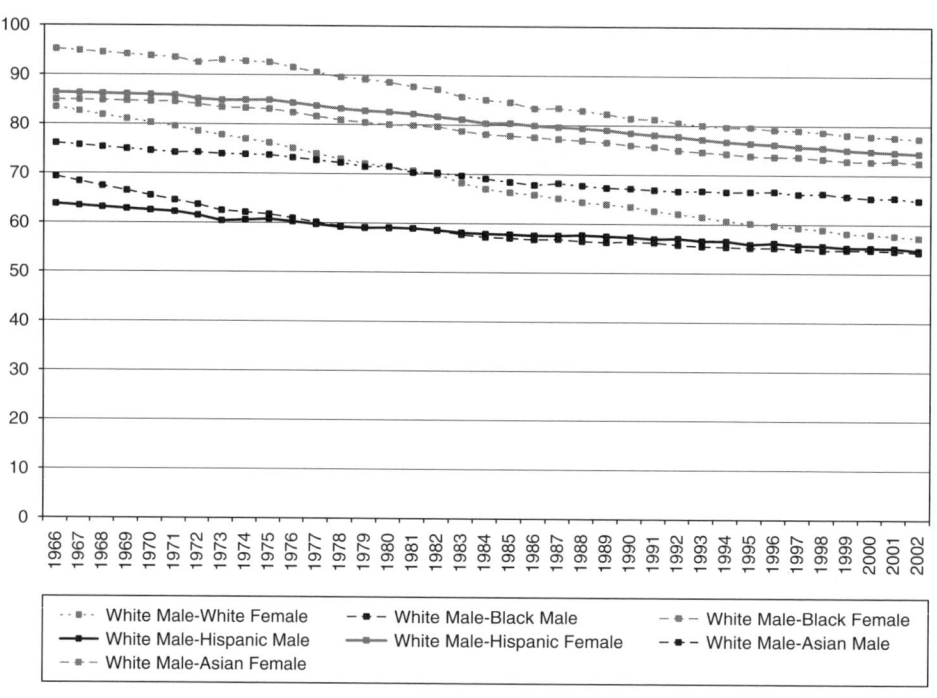

FIGURE 2
TRAJECTORY OF EQUAL EMPLOYMENT OPPORTUNITY (EEO) REPORTING WORKPLACE SEGREGATION RELATIVE TO WHITE MALES

across the twentieth century. Many scholars have researched housing segregation trends in the United States, but almost none have looked at workplace level segregation trends. Equal opportunity in workplaces requires employers to not simply hire minority employees but also to hire them on the same terms as whites. What progress has been made to desegregate private sector workplaces?

Figure 2 displays the trends in workplace occupational segregation from white men since 1966 in private sector regulated workplaces. We focus on white men since in all historical accounts it is white males' control of desirable jobs that was being challenged by the Civil Rights Act and associated legal and regulatory pressures. We measure segregation with the conventional index of dissimilarity (D). The index equals 100 when groups are completely segregated from each other. The level of the index suggests what proportion of a group would have to switch occupations to end segregation in employment. Because these data refer to occupations within workplaces, rather than job titles within workplaces we underestimate actual workplace segregation.[2] Given this limitation, in 1966 we estimate that the segregation of white men relative to women was between 85 and 95. In 1966, white men almost never worked with women of any race in the same occupation in the same workplace. Segregation from Asian women was highest (95), followed by Hispanic women (86), black women (85), and white women (83) in 1966. Overwhelmingly, white men simply did not work as peers with women at the beginning of the legal period mandating EEO. White men were more likely to work with black men (69) and Hispanic men (64) and Asian men (76), but employment segregation was still quite high. It is quite possible that by 1966 some employment segregation among men had already been reduced by reactions to the civil rights movement, state-level Fair Employment Practice (FEP) laws (Stainback, Robinson, and Tomaskovic-Devey 2005), and the 1964 Civil Rights Act. Although the Civil Rights Act outlawed sex segregation, the political target was primarily minority male employment, and early enforcement, as well as earlier FEP laws, which were also concerned with providing increased opportunities for minority men.

Currently white male employment segregation remains quite high in all comparisons, dropping to its lowest level with minority men and white women. Even then, the index of dissimilarity remains in the high 50s. Almost forty years after the Civil Rights Act, substantially more than 50 percent of workers would have to exchange jobs to produce workplaces in which white men were integrated with minority workers and white women.

If we focus on the early civil rights periods, when uncertainty was highest and most political pressure was focused on discrimination against black men, we see the steepest decline in workplace segregation between white and black men. Black-white segregation among males dropped 7 points between 1966 and 1973. Interestingly, segregation between white men and white women also dropped substantially in this early period, even as segregation between white men and minority women barely changed at all in the immediate post–Civil Rights Act period. Hispanic men made limited gains between 1966 and 1973, with a 3-point drop in workplace segregation from white men. Asian males begin with the highest male segregation compared to white men (87) and show the smallest integration with white males (2 points). Black men, the intended beneficiaries of EEO/affirmative action law, were the immediate big winners, gaining access at a faster rate to positions occupied by white men than any other group. White women, however, showed rapid gains in access to white male jobs during this early period as well. There is essentially no change, however, in white male workplace segregation from minority women during the earliest years of formal equal opportunity and the illegality of workplace segregation on the basis of sex, race, and ethnicity.

Beginning in the early 1970s, organizations began to adopt personnel practices intended to at least symbolically demonstrate their commitment to EEO principles, federal regulatory capacity through the EEOC and the OFCCP was at its peak, and discrimination case law supported discrimination claims based on disparate impact (e.g., *Griggs v. Duke Power* in 1971). It is in this period that some prior researchers expected the greatest gains in equal opportunity. We observe, however, a substantial slowdown in the rate of integration of minority men with white men. Among males, Hispanic-white segregation essentially plateaus after 1973, dropping only 5 points over the next thirty years. Black-white workplace segregation among males continues to drop, although at a slower rate, through the early 1980s, but becomes fairly stable thereafter. Among males, Asians remain the most segregated from white males across the entire period, and by 2002, white males and Asian males display D values that are 10 points higher than white males compared to black males or Hispanic males.

After 1973, white males become increasingly integrated in their places of employment with women. White male workplace segregation from black and Hispanic women remains remarkably high to this day, although displaying a weak, but nearly linear, decline across the entire period. Much more striking has been the rapidly declining workplace segregation between white men and women. In 1966, white men and women were nearly totally segregated at work, residing in separate and typically unequal work. While white sex segregation remains high today, it is now lower than white male–Asian male segregation and almost as low as white male segregation from other minority men. Researchers have routinely assumed that sex segregation was higher than race segregation. This was clearly true in 1966, but by the year 2002 it seems more reasonable to say that the workplace barriers between white men and white women are now equivalent to those between white men and minority men. White women have clearly benefited the most from the legal and institutional prohibitions against workplace segregation.

We wondered if this meant that white women were becoming more integrated with all groups or if this signified the decline of sex distinctions among whites, even as race employment distinctions remain strong. Figure 3 makes the integration comparisons between white women and the other groups. There is substantial black-white integration among females in the earliest period following the passage of Title VII. Between 1966 and 1973, segregation between white women and black women fell by 6 points; however, the two have become increasingly segregated since. By 2002, white women and black women are as segregated as they were in 1966. Over the entire 1966 to 2002 period, white women are increasingly segregated from Hispanic women and Asian women. There was a short period of rapid desegregation relative to black women during the initial EEO period. In fact, the integration of black and white women immediately after the Civil Rights Act was more rapid than any other comparison or time shown in Figures 2 and 3. Evidently, race integration among women was easier to accomplish than race integration among men. On the other hand, it was less sustained and characterized by resegregation for the next thirty years.

The patterns of workplace desegregation among regulated private sector employers are only partially consistent with our original expectations. Within sex, black-white employment desegregation made rapid progress in the initial post–Civil Rights Act period, when firms were experimenting with human resources practices and uncertain as to which practices would signal compliance with the new legal expectations. There was essentially no cross-sex, cross-race progress in the earliest period. Sex segregation between whites and minorities was undisturbed by the initial set of firm responses to equal opportunity law. It is also the case that after 1980 when political pressure faded, so did further progress in black-white segregation among men.

FIGURE 3
TRAJECTORY OF EQUAL EMPLOYMENT OPPORTUNITY (EEO) REPORTING WORKPLACE SEGREGATION RELATIVE TO WHITE FEMALES

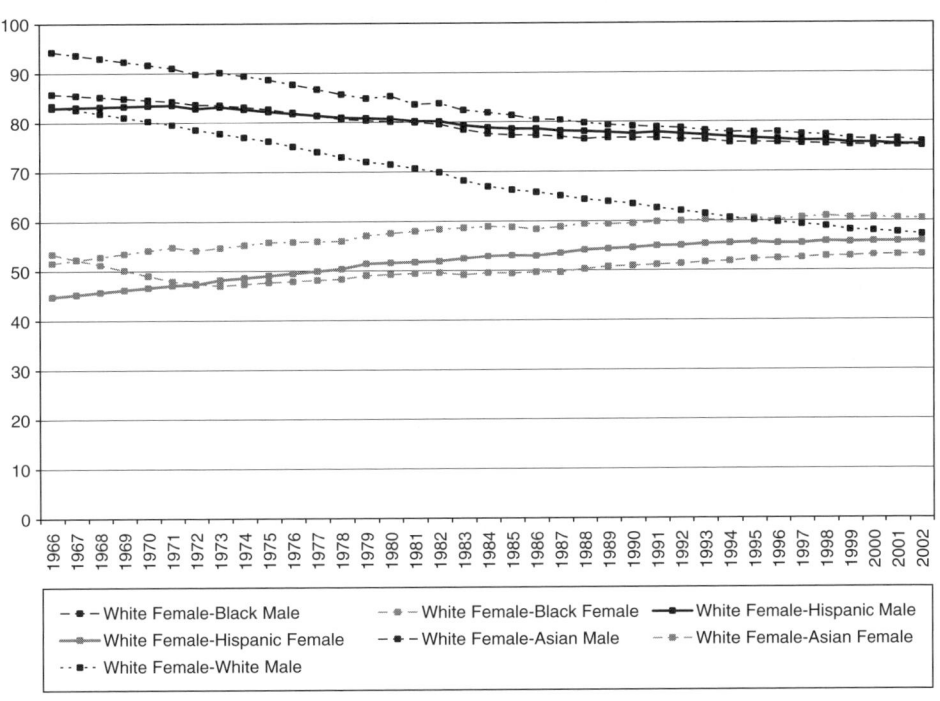

We also have a set of remarkable findings about the segregation patterns of white women. Across the entire post–Civil Rights Act period, white women have been rapidly integrating employment settings with white men, have slowly integrated with minority men, and are increasingly segregated from minority women. This rise in workplace segregation from minority women is dramatic and troubling. Overall, forty years after the law changed to make workplace segregation illegal, it remains high. Most whites work with other whites. Increasingly, white women work with white men. The big success story of the equal rights revolution in the private sector is the integration of white men and women. Cross-race progress among men stalled in the 1980s and among women has worsened since the mid-1970s.

Access to desirable occupations

Analyses of employment and segregation tell us something about the social distance between status groups but nothing about the quality of employment. In this section, we examine trends in access to craft production, managerial, and professional occupations. Craft occupations include skilled manual trades such as carpenters, plumbers, and machinists. These jobs typically have substantial autonomy, high skill, and relatively high wages. They are traditionally the most desirable working-class jobs. They are also traditionally male jobs. Managerial and professional jobs are typically the best-paid, most respected, and often most self-directed jobs in workplaces. They differ in the degree to which they require educational certification. Managerial jobs tend to require a diffuse set of background characteristics and can often be attained through experience even in the absence of a generalist college degree. In contrast, professional jobs typically require quite specific college or professional degrees (e.g., a BS in engineering, a BA in accounting, or a JD in law).

We focus on these three occupational destinations because they clearly represent the most desirable employment destinations and because we have different expectations as to the degree of discrimination likely to be involved. Craft jobs because they are the most valuable working-class jobs and because skills are largely transmitted from the current generation of workers to the next, either through apprenticeships or on-the-job training, should be relatively difficult for minorities (and women) to get access to. It is in these jobs where workplace formalization is likely to be at its weakest and the opportunity for incumbents to exclude out-groups the highest. Managerial jobs should show similar barriers but are even more likely to be hoarded by powerful decision makers. Managerial jobs are more likely to be subject to formal internal labor market policies and to be the object of discrimination lawsuits and external regulatory attention. Entrance to professional jobs, which are clearly desirable and such potentially discriminatory targets from a social closure perspective, is at least initially governed by objective educational requirements. It is among professionals that we expect to see the most EEO progress, because specific educational requirements can clearly define one aspect of qualification and so mute the influence of status-based discriminatory selection of job candidates.

For the analyses in this section, we compare the relative probability of attaining craft, managerial, and professional jobs. Doing this produces some methodological problems that were not present in the segregation analysis and ignorable (at least for the purposes of this article) in the workplace homogeneity analysis. It is particularly useful to control for the supply of different groups when comparing their relative probability of being in specific jobs. The proportion of the labor force that is white male has declined tremendously since the enactment of the Civil Rights Act, even as the proportions of white women and Hispanic and Asian men and women have grown. Thus, we would expect white males to decline in desirable jobs because they are simply a smaller proportion of the labor force. To make matters more complicated, the distribution of both employment and the Hispanic and Asian labor forces have changed across places over time, thus comparing relative employment frequencies requires some adjustment for both temporal and spatial labor supply. We do this in the following charts by calculating employment representation as the proportion of craft employment in a group (e.g., percentage of black males in craft occupations) divided by the proportion of all employment in the local labor market in that group (i.e., percentage

FIGURE 4
TRAJECTORIES OF RELATIVE ACCESS TO CRAFT PRODUCTION JOBS IN EQUAL EMPLOYMENT OPPORTUNITY COMMISSION (EEOC) REPORTING WORKPLACES

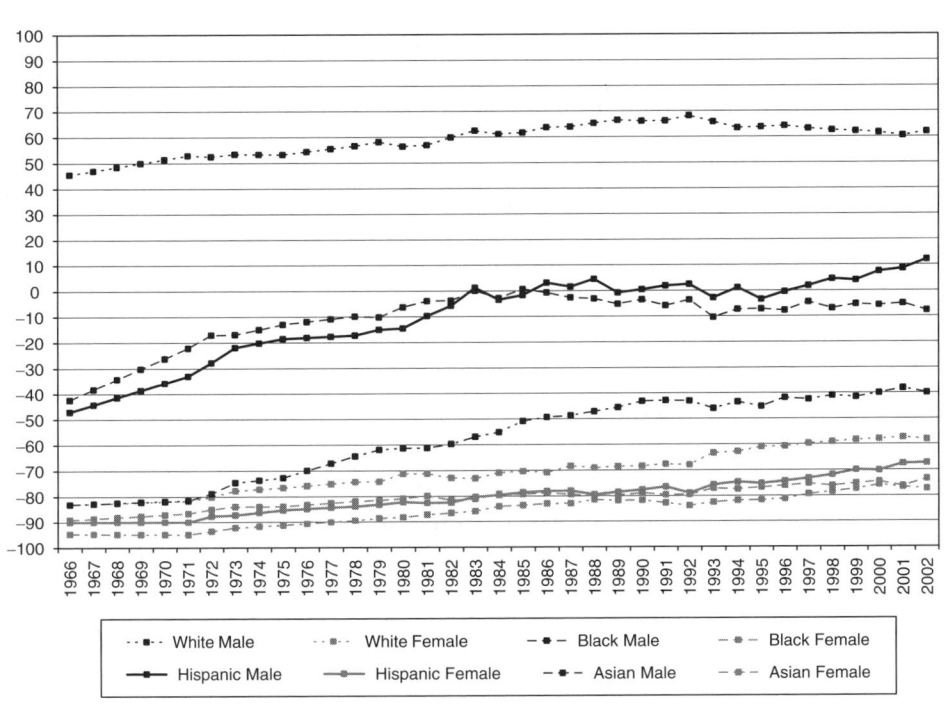

of black male employment in local labor market).[3] Thus, our comparisons are the occupational percentage difference from labor market participation.[4] A score of 0 indicates that a group is represented on average at the same rate as it is employed in local labor markets. A score of 40 indicates that a group is overrepresented by 40 percent, and a score of –40 means that the group is underrepresented by the same percentage relative to their relative labor force size. Positive scores suggest net advantage in access to jobs.[5]

Craft occupations employment trends

Blue-collar or working-class jobs vary dramatically in their desirability. Among these jobs, craft production jobs stand out as highly rewarded, relatively autonomous, and clearly desirable positions. Figure 4 outlines the trajectory of employment among these jobs. Since 1966, as the economy shifted from goods to service production, craft occupations decline as a percentage of all occupations.

The graph shows a clear distinction between male and female employment, with craft production jobs showing very strong male bias.

In 1966, white males were overrepresented in craft jobs at 44 percent. Hispanic males were underrepresented by 47 percent and black males by 42 percent, while Asian males were nearly absent from craft jobs altogether (83 percent underrepresented). While white males were far and away the most advantaged in access to the most desirable working-class jobs, because of sex segregation in access to these jobs, minority men were also advantaged relative to women in access to craft jobs.

The early period trends show a gradual increase in white males' privileged access to craft jobs. This reflects the initial hiring of minority men into low-skilled jobs in EEOC reporting workplaces directly after the Civil Rights Act. White males' privileged access to craft production jobs grows until 1990, peaking at 68 percent overrepresentation in these desirable blue-collar jobs. Thereafter, there is some decline in white male control of the best blue-collar jobs, although they are still overrepresented by 62 percent in 2002.

Black and Hispanic men, but not Asian men, made substantial gains in the 1966 to 1972 period, followed by slower gains across the 1970s. After 1985, black males' access to craft jobs declines slightly over time, ending the period of just under proportional representation. In the 1980s, Hispanic males' access to craft jobs stagnates around proportional representation; however, after 1994, there appears to be fairly strong gains, ending the period about 12 percent overrepresented in craft jobs. Asian males show an entirely different pattern. They begin with practically no representation in craft jobs, followed by increased access from 1971 to 1990, and stagnating thereafter. By 2002, Asian males were still 40 percent underrepresented in craft production jobs. White males' privileged access to craft production jobs was not eroded as a result of the Civil Rights Act, legal or regulatory pressures, or changes in human resource practices.

Black males and especially Hispanic males made significant gains between 1966 and 1985, but this seems to have been produced by the decline in white males as a proportion of the labor force and the absence of effective competition from female labor for these jobs. All women are underrepresented in craft production jobs across the entire period by 60 to 80 percent. After 1990, there is slight increased representation of white, black, Hispanic and Asian women in craft jobs, although underrepresentation for all women remains extreme.

Managerial occupations employment trends

Managerial jobs are the most powerful in most workplaces. These are employees trusted to make hiring and firing decisions, invest capital, direct product development, and enforce equal opportunity laws—or not. Diversity in top managerial positions is often used to gauge whether a company is committed to diversity. Discrimination lawsuits are often filed around denied access to or promotion within managerial positions. Arguably, it is around access to managerial jobs that environmental equal opportunity pressures are most intense. On the other hand,

FIGURE 5
TRAJECTORIES OF RELATIVE ACCESS TO MANAGERIAL JOBS IN EQUAL EMPLOYMENT OPPORTUNITY COMMISSION (EEOC) REPORTING WORKPLACES

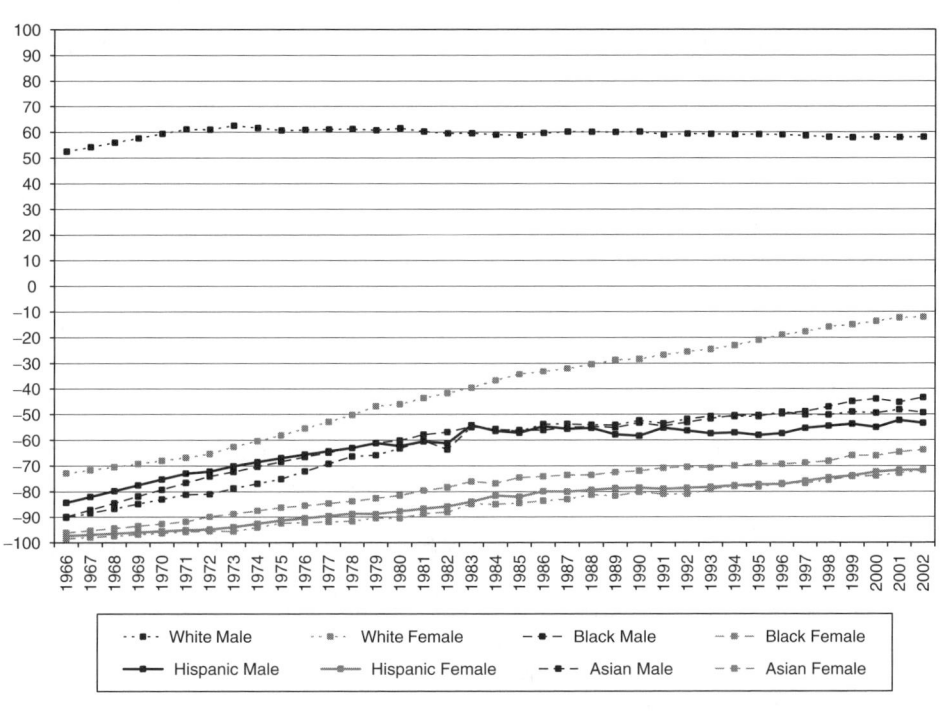

from a social closure point of view, it is precisely managerial jobs that will be most protected from out-group competition. The pressures for "homosocial reproduction" are at their highest among managerial positions both because of the responsibility and the rewards associated with these jobs.

The most striking pattern revealed in Figure 5 is that white males' advantaged access to managerial jobs is uniformly high across the entire post–Civil Rights Act period and never declines appreciably. As we saw for craft jobs, white men's privileged access to managerial jobs actually increased in the early period, as all women and minority men gained access to lower-level jobs in the EEOC regulated private sector.

Even more striking is the rapid increase in white women's access to managerial jobs after 1971. White women move from being underrepresented in managerial jobs by 70 percent to being underrepresented by only 12 percent at the turn of the century. While they have not yet reached parity, white women have made remarkable and consistent gains. Black males also have made gains in private sector managerial employment, although their advances are not as dramatic or consistent. Black males were barely represented among managers in this EEOC reporting sample in 1966, being underrepresented by 90 percent relative to their employment in the sector. They made sustained improvements through 1983, although they were still substantially underrepresented at –54 percent of their general labor market employment. No further progress was made through the 1980s, but progress began again across the 1990s. Hispanic males were less disadvantaged (–84 percent) in their access to managerial jobs than other minorities in 1966, saw increased access through 1983, but saw stagnating representation thereafter. The stall in progress may be the result of the new immigration of low-education Hispanic workers to the United States during this period. Asian males are equally underrepresented with black males in 1966 and make fewer gains than black males from 1966 to 1972; however, the trends for these two groups of males converge around 1983, and slow gains are made in the 1990s. By 2002, black males and Asian males were 43 and 49 percent underrepresented in managerial jobs, respectively. Black, Hispanic, and Asian women are grossly underrepresented in managerial jobs across the entire period; although all demonstrate increased relative access to managerial jobs, they remain underrepresented by more than 60 percent four decades after the Civil Rights Act.

White males' privileged control of managerial jobs has not been challenged in the private EEOC regulated sector of the economy. While other groups have increased access, and white women in particular are approaching parity with their representation in the labor force, this has been accomplished not by displacing white male labor but because white males are a smaller proportion of the overall economy and to some extent because of an increased supply of managerial jobs.

In other research, we found that all groups are more likely to be managers within workplaces that employ a greater number of similar others who are nonmanagers (Stainback and Tomaskovic-Devey 2006). This is consistent with a "bottom-up" ascription version of social closure theory (Elliott and Smith 2001; Smith and Elliott 2002). While we found that groups are most likely to manage similar others, there is an interesting intersectionality finding as well. White women are least likely to be managers in workplaces with higher percentages of white male, black male, or other minority male nonmanagers. White women are much more likely to be managers in workplaces with increasing percentages of minority females in the nonmanagerial workforce. This suggests that white women benefit from their racial privilege in what remain sex-segregated managerial roles. They are, however, least likely to manage men of any race. Black men occupy an even more precarious position of being advantaged by sex privilege, but only in the management of black women. Black males are least likely to manage white women and white men. African American women's experiences are further constrained. They benefit only from increasing percentages of black female nonmanagers. Therefore, they are disadvantaged by both their sex and race. With the exception of white men, all status groups are most likely to become managers in workplaces when a large population of similar people are employed among nonmanagers.

Professional occupations employment trends

Professional jobs, while highly desirable for their relative autonomy and high pay, are obvious objects for social closure attempts. In fact, educational credentials are the primary mechanism through which professions reserve employment positions for similar others. Thus, while social closure is a primary part of the allocation of people to professional jobs, it is typically organized around educational credentials rather than sex or race. Thus, we expect that among these jobs, women and minorities are least likely to be excluded by discriminatory mechanisms of cognitive bias or social closure. It is also likely that in these jobs the formalization of human resource practices inspired by EEO goals can be expected to be most successful. Since formalization typically implied the creation of formal job descriptions that included specific skill requirements and the broad advertisement of open positions, it is precisely among professional jobs that we would suspect that information would reach minority job candidates, often through schools and professional associations, and that employers would have to screen on professional certification and experience before any race (or gender) bias could come into play. Thus, we expect that progress toward EEO is more likely among professional jobs than we have already observed among craft and managerial occupations (see Figure 6).

White males again begin the period with the strongest advantage, being overrepresented by 45 percent in 1966. Unlike craft and managerial occupations, we see no improved advantages in white male hiring into professional jobs in the initial equal opportunity period, and a slow decline thereafter. By the turn of the century, white males' overrepresentation in professional jobs dropped from 45 to 25 percent. While white males are still the most privileged group in terms of access to professional jobs, that privilege has clearly eroded. We see gains for all other groups, except Hispanic males, whose trend is nearly flat, in access to professional jobs across the entire post–Civil Rights Act period. White women have dramatically gained access to professional jobs, beginning the period 60 percent underrepresented, reaching proportional representation by the late 1980s, and continuing to gain through the remainder of the period. By 2002, white women are nearly 17 percent *overrepresented* in professional jobs relative to their share of the private sector labor market.

Black males and females were almost absent in professional jobs in EEOC reporting workplaces in 1966. By the year 2002, they were still much less likely to be found in professional jobs than their presentation in the EEOC regulated labor force, but they had made gains from roughly 90 percent underrepresentation to 63 percent for black males and 52 percent for black females. While in Figure 5 we saw that black males were advantaged relative to black females in their access to managerial jobs, by the year 2002 black women have relatively higher access to professional jobs than do black men. This no doubt represents at least in part the superior educational credentials of black women relative to black men at the end of the twentieth century.

FIGURE 6
TRAJECTORIES OF RELATIVE ACCESS TO PROFESSIONAL
JOBS IN EQUAL EMPLOYMENT OPPORTUNITY COMMISSION
(EEOC) REPORTING WORKPLACES

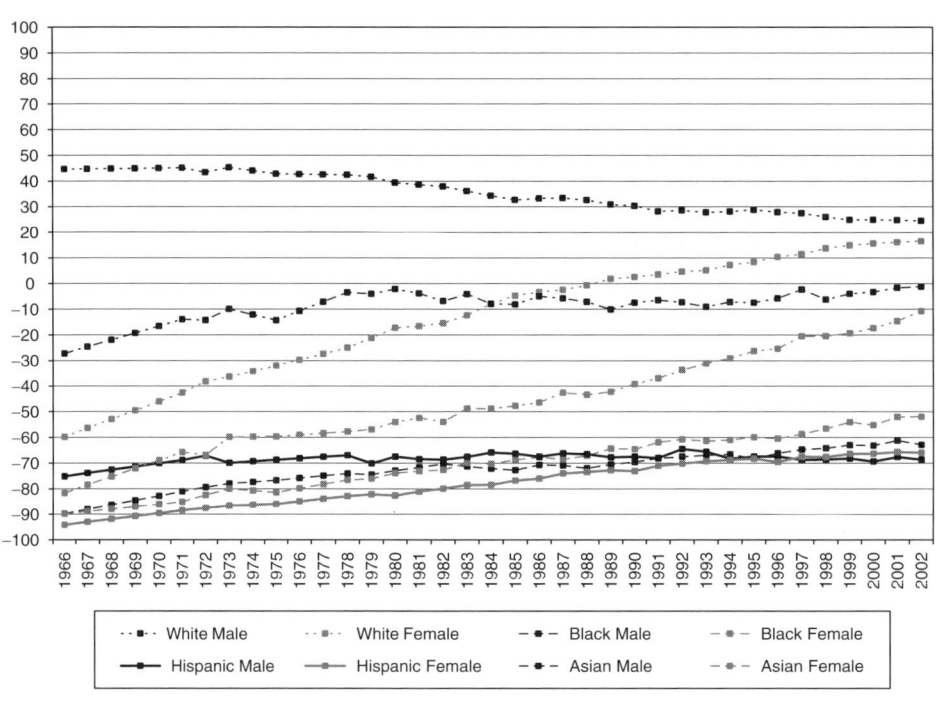

The trends for Hispanic men and women are quite a bit different from each other. While Hispanic men were actually underrepresented among professionals in 1966 by 75 percent, their relative employment in these high-education jobs is virtually stagnant across the entire period. This reflects the change in the composition of the Latino population, as new low-education immigrants became an increasing proportion of the total Latino labor force. Hispanic women, although they remain grossly underrepresented among professionals in the private EEOC regulated economy, made slow continuous gains in access to professional positions throughout the entire period.

Asian men and to a greater extent Asian women made gains into professional jobs during the 1966 to 2002 period. Asian males were 27 percent underrepresented in 1966 and gain a greater share of professional jobs through the early 1970s. After 1976, Asian males fluctuate between 10 percent underrepresented and proportional representation. Asian women make remarkable gains in access to professional jobs from being 81 percent underrepresented in 1966 to about 10 percent underrepresented by 2002.

Our expectation that EEO progress would be stronger in professional occupations than in managerial or craft occupations receives support for all groups, except Hispanic men. Most striking is that white women end the period overrepresented in professional positions by more than 16 percent, only 8 points less advantaged than white men. In fact, if current trends were to continue, one would predict that white women became more advantaged than white men on average in their access to these highly desirable jobs in 2005. Our supposition that educational criteria might increasingly replace race, ethnic, and sex criteria in access to private sector professional jobs is consistent with these patterns.

Conclusions

Title VII of the 1964 Civil Rights Act made discrimination and segregation in employment illegal in the United States. That same legislation created the EEOC to monitor private sector progress in firms with at least fifty employees. Later legislation and legal cases expanded the scope of the EEOC and added other federal and legal resources toward fighting employment discrimination.

As Burstein (1985) and others have pointed out the enactment of law does not produce social change; it is the political process through which law becomes implemented that determines the law's eventual impact. There are many reasons to predict that the Civil Rights Act would have limited impact on EEO. First, at the level of decision makers, there are many reasons to expect continued bias and discrimination against minority workers. These include cultural prejudice against minorities, cognitive biases in the evaluation of minority and majority employees, statistical discrimination by employers, and social closure around desirable jobs from white and male workers. Second, most workplaces respond reluctantly to environmental pressures, often adopting strategies of symbolic compliance with legal mandates, rather than fundamental reorganizations of their core divisions of labor and behavioral expectations. Since political pressures for EEO have waned, particularly since 1980, there may be less incentive now than there was immediately after the Civil Rights Act and during the period of peak enforcement of the 1970s to expand minority representation in private sector workplaces.

On the other hand, we do expect some progress as a result of the Civil Rights Act and associated EEO innovations in legislative, legal, and human resource support for a more just American workplace. First, we believe such progress is most likely when uncertainty is high, and organizations demonstrate compliance with the law prior to the establishment of a set of symbolically legitimate practices that demonstrate compliance, even while sheltering the organization from further change. Thus, we expect the most rapid equal opportunity gains among regulated private sector firms directly after the enactment of the Civil Rights Act. Second, progress will be more rapid when the stakes are low. It should be easier to desegregate a workplace than coveted managerial or craft jobs, because minorities can be given access to less desirable jobs that privileged white male workers find less desirable. Third, minority EEO progress should continue during the 1970s when regulatory pressure was high and human resource practices were evolving to create the contemporary set of generally accepted equal opportunity personnel practices. Finally, equal opportunity progress should be stronger and more sustained in professional occupations because required educational credentials will take precedence in decision making over preferred race, ethnicity, or even sex. Finally, although we did not develop the idea theoretically, it is possible that general cultural change will lead to widespread equal opportunity. It is difficult to imagine this happening, with what we know about organizational inertia and group bias, but it is at some level the ultimate preferred destination of a nondiscriminatory social order.

> *The enactment of law does not produce social change; it is the political process through which law becomes implemented that determines the law's eventual impact. There are many reasons to predict that the Civil Rights Act would have limited impact on [equal employment opportunity].*

Our empirical findings are nowhere near as straightforward as our theoretical expectations. The general expectation that EEO progress will be difficult and uneven is strongly supported. Nearly four decades after the Civil Rights Act, many workplaces are racially homogeneous, within-workplace segregation remains high, and African American and Hispanic employees are still grossly underrepresented among managerial and professional workers. Hispanic and black men have achieved better representation among the most desirable blue-collar jobs—the various skilled craft occupations—although this represents their male privilege relative to all women in these good jobs, rather than gains relative to white men.

For African Americans, progress on all dimensions was rapid in the period immediately after the enactment of the Civil Rights Act but before there was significant regulatory, legal, or human resource support for its provisions. During this period, the proportion of regulated private sector workplaces with no black men or women dropped sharply, and the segregation of black men from white men and black women from white women did as well. During this period, the segregation of Hispanic men from white men also dropped, if less dramatically. The organizational uncertainty around initial compliance with equal opportunity law seems to have been most closely tied to the fate of African Americans, and there within a highly sex-segregated work world. This initial period saw no gains for minority workers in craft jobs but strong gains from practically total prior exclusion in managerial and professional employment.

For African Americans, progress on all dimensions was rapid in the period immediately after the enactment of the Civil Rights Act but before there was significant regulatory, legal, or human resource support for its provisions. The expectation that equal opportunity progress for minorities might stall after the Reagan Revolution of the 1980s received a good deal of support.

The expectation that equal opportunity progress for minorities might stall after the Reagan Revolution of the 1980s received a good deal of support. Declines in racially homogeneous establishments and workplace segregation relative to white men, as well as increased access to managerial jobs, all slowed down or stopped entirely in the 1980s. Hispanic and black women actually were increasingly segregated from white women after the mid-1970s, suggesting that whatever political pressure there was to racially integrate female jobs dissipated at about the same time human resource professionals institutionalized a set of legitimate compliance signaling practices. It looks as if white men and white male jobs continued to be the target of equal opportunity innovation at least through 1980, while almost all race desegregation among women happened prior to the period of institutionalization.

We find continued undisturbed white male privilege in access to the peak blue-collar and white-collar jobs. White males' disproportionate access to craft production and managerial jobs actually increased as workplaces hired more minority and female employees in low-level jobs. Thereafter, white privilege was undisturbed in these jobs. In other research we have found that when black and Hispanic men and women as well as white women get access to managerial jobs, it tends to be in low-wage industries and in workplaces where they can manage workers from their own status group (Stainback and Tomaskovic-Devey 2006). Thus, substantial evidence suggests that progress has taken place where white males' advantages are not being challenged. Very little evidence shows any erosion of white males' dominance of craft and managerial jobs. Other groups have achieved increased access to these jobs primarily because white males are a smaller proportion of the labor force, not because they have had to acclimate themselves to a lower-opportunity environment.

> *[S]ubstantial evidence suggests that [racial] progress has taken place where white males' advantages are not being challenged.*

There is also some good news among this fairly disappointing story. Among professionals, all groups have made strong gains, and white males' privileged position, while still substantial, has been eroded. Among professional jobs, we see the promise of the Civil Rights Act realized. We think that what is important here is that the screening mechanism for professional jobs is not lodged in the employment practices of workplaces, but in the admission practices of colleges and universities. The desegregation of higher education has probably produced much more EEO progress among desirable jobs than any workplace lawsuits or innovations in human resource practice.

Finally, white women have made uninterrupted progress in every dimension we have examined, except access to craft production jobs. At the turn of the century almost no workplaces had no white female employment. Segregation relative to white males had dropped so quickly and stably that forty years after the Civil Rights Act, sex segregation of white women from white men had reached the level of race segregation among men. Among managerial jobs, white women have almost reached proportional representation, although white males' advantages are still quite large. The greatest gains have come in professional employment, in which white women are now overrepresented relative to their overall employment and may have already gained representational, if not earnings or field, parity with white men. It is certainly an ironic outcome that legislation that was originally targeted at ending racial segregation and discrimination and only included sex in a last-ditch effort to undermine the legislation (Deitch 1993) has produced the most sustained benefits for white women. It may be that an unanticipated consequence of the Civil Rights Act was to reduce sex distinctions among whites, even as it both challenged and reinforced race and ethnic distinctions between whites and others.

That white women have become increasingly segregated from black and Hispanic women in the private sector is particularly discouraging. Although racial equal opportunity progress relative to white men has been limited, posed no particularly threat to white male advantage, and stalled after 1980, no strong evidence reveals increased inequality or segregation between white men and minority men and women. White women, on the other hand, are increasingly racially isolated in the regulated private sector, a disturbing result requiring explanation and exploration.

Notes

1. This was changed in 1983 to one hundred employees, fifty for federal contractors.

2. The Equal Employment Opportunity Commission (EEOC) reporting forms collect occupational distributions (e.g., managers, professionals, technical, sales, clerical, craft, operation, laborer, and service), and so ignore within-occupation segregation. We treat this as a form of measurement error and adjust reported segregation measures to take into account observed occupational heterogeneity at the workplace level. The technical discussion behind this adjustment can be found in Tomaskovic-Devey et al. 2006.

3. For example we calculate craft representation (CR) as follows:

$$CR = \{[(Xc_{it}/Tc_{it})/ \sum (X_{ijt}/ \sum T_{ijt})]-1\} \times 100,$$

where Xc_{it} is the number of status group members (e.g., white males) in the craft occupational category within an establishment in a given year. Tc_{it} is the total number of individuals in the craft occupational category (c) within establishment (i) in a given year (t). $\sum (X_{ijt})$ is the total number of status group X members in commuting zone j in a given year t, and $\sum (T_{ijt})$ is the sum of employment across all establishments in commuting zone j for a specific year t.

4. Commuting zones are aggregations of counties, not confined to state boundaries, and are calculated based upon decennial census surveys documenting the distance individuals travel to work from where they live (Tolbert and Sizer 1996). Therefore, they describe local labor markets. We impose 1990 commuting zone boundaries on all years of data in these analyses for consistency purposes. The use of stable geography allows us to compare localities over time. While the use of commuting zones is novel and we think preferably for theoretical reasons, the comparison of stable geography at the county, metropolitan statistical area (MSA), state, and nation level is conventional. Commuting zone composition does not change radically over time.

5. All unemployment-produced discrimination is ignored in these estimates. To the extent that discrimination toward minorities leads to lower labor force participation, we are underestimating minority disadvantage in access to these jobs.

References

Anderson, Cynthia, and Donald Tomaskovic-Devey. 1995. Patriarchal pressures: An exploration of organizational processes that exacerbate and erode sex earnings inequality. *Work and Occupations* 22:328-56.

Baron, James N. 1991. Organizational evidence of ascription in labor markets. In *New approaches to economic and social analyses of discrimination*, ed. R. Cornwall and P. Wunnava. Westport, CT: Praeger.

Baron, James N., Brian S. Mittman, and Andrew E. Newman. 1991. Targets of opportunity: Organizational and environmental determinants of gender integration within the California Civil Service, 1979-1985. *American Journal of Sociology* 96:1362-1401.

Bergmann, Barbara R. 1996. *In defense of affirmative action*. New York: Basic Books.

Bielby, William T. 2000. How to minimize workplace gender and racial bias. *Contemporary Sociology* 29:190-209.

Bodenhausen, G. V., and C. N. MacCrae. 1996. The self regulation of intergroup perception: Mechanisms and consequences of stereotype suppression. In *Stereotypes and stereotyping*, ed. C. N. MacRae, C. Stangor, and M. Hewstone, 227-53. New York: Guilford.

Braddock, J. H., and J. M. McPartland. 1987. How minorities continue to be excluded from equal employment opportunities: Research on labor market and institutional barriers. *Journal of Social Issues* 43:5-39.

Brewer, M. B., and R. M. Kramer. 1985. The psychology of intergroup attitudes and behaviors. *Annual Review of Psychology* 36:219-43.

Burstein, Paul. 1985. *Discrimination, jobs and politics: The struggle for equal employment opportunity in the United States since the New Deal*. Chicago: University of Chicago Press.

Carlson, Susan M. 1992. Trends in race/sex occupational inequality: Conceptual and measurement issues. *Social Problems* 39:268-90.

Cockburn, Cynthia. 1991. *In the way of women*. Ithaca, NY: Industrial and Labor Relations Press.

Cohen, Lisa, Joseph Broschak, and Heather Haveman. 1998. And then there were more? The effect of organizational sex composition on hiring and promotion. *American Sociological Review* 63:711-27.

Deitch, Cynthia. 1993. Gender, race, and class politics and the inclusion of women in the 1964 Civil Rights Act. *Gender & Society* 7:183-203.

Devine, P. G. 1989. Stereotypes and prejudice: Their automatic and controlled components. *Journal of Personality and Social Psychology* 56 (1): 5-18.

DiMaggio P. J., and W. W. Powell. 1983. The iron cage revisited: Institutional isomorphism and collective rationality in organizational fields. *American Sociological Review* 48:147-60.

Dobbin, Frank, John Sutton, John Meyer, and Richard Scott. 1993. Equal opportunity law and the construction of internal labor markets. *American Journal of Sociology* 99:396-427.

Edelman, L. B. 1992. Legal ambiguity and symbolic structures: Organizational mediation of civil rights law. *American Journal of Sociology* 97:1531-76.

Elliott, James R., and Ryan A. Smith. 2001. Ethnic matching of supervisors to subordinate work groups: Findings on bottom-up ascription and social closure. *Social Problems* 48:258-76.

Fiske, Susan T. 1998. Stereotyping, prejudice and discrimination. In *Handbook of social psychology*, ed. D. T. Gilbert, S. T. Fiske, and G. Lindzey, 357-411. New York: McGraw-Hill.

Hamilton, D. L., and J. W. Sherman. 1994. Stereotypes. In *Handbook of social cognition*, 2nd ed., ed. R. S. Wyer Jr. and T. K. Scrull, 1-68. Mahwah, NJ: Lawrence Erlbaum.

Hannan, Michael T., and John Freeman. 1984. Structural inertia and organizational change. *American Sociological Review* 49:149-64.

Hewstone, M. 1990. The "ultimate attribution error"? A review of the literature on intergroup causal attribution. *European Journal of Social Psychology* 30:311-35.

Hilton, J. L., and W. Von Hipple. 1996. Stereotypes. *Annual Review of Psychology* 47:237-71.

Hirsh, Elizabeth. 2005. Organizing equal opportunity: The effect of EEO enforcement on sex and race segregation in the workplace. Presented at the American Sociological Association annual meeting, Philadelphia, August 16.

Holzer, Harry J. 1996. *What employers want: Job prospects for less educated workers*. New York: Russell Sage Foundation.

Hultin, Mia, and Ryzard Szulkin. 1999. Wages and unequal access to organizational power: An empirical test of gender discrimination. *Administrative Science Quarterly* 44:453–72.

Ibarra, Henry. 1993. Personal networks of women and minorities in management: A conceptual framework. *Academy of Management Review* 18:46-87.

———. 1995. Race, opportunity and diversity of social circles in managerial networks. *Academy of Management Journal* 38:673-703.

Kanter, Rosabeth Moss. 1977. *Men and women of the corporation*. New York: Basic Books.

Leonard, Jonathan S. 1984a. Employment and occupational advance under affirmative action. *Review of Economics and Statistics* 66:377-85.

———. 1984b. The impact of affirmative action on employment. *Journal of Labor Economics* 19:439-63.

———. 1990. The impact of affirmative action regulation and equal employment opportunity law on black employment. *Journal of Economic Perspectives* 4:47-63.

McTague, Tricia, Kevin Stainback, and Donald Tomaskovic-Devey. 2006. Is organizational theory useful for understanding workplace inequality? Manuscript, University of Massachusetts, Amherst.

Moss P., and C. Tilly. 2001. *Stories employers tell.* New York: Russell Sage.

Neckerman, K. M., and J. Kirschenman. 1991. Hiring strategies, racial bias and inner-city workers. *Social Problems* 38:801-15.

Parkin, Frank. 1979. *Marxism and class theory: A bourgeois critique.* New York: Columbia University Press.

Perdue, C. W., J. F. Dovidio, M. B. Guttman, and R. B. Tyler. 1990. "Us" and "them": Social categorization and the process of intergroup bias. *Journal of Personality and Social Psychology* 59:475-86.

Pfeffer, Jeffrey, and Gerald R. Salancik. 1978. *The external control of organizations.* New York: Harper & Row.

Reskin, Barbara F. 1988. Bringing the men back in: Sex differentiation and the devaluation of women's work. *Gender & Society* 2:58-81.

———. 2000. The proximate causes of employment discrimination. *Contemporary Sociology* 29:319-28.

Reskin, Barabara F., and Debra Branch McBrier. 2000. Why not ascription? Organizations' employment of male and female managers. *American Sociological Review* 65:210-33.

Reskin, Barbara F., and Patricia A. Roos. 1990. *Job queues, gender queues: Explaining women's inroads into male occupations.* Philadelphia: Temple University Press.

Ridgeway, Cecilia. 1997. Interaction and the conservation of gender inequality: Considering employment. *American Sociological Review* 62:218-35.

Salancik, Gerald R. 1979. Interorganizational dependence and responsiveness to affirmative action: The case of women and defense contractors. *Academy of Management Journal* 22:375-94.

Schuman, Howard, Charlotte Steeh, Lawrence D. Bobo, and Maria Krysan. 1997. *Racial attitudes in America: Trends and interpretations.* Cambridge, MA: Harvard University Press.

Sears, David O., P. J. Henry, and Rick Kosterman. 2000. Egalitarian values and contemporary racial politics. In *Racialized politics: The debate about racism in America*, ed. David O. Sears, Jim Sidanius, and Lawrence Bobo, 75-117. Chicago: University of Chicago Press.

Selznick, Philip. 1949. *TVA and the grass roots: A study of politics and organization.* Berkeley: University of California Press.

Smith, Ryan A., and James R. Elliott. 2002. Does ethnic concentration influence employees' access to authority? An examination of contemporary urban labor markets. *Social Forces* 81:255-79.

Stainback, Kevin. 2006a. Politics, uncertainty and organizational change: Workplace segregation in the post-civil rights era, 1966-2002. Paper presented at the American Sociological Association annual meeting, August 12, Montreal, Canada.

———. 2006b. Race, social networks and job-level segregation. Manuscript.

Stainback, Kevin, Corre Robinson, and Donald Tomaskovic-Devey. 2005. Racial integration: A "politically-mediated" process? *American Behavioral Scientist* 48:1200-1228.

Stainback, Kevin, and Donald Tomaskovic-Devey. 2006. Managing privilege: The stable advantage of white males in U.S. labor markets, 1966-2000. Manuscript.

Stinchcombe, Arthur L. 1965. Social structure and organizations. In *Handbook of organizations*, ed. James G. March, 142-93. Chicago: Rand McNally.

Sutton, J. R., F. Dobbin, J. W. Meyer, and W. R. Scott. 1994. The legalization of the workplace. *American Journal of Sociology* 99:944-71.

Szafran, Robert. 1982. What kinds of firms hire and promote women and blacks—A review of the literature. *Sociological Quarterly* 23:171-90.

Thernstrom, Stephen, and Abigail Thernstrom. 1997. *America in black and white: One nation, indivisible.* New York: Simon & Schuster.

Tilly, Charles. 1998. *Durable inequality.* Berkeley: University of California Press.

Tolbert, Charles M., and M. Sizer. 1996. U.S. commuting zones and labor market areas: A 1990 update. Staff Paper no. AGES-9614, Rural Economy Division, Economic Research Service, U.S. Department of Agriculture, Washington, DC.

Tomaskovic-Devey, Donald. 1993. *Gender & racial inequality at work: The sources and consequences of job segregation*. Ithaca, NY: ILR Press.

Tomaskovic-Devey, Donald, Catherine Zimmer, Kevin Stainback, Corre Robinson, Tiffany Taylor, and Tricia McTague. 2006. Documenting desegregation: Segregation in American workplaces by race, ethnicity, and sex 1966-2000. *American Sociological Review* 71:565-88.

Wilson, George. 1997a. Pathways to power: Racial differences in the determinants of job authority. *Social Problems* 44:38-54.

———. 1997b. Payoffs to power among males in the middle class: Has race declined in its significance? *Sociological Quarterly* 38:607-22.

Wilson, George, Ian Sakura-Lemessy, and Jonathan West. 1999. Reaching the top: Racial differences in mobility paths to upper-tier occupations. *Work & Occupations* 26:165-86.

Racial Composition of Workgroups and Job Satisfaction among Whites

By
DAVID J. MAUME
and
RACHEL SEBASTIAN

Despite decades of research on job satisfaction, few analysts have examined the relative explanatory power of the demographic composition of the workgroup against traditional predictors that focus on the characteristics of workers' jobs. This article drew from the organizational demography and status composition perspectives to examine the effects of workgroup racial composition on white job satisfaction. The sample consisted of non-Hispanic whites who responded to the 2002 National Study of the Workforce. The findings showed that an increase in the number of minority coworkers negatively affected job satisfaction among whites, until the characteristics of jobs were controlled. The results support the status composition perspective in suggesting that whites are not overtly biased against minority coworkers but rather become dissatisfied with the less favored jobs they share with minorities.

Keywords: job satisfaction; race; organizational demography; workgroup composition

Segregation is a pervasive feature of the labor market, yet researchers pay more attention to gender segregation than to racial segregation. Few would dispute the proposition, however, that the labor force will be increasingly diverse in the future (Milliken and Martins 1996) and that whites and minorities will increasingly interact with each other as firms adopt team-based forms of production (Hodson 2001). And it is at the workplace where intergroup contact is likely to be highest, since whites and minorities are unlikely to interact in other settings like neighborhoods, churches, and schools (Brown et al. 2003).

These statements serve to remind us, as Simpson (1989) did nearly two decades ago, that work is fundamentally a social experience. Simpson urged social scientists to remember that at work individuals are more than simply trying to maximize utility; they also become embedded in a workgroup whose orientations, rituals, and expectations affect how work is experienced. Organizational demographers

DOI: 10.1177/0002716206295396

appear to have embraced Simpson's argument, in that a growing body of scholarship shows that net of individual traits, the demographic characteristics of the workgroup affects the behavior and attitudes of its members (Reskin, McBrier, and Kmec 1999).

Of course, the attitudes and outcomes of interest may have positive as well as negative overtones. In the case of the racial composition of the workgroup, researching its effects on job satisfaction among whites may contribute to an understanding of the contemporary labor market. For example, managing the diverse workforce of the future may be increasingly difficult if white job dissatisfaction grows with increased contact with minority coworkers (Milliken and Martins 1996). As well, the empirical nature of this relationship may bear on the proposition that race has "declined in significance" (Wilson 1980). Past research found that whites were *less* satisfied with their jobs when the number of minority coworkers increased, but these studies relied on older data or sampled workers within a single firm. If race has declined in significance, there should be no association between the racial composition of coworkers and job attitudes in a representative sample of contemporary whites.

This article investigated these propositions by drawing on a broad 2002 cross-section of U.S. workers. The primary relationship of interest is the effect of the racial composition of coworkers on the job satisfaction of whites. This article drew on studies of organizational demography and the status composition of jobs to develop and specify a causal model of white job attitudes. The next section reviews prior literature on the effects of racial segregation, followed by a section discussing the data and measures used in the analyses.

Background

There is a voluminous literature on the causes and consequences of sex segregation at work, but racial segregation is similarly problematic in the labor market.

David J. Maume is a professor of sociology, and director, Kunz Center for the Study of Work & Family, at the University of Cincinnati. His teaching and research interests are in labor market inequality and work-family issues, with recent publications appearing in the Journal of Marriage and Family, Work & Occupations, *and* Social Problems. *He is currently researching gender differences in providing urgent child care in dual-earner families, gender differences in the effects of supervisor characteristics on subordinates' job attitudes, and the effects of shift work on the work and family lives of retail food workers (funded by the National Science Foundation).*

Rachel Sebastian is a graduate student in the Department of Sociology at the University of Cincinnati. Her research interests include family and work conflict and structural inequality, especially as it relates to families. Her research has included examining the experiences of homeless women and children in shelters and evaluation of child care quality. Currently, she is examining parents' choices of child care arrangements.

NOTE: This research was supported by grants to the first author from the National Institute of Child Health and Human Development (R03-HD42411-01A1) and the Charles Phelps Taft Memorial Fund at the University of Cincinnati.

Blacks are underrepresented in most places of employment (Reskin, McBrier, and Kmec 1999), and careers are affected for those working in minority-dominated jobs (Tomaskovic-Devey 1993). Those who have examined the segregation of Hispanics reported similar findings (e.g., see Bayard et al. 1999). A smaller body of research has examined the link between racial heterogeneity and job attitudes. The existing literature primarily draws on perspectives in *organizational demography* to interpret the typically negative effect of racial segregation on white job attitudes. The *status composition* perspective has been used to examine the effects of heterogeneity on individual pay and promotions, with relatively few instances in which analysts have tested the explanatory power of this perspective against the organizational demography perspective in predicting individual job attitudes. Below, we elaborate on these perspectives and review prior studies of the effects of racial integration on job attitudes.

Organizational demography perspective

In an often-cited article, Pfeffer (1983, 303-4) asserted that "the relative proportions of groups condition the form and nature of social interaction . . . that affects workers' psychological well-being and attitudes." Much research sprang from this insight, but organizational demographers typically invoke two social psychological processes by which group proportions affect individual attitudes.

First, the similarity-attraction paradigm contends that in the absence of detailed information about others, individuals tend to like those who are similar to them on visible characteristics like race and gender (Byrne 1971). Individuals tend to think that similar others had similar life experiences and have similar values, and consequently, communication is easier (Kanter 1977). At the same time, interacting with similar others enhances one's own self-esteem and fosters a motivation to identify with the group (Riordan and Shore 1997). Second, the social categorization paradigm suggests that individuals tend to define others as either part of one's social circle or outside it, and out-group members are less likely to be viewed as honest and trustworthy (Tajfel and Turner 1986). Sociologists have also drawn on Blalock (1967), who contended that as a minority group grows in size, the majority group views it as a greater threat in the competition for valued resources. Of course, when these arguments are placed in the context of the history of race relations in the United States, it is plausible to hypothesize that white unhappiness in working with minorities simply reflects racial prejudice.

For the most part, empirical findings on these propositions have been supportive. For example, Tsui, Egan, and O'Reilly (1992) examined the racial diversity of workgroups and found that heterogeneity was associated with higher absenteeism and turnover intentions. Similar results were reported by Wharton, Rotolo, and Bird (2000) and by Pelled, Eisenhardt, and Xin (1999), who reported lower levels of satisfaction in more diverse work groups.

Although provocative, these results were based on older and/or unique samples of workers. For example, the Tsui, Egan, and O'Reilly (1992) sample was drawn a generation ago when overt racism may have been higher among whites (see Brown et al. 2003). The sample in the Wharton, Rotolo, and Bird (2000) study was drawn more recently, but these respondents worked at a university where employment relations are likely to differ from those in the private sector. Finally, the unit of analysis in the Pelled, Eisenhardt, and Xin (1999) study was the workgroup, and their analysis estimated a model of *group* unhappiness that failed to control for individual-level correlates of job satisfaction, such as pay and job security. Thus, to fully test the theory that white job dissatisfaction grows with the integration of workgroups, further research is needed that estimates a fully specified model in a general sample of workers.

Organizational demographers further contend that workgroup composition affects the volume and nature of contacts between majority and minority groups. Thus, several studies have examined the mediating influence of intergroup relations on the association between the workgroup demography and individual job attitudes. Again, the bulk of this research examined women's reactions to diversity in the workgroup (following Kanter's [1977] classic statement on tokenism). Tolbert, Graham, and Andrews (1999) reviewed this literature and found that when women were tokens they were isolated from the workgroup and contended with stereotypes about their gender. As their representation in the workgroup increased, the number of contacts with men increased and job satisfaction likewise increased.

Few studies have examined these relationships as they pertain to racial segregation, but there are two notable exceptions. Jackson, Thoits, and Taylor (1995) surveyed elite African Americans and found that as racial heterogeneity increased, depression and anxiety among blacks decreased. Although these findings are provocative, it is possible that anxiety and depression were caused by stressors in the home or in the community, rather than on the job. Furthermore, if job conditions did cause psychological distress, this study did not test for the mediating influence of relations with coworkers. Finally, while it is important to study black attitudes to assess progress in race relations, whites are the majority group in most work settings and thus most capable of acting on their prejudice.

Some of these issues were addressed by Mueller et al. (1999), who found that the negative effect of racial composition of schools on teachers' job satisfaction was eliminated once coworker support was taken into account. It is also important to note that this study controlled for several intrinsic and extrinsic factors in a manner consistent with much prior research on job satisfaction (for an overview, see Hodson 2001). Yet Mueller et al.'s sample was composed of elementary and secondary school teachers in one of the largest urban areas in the country, raising the question of whether their findings generalize to all workers.

In sum, the organizational demography perspective posits that workgroup composition directly affects individual job attitudes and/or that relations with coworkers mediate this relationship. But few studies explicitly examine white reactions to black coworkers, and those that do often fail to control for important determinants of job attitudes. Furthermore, the existing literature relies on older and/or unique samples that may not characterize the typical white worker today. This study will attempt to address these deficiencies in the existing literature.

Status composition perspective

In essence, the organizational demography perspective focuses on white prejudice (expressed either as a preference for in-group members, or a distrust of out-group members, or both) as the mechanism by which heterogeneity affects job attitudes, either directly or indirectly. The status composition perspective also identifies bias as the mechanism by which workgroup heterogeneity affects individual job rewards, although here the bias is located in organizations rather than in individuals. That is, when jobs are increasingly held by minorities, the organization *devalues* those jobs in its pay and promotion policies. Again, much of the prior research focused on the effects of sex segregation on job rewards,[1] but racial segregation has also received a fair amount of attention.

> *[T]he organizational demography perspective posits that workgroup composition directly affects individual job attitudes and/or that relations with coworkers mediate this relationship.*

For example, Tomaskovic-Devey (1993) surveyed residents of North Carolina and found that more than half his sample would have to change jobs to achieve racial job integration. Perhaps more important, Tomaskovic-Devey found that the proportion of coworkers who were black had a significant negative effect on wages in the presence of extensive controls. Similar results were reported by Sorenson (1989) using national data, and by Baron and Newman (1989), who examined pay differentials in the California Civil Service. Other studies showed that those who worked in jobs dominated by blacks were less likely to be promoted and had higher turnover rates than incumbents in white-dominated jobs (Barnett, Baron, and Stuart 2000; Maume 1999; Sørensen 2004).

If this perspective is correct in asserting that organizations discriminate against *jobs* held by minorities, then it suggests a different mechanism by which the composition of the workgroup affects white job attitudes. That is, when whites work with minorities, it is not the presence of minority coworkers per se that lowers job satisfaction but rather the growing realization among whites that they have been placed in jobs that are devalued by their employers. Working beside minorities is likely to be associated with lower pay and flat career profiles, irrespective of the talents and contributions of individual workers. A likely outcome of this realization is that whites become dissatisfied with their jobs.

Dozens of studies have examined the impact of job conditions on job satisfaction, and Hodson (2001) thoroughly reviewed this literature. In brief, analysts have identified intrinsic and extrinsic job conditions as important determinants of job satisfaction. When work is intrinsically satisfying, individuals are in jobs that rely upon and expand their creative skills to offer a good or service of benefit to the community. Intrinsically satisfying jobs are also free from overbearing supervision, offering workers a chance to exercise their judgment and control how they spend their time. At the same time, extrinsically satisfying jobs pay good wages, are secure, and offer opportunities for promotion.

The status composition perspective . . . [suggests that] when jobs are increasingly held by minorities, the organization devalues those jobs in its pay and promotion policies.

Numerous studies control for extrinsic and intrinsic job conditions in models of job satisfaction but fail to consider the effects of workgroup diversity. The few studies that explicitly examined racial integration's effect on job satisfaction (cited above) incompletely specified their analytic models. For example, Wharton, Rotolo, and Bird's (2000) study of university employees controlled for the autonomy and complexity of jobs but not for pay, job security, or promotion chances. Similarly, Pelled, Eisenhardt, and Xin (1999) and Tsui, Egan, and O'Reilly (1992) controlled for the nature of tasks and the characteristics of the workgroup but ignored several intrinsic and extrinsic factors that might affect job satisfaction. This may not be problematic because these studies drew samples of workers that were firm- or job-specific, and thus these factors may be implicitly controlled in the sampling process. The Mueller et al. (1999) study was the most comprehensive in terms of controlling for a variety of job conditions as well as workgroup diversity, but their sample of teachers in a large city may not represent the experiences of most workers. Thus, this study will estimate a comprehensive model of job satisfaction in a representative sample of workers.

Hypotheses

After estimating a fully specified model of job satisfaction, the perspectives above imply a particular pattern of findings. First, if the organizational demography perspective is correct that whites prefer to associate with other whites and eschew contact with nonwhites, then workgroup integration should be negatively related to job satisfaction irrespective of other controls in the model. Such a finding would also imply that race has *not* declined in significance, as Wilson (1980) argued a generation ago. Of course, if contemporary whites are no longer prejudiced against blacks, then the composition of the workgroup will have no impact on white job satisfaction, even in a baseline model with few controls. Second, the organizational demography perspective also suggests that white prejudice is reduced when individuals enjoy good relations with their coworkers. If so, then the relationship between workgroup diversity and white job satisfaction will disappear when the quality of workgroup relations is controlled. Third, the status composition perspective also implies a spurious association between workgroup diversity and white job satisfaction, in that this relationship will disappear once intrinsic and extrinsic job conditions are controlled. Such a finding would imply that whites are not personally biased against black coworkers but rather are concerned for their careers when they work beside minorities.

Data

The data source for this article is the 2002 National Study of the Changing Workforce (NSCW), designed by the Families and Work Institute and administered by Harris Interactive. This is the third in a series of cross-sectional surveys designed to examine important issues affecting the U.S. labor force. Unlike the first two versions of the NSCW, the 2002 edition had detailed characteristics on the racial composition of the workgroup.

The NSCW was administered over the phone to a sample selected by random-digit-dialing methods. Eligible respondents were adults who worked for pay and resided in a dwelling that had a telephone in one of the contiguous forty-eight states. When interviewers reached an eligible respondent, interviews were completed 98 percent of the time. Yet the eligibility status of a substantial number of households could not be determined after twenty-plus attempts, and numerous households were known to be eligible but an interview was not completed. The completion rate was estimated at 52 percent after taking known and unknown eligible households into account. Yet the NSCW sample is representative of the labor force on several demographic and economic traits when compared to the March 2002 Current Population Survey (Bond et al. 2003).

The sample consists of 2,810 wage and salaried workers, but one selection criterion was imposed to get an appropriate analytic sample for an analysis of white job attitudes. That is, respondents were asked several questions about their race and ethnicity, and those who self-identified as white and non-Hispanic were retained for analysis. After selecting these respondents, 2,179 respondents remained in the analytic sample, but scattered missing data on variables in the model further reduced the sample to the 2,099 cases shown in Table 1. Weights were provided to correct for potential design effects, but weighted and

TABLE 1
DESCRIPTIVE STATISTICS ON VARIABLES IN ANALYSIS OF JOB SATISFACTION, WHITE NON-HISPANICS, 2002 NATIONAL STUDY OF THE CHANGING WORKFORCE (NSCW) (N = 2,099)

Variable (Low; High)	M	SD
Dependent variable		
Job satisfaction (1 = *not satisfied*; 3 = *very satisfied*)	2.47	0.62
Workgroup composition and relations		
Minorities as percentage of workgroup (1 = 0%; 6 = 100%)	2.38	1.08
Number of problems with coworkers (0; 3)	0.28	0.65
Intrinsic and extrinsic job characteristics		
Supervises others (0; 1)	0.37	0.48
Creativity index (1 = *low*; 5 = *high*)	4.31	0.81
Autonomy index (1 = *low*; 5 = *high*)	3.77	1.01
High-pressure index (1 = *low*; 5 = *high*)	3.65	0.95
Job is physically demanding (1 = *strongly disagree*; 5 = *strongly agree*)	2.81	1.60
Log of hourly wage (0.76; 6.48)	2.76	0.70
Chance for advancement (1 = *poor*; 4 = *excellent*)	2.57	1.03
Job is secure (1 = *low*; 4 = *high*)	3.06	0.91
Control variables		
Age in years (18; 63)	42.082	11.82
Years of education (9; 20)	14.62	2.81
Male (0; 1)	0.42	0.49
Works full-time (0; 1)	0.78	0.41
Log of years of tenure (0; 4.16)	1.79	0.97
Log of establishment size (2.56; 9.62)	4.63	1.89

unweighted analyses yielded substantively similar results. Thus, all analyses presented below were based on unweighted samples.

Measures

Job satisfaction

Job satisfaction has long been considered a core indicator of workers' evaluations of their jobs (for a review, see Hodson 2001). Of course, it is possible that workers like and dislike various aspects of their jobs, and much research has examined satisfaction with various facets of work. As a concept, job satisfaction assumes that workers evaluate all aspects of their job situations, consider their alternatives, and through an internal calculus arrive at an overall evaluation of the quality of their jobs. Thus, the dependent variable in this analysis is the summary *job satisfaction* indicator in which workers responded to the question, "All in all, how satisfied are you with your job?" Response options included 3 = *very satisfied*, 2 = *somewhat satisfied*, and 1 = *not satisfied*. Table 1 shows that the typical worker has a mean satisfaction score of 2.47 on a 3-point scale; an inspection of frequency counts (not shown) revealed that 53 percent of workers were *very satisfied* and only 7 percent were *not satisfied*.[2]

Workgroup composition and relations

To measure the diversity of the workgroup, NSCW respondents were asked, "About what percentage of your coworkers are people from your racial, ethnic, or national background?" Response options included 1 = *100 percent of coworkers*, 2 = *75-99 percent*, 3 = *50-74 percent*, 4 = *25-49 percent*, 5 = *less than 25 percent but more than 0*, and 6 = *0 percent*. Given that the sample consists entirely of respondents who self-identified as white non-Hispanics, rising values indicate an increased presence of minorities in the workgroup.[3] Approximately 85 percent of respondents were employed in majority-white workgroups (i.e., they answered categories 1, 2, or 3), and only 15 percent of whites were in minority-dominated workgroups (categories 4, 5, and 6). We experimented with several categorical representations of workgroup mix, but none of them improved model fit. Thus, the ordinal measure was used in the analyses below.

The nature of relations with coworkers was assessed by three items: (1) I feel I am really a part of the group of people I work with, (2) I have the support from coworkers that I need to do a good job, and (3) I have support from coworkers that helps me to manage my work and personal or family life. Responses to these items were in 5-point Likert format, with *don't know* as the middle category. Preliminary analyses revealed that on all three items, 92 to 95 percent of respondents *agreed* or *strongly agreed* that they had the support of their coworkers. Thus, rather than scaling together items that were skewed, we created a count measure of *problems with coworkers*, as the number of items above to which respondents responded *disagreed* or *strongly disagreed*.

Intrinsic job traits

The first measure of intrinsic rewards is whether the respondent *supervises others* (measured as a binary variable). Other rewarding aspects of work include the extent to which work requires individuals to be creative or offers them autonomy in deciding what to do and when. Both of these concepts were measured by composite indices consisting of 5-point Likert items with *don't know* as the middle response value. The *creativity index* was calculated by taking the mean of four items (e.g., My job lets me use my skills and abilities), and the *autonomy index* was also constructed from the mean of four items (e.g., I have the freedom to decide what I do on my job).[4] Work may also be intrinsically unrewarding in *high-pressure* jobs or if the work is *physically tiring*. The high-pressure job index was calculated by taking the mean of three items that tapped the pressures at work (e.g., I never seem to have enough time to get everything done on my job), all of which were in 5-point Likert response format.[5] Finally, the NSCW stated, "My job is very physically demanding and tiring," and workers could respond from 1 = *strongly disagree* to 5 = *strongly agree*.

Extrinsic job traits

The most basic extrinsic job trait is the *hourly wage* on the main job. This measure was calculated by NSCW staff as the typical earnings (including bonuses and overtime pay) in a pay period (e.g., week, month, year, etc.) divided by the usual number of hours worked in the pay period. The resulting wage quotient was logged to correct for a rightward skew.[6] In addition, jobs are extrinsically rewarding if they offer *job security* and *advancement opportunities*. The latter was measured by the item, "How would you rate your own chance to advance in your organization?" with responses ranging from 1 = *poor* to 4 = *excellent*. Job security was assessed by the item, "How likely is it that during the next couple of years you will lose your present job and have to look for a job with another employer?" Responses ranged from 1 = *very likely* to 4 = *not at all likely*.

Controls

Several additional factors may affect job satisfaction including *years of education*, *gender* (1 = male, 0 = female), works *full-time* (forty-plus hours per week) on the main job, *years of tenure* with the employer, and *establishment size* (the last two measures were logged to correct for their rightward skew). The rationale for controlling for these measures will be discussed when the results are shown below.[7]

Method

Given the ordinal nature of the dependent variable and the skewed distribution of responses, analyzing these measures with ordinary least squares (OLS) regression would likely produce misleading results. Rather, these measures will be analyzed with ordered logistic regression. This technique is an extension of binary logistic regression and is often referred to as the "cumulative logistic regression model." That is, the technique estimates a series of tau thresholds or cut points, giving the cumulative log odds of scoring at or below a given threshold of job satisfaction. The number of thresholds is always one less than the number of categories on the dependent variable (since by definition, all responses are in the highest response category or lower). The slope parameters in ordered logit regression indicate changes in the cumulative distribution of responses at the cut points given unit increases in predictor variables; significance tests are conducted in the usual manner (i.e., dividing the slope parameter by its standard error).[8] As in logistic regression, the ordered logistic regression model estimates a model chi-square (with *df* equal to the number of predictor variables in the model) that

TABLE 2
ORDERED LOGISTIC REGRESSION MODEL OF JOB SATISFACTION, WHITE NON-HISPANICS, 2002 NATIONAL STUDY OF THE CHANGING WORKFORCE (NSCW) (N = 2,099)

Predictor	Model 1 b	SE	Model 2 b	SE	Model 3 b	SE	Model 4 b	SE
Minorities as percentage of workgroup	-0.09	0.04**	-0.09	0.04**	-0.04	0.04	-0.04	0.05
Number of problems with coworkers	—	—	-1.15	0.07****	—	—	-0.75	0.08****
Supervises others	—	—	—	—	-0.26	0.10**	-0.22	0.10**
Creativity index	—	—	—	—	0.94	0.07****	0.87	0.07****
Autonomy index	—	—	—	—	0.42	0.05****	0.37	0.05****
High-pressure index	—	—	—	—	-0.41	0.06****	-0.40	0.06****
Job is physically demanding	—	—	—	—	-0.07	0.03**	-0.06	0.03*
Hourly wage (logged)	—	—	—	—	0.01	0.08	0.04	0.08
Chance for advancement	—	—	—	—	0.47	0.05****	0.41	0.05****
Job is secure	—	—	—	—	0.38	0.05****	0.35	0.06****
Age in years	0.02	0.00****	0.02	0.00****	0.02	0.00****	0.02	0.00****
Years of education	0.03	0.02**	0.02	0.02	-0.06	0.02**	-0.06	0.02**
Male	-0.40	0.09****	-0.32	0.09****	-0.56	0.10****	-0.50	0.10****
Works full-time	0.15	0.11	0.16	0.11	-0.06	0.13	-0.04	0.13
Years of tenure (logged)	0.14	0.05***	0.10	0.05*	0.12	0.06*	0.09	0.06
Establishment size (logged)	-0.06	0.02**	-0.03	0.02	0.01	0.03	0.01	0.03
τ_1 ("not satisfied")	-1.66	0.29****	-2.26	0.30****	2.64	0.45****	1.78	0.46****
τ_2 ("somewhat satisfied")	0.86	0.28****	0.62	0.29**	5.98	0.47****	5.32	0.48****
Model chi-square	89.3****		359.6****		769.1****		859.5****	
df	7		8		15		16	

°$p < .10$. °°$p < .05$. °°°$p < .01$. °°°°$p < .001$.

shows the reduction in the log likelihood compared with a model containing only the intercept.

Results

In Table 2, a series of models are estimated that test the propositions advanced by the organizational demography and status compositions perspectives above. Model 1 is a baseline model that tests for the effect of racial representation in the workgroup on job satisfaction in the presence of controls. Model 2 takes into account problems with coworkers, while model 3 accounts for job characteristics. Model 4 is a comprehensive model that includes all predictors of job satisfaction. In the table, positive slopes indicate that job satisfaction increases with a unit change in a given predictor. The bottom of Table 2 shows that the predictive power of the analytic model increases with the number of predictors.

Before examining the variables of interest, we make several observations on the effects of the control variables. First, model 1 shows that age and tenure have positive effects on job satisfaction. Most analysts suggest that with time individuals increasingly find and settle into jobs for which they were suited and/or they lower their expectations in what they want from their jobs (Hodson 2001). In either case, job satisfaction is higher among older and/or more senior workers.

Second, most studies report that more educated workers have higher standards in what they expect from a job, and their current jobs often fail to meet those standards, producing lower levels of job satisfaction (for a review, see Burris 1993). The contrary education slope in model 1 likely results from the failure to control for job characteristics; once these characteristics are controlled in models 3 and 4, the expected negative effect of education on job satisfaction is observed.

Third, men are less satisfied with their jobs than women, which is consistent with findings from prior studies (e.g., Phelan 1994). Buchanan (2005) explained the gender differential in job satisfaction by using reference group theory. That is, given the prevailing levels of gender inequality in the labor market, women often compare their job situations to those of other women, many of whom are struggling to achieve economic parity with men. Men, on the other hand, compare themselves to other men, and there are more examples of highly successful men than highly successful women. Thus, reference group theory suggests that men are more likely than women to be dissatisfied with their jobs.[9]

Finally, job satisfaction tends to be lower in larger firms, which are more impersonal and bureaucratic (Hodson 2001). This expected negative effect of establishment size on job satisfaction is observed in the baseline model, but this effect vanishes when the number of coworker problems and job characteristics are controlled.

Turning now to the variables of interest, model 1 shows that as the minority presence in the workgroup increases, whites are less satisfied with their jobs. The significant negative effect of minority representation in the workgroup on job satisfaction holds up when the quality of coworker relations is controlled. Model 2 shows that the magnitude of the slope for minority representation is unchanged ($b = -.09$, $p < .05$) compared to the baseline model 1. Furthermore, the number of problems with coworkers significantly reduces job satisfaction in a manner predicted by organizational demographers, and the explanatory power of the model is greatly enhanced when this measure is included (compare the model chi-square values between models 1 and 2). If the analysis ceased at this point, one would conclude that whites are increasingly unhappy with their jobs as workgroups integrate and that white bias persists even when relations with coworkers is controlled.

Model 3 includes controls for the intrinsic and extrinsic nature of respondents' jobs, and the majority of these factors predict job satisfaction in accordance with expectations. Those who work in jobs requiring creativity are more satisfied, as are those who exercise autonomy in deciding what tasks to perform and when to do them. Similarly, job satisfaction rises when respondents perceive that their jobs are secure and/or they have a chance to advance in their firms. Workers are less satisfied when they are in high-pressure jobs and/or ones that are physically demanding. Contrary to expectations, supervisors are less satisfied with their jobs. One plausible explanation for this unexpected effect is that the model controls for the *benefits* of being a supervisor (e.g., higher pay and more autonomy), and the binary measure is now tapping the *stress* of supervising others. For example, Kanter (1977) argued that the effectiveness and success of supervisors is dependent on the commitment and behaviors of subordinates, a stressful situation that may manifest itself in lower job satisfaction among supervisors.

Yet for our purposes, the more important finding that emerges from model 3 is that the size of the minority presence in the workgroup no longer significantly predicts job satisfaction when job characteristics are controlled. This finding supports the status composition perspective, which contends that organizations provide fewer rewards to incumbents of minority-dominated jobs. If whites are reluctant to work with minorities, this may not be because of overt racial prejudice, but rather reflects a concern that one is located in a job that is devalued in the eyes of one's employer. In the fully specified model these interpretations hold up, in that the number of problems with coworkers and job conditions continue to strongly determine levels of job satisfaction, while the effect of minority representation in the workgroup has no effect on job satisfaction.

Of course, with eight factors tapping the status composition perspective, there is a greater chance that it will receive support in the findings than the organizational demography perspective (which is tapped by two predictors). In this situation, one is tempted to examine the relative strength of variables predicting job satisfaction. Ordered logistic regression can approximate standardized slopes in OLS by examining predicted responses on the job satisfaction measure when predictors are set at the values of their 5th and 95th percentile scores (and all other predictors are held constant at their means). The summed products of slopes and predictor values are subtracted from each tau threshold to yield the log odds that respondents scored *at that threshold or lower* on the dependent variable. The cumulative logits are then transformed to cumulative probabilities,

TABLE 3
ESTIMATED PROPORTION OF *VERY SATISFIED* RESPONDENTS AT THE MINIMUM AND MAXIMUM VALUES ON PREDICTORS, WHITE NON-HISPANICS, 2002 NATIONAL STUDY OF THE CHANGING WORKFORCE (NSCW) (N = 2,099)

Predictor	Min Value[a]	Max Value[a]	Proportion at Min	Proportion at Max	Change
Minorities as percentage of workgroup	1	5	0.532	0.488	–0.044
Number of problems with coworkers	0	2	0.568	0.226	–0.342
Supervises others	0	1	0.537	0.482	–0.054
Creativity index	2.46	4.50	0.177	0.558	0.381
Autonomy index	1.75	5	0.334	0.628	0.294
High-pressure index	2	5	0.673	0.384	–0.288
Job is physically demanding	1	5	0.544	0.483	–0.061
Hourly wage (logged)	1.61	3.79	0.505	0.526	0.021
Chance for advancement	1	4	0.359	0.657	0.299
Job is secure	1	4	0.344	0.596	0.252
Age in years	21	62	0.403	0.622	0.218
Years of education	9	20	0.597	0.438	–0.159
Male	0	1	0.568	0.444	–0.125
Works full-time	0	1	0.525	0.514	–0.011
Years of tenure (logged)	0	3.30	0.477	0.549	0.072
Establishment size (logged)	2.56	8.16	0.509	0.529	0.019

NOTE: Italicized variables were insignificant predictors of job satisfaction in Table 2.
a. Min values are 0 for binary measures or the 5th percentile score for continuous measures; max values are 1 for binary measures or the 95th percentile score for continuous measures.

which in turn yield the proportion of respondents in each response category. When the predicted distributions on the dependent variable is calculated at the 5th and 95th percentiles across a set of covariates, this approximates the amount of change in responses on the dependent variable that would be expected given similar amounts of change in a set of predictors. For categorical predictors, the predicted probabilities are estimated when the predictors are set at values of 0 and 1.

Table 3 presents the change in the estimated proportion of respondents who said they were *very satisfied* with their jobs as predictors varied from their minimum to maximum values. For example, at the 5th percentile score, whites have no minority coworkers (response value = 1), and 53.2 percent of them are *very satisfied* with their jobs. At the 95th percentile score (response value = 5, or 75 to 99 percent of coworkers are minorities), 48.8 percent of whites are *very satisfied* with their jobs. Thus, as workgroup integration increases from 5th to 95th percentile scores, the proportion of workers who are *very satisfied* with their jobs declines by 4.4 percent. This relatively small change in predicted maximum job satisfaction further illustrates the insignificant effect of this measure in the fully specified model in Table 2.

By contrast, the creativity index has the strongest effect on job satisfaction. When their jobs require little or no creativity (5th percentile = 2.46 on a 5-point scale), only 18 percent of respondents are expected to be *very satisfied* with their jobs. Yet 56 percent of respondents are expected to be *very satisfied* with their jobs at the 95th percentile score on the creativity index. The 38 percent increase in the expected proportion of *very satisfied* workers is the largest increase of any continuous predictor across the range from the 5th to the 95th percentile score observed in Table 3. Yet numerous other measures of job traits also contribute to maximum satisfaction on the job, including (in order of magnitude) chance for advancement, job autonomy, the high-pressure job index, and job security.

The results support the status composition perspective in suggesting that whites are not overtly biased against minority coworkers but rather become dissatisfied with the less favored jobs they share with minorities.

Nevertheless, the number of problems with coworkers is the second strongest predictor of maximum job satisfaction. When they do not have any problems with their coworkers, 57 percent of workers are *very satisfied* with their jobs. The proportion of *very satisfied* respondents declines to 23 percent when they have problems with their coworkers in two domains in this index. Although the demographic composition of the workgroup fails to exert a direct influence on individual job satisfaction, the organizational demography perspective is clearly supported by the importance of the quality of coworker relations in determining contentment with one's job.

Summary

Despite decades of research on job satisfaction, few analysts have contrasted the explanatory power of the organizational demography and status composition perspectives in predicting job satisfaction in a representative sample of whites. This study drew a representative sample of workers from the 2002 NSCW. This study tested for the direct effect of racial composition on the job satisfaction of whites and the possibility that problems with coworkers mediated this relationship. Alternatively, white job dissatisfaction in working with minorities may be due to a realization that employers devalued jobs with a significant number of minority incumbents, such that controlling for job characteristics would eliminate the effect of workgroup composition on white job attitudes. The findings showed that an increase in the number of minority coworkers negatively affected job satisfaction, until the characteristics of jobs were controlled. The results support the status composition perspective in suggesting that whites are not overtly biased against minority coworkers but rather become dissatisfied with the less favored jobs they *share* with minorities. Although problems with coworkers failed to eliminate the effect of workgroup composition on job satisfaction, it exerted a strong negative effect on job satisfaction.

Discussion

The workforce of the future will be increasingly diverse, and adults spend many of their waking hours at work. In this context, it is important to know how whites react to minority coworkers, not only because of what the findings imply for the current state of race relations, but also because of its implications for managing an increasingly diverse workforce. The finding of this study suggests that whites are not overtly prejudiced against minority coworkers as much as they are concerned for their careers when they work in devalued jobs beside minorities.

Of course, this distinction may be lost on those minorities who work beside whites. If whites become increasingly dissatisfied out of a concern for their job situations in the presence of minority coworkers, this may be hard to distinguish from overt racial prejudice by minorities themselves. And without better data on the nature of relations between coworkers, minority concerns cannot be discounted. One limitation of this study is that it takes into account the *number* of problems with coworkers, but not the *content* of those problems. It is entirely possible that as workgroups become more racially diverse, racial tensions and misunderstandings increase, which produces more conflict with coworkers. To fully investigate this possibility, it is necessary to investigate whether race-related conflict increases with minority representation in the workgroup and how this impacts on white attitudes and performance.[10] If this is the case, it suggests that white prejudice against minority coworkers is persistent and contradicts the notion of a declining significance of race. If this is not the case, however, it suggests that employers need to pay attention to other factors that might affect coworker relations and, by extension, job satisfaction.

In his analysis of 108 workplace ethnographies, Hodson (2004) confirmed the conventional wisdom that well-run organizations, with clearly defined and fairly administered personnel policies, have more contented workers. To quote Hodson, "positive managerial behavior supportive of workers' dignity and productivity, not only encourages meaning and satisfaction at work but it also reduces both vertical and *horizontal conflict*" (p. 311, italics added). In other words, when management treats all workers with dignity and respect, workers are more satisfied with their jobs irrespective of the racial composition of workgroups. Thus, increased workforce diversity in the future does not necessarily mean more racial conflict when managers are concerned with promoting worker dignity. A priority of future research, then, should be to examine the determinants of managerial decisions to eschew an adversarial stance toward workers, in favor of policies that treat them as valued partners in the production process.

Notes

1. Tomaskovic-Devey (1993) and Reskin, McBrier, and Kmec (1999) provided good overviews of the literature on the effects of sex segregation on the pay, promotion prospects, and turnover of individuals. For the most part, incumbents are paid less, are promoted less, and have faster turnover when they are employed in female-dominated jobs. There is, however, a growing literature suggesting that the effects of segregation are asymmetric. That is, when men are employed in female-dominated jobs, they are more likely to be promoted than similarly situated women (Hulton 2003; Maume 1999). These findings were inspired by Williams (1992), who referred to men's greater likelihood of promotion out of female-dominated jobs as a "glass escalator."

2. Category 1 was originally composed of workers who were either *not too satisfied* (5.3 percent of responses) or *not satisfied at all* with their jobs (1.7 percent of respondents). The fit of the analytic models to the data were slightly improved when these two response categories were combined into a category reflecting *dissatisfaction* with one's job.

3. Seven respondents volunteered the response that they had no coworkers, and these answers were treated as missing data. Twenty respondents said they "don't know" how many racially and ethnically different coworkers they had. Rather than treating these responses as missing, they were recoded to the modal response on the composition measure (i.e., 2 = 75 to 100 percent).

4. The other three items in the creativity index were (1) my job requires that I keep learning new things, (2) the work I do on my job is meaningful to me, and (3) my job requires that I be creative. The remaining items in the autonomy index were (1) it is basically my own responsibility to decide how my job gets done, (2) I have a lot of say about what happens on my job, and (3) I decide when I take breaks. The creativity and autonomy indices had Cronbach's alpha scores of .73 and .72, respectively.

5. The other two items in the scale were "my job requires that I work very fast" and "my job requires that I work very hard." The high-pressure job scale had a Cronbach's alpha score of .52.

6. Approximately 7 percent of respondents refused to divulge their earnings. Rather than deleting these respondents from the analysis, they were assigned the mean value on earnings. A binary measure was created to control for mean assignment on hourly pay, but it had no impact on job satisfaction and was dropped from the analytic models shown below.

7. In addition, we constructed a vector of six binary measures for industry (manufacturing was the reference category) and a vector of six dummy variables for occupation (with mangers and professionals serving as the reference category). The controls for occupation and industry failed to predict job satisfaction, most likely because of the presence of numerous controls for proximate work conditions. Thus, the binary measures for occupation and industry were omitted from the analytic models. Finally, 14 percent of National Study of the Changing Workforce (NSCW) respondents worked two or more jobs, and some of the predictors in the analytic model specifically reference the respondent's main job while others do not. Rather than limiting the sample to workers with a single job, the models included a binary control for *working two or more jobs*. This measure failed to significantly predict job satisfaction and was dropped from the models.

8. The ordered logit technique assumes that the slopes effects are the same at each threshold of the dependent variable. For example, if there were only a single predictor of job satisfaction, one would graph

this as a series of parallel lines. That is, the lines would intersect the y-axis at their respective tau thresholds, but the lines would be parallel because the slope was the same magnitude at each cut point. To test this assumption the ordered logit procedure produces a chi-square statistic, in which the null hypothesis is that the slopes are the same at each cut point (the alternative hypothesis is that the slopes differ depending on the tau threshold, suggesting that multinomial analysis is the more appropriate technique). This parallel lines chi-square test was insignificant in seven of the eight models shown in Tables 2 and 3 (the only exception being the baseline model 1 in Table 2), thereby confirming that the slopes are indeed the same at each cut point on the dependent variable.

9. Not only do some analysts suggest that the determinants of job satisfaction vary by gender, but other analysts suggest that women are less prejudiced against minorities than are men (e.g., see Hughes and Tuch 2003). If so, then gender may interact with the determinants of job satisfaction, including the racial composition of workgroups. To test this proposition, a vector of product terms was constructed in which gender was multiplied by the other variables in the model. Yet the presence of these interaction terms failed to improve the fit of the models to the data, and almost without exception they had insignificant effects on job satisfaction.

10. In a supplemental analysis, we regressed problems with coworkers onto the predictors shown in Table 2. In baseline models including the control variables, the number of problems with coworkers *increased* with minority representation in the workgroup. But once job characteristics were controlled, workgroup composition no longer had a significant effect on problems with coworkers. This lends further support to the status composition model, which suggests that the intrinsic and extrinsic nature of jobs in which they are placed plays a more consequential role in determining job attitudes than the racial composition of their coworkers per se. Nevertheless, this study's inability to examine the nature and content of disputes with coworkers suggests the need for further research on these issues.

References

Barnett, William P., James N. Baron, and Toby E. Stuart. 2000. Avenues of attainment: Occupational demography and organizational careers in the California civil service. *American Journal of Sociology* 106:88-104.

Baron, James N., and Andrew E. Newman. 1989. Pay the man: Effects of demographic composition on prescribed wage rates in the California civil service. In *Pay equity: Empirical inquiries*, ed. Robert T. Michael, Heidi I. Hartmann, and Brigid O'Farrell, 107-30. Washington, DC: National Academy Press.

Bayard, Kimberly, Judith Hellerstein, David Neumark, and Kenneth Troske. 1999. Why are racial and ethnic wage gaps larger for men than for women? In *The creation and analysis of employer-employee matched data*, ed. John C. Haltiwanger, Julia Lane, James Spletzer, Jules Theeves, and Kenneth Troske, 175-203. Amsterdam: Elsevier Science.

Blalock, Hubert M. 1967. *Toward a theory of minority-group relations*. New York: Wiley.

Bond, J. T., C. Thompson, E. Galinsky, and D. Prottas. 2003. *Highlights of the 2002 National Study of the Changing Workforce*. New York: Families and Work Institute.

Brown, Michael K., Martin Carnoy, Elliot Currie, Troy Duster, David B. Oppenheimer, Marjorie M. Schultz, and David Wellman. 2003. *Whitewashing race: The myth of a color-blind society*. Berkeley: University of California Press.

Buchanan, Tom. 2005. The paradox of the contented female worker in a traditionally female industry. *Sociological Spectrum* 25:677-713.

Burris, Beverly H. 1993. *Technocracy at work*. Albany: State University of New York Press.

Byrne, Donn. 1971. *The attraction paradigm*. New York: Academic Press.

Hodson, Randy. 2001. *Dignity at work*. Cambridge: Cambridge University Press.

———. 2004. Demography or respect? Work group demography versus organizational dynamics as determinants of meaning and satisfaction at work. *British Journal of Sociology* 53:291-317.

Hughes, Michael, and Steven A. Tuch. 2003. Gender differences in whites' racial attitudes: Are women's attitudes really more favorable? *Social Psychology Quarterly* 66:384-401.

Hulton, Mia. 2003. Some take the glass escalator, some hit the glass ceiling? Career consequences of occupational sex segregation. *Work & Occupations* 30:30-61.

Jackson, Pamela Braboy, Peggy A. Thoits, and Howard F. Taylor. 1995. Composition of the workplace and psychological well-being: The effects of tokenism on America's black elite. *Social Forces* 74:543-57.

Kanter, Rosabeth Moss. 1977. *Men and women of the corporation*. New York: Basic Books.

Maume, David J. 1999. Glass ceilings and glass escalators: Occupational segregation and race and sex differences in managerial promotions. *Work & Occupations* 26:483-509.

Milliken, F. J., and L. L. Martins. 1996. Searching for common threads: Understanding the multiple effects of diversity in organizational groups. *Academy of Management Review* 21:402-33.

Mueller, Charles W., Ashley Finley, Roderick D. Iverson, and James L. Price. 1999. The effects of group racial composition on job satisfaction, organizational commitment, and career commitment: The case of teachers. *Work & Occupations* 26:165-86.

Pelled, Lisa H., Kathleen M. Eisenhardt, and Katherine Xin. 1999. Exploring the black box: An analysis of work group diversity, conflict, and performance. *Administrative Science Quarterly* 44:1-28.

Pfeffer, Jeffrey. 1983. Organizational demography. *Research in Organizational Behavior* 5:299-357.

Phelan, Jo. 1994. The paradox of the contented female worker: An assessment of alternative explanations. *Social Psychology Quarterly* 57:105-7.

Reskin, Barbara F., Deborah Branch McBrier, and Julie A. Kmec. 1999. The determinants and consequences of workplace sex and race composition. *Annual Review of Sociology* 25:335-61.

Riordan, Christine M., and Lynn F. Shore. 1997. Demographic diversity and employee attitudes: An empirical examination of relational demography within work units. *Journal of Applied Psychology* 82:342-58.

Simpson, Ida H. 1989. The sociology of work: Where have all the workers gone. *Social Forces* 67:563-81.

Sørensen, Jesper B. 2004. The organizational demography of racial employment segregation. *American Journal of Sociology* 110:626-71.

Sorenson, Elaine. 1989. Measuring the effect of occupational sex and race segregation on earnings. In *Pay equity: Empirical inquiries*, ed. Robert T. Michael, Heidi I. Hartmann, and Brigid O'Farrell, 49-69. Washington, DC: National Academy Press.

Tajfel, Henri, and John C. Turner. 1986. The social identity theory of intergroup behavior. In *Psychology of intergroup relations*, ed. S. Worchel and W. G. Austin. Chicago: Nelson-Hall.

Tolbert, Pamela S., Mary E. Graham, and Alice O. Andrews. 1999. Group gender composition and work group relations: Theories, evidence, and issues. In *Handbook of gender & work*, ed. Gary N. Powell, 179-202. Thousand Oaks, CA: Sage.

Tomaskovic-Devey, Donald T. 1993. *Gender and racial inequality at work*. Ithaca, NY: ILR Press.

Tsui, Anne, Terri D. Egan, and Charles A. O'Reilly. 1992. Being different: Relational demography and organizational attachment. *Administrative Science Quarterly* 37:549-79.

Wharton, Amy S., Thomas Rotolo, and Sharon R. Bird. 2000. Social context at work: A multilevel analysis of job satisfaction. *Sociological Forum* 15:65-90.

Williams, Christine L. 1992. The glass escalator: Hidden advantages for men in nontraditional occupations. *Social Problems* 39:253-67.

Wilson, William Julius. 1980. *The declining significance of race*. 2nd ed. Chicago: University of Chicago Press.

The Use of Field Experiments for Studies of Employment Discrimination: Contributions, Critiques, and Directions for the Future

By
DEVAH PAGER

Have we conquered the problems of racial discrimination? Or have acts of discrimination become too subtle and covert for detection? This discussion serves to situate current debates about discrimination within the context of available measurement techniques. In this article, the author (1) considers the arguments from recent debates over the contemporary relevance of labor market discrimination; (2) provides a detailed introduction to experimental field methods for studying discrimination (also called audit studies), including an overview of the findings of recent audit studies of employment; (3) addresses the primary critiques of the audit methodology and the potential threats to the validity of studies of this kind; and (4) considers how we might reconcile evidence from field experiments with those from analyses of large-scale survey data, each of which points to markedly different conclusions. Only by gathering rigorous empirical evidence can we begin to understand the nature of race and racial discrimination in labor markets today.

Keywords: discrimination; race; employment; field experiment; audit study

In December 2002, the Equal Employment Opportunity Commission (EEOC) filed a lawsuit in the Wisconsin Federal Court against the Target Corporation, alleging discrimination against black job applicants at nearly a dozen Wisconsin stores. In depositions for the lawsuit, Target employees admitted to routinely

Devah Pager is an assistant professor of sociology and faculty associate of the Office of Population Research at Princeton University. Her research focuses on institutions affecting racial stratification, including education, labor markets, and the criminal justice system. Her current research has involved a series of field experiments studying discrimination against minorities and ex-offenders in the low-wage labor market. Recent publications include "Walking the Talk: What Employers Say versus What They Do" (American Sociological Review, 2005, with Lincoln Quillian) and "The Mark of a Criminal Record" (American Journal of Sociology, 2003).

NOTE: Support for this research comes from an NSF CAREER Award (NES-0547810). Views expressed in this document are those of the author and do not necessarily represent those of the granting agency.

DOI: 10.1177/0002716206294796

destroying the job applications of black individuals who attended job fairs held at several Milwaukee universities.[1]

Examples of blatant forms of discrimination appear sporadically in a blitz of media attention. As much as these examples provide vivid illustration of lingering forms of racial bias, they simultaneously reinforce the notion that acts of discrimination in contemporary America are rare events committed by unusually malevolent actors. Under more typical circumstances, discrimination in America appears to have all but disappeared. Indeed, the presence of prominent black personalities, athletes, actors, and politicians provides an image of an open door to opportunity for blacks, one no longer conditioned by the stigma of skin color. In his book *Creating Equal: My Fight against Racial Preferences* (2000), Ward Connerly (sponsor of the successful proposition in California to end affirmative action) argued that liberals cling to a misguided belief in the persistence of racism, characterized by the "need to believe that Rosa Parks is still stuck in the back of the bus, even though we live in a time when Oprah is on a billboard on the side of the bus."[2] Perhaps, then, periodic examples of discriminators "caught in the act" represent only extreme aberrations. Dramatic cases of discrimination may get extensive publicity even if they represent rare occurrences overall.

On the other hand, contemporary forms of discrimination may be simply more subtle and covert, leading to less frequent detection and awareness by the general public. In the contemporary United States, social and legal proscriptions against discrimination are strong, placing pressure on potential discriminators to conceal their motives in ways that are consistent with norms of color blindness. Employers (or other gatekeepers) who retain strong preferences for members of a particular race thus face clear incentives to mask their discriminatory actions behind nonracial justifications. It could be the case, then, that discrimination remains fairly routine in certain contexts, despite infrequent public exposure.[3]

Debates about the contemporary relevance of discrimination have been difficult to resolve, in part because of the challenges in identifying, measuring, and documenting its presence or absence in all but extreme cases. In this article, I consider the utility of one approach—the field experiment—as a tool for measuring employment discrimination. Though field experiments in this context are not without limitations, they offer certain unique advantages—namely, the opportunity to observe discrimination directly. The following discussion proceeds in four sections: First, I consider the arguments from recent debates over the contemporary relevance of discrimination in shaping employment opportunities. Second, I provide a detailed introduction to experimental field methods for studying discrimination (also called audit studies), an approach still relatively rare in studies of employment. I also present an overview of the findings of recent audit studies of employment. Third, I address the primary critiques of the audit methodology and examine potential threats to the validity of studies of this kind. Finally, I consider how we might reconcile evidence from field experiments with those from analyses of large-scale survey data, each of which points to markedly different conclusions about the relevance of discrimination in contemporary labor markets. Overall, this discussion serves to situate current debates about discrimination within the context of available measurement techniques. It is only by gathering rigorous empirical evidence that we can make headway in understanding the nature of race and racial discrimination in labor markets today.

Debates about the contemporary relevance of discrimination have been difficult to resolve, in part because of the challenges in identifying, measuring, and documenting its presence or absence in all but extreme cases.

The Declining Significance of Race (as an Explanatory Variable)

Much has changed in American race relations since the middle of the twentieth century. The civil rights movement brought with it a wave of reform, undermining the previously entrenched system rooted in a racialized allocation of opportunity. Historic legislative and court decisions banning segregated schools, prohibiting discrimination in employment and public accommodations, and extending the franchise created a new horizon of opportunities previously unavailable to African Americans. Antidiscrimination law and affirmative action provided twin vehicles for the enforcement and promotion of equal opportunity for America's racial minorities, spurring an unprecedented growth of black upward mobility (Wilson 1978; Harrison and Bennett 1995). With the shifting legal context, the social context of discrimination was transformed dramatically as well. Whereas in 1940 fewer than half of Americans believed that blacks should attend the same schools as whites or have the same chances of getting a job, by 1970 the balance had shifted toward an endorsement of the principles of racial equality; by 1995 more than 95 percent of Americans would support the ideals of racial integration and equality of opportunity.[4] In the wake of this historic transformation, many grew confident that American society had moved beyond the fault lines of race. Lingering signs of racial inequality could be viewed as the eroding vestiges of the previous era rather than as the continuing product of contemporary racial injustice.

Prominent intellectuals of the post–civil rights era were quick to document this transformation. Most notably, in 1978, William Julius Wilson published the now classic treatise on black America, titled *The Declining Significance of Race*, in which he skillfully argued that the problems facing African Americans in the modern industrial period had more to do with class than race. Discrimination, Wilson argued, was no longer paramount in shaping the outcomes of blacks; rather, issues of poverty, education, and employment opportunities were far more important to improving the well-being of individuals from all race groups. Discrimination was not the problem, but rather a lack of jobs, caused by structural changes in the economy, which underlay black—and other groups'—disadvantage. Wilson's book clearly picked up the developing zeitgeist of the time. Indeed, in the thirty years since its publication, we have seen a notable decline in attention to the problems of racial discrimination in academic and policy discussions.[5]

Consistent with notions of a "declining significance of race," racial disparities on a number of key indicators have diminished or disappeared since the 1960s. Rates of high school graduation have narrowed to just a few percentage points difference, and the black-white test score gap appears to be following a similar trajectory (Jencks and Phillips 1998).[6] These improvements in the human capital attainment of blacks, along with a liberalization of opportunity, have facilitated greater performance in the labor market, with blacks becoming increasingly well represented in occupational sectors previously dominated by whites, and a shrinking of the wage gap through 1980 (Farley 1997; Mare 1995; Harrison and Bennett 1995).

Despite visible improvements, however, blacks continue to lag behind whites on key dimensions of inequality. Particularly among those at the bottom half of the distribution, rapid gains beginning in the 1960s slowed, and in some cases reversed, during the 1980s and 1990s. Even at the high point of economic expansion in the late 1990s when unemployment rates were dropping steadily for all groups, black men were still more than twice as likely to be unemployed relative to their white counterparts. Over time blacks, and young black men in particular, have become increasingly likely to drop out of the labor market altogether when faced with the prospect of long-term unemployment or marginal employment opportunities (Holzer, Offner, and Sorensen 2005).[7]

How can we explain these persistent disparities? The truth of the matter is, the employment problems of blacks are vastly overdetermined. Far more factors contribute to black employment problems than would be necessary to produce the trends we observe: the manufacturing sector declined, jobs moved from the central city, black test scores have lagged behind those of whites as the returns to skill have increased, blacks have less effective social networks for finding work, blacks face increasing competition from women and immigrants (Wilson 1987; Freeman and Holzer 1986; Murnane, Willett, and Levy 1995; Waldinger 1999). Interestingly, in this litany of possible explanations, rarely nowadays do we hear mention of the oldest and most basic interpretation. Does discrimination continue to contribute to the employment problems of African Americans?

According to most Americans, the answer is no. The majority of white Americans believe that a black person today has the same chance at getting a job as an equally qualified white person, and only a third believe that discrimination is an important explanation for why blacks do worse than whites in income, housing, and jobs.[8] Public opinion thus favors the idea that discrimination is of vanishing importance, at least as a direct cause of present-day inequalities.

Scholarly opinion likewise remains divided on the question of discrimination. Social psychologists have extensively documented the subtle distortions that take place when race is involved in the course of reasoned evaluations. Despite the widespread conscious endorsement of racial equality, deep-seated stereotypes about the intelligence, work ethic, criminality, and cultural dispositions of various groups continue to frame our evaluations and decision making in social situations.[9]

In contrast to social psychological research that shows a strong persistence of racial stereotypes and discrimination, a growing body of research in sociology and economics has challenged the notion that contemporary labor market outcomes are influenced by race. Wilson's work, mentioned earlier, highlights the importance of structural changes in the economy that, although disproportionately affecting poor and working-class blacks, are race-neutral in origin. More recent work has moved from structural to individual explanations, emphasizing the growing importance of skill in today's economy and the persistent black-white skill gap as a key source of contemporary racial disparities. A series of influential studies, for example, indicate that when relevant individual characteristics—in particular, cognitive ability—have been accounted for, racial disparities in wages among young men narrow substantially or disappear (Farkas 2003; Farkas and Vicknair 1996; Murnane, Willett, and Levy 1995; O'Neill 1990). Neal and Johnson (1996), for example, used data from the National Longitudinal Study of Youth to analyze the black-white wage gap for a cohort born between 1958 and 1963. They found that a measure of cognitive ability (AFQT) explains fully three-quarters of the wage gap for young men. This line of research has reinforced the view that the vast majority of the employment problems of young minority men can be explained by skill or other individual deficiencies, rather than any direct effect of discrimination. Economist James Heckman (1998, 101) summarized this position most clearly: "Most of the disparity in earnings between blacks and whites in the labor market of the 1990s is due to differences in skills they bring to the market, and not to discrimination within the labor market." He went on to describe discrimination as "the problem of an earlier era."

Have we conquered the problems of racial discrimination? Or have acts of discrimination become too subtle and covert for detection? These questions are difficult to answer using standard techniques of observation and analysis. In the following discussion, I consider the use of field experiments for studying discrimination in low-wage labor markets. Because field experiments remain relatively uncommon in studies of employment (and thus fewer resources exist for those interested in pursuing this methodology), there is some value to providing a fairly detailed description of both the conceptual and practical dimensions of this approach.

The Methodology of Field Experiments for Studies of Discrimination

Experimental methods provide a powerful means of isolating causal mechanisms. Traditional experiments typically begin with clearly defined "treatment" and "control" conditions, to which subjects are randomly assigned.[10] All other environmental influences are carefully controlled. A specific outcome variable is then recorded to test for differences between groups. Often subjects are not told the purpose of the experiment to ensure a naive or "natural" reaction to the experimental condition. *Field experiments* blend experimental methods with field-based research, relaxing certain controls over environmental influences to better simulate real-world interactions. While retaining the key experimental features of matching and random assignment important for inferences of causality, this approach relies on real contexts (e.g., actual employment searches, real estate markets, consumer transactions, etc.) for its staged measurement techniques. For example, rather than asking undergraduate subjects to rate hypothetical job applicants in a lab experiment, a field experiment would present two equally qualified job applicants to real employers in the context of real job searches.

> *Field experiments blend experimental methods with field-based research, relaxing certain controls over environmental influences to better simulate real-world interactions.*

Field experiments designed specifically for the measurement of discrimination are typically referred to as audit studies. The audit methodology was first pioneered in the 1970s with a series of audits conducted by the Department of Housing and Urban Development to test for racial discrimination in real estate markets (Yinger 1995; Wienk et al. 1979; Hakken 1979). The approach has since been applied to numerous settings, including mortgage applications, negotiations at a car dealership, and hailing a taxi (Turner and Skidmore 1999; Ayres and Siegelman 1995; Ridley, Bayton, and Outtz 1989; Yinger 1995; Massey and Lundy 2001; Cross et al. 1990; Turner and Skidmore 1991; Bendick, Jackson, and Reinoso 1994; Neumark 1996).[11] In the case of employment discrimination, two main types of audit studies offer useful approaches: correspondence tests and in-person audits.

Correspondence tests

The correspondence test approach, so named for its simulation of the communication (correspondence) between job applicants and employers, relies on fictitious matched resumes submitted to employers by mail or fax. In these studies, two or more resumes are prepared reflecting equal levels of education and experience. The race (or other group characteristic) of the fictitious applicant is then signaled through one or more cues, with race randomly assigned to resume type across employers (i.e., minority status is assigned to one resume for half the employers, the other resume for the other half; this is to ensure that any unobserved differences between resumes will not be correlated with the measured effects of race).[12] Reactions from employers are then typically measured by written responses (to staged mailing addresses) or callbacks (to voice mail boxes) for each applicant. An exemplary study of this kind was recently conducted by Marian Bertrand and Sendhil Mullainathan (2004).[13] In this study, the researchers prepared two sets of matched resumes reflecting applicant pools of two skill levels. Using racially distinctive names to signal the race of applicants, the researchers mailed out resumes to more than thirteen hundred employers in Chicago and Boston, targeting job ads for sales, administrative support, and clerical and customer services positions. The results of their study indicate that white-sounding names were 50 percent more likely to elicit positive responses from employers relative to equally qualified applicants with "black" names.[14] Moreover, applicants with white names received a significant payoff to additional qualifications, while those with black names did not. The racial gap among job applicants was thus higher among the more highly skilled applicant pairs than among those with fewer qualifications.

The advantage of the correspondence test approach is that it requires no actual job applicants (only fictitious paper applicants). This is desirable for both methodological and practical reasons. Methodologically, the use of fictitious paper applicants allows researchers to create carefully matched applicant pairs without needing to accommodate the complexities of real people. The researcher thus has far more control over the precise content of "treatment" and "control" conditions. Practically, the reliance on paper applicants is also desirable in terms of the logistical ease with which the application process can be carried out. Rather than coordinating job visits by real people (creating opportunities for applicants to get lost, to contact the employer under differing circumstances [e.g., when the employer is out to lunch, busy with a customer, etc.], and so on), the correspondence test approach simply requires that resumes are sent out at specified intervals. Additionally, the small cost of postage or fax charges is trivial relative to the cost involved in hiring individuals to pose as job applicants.

While correspondence tests do have many attractive features, certain limitations of this design have led other researchers to prefer the in-person audit approach.

Problems signaling key applicant characteristics. Because correspondence tests rely on paper applications only, all relevant target information must be conveyed without the visual cues of in-person contact. In the case of gender or ethnicity, identifiable names can easily convey the necessary information using gender-specific or ethnically identifiable names (see Riach and Rich 2002; Lahey 2005). In the case of age discrimination, several studies have relied on high school graduation dates to convey the applicants' age difference (Bendick,

Brown, and Wall 1999; Lahey 2005). Researchers who wish to study black-white differences, on the other hand, face a somewhat more challenging task. The Bertrand and Mullainathan (2004) study discussed above, for example, used racially distinctive names to signal the race of applicants. Names like "Jamal" and "Lakisha" signaled African Americans, while "Brad" and "Emily" were associated with whites. While these names are reliably associated with their intended race groups, some critics have argued that the more distinctive African American names are also associated with lower socioeconomic status, thus confounding the effects of race and class. Indeed, mother's education is a significant (negative) predictor of a child having a distinctively African American name.[15] The use of names to test for black-white differences, then, is complicated by the social context in which racially distinctive names are situated.

Other correspondence test studies have used the "extracurricular activities" or "voluntary memberships" section of the resume to bolster the signal of the applicant's race.[16] Membership in the student league of the NAACP, for example, would strongly signal an African American applicant. The matched "white" applicant would then be given a race-neutral activity (e.g., Student Democratic Alliance), which, in the absence of any racial identifiers, is typically (by default) associated with whites.[17] Whatever strategy is used, it is important that resumes are pretested carefully before using them in the field. Names, extracurricular activities, neighborhoods, and high schools may each have connotations that are not readily apparent to the researcher. Directly assessing these connotations/associations is an important first step in developing the materials necessary for a strong test of discrimination.

Limited sample of jobs. One other important limitation of the correspondence test method relates to the types of jobs available for testing. The type of application procedure used in correspondence tests—sending resumes by mail—is typically reserved for studies of administrative, clerical, and other white-collar occupations. The vast majority of entry-level jobs, by contrast, more often require in-person application procedures. For jobs such as busboy, messenger, laborer, or cashier, for example, a mailed-in resume would appear highly out of place. Any study of the low-wage labor market then would require in-person application procedures. While in-person audit studies also face a restricted range of job openings, in-person application procedures allow for a substantially wider pool than can be achieved through paper applications alone.

In-person audits

The use of in-person audits, as opposed to mail-in resumes, represents a more elaborate simulation of the hiring process.[18] In-person employment audits involve the use of matched pairs of individuals (called testers) who pose as job applicants in real job searches. Applicants are carefully matched on the basis of age, height, weight, physical attractiveness, interpersonal style, and any other employment-relevant characteristics to which employers may respond in making hiring decisions. As with correspondence tests, resumes are constructed for each applicant that reflect equal levels of schooling and work experience. In addition, the in-person presentation of confederate job seekers must be carefully controlled. Testers must participate in extensive training to familiarize themselves with the details of their profile and to learn to present themselves to employers according to a highly structured protocol. Daily debriefings are necessary to ensure that the implementation of each test proceeds according to plan (see the appendix). Though in-person audits are time-consuming and require intensive supervision, the approach offers several advantages over correspondence studies. In-person audits provide a clear method for signaling race (through the physical presentation of job applicants); they allow for a wide sample of entry-level job types (which often require in-person applications); and they provide the opportunity to gather both quantitative and qualitative data, with information on whether the applicant receives the job as well as how he or she is treated during the interview process. For those readers interested in the nuts and bolts of audit design, I include a detailed methodological appendix at the end of this article.

In-person employment audits involve the use of matched pairs of individuals (called testers) who pose as job applicants in real job searches.

Table 1 presents the results of a number of recent audit studies conducted in cities across the country. Each study comes to the same basic conclusion—that race matters in hiring decisions. Estimates of the magnitude of discrimination do, however, vary across studies, with whites anywhere from 1.5 to 5 times more likely to receive a callback or job offer relative to equally qualified black applicants.[19] Differences across cities may account for some degree of variation (with Washington, D.C., demonstrating the highest levels of discrimination), as well as differences in the specific design of each experiment (e.g., the level of education presented, the gender of testers, the outcomes measured, etc.). Relative to in-person audits, the correspondence test shows less evidence of discrimination, in part because call-back rates are much lower overall in response to mailed applications.[20] At the conclusion of this article, I consider some future directions for audit research that would improve the continuity across studies to allow for more straightforward interpretations of the nature of variation in discrimination across labor markets.

TABLE 1
SUMMARY OF RECENT AUDIT STUDIES OF RACIAL
DISCRIMINATION IN EMPLOYMENT[a]

Audit Study	Application Method	Location	Sample Size	Interacting Characteristics	Gender of Testers	Education on Resumes	Outcome Measure	Ratio (White/Black)
Pager and Western (2005)	In-person	New York	522	Criminal record	Men	High school diploma	Callback or job offer	2.0
Bertrand and Mullainathan (2004)[b]	Correspondence	Chicago; Boston	1,323	Skill level; neighborhood	Men and women	High school diploma to college grad	Callback	1.5
Pager (2003)[c]	In-person	Milwaukee	350	Criminal record	Men	High school diploma	Callback	2.4
Bendick, Jackson, and Reinoso (1994)[d]	In-person	Washington, D.C.	149	None	Men and women	Two years' college	Job offer	5.0
Turner, Fix, and Struyk (1991)[e]	In-person	Chicago; Washington, D.C.	476	None	Men	High school diploma	Job offer	3.0

a. A similar (more inclusive) table was put together by Marc Bendick Jr. and is available at http://www.bendickegan.com/pdf/Bendick%20SPSSI%202004%20Testing.pdf, Table 1. For a similar overview of correspondence studies in comparative context, see Riach and Rich (2002).
b. The reported sample size for the Bertrand and Mullainathan (2004) study is derived from their Table 2. This study finds no difference in the rate of discrimination between Boston and Chicago. The study found no gender differences in overall callback rates (1.52 vs. 1.49 for males and females, respectively); when comparing males and females in sales jobs, however (male resumes were sent almost exclusively to sales positions), they found a much larger race effect for men (1.52 vs. 1.22 for males and females in sales jobs, respectively).
c. Estimates of race differences are based on between-pair comparisons.
d. The white/black ratio for this study is calculated by multiplying the percentage of testers who were interviewed (48.3 and 39.6 percent for whites and blacks, respectively) by the percentage of testers who, given an interview, were offered jobs (46.9 and 11.3 percent, respectively). Bendick, Jackson, and Reinoso (1994) found a somewhat higher incidence of discrimination against African American women than men.
e. Turner, Fix, and Struyk (1991) found rates of discrimination that are significantly higher in Washington, D.C., than in Chicago.

Variation notwithstanding, in all cases we come to the conclusion that race has large effects on employment opportunities, with a black job seeker anywhere between 50 and 500 percent less likely to be considered by employers as an equally qualified white job applicant. The matched designs allow us to separate speculation about applicant qualifications (supply-side influences) from the racial attributions or biases of employers (demand-side influences). While these studies remain silent on the many supply-side factors that may also contribute to the employment difficulties of young black men, they speak loud and clear about the significance of employer demand in shaping the opportunities available to young black and white job seekers. Before applicants have an opportunity to demonstrate their capabilities in person, a large proportion are weeded out on the basis of a single categorical distinction. Results from audit studies thus provide one clear source of evidence with which to address debates about the contemporary relevance of discrimination.

We come to the conclusion that race has large effects on employment opportunities, with a black job seeker anywhere between 50 and 500 percent less likely to be considered by employers as an equally qualified white job applicant.

Critiques of the Audit Method

While most researchers view the audit methodology as one of the most effective means of measuring discrimination, the approach is not without its critics. Before assuming that a field experimental design automatically confers high levels of both internal and external validity, the possible vulnerabilities of the audit methodology deserve careful consideration. Economist James Heckman is among the most vocal critics of the audit methodology, particularly when used to study the effects of race. Heckman's primary criticism focuses on the problems of effective matching.[21] The validity of an audit study relies on its success in presenting two otherwise equally qualified job applicants who differ only by race. Given the vast number of characteristics that can influence an employer's evaluation, however, it is difficult to ensure that all such dimensions have been effectively controlled. Because, race is not something that can be experimentally assigned, we must believe that audit researchers have been successful in identifying and matching on all relevant characteristics—something that, according to Heckman, leaves substantial room for bias. Heckman's primary critique focuses on the problem of unobservables—those characteristics "unobservable to the audit study [researchers], but . . . at least somewhat visible to the prospective employer and acted on in hiring . . . decisions" (Heckman 1998, 109). According to Heckman, blacks and whites (at the population level) may differ in the average and/or distribution of important characteristics. As an example, consider a hypothetical case in which whites on average have a faster response time in interview interactions than blacks. That is to say, the delay in seconds between a question posed by an interviewer and the initiation of response is shorter on average for whites than for blacks. (To be sure, response time is just one potential example, and I emphasize that it is a case that to my knowledge has no empirical basis. Heckman himself does not suggest any concrete examples of potentially relevant unobservables that could affect hiring outcomes; but it is instructive to consider a concrete hypothetical case for the purpose of clarity.) Because any difference in response time would be extremely subtle, it may not be immediately recognizable to researchers and may even register for employers only at a subliminal level. Nevertheless, if this trait produces an incremental advantage for the individual with a faster response time—because he or she is perceived as sharper or more engaged—we may mistake the employer's response for discrimination when in fact nonracial evaluations are driving the differential response.

A related problem emerges if blacks and whites differ on key characteristics, not on the average, but in the level of dispersion. To continue with the same example, imagine a case in which blacks and whites each have a mean response time of 0.5 seconds, but blacks demonstrate greater heterogeneity along this dimension than whites. Differential results may then be observed depending on the overall qualifications of the testers relative to the requirements of the job. If testers are highly qualified relative to the positions they apply for (which tends to be the case in audit studies), differential dispersion on any key variable will favor the group with lower dispersion (because a smaller proportion of applicants in this group will be at the low end of the tail relative to a high-dispersion group).

Heckman's critique raises some important considerations and surely encourages a more rigorous scrutiny of the audit methodology. In each case, it is worth considering when and how these concerns can be effectively addressed. Heckman's concern is that if, on average, blacks and whites differ in the mean or variance on any unobserved productivity-related variable, estimates from matched-pair studies will be biased by design. If auditors were randomly drawn from the population and matched on a rote basis according to readily measurable characteristics, this critique would surely be valid. It is a mistake, however, to assume that the researcher is at a necessary disadvantage relative to the employer in identifying productivity-related characteristics. In fact, the researcher is herself or himself an employer in the planning and implementation of an audit study.

The job of a tester is not an easy one, and finding a suitable team to complete this type of project requires extensive screening and careful selection. The job requires solid writing skills (for the written narratives that follow each audit), good communication skills (to communicate the necessary information in an interview, to make a good impression on the employer); high levels of motivation (to keep up day after day), reliability (to accurately conduct and report each test), navigation skills (to find locations throughout the city); and an endless number of other qualifications. Thus, apart from the more explicit traits of height, weight, race, and age, researchers must search for testers who can perform well in an intensely demanding position.[22] As an employer, the researcher must identify subtle cues about applicants that indicate their ability to perform. Whether or not these cues are explicit, conscious, or measurable, they are present in a researcher's evaluation of tester candidates as they are for employers' evaluations of entry-level job applicants. Like employers, researchers are affected by both objective and subjective/subconscious indicators of applicant quality in their selection and matching of testers, in ways that should ultimately improve the nuanced calibration of test partners.

A related concern of Heckman has to do with the possibility that matching (even when done successfully) may itself produce distortions in the hiring process. Because audit partners are matched on all characteristics that are most directly relevant to the hiring process (education, work experience, physical appearance, interpersonal skills, etc.), employers may be forced to privilege relatively minor characteristics simply out of necessity of breaking the tie. "By taking out the common components that are most easily measured, differences in hiring rates as monitored by audits arise from the idiosyncratic factors, and not the main factors, that drive actual labor markets" (Heckman 1998, 111). If employers care only marginally about race, but are confronted with two applicants equal on all other dimensions, race may take on greater significance in that particular hiring decision than is true under more normal circumstances, when evaluating real applicants who differ according to multiple dimensions.

Again, this critique is an important one, though in this case one that can be addressed more easily. If the only outcome of interest in an audit study is whether an applicant gets the job, Heckman's concern is certainly relevant. If forced to choose a single hire, employers will use whatever basis for differentiation exists, whether that particular attribute is valued highly or not. Audit studies that measure callbacks as an outcome variable, by contrast, avoid situations in which employers can choose only one applicant. In fact, employers typically interview an average of eight applicants for each entry-level job they fill. If race is only a minor concern for employers, we would expect both members of an audit pair to make it through the first cut. To the extent that race figures prominently even in these early rounds of review, we can infer that race is invoked as more than a mere tie-breaker. In these cases, the evidence of race-based decision making is quite strong.[23]

A third important critique of the audit methodology raises the problem of experimenter effects, or the possibility that the expectations or behaviors of testers can influence the audit results in nonrandom ways. For example, if a tester expects to be treated poorly by employers, he or she may appear more withdrawn, nervous, or defensive in interactions. The nature of the interaction may then create a self-fulfilling prophecy in which the tester experiences poor outcomes, but for reasons unrelated to the experimental condition (e.g., his or her race). Indeed, the possibility of experimenter effects represents one of the most serious threats to the validity of the audit experiment. While there is no way to conclusively rule out the possibility of experimenter effects, several precautions can be taken to minimize the problem. First, effective training and supervision are critical to the successful implementation of an audit study. Testers must be exceedingly familiar with their assumed profiles and the audit protocol, such that appropriate responses to employer queries become almost automatic. Extensive role-plays, videotaped interviews, and practice audits help testers to become comfortable with their role and to gain important feedback on their performance. Likewise, during the course of the fieldwork, daily debriefings and regular troubleshooting sessions are critical to identify any potential problems or to refine the protocol in ways that best suit the specifics of the study. Finally, after the fieldwork is completed, it is possible to conduct an indirect check on the problem of experimenter effects. Typically a significant proportion of tests are conducted with little or no in-person contact, either because the employer is not present or does not have time to meet with the applicant. By comparing audit outcomes for testers who did and did not interact with employers, we can assess the degree to which in-person interaction leads to a different distribution of results. If testers are acting in ways that fulfill their expectations of discrimination, we would expect outcomes for those tests conducted with interaction to show greater evidence of differential treatment than those without. If the results show no difference, or show weaker evidence of differential treatment, we can be more confident that experimenter effects are not driving the results.[24] As a final note, it is worth reiterating that a key advantage of correspondence tests (relative to in-person audits) is the ability to present matched pairs of resumes to employers without the use of real testers. That these studies typically also demonstrate consistent evidence of discrimination provides one further reassurance that the outcomes from in-person audit studies are not merely the product of mismatched testers or participants' enacted expectations (Bertrand and Mullainathan 2004).

Reconciling Competing Measures of Discrimination

If employment discrimination is indeed as great a problem as the results of field experiments suggest, how can we reconcile this conclusion with competing evidence demonstrating a small or nonexistent wage gap between equally qualified blacks and whites? As mentioned earlier, recent analyses of large-scale survey data indicate that after statistically controlling for a wide range of individual characteristics (cognitive ability, in particular), most or all of the wage gap between young black and white men can be eliminated. The implication of this line of research is that discrimination plays little role in determining the economic attainment of young men. How then can we account for the substantial evidence of discrimination indicated by the audit results?

I consider this discrepancy from several perspectives. In this discussion, I do not interrogate the validity of specifications used in existing studies of wage inequality, taking at face value the reliability of the analyses. It should be acknowledged, however, that a wide range of estimates of the black-white wage gap exist within the survey literature, with numerous studies reporting a large and persist racial gap (see, e.g., Cancio et al. 1996; Neumark 1999). Likewise, analysis following the Neal and Johnson (1996) paper has found some evidence that the original results overstate the extent to which cognitive ability can account for racial disparities in wages. Carneiro, Heckman, and Masterov (2003), for example, found that adjustments for years of schooling at the time the respondent's cognitive ability was measured lead to the reemergence of a substantial wage differential. Tomaskovic-Devey, Thomas, and Johnson (2005, 76) found that, while wages measured in early adulthood show little evidence of racial inequality (because there is little wage dispersion to begin with), the racial wage gap then grows across the life course, reaching 14 percent by the time these men reach forty (controlling for cognitive ability and other person-specific characteristics). It thus remains an open question exactly how much of the wage gap can be explained by individual attributes like cognitive ability. Nevertheless, this discussion takes as its starting point the argument that, after extensive controls, analyses of black-white wage disparities can be largely explained by observed individual characteristics. In contrast to evidence from audit studies, these survey results suggest little reason to be concerned with the problems of discrimination.

Before we dismiss discrimination as "the problem of an earlier era," however, it is worth considering under what circumstances these discrepant findings could be meaningfully reconciled. First, it is important to keep in mind that the employment relationship is characterized by a number of discrete decisions, including hiring, wage setting, promotion, and termination. Discrimination may affect all, none, or some of these decisions. Varying incentives or constraints characteristic of different employment decisions can mediate the emergence of discrimination in important ways. For example, there is reason to believe that decisions about whom to interview and whom to hire may be more susceptible to discriminatory bias relative to those decisions made at later stages of the employment relationship. Both economic theories of statistical discrimination and social-psychological theories of unconscious bias predict that discrimination will be most pronounced when objective information about the target is limited or unreliable.[25] Indeed, the amount of information employers have about applicants at this point of introduction is at a minimum. We would expect, then, that, whether exerted consciously or not, underlying assumptions about race and productivity will be most likely to color evaluations of blacks at earlier stages in the employment process (i.e., hiring) than at later stages (i.e., wage setting/termination decisions), when more objective performance indicators have become available.[26] Likewise, we would expect to see the effects of discrimination reflected in differential employment rates rather than wage rates.

In addition to information asymmetries that affect employers' perceptions about workers, workers' perceptions of employer decision making is likewise most limited at the point of hire. Uncertainty about the competing applicant pool, about the employer's preferences, and about the job itself makes acts of discrimination particularly difficult to detect at the initial point of contact. At later stages, by contrast, workers have more information with which to compare their treatment to others in comparable positions. Employers concerned about detection, or even accusations of discrimination, will thus be safer eliminating black applicants early on.

Finally, aside from the distinct conditions that characterize different stages of the employment process, it is important also to consider their interdependence. If individuals who have been refused employment opportunities are excluded from estimates of wage disparities, hiring discrimination against blacks will result in a more select sample of black wage earners than whites. In fact, barriers to labor market entry—including but not limited to hiring discrimination—will lead young black men to remain unemployed longer and may cause them to drop out of the labor force altogether. In this case, our estimates of wage disparities may be distorted by the large numbers of black men missing from the sample of wage earners. Trends in labor force participation indeed show high levels of labor force nonparticipation among young black men and a growing black-white disparity in rates of joblessness.[27] Because individuals who are not working and not looking for work are excluded from standard economic analyses, increases in labor force nonparticipation among blacks can substantially distort conventional measures of racial wage disparities.[28] According to Western and Pettit (2005, 573), "By 1999, the high rate of black joblessness inflated black relative earnings by between 7 and 20% among working age men, and by as much as 58% among young men." According to this and other analyses, black-white wage equality is in large part an artifact of decreasing labor force participation among the most disadvantaged young black men. Without effectively accounting for the processes that precede labor force participation—such as discrimination, discouragement, incarceration, or other sources of selection—wage estimates can account for only one incomplete picture of the larger employment process.

Discrepancies between wage estimates and measures of discrimination at the point of hire may then reflect one (or both) of two processes: First, incentives to discriminate at the point of hire are greater than those at later stages, due to information asymmetries that affect both employer and worker perceptions. In this case, wage estimates and hiring discrimination estimates may both represent accurate reflections of discrimination at different stages of the employment relationship. Second, discrimination at the point of hire may distort wage estimates by contributing to the large numbers of young black men who are unemployed or who drop out of the labor force altogether. In this case, wage estimates reflect only the more "select" members of the black population, artificially reducing the contrast with less select white workers. In either scenario, discrimination at the point of hire remains an active barrier to employment for young black men. Indeed, the magnitude of the results shown here, across a wide range of studies, suggests that barriers to labor market entry are likely to represent a serious constraint on the achievement of economic self-sufficiency among young black men today.[29]

Directions for the Future

This article has sought to familiarize readers with the audit methodology and to consider how we might reconcile the findings from audit studies with those from recent analyses of survey data. But there is much more to be done. In this final section, I consider several directions for future research that could substantially improve our estimates and interpretation of audit results measuring employment discrimination.

First, it would be useful for future research to develop a standardized audit framework that could be replicated across testing sites and over time, similar to the model pursued in recent housing audits (Turner et al. 2002). Though several researchers have conducted multicity studies, no researcher has attempted to include more than two sites, thus limiting our comparative perspective on discrimination across labor markets and over time. Second, the introduction of additional experimental variables (e.g., skill, education, written references, etc.) would allow researchers to calibrate the effects of race against other key labor market determinants. The effects of race matters *relative to what?* As shown in Table 1, a few prior studies have included one or more variables in addition to race. Pursuing such designs would help to translate the effects of race into another meaningful metric. We might ask, for example, How do the advantages of whiteness compare to the advantages of having a high school degree? How many years of additional work experience would a black applicant need to be competitive with an otherwise comparable white applicant? Though experimental designs are constrained in the number of conditions that can be included in any single study, the inclusion of key comparison variables would greatly contribute to the interpretation and translation of audit results.

Finally, additional research should make efforts to empirically map the findings from audit studies onto population surveys of job search and employment patterns. This next step is important in helping us to assess how the prevalence of discrimination encountered by testers corresponds to discrimination experienced by real job seekers with similar characteristics. Indeed, Heckman (1998) warns us not to interpret the findings from audit studies as accurate measures of the prevalence of discrimination in everyday life. "The impact of market discrimination is not determined by the most discriminatory practices in the market, or even by the average level of discrimination among firms, but rather by the level of discrimination at the firms where ethnic minorities or women actually end up buying, working and borrowing. It is at the margin that economic values are set. . . . Purposive sorting within markets eliminates the worst forms of discrimination" (pp. 102-3). Heckman's argument suggests that minority workers are likely to avoid applying for jobs at discriminatory firms, thus reducing actual experiences of discrimination. Provided there are a sufficient number of employers who are willing to hire minorities, blacks and whites can sort into different labor markets without experiencing any direct discrimination.

How can we assess the validity of these claims? First, we need better information about how and where black and white job seekers search for work and how similar or different the distribution of employers encountered in real searches is to that achieved in the simulated search process of audit studies. This information can help us understand how the audit results map onto the direct experiences of actual job seekers.[30] Second, we need more information about how black job seekers make decisions about search behavior. Do blacks consciously avoid employers or industries in which discrimination is known to be prevalent? This information can help us understand the extent to which perceived discrimination may shape or constrain the search process of minority job seekers in ways that indirectly affect employment outcomes. And finally, what distortions in labor market sorting might discrimination produce, apart from its direct effects on hiring decisions? Economic models assume that, in the presence of discrimination, blacks and whites can sort into different labor markets with little consequence. This assumption is true only if those employers willing to hire blacks are no different (in compensation, security, number of vacancies, opportunities for promotion, etc.) from those employers who prefer to hire whites. By contrast, previous research suggests that occupational segregation (or crowding) within labor markets (whether due to discrimination or self-selection) is often associated with lower wages, less job security, longer search times, and/or reduced labor force participation (e.g., Parcel and Mueller 1983, chap. 5). Assessing the possible indirect effects of discrimination, in addition to any direct effects on hiring decisions, would provide a more complete understanding of the role of discrimination in contemporary labor markets.

Research on discrimination poses numerous complications, with issues of measurement of central concern. This discussion sought to provide an overview of some of the recent debates about the relevance of discrimination in contemporary labor markets, the measurement tools used to study discrimination, and the varying results in the empirical literature. While little consensus remains among researchers about the appropriate techniques for studying discrimination, active comparisons across studies can help to shed light on the relative strengths and weaknesses of existing approaches. While no research method is without flaws, careful consideration of the range of methods available helps to match one's research question with the appropriate empirical strategy. This article focused primarily on the strengths and limitations of the audit methodology for studying discrimination. Although the audit design cannot address all relevant aspects of labor market disadvantage, it can provide strong and direct measures of discrimination at the point of hire, a powerful mechanism regulating the broader array of labor market opportunities. Future research should extend this focus to include a broader perspective on the employment process, from search decisions to hiring behavior to wages, tenure, and promotion, comparing findings across studies for a more complete picture of discrimination in labor markets today.

Appendix
The Implementation of an In-Person Audit Study

This appendix is intended to provide a general orientation to the nuts and bolts of designing and implementing an in-person audit study. This discussion addresses the selection and matching criteria necessary for ensuring high-quality and well-aligned applicant pairs, training and supervision requirements, outcome measures, and the ethics of audit research.

Matching. The selection of testers who will play the role of job applicants is one of the most critical components in the design of an employment audit and arguably one of the most time-intensive. Testers must be chosen based on personal attributes that make them individually well qualified to perform what can be a highly demanding job requiring a substantial degree of autonomy, but they must also be chosen based on personal attributes that make them a good match for another well-qualified individual (their test partner). Taking into account the wide range of characteristics employers may pay attention to in evaluating applicants, testers should be matched on concrete factors: such as age, height, weight, and level of education; in addition to more subjective criteria: articulateness, ease of personal interaction, physical attractiveness, and nonverbal communication style. Though the relevance of these characteristics may vary by job type or employer, they are all nevertheless potentially influential in hiring decisions and thus must be considered in deciding on potential matches. Taking all these considerations into account, it is not unusual to interview between eighty to one hundred applicants for each tester hired.

The matching process itself is an art as much as it is a science (an issue that has provoked criticism by some) (Heckman and Siegelman 1993). While a number of psychometric scales exist to measure personality attributes, verbal ability, and so on, certain intangible qualities are arguably more important in making a first impression. Including a wide range of external evaluators (individuals not directly involved in the research project) can provide important feedback about the holistic impressions formed by each potential tester and the degree of similarity between proposed pairs.

Note that audits of contexts other than employment require less attention to physical appearance and personality characteristics. Housing audits and audits of consumer markets, for example, are typically based on a far narrower (and easier to control) set of tester characteristics. Likewise, requirements are less stringent when treatment conditions can be randomly assigned. In testing the effects of a criminal record, for example, testers can alternate which individual presents himself as the ex-offender over the course of the study, thus evening out any unobserved differences within the tester pair. If one tester is slightly more attractive, for example, in certain cases he or she will be a slightly more attractive offender and in other cases a slightly more attractive nonoffender. Any individual differences will even out if each tester serves in the treatment and control condition in an equal number of cases.[a] In testing the effects of race, by contrast, the treatment condition cannot be randomly assigned. The quality of the matches thus becomes extremely consequential, as race can be fully confounded with any other individual characteristic. To the extent that differences will persist, researchers should err in the direction of choosing black testers with slightly more desirable attributes. Results will then represent a conservative test of discrimination.

Constructing resumes. Once tester pairs have been matched, they are assigned resumes reflecting equal levels of education and experience. Substantial thought must go into choosing high schools and neighborhoods that have similar reputations and student/resident compositions; likewise, work histories must be developed to reflect not only equal amounts of prior work experience but also similar types of work experience.[b] In addition to pretesting resumes to assess their comparability, ideally resume types can be assigned independent of treatment condition (e.g., any given resume will be used by both black and white testers, to control for any unmeasured differences). In some cases, the resume will be the only point of contact between the tester and the employer (e.g., in cases where the person in charge of hiring is not present at the time of the test, and the tester leaves a resume); it is thus important that all relevant information can be effectively conveyed on this single-page document.

Training. No matter how carefully matched two testers may be, they can only act as successful as audit partners if they learn to interact with employers in similar ways. A wide range of questions can come up in the course of a conversation or interview with an employer, and testers must be prepared to share similar information and communicate similar types of profiles in their descriptions of past (fictitious) experiences. Before starting actual fieldwork for an audit study, testers typically participate in an extensive training period during which they rehearse the content of their profile, the appropriate way to phrase answers to interview questions, and work on aligning their responses with those of their test partner. Training can consist of videotaped mock interviews, practice interviews with employer confederates, and practice audits with real employers. In addition to the initial training period, daily debriefings with testers can help to identify problems that may arise or additional content that needs rehearsing.

Problems of implementation. With any field experiment, the unpredictabilities of the real world often interfere with carefully planned research designs.

Traffic can back up (or public transportation can break down), making it impossible for one tester to make it to an employer at the specified time; a job can get filled in between the time the two testers come to apply; a tester may run into someone he knows during an audit; an employer may know the manager of a fictitious job listed on the tester's resume. The key to maintaining the integrity of the experimental design lies in the ability to respond quickly to unexpected happenings and to constantly tweak existing protocols to take account of new situations. In cases where the protocol appears not to have been fully (or effectively) implemented, the test should be cancelled. While it is impossible to catalogue the countless number of potential disruptions that may arise, researchers must be vigilant throughout the course of the study. Effective and continual supervision of the testing process is one of the most important elements of a successful audit study.

Supervision. The quality of the data from an audit study depends on the degree to which testers effectively follow the established protocol. And yet evaluating testers' performance is difficult, since the majority of the testers' work is completed with no direct supervision. To monitor the quality of the testing process, a number of formal procedures can be put into place. First, immediately following each visit to an employer, testers are typically required to fill out an extensive summary form, including a large number of closed-ended questions (e.g., job title, race/gender/age of employer, screening tests required? asked about criminal background? etc.). In addition, testers write a lengthy open-ended narrative, describing their contact with the employer and the content of interactions they had during the test. These summary forms allow researchers to monitor the relative experiences of tester pairs and to identify any anomalies in the testing experiences that may confound measurement of the treatment variable. Second, the researcher (or project manager) should be available for daily debriefings with each of the testers, following the completion of each day's work. On occasions where something unexpected occurs, the project manager should be contacted immediately. Third, weekly meetings can be useful to allow testers the opportunity to brainstorm together about how to make the logistics of testing as efficient and controlled as possible. And finally, spot checks of tester performance can provide helpful tools for surveillance and continued training. For example, researchers can arrange for testers to unknowingly apply for jobs with confederate employers (i.e., employers who are collaborators of the researcher), to allow for an external assessment of their performance. Arranging for hidden cameras to record these spot checks can provide an additional training tool, as the audit team can watch and discuss the videotapes to identify differences in presentation style between tester pairs. The vast majority of problems that arise in the course of fieldwork for an audit study are relatively minor and can be resolved quickly, provided effective monitoring. It is only when problems continue unchecked that they can pose a significant threat to the validity of the research.

Quantitative and qualitative outcomes. One of the attractive features of the in-person audit design is its ability to measure a wide range of outcome variables, reflecting a range of applicant experiences. The primary outcome variable is typically a quantitative indicator of positive response by the employer: a callback or job offer. In addition, however, the audit process can detect a number of more subtle indicators of differential treatment. In some cases, for example, testers are channeled into jobs other than the ones originally advertised (e.g., the job ad was for a retail sales clerk, but the employer offers the tester a job as a stock boy). In other cases, employers may express revealing comments in the course of a conversation or interview. Tracking the level of attention, encouragement, or hostility testers elicit can provide important information about the experiential aspects of the job seeking process. Indeed, by observing the kinds of treatment testers receive in their ongoing job searches, one can identify the experiences that may lead certain workers to become discouraged from seeking work altogether.

Testing for litigation versus research. One of the common questions about the audit methodology concerns how it can be used to reduce the problems of discrimination. The audit method was initially designed for the enforcement of antidiscrimination law. Testers were used to detect racially discriminatory practices among real estate agents, landlords, and lenders, providing the evidence necessary to pursue litigation.[c] Audit studies for research purposes, by contrast, are oriented not toward a specific intervention but rather toward obtaining accurate measures of the prevalence of discrimination across a broad sector or metropolitan area. The difference between these two types of studies is further reflected in the design of the study. Testing for litigation requires multiple audits of the same employer (or real estate agent, etc.) to detect consistent patterns of discrimination by that particular individual and/or company. Testing for research, by contrast, typically includes no more than a single audit per employer, with discrimination detected through systematic patterns across employers, rather than repeated acts of discrimination by a single employer. The distinction here is important in what we can tell from audit studies intended for research purposes. In these studies, *it is not possible to draw conclusions about the discriminatory tendencies of any given employer*. Indeed, even in the complete absence of discrimination, an employer confronted with two equivalent candidates will choose the white applicant in 50 percent of cases. Using a single test of each employer, therefore, does not allow for individual-level assessments of discrimination; only by looking at systematic patterns across a large number of employers can we determine whether hiring appears influenced by race or other stigmatizing characteristics.[d] The point of research-based audit studies, therefore, is to assess the prevalence of discrimination across the labor market, rather than to intervene in particular sites of discrimination. While the objective is different, research audit studies provide important information about discriminatory practices that can support calls for strengthening antidiscrimination policy or other policy initiatives designed to protect vulnerable workers.

Ethics of audit research. Discussions of audit studies inevitably lead to questions about the ethics of research of this kind. Audit studies require that employers are unwittingly recruited for participation and then led to believe that the testers are viable job candidates. Contrary to the ethical standards for research established by the federal government, this design does not allow for the use of informed consent by research subjects for participation and often avoids debriefing subjects after the study's completion. How then are audit studies permitted to take place? As it turns out, there are specific criteria that regulate the use of research of this kind, and a well-designed audit study can arguably meet each of them. Below I provide a discussion of the relevant concerns and potential solutions to the ethical problems posed by research of this kind.

The use of deception in social science has long been met with suspicion. While individual researchers may feel they can clearly distinguish between appropriate and improper research practices, examples from the past indicate that researchers' individual judgments may not always conform to the standards of the discipline (e.g., Milgram 1974). Because of past transgressions, legislation concerning the use of human subjects now governs all social science research and includes, as one of its fundamental criteria, the use of informed consent from all research participants.[e] In the case of audit studies, however, the nature of the research requires that subjects remain unaware of their participation, and the condition of informed consent therefore cannot be met.

While current federal policy governing the protection of human subjects strongly supports the use of informed consent, there is recognition that certain types of research that fail to obtain formal consent can be deemed permissible. According to the regulations, a human subjects institutional review board (IRB) "may . . . waive . . . informed consent provided (1) the research involves no more than minimal risk to human subjects; (2) the waiver or alteration will not adversely affect the rights and welfare of the subjects; (3) the research could not practicably be carried out without the waiver or alteration; and (4) whenever appropriate, the subjects will be provided with additional information after participation."[f] Each of these conditions can arguably be satisfied in the context of audit studies of discrimination. While there are potential risks to subjects, reasonable efforts can be made to reduce the costs to subjects and thereby impose only minimal risk.

Most audit research poses two primary potential risks to subjects: (1) loss of time and (2) legal liability. In the first case, subjects are asked to evaluate a pair of applications submitted by phony applicants. Time spent reviewing applications and/or interviewing applicants will therefore impose a cost on the subject. Most employment audit studies limit their samples to employers for entry-level positions—those requiring the least intensive review—in part to minimize the time employers spend evaluating phony applicants. Entry-level positions are typically filled on the basis of cursory overviews of applications and limited personal contact (Fix and Struyk 1993). Contact with subjects is thus minimal, consisting of requesting an application and/or answering a few brief questions. Audits of higher-skill jobs, by contrast, impose a greater burden on employers, as the hiring process for such positions typically requires a greater investment of time and effort.[g]

A second potential risk posed by audit research is the potential for employers and/or firms to be held liable for discrimination if evidence were to be publicly released as to their performance in the audit. In fact, as mentioned above, the evidence provided by audit studies intended for research cannot support claims of discrimination against any individual employer. Nevertheless, efforts must be taken to protect employer identities so that even association with a study on discrimination cannot be made. To this end, identifying information should be kept in a secure location, and any publicly released publications or presentations should omit all identifying characteristics of individuals and firms.

The issue of debriefing subjects following the completion of the audit study is a complicated one. Though typically IRB protocol supports the debriefing of subjects whenever possible, in certain cases acknowledging the occurrence or nature of a research study is deemed undesirable. It could be argued, for example, that subjects could be placed at greater risk should their behavior, as a result of the audit study, fall under greater scrutiny by superiors. For human resource personnel or managers who are thought to be discriminating, the consequences may be more serious than if no attention were brought to the audit whatsoever. While the chances that negative consequences would result from this research in any case are very small, some IRB committees take the view that eliminating the debriefing stage is the most prudent strategy. The purpose of audit research is *not* to harm individual employers. Rather, the research seeks to improve our understanding of the barriers to employment facing stigmatized groups in their search for employment.

As a final matter, it should be emphasized that the ethics of audit research is not only of concern in a university context. The legal standing of testers has likewise received close scrutiny by the courts. In fact, the issue of testing has reached the highest judicial body, with the United States Supreme Court upholding the standing of testers in its 1982 decision.[h] A more recent ruling by the 7th Circuit Court again upheld the standing of testers in cases of employment discrimination, broadening their endorsement of this methodology. In each of these rulings, the courts have been primarily concerned with the use of testing for pursuing litigation against employers (rather than for pure research, as is the case here). Implicit in these holdings, however, is the belief that the misrepresentation involved in testing is worth the unique benefit this practice can provide in uncovering discrimination and enforcing civil rights laws. According to former Equal Employment Opportunity Commission (EEOC) Chairman Gilbert Castellas, "Using employment testers in a carefully controlled manner is an important tool for measuring the presence or absence of discrimination. If we can shed light on barriers to fair hiring in entry-level jobs, which are the gateway to self-sufficiency and economic independence, we will have made an important step in assuring equal opportunity for everyone."[i] Indeed, despite certain burdens imposed by audit studies, the ultimate benefit from research of this kind extends far beyond the contribution of a single study. Rigorous and realistic measurement of discrimination is fundamental to understanding and addressing persistent barriers to employment facing members of stigmatized groups.

---

a. Note that even in cases where the experimental condition can be randomly assigned, it is nevertheless desirable to match testers as closely as possible, so as to minimize extraneous "noise" in the comparisons of tester outcomes.

b. Typically resumes are constructed to reflect a range of entry level work experience, including, for example, jobs in sales, restaurants, and manual labor.

c. In these discrimination cases, testers serve as the plaintiffs. Despite the fact that the testers themselves were not in fact seeking housing (or employment) at the time their application was submitted, their treatment nevertheless represents an actionable claim. This issue has received close scrutiny by the courts, including rulings by the highest federal courts. The U.S. Supreme Court upheld the standing of testers in its 1982 decision (*Havens Realty Corp. v. Coleman*, 455 U.S. 363, 373 [1982]). A more recent ruling by the 7th Circuit Court again upheld the standing of testers in cases of employment discrimination, broadening their endorsement of this methodology.

d. This feature has certain desirable properties from the perspective of gaining approval from an institutional review board (i.e., university ethics committees). Concerns about confidentiality and risks to employers are reduced when no single participant can be identified as a discriminator.

e. DHHS CFR45.46.116.

f. 56 *Federal Register* 117, p. 28017, June 18, 1991.

g. In the present research, I further limit imposition on employers by restricting audits to the first stage of the employment process. In most cases, then, I look only at whether or not an employer invites the tester for an interview, rather than including the interview and job offer stages as well. Limiting the research design to the initial process can thus further reduce the burden to subjects.

h. *Havens Realty Corp. v. Coleman*, 455 U.S. 363, 373 (1982).

i. This statement was drawn from a press release issued on December 5, 1997, and can be found at http://www.eeoc.gov/press/12-5-97.html.

Notes

1. *EEOC v. Target Corporation*, case no. 02-C-146. As of this writing, the case was pending appeal at the 7th Circuit Court, case no. 04-3559.

2. Connerly (2000, 20-21).

3. Dovidio and Gaertner (2000), for example, measured racial attitudes and discrimination at two points in time (late 1980s and late 1990s). They found substantial declines in self-reported racial prejudice. Evidence of discrimination, by contrast, remained stable. To test for discrimination, the researchers performed a simulated hiring experiment in which subjects were asked to evaluate the application materials for black and white job applicants of varying qualification levels. When applicants were either highly qualified or poorly qualified for the position, there was no evidence of discrimination. When applicants had acceptable but ambiguous qualifications, however, subjects were nearly 70 percent more likely to recommend the white applicant than the black applicant. This finding was consistent across the two time periods.

4. In 1942, only 32 percent of Americans believed that "white students and black students should go to the same schools"; by 1995, this proportion increased to 96 percent. In 1944, 45 percent believed that blacks "should have as good a chance as white people to get any kind of job"; by 1972, this proportion had increased to 97 percent (Schuman et al. 1997, 104-5).

5. As one simple empirical measure of this trend, I calculated the number of articles included in *Sociological Abstracts* that have the words "race" or "racial" and "discrimination" in their title relative to the proportion that merely reference "race" or "racial." Nearly 20 percent fewer articles in the period 1986 to 2002 reference the word "discrimination" in their title relative to those articles about race written between 1963 and 1985; among those written in 2003 to 2004, nearly 40 percent fewer articles about race directly indicate an emphasis on discrimination in their titles. In recent years, therefore, an explicit emphasis on discrimination seems increasingly uncommon in sociological research. Political resources devoted to the problems of racial discrimination have likewise declined. For example, the proportion of Equal Employment Opportunity Commission (EEOC) cases addressing racial discrimination declined steadily in the 1990s, relative to increases in claims focusing on discrimination by gender or disability (Donohue and Siegelman 2005).

6. Note, however, that the black-white test score gap remains large and statistically significant.

7. Current Population Survey data show that in the early 1980s, only 14 percent of white men, aged twenty to thirty-five, with a high school diploma, were not working compared to 25 percent of their black counterparts. By 2000, the jobless rate for young high school educated white men had dropped below 10 percent, but joblessness among black men of the same age and education was around 22 percent. Racial inequality in joblessness had thus increased and employment rates for young noncollege blacks at the height of the economic boom in 2000 was little better than during the recession of the early 1980s.

8. The most common explanation for black disadvantage is "a lack of motivation or willpower," with over half of white respondents endorsing this view. By contrast, fully two-thirds of black respondents believe that discrimination is an important explanation, with "poor quality education" representing the second most common choice. Author's calculations from the 2000 General Social Survey.

9. Fiske (1998); Bodenhausen (1988); Trope and Thomson (1997); Banaji, Hardin, and Rothman (1993). Despite the progressive changes in racial attitudes generally, research indicates that the content of racial stereotypes has changed little over time (Devine and Elliot 1995); what has changed is the conscious effort on the part of nonprejudiced individuals to inhibit the activation of these stereotypes (Devine 1989). While these conscious strategies have successfully resulted in a substantial reduction in the expression of racial bias, actions taken under pressure or in cognitively demanding situations remain vulnerable to the influence of implicit racial attitudes (Gilbert and Hixon 1991).

10. Random assignment helps to remove the influence of any respondent characteristics that may affect their outcomes by breaking the link between respondent characteristics and selection into treatment conditions.

11. For a review of experimental field experiments in international contexts, see Riach and Rich (2002).

12. The present discussion focuses on the case of racial discrimination, but these methods can be readily applied to studies of discrimination on the basis of gender, age, neighborhood, and numerous other social categories.

13. In fact, very few correspondence studies have been conducted in the United States. This approach has been more widely used in European and Australian contexts. See Riach and Rich (2002) for a review.

14. White male names triggered a callback rate of 9.19 percent, compared to 6.16 percent among black male names.

15. Fryer and Levitt (2004, 786) reported that "Blacker names are associated with lower income zip codes, lower levels of parental education, not having private insurance, and having a mother who herself has a Blacker name."

16. See Bendick, Jackson, and Reinoso (1994). It would be undesirable, however, to use only extracurricular activities to signal race. This subtle cue would likely be missed by many employers in the course of their cursory review.

17. To the extent that applicants presenting "race-neutral" extracurricular activities are not assumed to be white in 100 percent of cases, more conservative results will be obtained. For an example of this approach, see Dovidio and Gaertner (2000).

18. For an in-between approach using telephone contact (with voice and style of speech signaling race, class and gender), see Massey and Lundy (2001).

19. When comparing the results across studies, I find it useful to calculate relative differences (ratio tests) rather than percentage point differences. Because baseline response rates differ across studies, ratio measures allow for more straightforward comparisons.

20. In the Bertrand and Mullainathan (2004) study, even among high-skilled white applicants the callback rate was less than 11 percent. Lower callback rates can depress evidence of differential treatment. If, for example, 5 percent of employers call back *all* applicants as a matter of policy, the resulting contrast would be based on a very small number of employers who conduct any type of screening at the resume submission stage.

21. Heckman (1998, 107-11). Elsewhere, Heckman and Siegelman (1993) identified five potential threats to the validity of results from audit studies: (1) problems in effective matching, (2) the use of "overqualified" testers, (3) limited sampling frame for the selection of firms and jobs to be audited, (4) experimenter effects, and (5) the ethics of audit research. Each of these issues is addressed in detail in Pager (forthcoming, Appendix 4A). See also the series of essays published in Fix and Struyk (1993). In addition to the criticisms expressed by Heckman, audit studies are often costly and difficult to implement and can only be used for selective decision-points (e.g., hiring decisions but not promotions).

22. Given these extensive demands, it is common for researchers to screen between fifty and one hundred applicants (already selected on age, race, and gender) before finding a single matched pair.

23. Indeed, we see evidence of more discrimination in audit studies testing actual job offers. This could be due to the kinds of tiebreaker effects discussed by Heckman (1998), though it may also result from the fact that job offers are more consequential, and thus employers may exert their preferences more forcefully at this final stage.

24. See Pager (2003, Appendix A) for an example of such a test.

25. Aside from active assumptions about general productivity by race, mere uncertainty can likewise lead to bias. Specifically, the problem of erroneous statistical discrimination is aggravated by racial disproportionality among employers. Generally, individuals have access to more and more reliable information about members of their own group (whether due to familiarity with their neighborhoods, schools, social networks, or simply due to a greater ability to recognize individuating information) (Strauss 1991; Anderson 1990). If the information white employers have about black applicants is seen as less reliable (simply as a result of lesser familiarity), risk-averse employers will be less inclined to consider these workers (Aigner and Cain 1977). Pervasive occupational and residential segregation by race may contribute to the preservation of inaccurate assumptions and/or the simple enhancement of uncertainty (Arrow 1998; Tomaskovic-Devey and Skaggs 1999).

26. See Altonji and Pierret (1997). While there is evidence that on-the-job evaluations may continue to be affected by racially biased perceptions, these effects can be mediated to some degree by objective performance indicators (Castilla 2005).

27. Current Population Survey data show that in 2000, joblessness among black men, aged twenty to thirty-five, with a high school diploma, was around 22 percent compared to less than 10 percent for white men of the same age and education.

28. For example, Neal and Johnson (1996) included a correction for labor force participation by assigning all nonparticipants a wage of zero. This correction produces a race coefficient nearly double in size to the original (.134 versus .072) and reduces the amount of the race gap explained by cognitive ability from roughly 70 to 60 percent (pp. 881-85). See also Butler and Heckman (1977); Mare and Winship (1984); Western and Pettit (2005); Chandra (2000); Fairlie and Sundstrom (1997).

29. This discussion focuses on discrimination against African Americans without college education, as the majority of audit studies focus on the experiences of job candidates with no more than a high school degree. Patterns of discrimination would likely differ at higher levels of the occupational hierarchy, with college-educated blacks less likely to experience barriers to access and more likely to experience channeling or barriers to mobility within the organizational setting (see Feagin and Sikes 1994; Collins 1989, 1993; Grodsky and Pager 2001).

30. Previous research, for example, indicates that roughly 20 to 25 percent of search time is spent on contacts generated by newspaper advertising, with friends and relatives and direct contact of firms by applicants representing much more common sources of new employment (Holzer 1988). At the same time, minorities appear more successful in job searches generated by general newspaper ads than through other means (Holzer 1987). Some have argued that the samples generated for audit studies (primarily from classified ads) yield a conservative test of discrimination: firms who wish to discriminate, it is argued, are more likely to advertise job openings through more restrictive channels than the metropolitan newspaper, such as through referrals, employment agencies, or more selective publications (Fix and Struyk 1993, 32).

These claims could be usefully tested by drawing more direct comparisons between samples of firms contacted by real black and white job seekers and those included in audit studies.

References

Aigner, Dennis J., and G. Cain Glen. 1977. Statistical theories of discrimination in labor market. *Industrial and Labor Relations Review* 30:749-76.

Altonji, Joseph G., and Charles R. Pierret. 1997. Employer learning and statistical discrimination. NBER Working Paper 6279, National Bureau of Economic Research, Cambridge, MA.

Anderson, Elijah. 1990. *Streetwise: Race, class, and change in an urban community*. Chicago: University of Chicago Press.

Arrow, Kenneth J. 1998. What has economics to say about racial discrimination? *Journal of Economic Perspectives* 12 (2): 91-100.

Ayres, Ian, and Peter Siegelman. 1995. Race and gender discrimination in bargaining for a new car. *American Economic Review* 85 (3): 304-21.

Banaji, M. R., C. Hardin, and A. J. Rothman. 1993. Implicit stereotyping in person judgment. *Journal of Personality & Social Psychology* 65 (2): 272-81.

Bendick, Marc Jr., Lauren Brown, and Kennington Wall. 1999. No foot in the door: An experimental study of employment discrimination. *Journal of Aging and Social Policy* 10 (4): 5-23.

Bendick, Marc, Jr., Charles Jackson, and Victor Reinoso. 1994. Measuring employment discrimination through controlled experiments. *Review of Black Political Economy* 23:25-48.

Bertrand, Marianne, and Sendhil Mullainathan. 2004. Are Emily and Greg more employable than Lakisha and Jamal? A field experiment on labor market discrimination. *American Economic Review* 94 (4): 991-1013.

Bodenhausen, Galen. 1988. Stereotypic biases in social decision making and memory: Testing process models of stereotype use. *Journal of Personality and Social Psychology* 55 (5): 726-37.

Butler, Richard, and James Heckman. 1977. The government's impact on the labor market status of black Americans: A critical review. In *Equal rights and industrial relations*, ed. Farrell Bloch, 235-81. Madison, WI: Industrial Relations Research Association.

Cancio, A. Silvia, T. David Evans, and David J. Maume. 1996. Reconsidering the declining significance of race: Racial differences in early career wages. *American Sociological Review* 61:541-56.

Carneiro, Pedro, James J. Heckman, and Dimitriy V. Masterov. 2003. Labor market discrimination and racial differences in premarket factors. NBER Working Paper #10068, National Bureau of Economic Research, Cambridge, MA.

Castilla, Emilio 2005. Gender, race, and meritocracy in organizational careers. In *Culture and inequality workshop*. Princeton, NJ: Princeton University Press.

Chandra, Amitabh. 2000. Labor-market dropouts and the racial wage gap: 1940-1990. *American Economic Review* 90 (2): 333-38.

Collins, Sharon. 1989. The marginalization of black executives. *Social Problems* 36:317-31.

———. 1993. Blacks on the bubble: The vulnerability of black executives in white corporations. *Sociological Quarterly* 34:429-48.

Connerly, Ward. 2000. *Creating equal: My fight against racial preferences*. San Francisco: Encounter Books.

Cross, Harry, Genevieve Kenney, Jane Mell, and Wendy Zimmerman. 1990. *Employer hiring practices: Differential treatment of Hispanic and Anglo job seekers*. Washington, DC: Urban Institute Press.

Devine, Patricia. 1989. Stereotypes and prejudice: Their automatic and controlled components. *Journal of Personality and Social Psychology* 56:5-18.

Devine, P. G., and A. J. Elliot. 1995. Are racial stereotypes really fading? The Princeton trilogy revisited. *Personality and Social Psychology Bulletin* 21 (11): 1139-50.

Donohue, John J., III, and Peter Siegelman. 2005. The evolution of employment discrimination law in the 1990s: A preliminary empirical investigation. In *Handbook of employment discrimination research*, ed. L. B. Nielsen and R. L. Nelson, 261-85. Dordrecht, the Netherlands: Springer.

Dovidio, John F., and Samuel L. Gaertner. 2000. Aversive racism and selection decisions. *Psychological Science* 11 (4): 315-19.

Fairlie, Robert W., and William A. Sundstrom. 1997. The racial unemployment gap in long-run perspective. *American Economic Review* 87 (2): 306-10.

Farkas, George. 2003. Cognitive skills and noncognitive traits and behaviors in stratification processes. *Annual Review of Sociology* 29:541-62.

Farkas, George, and K. Vicknair. 1996. Appropriate tests of racial wage discrimination require controls for cognitive skill: Comment on Cancio, Evans, and Maume. *American Sociological Review* 61:557-60.

Farley, Reynolds. 1997. Racial trends and differences in the United States 30 years after the civil rights decade. *Social Science Research* 26:235-62.

Feagin, Joe R., and Melvin P. Sikes. 1994. *Living with racism: The black middle-class experience.* Boston: Beacon.

Fiske, Susan. 1998. Stereotyping, prejudice, and discrimination. In *The handbook of social psychology*, 4th ed., ed. Daniel Gilbert, Susan Fiske, and Gardner Lindzey, 357-411. Boston: McGraw-Hill.

Fix, Michael, and Raymond J. Struyk, eds. 1993. *Clear and convincing evidence: Measurement of discrimination in America.* Washington, DC: Urban Institute Press.

Freeman, Richard B., and Harry J. Holzer, eds. 1986. *The black youth employment crisis.* Chicago: University of Chicago Press, for National Bureau of Economic Research.

Fryer, Roland G., Jr., and Steven D. Levitt. 2004. The causes and consequences of distinctively black names. *Quarterly Journal of Economics* 119 (3): 767-805.

Gilbert, Daniel T., and J. Gregory Hixon. 1991. The trouble with thinking: Activation and application of stereotypic beliefs. *Journal of Personality and Social Psychology* 60 (4): 509-17.

Grodsky, Eric, and Devah Pager. 2001. The structure of disadvantage: Individual and occupational determinants of the black-white wage gap. *American Sociological Review* 66 (August): 542-67.

Hakken, Jon. 1979. *Discrimination against Chicanos in the Dallas rental housing market: An experimental extension of the housing market practices survey.* Washington, DC: U.S. Department of Housing and Urban Development.

Harrison, Roderick J., and Claudette E. Bennett. 1995. Racial and ethnic diversity. In *State of the union: America in the 1990s,* vol. 2, *Social trends,* ed. R. Farley, 141–210. New York: Russell Sage Foundation.

Heckman, James J. 1998. Detecting discrimination. *Journal of Economic Perspectives* 12 (2): 101-16.

Heckman, James, and Peter Siegelman. 1993. The Urban Institute audit studies: Their methods and findings. In *Clear and convincing evidence: Measurement of discrimination in America,* ed. Michael Fix and Raymond J. Struyk, 187-258. Washington, DC: Urban Institute Press.

Holzer, Harry. 1987. Informal job search and black youth unemployment. *American Economic Review* 77 (3): 446-52.

———. 1988. Search methods used by unemployed youth. *Journal of Labor Economics* 6 (1): 1-20.

Holzer, Harry, Paul Offner, and Elain Sorensen. 2005. What explains the continuing decline in labor force activity among young black men? *Labor History* 46 (1): 37-55.

Jencks, Christopher, and Meredith Phillips, eds. 1998. *The black-white test score gap.* Washington, DC: Brookings Institution.

Lahey, Joanna. 2005. Age, women, and hiring: An experimental study. NBER Working Paper #11435, National Bureau of Economic Research, Cambridge, MA. http://www.nber.org/papers/w11435.

Mare, Robert D. 1995. Changes in educational attainment and school enrollment. In *State of the union: America in the 1990s,* vol. 1, *Economic Trends,* ed. R. Farley, 155–213. New York: Russell Sage Foundation.

Mare, Rob, and Christopher Winship. 1984. The paradox of lessening racial inequality and joblessness among black youth: Enrollment, enlistment and employment, 1964-1981. *American Sociological Review* 49:39-55.

Massey, Douglas, and Garvey Lundy. 2001. Use of black English and racial discrimination in urban housing markets: New methods and findings. *Urban Affairs Review* 36:452-69.

Milgram, Stanley. 1974. *Obedience to authority: An experimental view.* New York: Harper & Row.

Murnane, Richard, John Willett, and Frank Levy. 1995. The growing importance of cognitive skills in wage determination. *Review of Economics and Statistics* 77:251-66.

Neal, Derek, and William Johnson. 1996. The role of premarket factors in black-white wage differences. *Journal of Political Economy* 104 (5): 869-95.

Neumark, David. 1996. Sex discrimination in restaurant hiring: An audit study. *Quarterly Journal of Economics* 111 (3): 915-41.

———. 1999. Wage differentials by race and sex: The roles of taste discrimination and labor market information. *Industrial Relations* 38 (3): 414-45.

O'Neill, June. 1990. The role of human capital in earnings differences between white and black men. *Journal of Economic Perspectives* 4:25-45.

Pager, Devah. 2003. The mark of a criminal record. *American Journal of Sociology* 108:937-75.

———. Forthcoming. *Marked: Race, crime, and finding work in an era of mass incarceration.* Chicago: University of Chicago Press.

Pager, Devah, and Bruce Western. 2005. Discrimination in low wage labor markets. Paper presented at the annual meeting of the American Sociological Association, August, Philadelphia.

Parcel, Toby L., and Charles W. Mueller. 1983. *Ascription and labor markets: Race and sex differences in earnings.* New York: Academic Press.

Riach, P. A., and J. Rich. 2002. Field experiments of discrimination in the market place. *Economic Journal* 112 (November): F480-F518.

Ridley, Stanley, James A. Bayton, and Janice Hamilton Outtz. 1989. Taxi service in the District of Columbia: Is it influenced by patrons' race and destination? Mimeograph, Washington Lawyers' Committee for Civil Rights under the Law, Washington, DC.

Schuman, Howard, Charlottee Steeh, Lawrence Bobo, and Maria Krysan. 1997. *Racial attitudes in America: Trends and interpretations.* Cambridge, MA: Harvard University Press.

Strauss, David A. 1991. The law and economics of racial discrimination in employment: The case for numerical standards. *Georgetown Law Review* 79:1619.

Tomaskovic-Devey, Donald, and Sheryl Skaggs. 1999. An establishment-level test of the statistical discrimination hypothesis. *Work and Occupations* 26 (4): 420-43.

Tomaskovic-Devey, Donald, Melvin Thomas, and Kecia Johnson. 2005. Race and the accumulation of human capital across the career: A theoretical model and fixed-effects application. *American Journal of Sociology* 111 (1): 58-89.

Trope, Yaacov, and Erik P. Thomson. 1997. Looking for truth in all the wrong places? Asymmetric search of individuating information about stereotyped group members. *Journal of Personality and Social Psychology* 73 (2): 229-41.

Turner, Margery, Michael Fix, and Raymond Struyk. 1991. *Opportunities denied, opportunities diminished: Racial discrimination in hiring.* Washington, DC: Urban Institute Press.

Turner, Margery Austin, Stephen L. Ross, George C. Galster, and John Yinger. 2002. Discrimination in metropolitan housing markets: National results from phase 1 HDS 2000. U.S. Department of Housing and Urban Development, final report. http://www.huduser.org/Publications/pdf/Phase1_Report.pdf.

Turner, Margery Austin, and Felicity Skidmore, eds. 1999. *Mortgage lending discrimination: A review of existing evidence.* Washington, DC: Urban Institute.

Waldinger, Roger. 1999. *Still the promised city? African-Americans and new immigrants in postindustrial New York.* Cambridge, MA: Harvard University Press.

Western, Bruce, and Becky Pettit. 2005. Black-white wage inequality, employment rates, and incarceration. *American Journal of Sociology* 111:553-78.

Wienk, Ronald E., Clifford E. Reid, John C. Simonson, and Frederick J. Eggers. 1979. *Measuring discrimination in American housing markets: The housing market practices survey.* Washington, DC: U.S. Department of Housing and Urban Development.

Wilson, William Julius. 1978. *The declining significance of race: Blacks and changing American institutions.* Chicago: University of Chicago Press.

———. 1987. *The truly disadvantaged: The inner city, the underclass, and public policy.* Chicago: University of Chicago Press.

Yinger, John. 1995. *Closed doors, opportunities lost.* New York: Russell Sage Foundation.

Family Background, Race, and Labor Market Inequality

By
DALTON CONLEY
and
REBECCA GLAUBER

For decades, social scientists have relied on sibling correlations as indicative of the effect of "global family background" on socioeconomic status. This study advances this line of inquiry by drawing on data from the Panel Study of Income Dynamics to analyze racial differences in siblings' labor market outcomes and socioeconomic outcomes. We find that African Americans have lower sibling correlations in labor market earnings and family income than whites. Across the life course, African American siblings move toward greater resemblance than whites. These findings suggest that the effect of family background on socioeconomic outcomes is weaker for African Americans than for whites. Volatility in earlier career stages may suppress the effect of family background on labor market outcomes, and this dynamic is especially pronounced for African Americans who lack resources to insulate themselves from volatile events.

Keywords: family background; stratification, racial inequality; labor markets; siblings

How similar are the labor market and socioeconomic statuses of black and white siblings in America? The current study aims to document the degree of sibling resemblance in labor market earnings, family income, and occupational prestige. It also aims to determine how racial inequality affects sibling resemblance over the life course. For nearly a century, behavioral geneticists have used sibling correlations as measures of the effects of genes and shared environment on behavioral traits (McGue and Bouchard 1998), and for more than three decades social scientists have used sibling correlations as "omnibus measures" (Solon, Page, and Duncan 2000, 383) of the effects of family and community on socioeconomic outcomes (Hauser, Sheridan, and Warren 1999; Jencks 1972; Solon et al. 1991). Despite this research tradition, two questions remain relatively unexplored: Do siblings converge or diverge in labor market and socioeconomic outcomes over the life course? Do siblings from racial groups that putatively differ on the degree of opportunity they enjoy and the level of resources at their command vary with respect to how similar they turn out?

DOI: 10.1177/0002716206296090

In answering these questions, we build on previous research and provide an analysis of how racial inequality and measurable and *unmeasurable* family background factors shape individual life chances and labor market outcomes over the life course. Our findings have important implications for stratification theories and for social policies aimed at ameliorating inequality over the life course. Though studies of sibling correlations have existed for decades and have helped researchers understand the global effects of family background on individual life chances, and though studies of racial inequality and life chances have also existed for decades (Blau and Duncan 1967; Featherman and Hauser 1978), the combination of these two pursuits has been nearly devoid in the research literature (especially when we consider life course dynamics). Our study of racial differences in sibling labor market and socioeconomic resemblances, therefore, provides new insights to a topic of central concern to scholars of inequality.

Previous Work on Sibling Resemblance

A long tradition of stratification and social mobility research deploys father-son correlations in socioeconomic outcomes. Father-son correlations were questionable measures of social mobility three decades ago (for debate over this, see Acker 1973; Goldthorpe 1983) and are even less adequate today given contemporary family fluidity (see, for example, Cherlin 1992; Furstenberg and Cherlin 1991) and women's increased educational and labor market statuses. As others before us, we argue instead for the use of sibling correlations as summative estimates of the combined effects of shared environmental factors, shared genetic factors, and intersibling effects on labor market and socioeconomic outcomes.

Studies of sibling resemblance on occupational and educational attainment find that the global effects of family background explain about half of the variance in schooling and a third of the variance in occupational status (Hauser and Mossel 1985; Hauser and Sewell 1986; Jencks et al. 1979). For example, Kuo and Hauser (1995) analyzed the Occupational Changes in a Generation (OCG) survey data and found that for education, sibling differences (within-family variance components) among various age groups of black and white brothers range

---

Dalton Conley is University Professor and chair of the Department of Sociology at New York University (NYU). He also holds appointments at NYU's Wagner School of Public Service, as an adjunct professor of community medicine at Mount Sinai School of Medicine, and as a research associate at the National Bureau of Economic Research. In 2005, Conley became the first sociologist to win the National Science Foundation's Alan T. Waterman Award. His research focuses on how socioeconomic status is transmitted across generations and on the public policies that affect that process. In this vein, he studies sibling differences in socioeconomic success; racial inequalities; the measurement of class and social status; and how health and biology affect (and are affected by) social position.

Rebecca Glauber is a PhD candidate in the Department of Sociology at New York University. Her research addresses the intersection of family and work, specifically the effects of parenthood on women's and men's labor market outcomes. She expects to complete her dissertation in the spring of 2007.

between 38 and 52 percent. Corcoran et al. (1990) estimated a brother-brother correlation in *permanent* income of .45 using data from the Panel Study of Income Dynamics (PSID). Mazumder and Levine (2003) used data from the 1966 and 1979 National Longitudinal Surveys[1] and found a significant increase in brothers' earnings correlations over the decade, but no significant increase in brothers' education correlations over the decade. Solon et al. (1991) used longitudinal data from the PSID and estimate correlations of .448 for men's permanent earnings, .342 for men's family income, and .276 for women's family income. Their findings suggest that earlier studies may have underestimated the effect of family background on income variables by using single-year income data.

While a handful of recent studies have examined *cohort* trends in father-son income elasticities (Lee and Solon 2006; Levine and Mazumder 2002; Mayer and Lopoo 2005), or cohort trends in father-son occupational mobility (Biblarz, Bengston, and Bucur, 1996; Grusky and DiPrete 1990; Hout 1988), few studies have examined *age* trends in sibling similarities. Warren, Sheridan, and Hauser's (2002) analysis comes closest to our study in that they used longitudinal data from the Wisconsin Longitudinal Survey (WLS) and found that siblings become less occupationally similar as they age. Warren, Sheridan, and Hauser (2002) and Hauser, Sheridan, and Warren (1999) also examined the extent to which sibling resemblances on some outcomes are part of their resemblances on other outcomes. We add to these studies an analysis of racial variation in sibling resemblances, as both of these studies have analyzed data from a nearly all-white, localized sample.

> *[E]arlier studies may have underestimated the effect of family background on income variables by using single-year income data.*

The current study makes several important contributions to the literature, specifically by examining life course and race differences in the strength of global family background on socioeconomic outcomes. Previous studies have been limited in their explanatory power due in part to their tendency to use all-male, white, young, and localized samples (data from the WLS; data from Kalamazoo, Michigan; and data from Lincoln, Nebraska). The current study benefits from its use of the PSID, in that it both allows for the inclusion of sisters and avoids the limitations inherent in a sample that is not nationally representative or includes only young adults. And most important, with the nationally representative PSID, we can examine racial differences in stratification dynamics across the life course. This has been notably missing in previous research.

Race and sibling resemblance

Previous qualitative research by Conley (2004) suggests that among disadvantaged households, sibling disparities tend to increase, since limited opportunities and resources may elicit parenting strategies that accentuate sibling differences by directing family resources to the better-endowed sibling for whom upward mobility is most likely. Other research suggests that resource-constrained parents may not be able to optimally invest in their children's human capital (Becker and Tomes 1986), and such underinvestment may lead to higher degrees of sibling resemblance since "high ability children from poor families may receive the same low level of education as a sibling with lower academic ability, compressing their earnings compared with similarly different siblings from a prosperous family" (Mazumder and Levine 2003, 16).[2] Behrman and Taubman (1990) found some support for this hypothesis as parent-child income elasticities for whites are lower than for nonwhites. However, when they included a squared parent's income term, findings do not lend support to Becker and Tomes's (1986) hypothesis.

Research also indicates that African Americans are more subject than whites to negative socioeconomic events. To use Jencks's (1972) terminology—African Americans experience more intervening "unlucky" events. African American workers are more likely to be laid off than similarly situated white workers (Wilson 1999), even among those in upper-tier occupations (Wilson and McBrier 2005). However, it is less than clear if these external shock events are concentrated in earlier stages of the life course and therefore mask black siblings' "true" family background, or if these external events are cumulative over the life course and push siblings away from each other with age.

Many studies have analyzed racial differences in social mobility, but they tend to focus on the effects of *observed* family background (Blau and Duncan 1967; Porter 1974; Portes and Wilson 1976). O. D. Duncan (1968) argued that racial inequality affects the status attainment process in two ways: African Americans begin from a more disadvantaged position than whites, and African Americans do not get as great a return to their resources as whites. Hauser and Featherman (1976) ran separate regression models for African Americans and whites for measured family background, but they did not provide separate models of sibling correlations that would shed light on racial differences in measurable and *unmeasurable* family background effects. Kuo and Hauser (1995) came closest to our analysis in that they use sibling correlations to study racial differences in the global effects of family background on socioeconomic attainment, but they focused only on educational attainment. Sibling correlations in labor market outcomes may be subject to even greater effects of racial stratification, and findings from the current study build on these previous models.

Data and Variables

The PSID began in 1968 with a nationally representative sample of five thousand American families and has followed them each year since. Needless to say, it

TABLE 1
DESCRIPTIVE STATISTICS: MEANS FOR FAMILIES WITH TWO OR MORE SIBLINGS (STANDARD DEVIATIONS AND WITHIN-FAMILY STANDARD DEVIATIONS BELOW)

	Occupational Prestige	Ln Earnings	Ln Total Family Income
Total sample	43.91	10.13	10.52
	14.48	0.91	1.32
	7.41	0.62	1.05
Black	0.07	0.06	0.08
	0.26	0.24	0.27
	0.00	0.00	0.00
Mother's educational attainment	11.92	11.89	11.85
(for outcome measure not missing)	2.64	2.66	2.68
	0.00	0.00	0.00
Family size (for outcome measure not missing)	4.16	4.21	4.22
	2.15	2.14	2.20
	0.00	0.00	0.00
Age (for outcome measure not missing)	36.58	34.96	36.75
	7.25	6.61	7.55
	4.64	4.05	4.76
Number of person-years	15,277	20,792	18,144
Number of individuals	1,388	1,876	1,871

is a complicated study design and cannot be done justice in the space allowed here. For a fuller description, see Hill (1992) or G. J. Duncan and Hill (1989). By virtue of this complex design, the study has information on the socioeconomic histories of families as well as on the outcomes of multiple children from the same families who were in the original sample, moved into it, or were born to sample members. We select adult respondents aged twenty-five and older who were head of their household or married to the head of household in any (or all) years between 1983 and 2001. Furthermore, these individuals had to have a valid person number for their mother; that is, their mother had to have been in the sample at some time. They were then linked to their siblings through this maternal connection. A trivial number (less than 1 percent) of respondents had a father in the sample but not a mother. The majority had both parents. But since many more of the fathers were missing, we decided to identify siblings based on their mother's identification. However, results are not statistically different if we rely on the father's identification or include only those who have both parents' sample identifiers. The reason we truncate the person-years at 1983 is that prior to that year "wives" were classified differently: there was no category for cohabiting women (what the PSID subsequently called "wife" in quotes). Furthermore, prior to 1981, occupation—one of our key dependent measures—was not coded in the same way (it was coded in a one- or two-digit format in contrast to the standard three-digit census classification used consistently from 1981 onward). For both of these reasons, we truncate the survey years at 1983. We also exclude from our analyses the Survey of Economic Opportunity (SEO) component, as questions have been raised about how representative this low-income sample is, especially among African Americans [Brown (1996); see also Lee and Solon (2006), footnote 5, for a critical evaluation of the SEO PSID sample].

The measures that we used to capture siblings' socioeconomic statuses are described below; the unit of analysis is the person-year. Mean values—which generally conform to national averages—are presented in Table 1.

Occupational prestige: This is based on Socioeconomic Index Scores (SEI) for 1970 U.S. Census occupational classification codes (Stevens and Featherman 1981). Hodge-Siegel-Rossi prestige scores (1964) return similar results (analyses not shown but available from the authors upon request).
Earnings: This is measured as the total labor market earnings (logged to the base e).
Family income: We tested a number of formulations of income including logged and unlogged forms, income-to-needs ratios and straight income, and total household income as well as individual income. We present sibling correlations for total household income (logged to the base e).
Race: The sample is divided along the lines of race (black versus white).
Life course: The sample is divided by stage in the life course. Here we compare individuals below age thirty to individuals aged thirty to forty and individuals over age forty. A frequency distribution of survey years for each stage in the life course reveals a relatively equal distribution across survey years. There are no individuals below age thirty in 2001, and less than 2 percent of observations of individuals below age thirty fall into years 1997, 1998, and 1999. However, these are the only exceptions, and all others are equally distributed across years.

Statistical Approach

The general approach that we take to estimate the sibling resemblance is a variance decomposition method, following the strategy for income used by Mazumder and Levine (2003) and Solon el al. (1991). The total variance of the outcome, Y_{ij}, can be expressed as

$$\sigma_\varepsilon^2 = E(\bar{\varepsilon} - \varepsilon_{ijt})^2. \tag{1}$$

This total variance can be decomposed into the sum of expected values of three components (as shown in equation [2] below): the between-family component in permanent status (that is, the difference between the mean for the family j and the grand mean), a within-family component (the difference between the mean for the individual i in family j from the mean for family j), and a within-subject component (the transitory component of income or earnings, that is, the differences between a given year's income or earnings and the mean for that individual). For our single-year measures—the maximized values—the third component essentially drops out of the equation.

$$\sigma_\varepsilon^2 = E[(\bar{\varepsilon}_j - \bar{\varepsilon})^2 + (\bar{\varepsilon}_{ij} - \bar{\varepsilon}_j)^2 + (\varepsilon_{ijt} - \bar{\varepsilon}_{ij})^2] \tag{2}$$

Multiplying this out gives us the well-known formula that the total variance equals the sum of the three variance components minus two times their respective covariances.

$$\sigma_\varepsilon^2 = E(\bar{\varepsilon}_j - \bar{\varepsilon})^2 + E(\bar{\varepsilon}_{ij} - \bar{\varepsilon}_j)^2 + E(\varepsilon_{ijt} - \bar{\varepsilon}_{ij})^2 \qquad (3)$$
$$- 2E(\bar{\varepsilon} - \bar{\varepsilon}_j)(\bar{\varepsilon}_{ij} - \bar{\varepsilon}_j) - 2E(\bar{\varepsilon}_{ij} - \bar{\varepsilon}_j)(\varepsilon_{ijt} - \bar{\varepsilon}_{jt}) - 2E(\bar{\varepsilon} - \bar{\varepsilon}_j)(\varepsilon_{ijt} - \bar{\varepsilon}_{jt})$$

Like others before us (for example, Solon et al. 1991; Mazumder and Levine 2003), we will proceed (for now) on the assumption that the covariance of between-family, between-sibling, and within-sibling differences is zero. This assumption is akin to positing

A. no relationship between where your family is on the distribution and how unstable your income (or occupation, education, or wealth) is,
B. no relationship between where you are relative to your family mean and how unstable your status is, and
C. no relationship between where your family is in the distribution and the degree of similarity among you and your siblings.

Because the validity of these assumptions may doubtful, we note that lemmas A and B are not needed in this analysis, as we interpret sibling correlations in permanent statuses and not sibling correlations in single year measures. We will revisit lemma C in the analysis of sibling resemblance by race, but in the meantime, with no covariance by design, the total variance in total SES can thus be represented merely as a sum of the three variance components:

$$\sigma_\varepsilon^2 = \sigma_a^2 + \sigma_u^2 + \sigma_v^2, \qquad (4)$$

where σ_a^2 is the variance between families, σ_u^2 is the variance within families in permanent status, and σ_v^2 is the variance in individual economic characteristics (or transitory SES). This assumption of zero covariance—not discussed thoroughly elsewhere—makes the variance decomposition possible and results in a sibling correlation in permanent status according to equation (5):

$$\rho = \frac{\sigma_a^2}{\sigma_a^2 + \sigma_u^2}. \qquad (5)$$

We examined estimates of sibling correlations in labor market and socioeconomic statuses (ρ) using several approaches. We decomposed the raw (unadjusted) value on a given measure for those families with two or more siblings with at least one valid person-year each in the sample. Inclusion of only children—which affects the denominator, that is, total variance—but not the numerator, does not substantially affect our results and these estimates are not presented, although they are available from the authors upon request.

We also estimated sibling resemblance in a residual purged of the effects of other socioeconomic outcomes—meaning that we purged occupational prestige of the effects of education; we purged earnings of the effects of occupational prestige and education; we purged income of the effects of earnings, occupational prestige, and education; and we purged wealth of the effects of income, earnings, occupational prestige, and education. This provides a descriptive account of the associations between sibling statuses as a result of socioeconomic-specific causal processes or as a result of life course sequencing. Hauser, Sheridan, and Warren (1999) and Warren, Sheridan, and Hauser (2001) found that sibling resemblance in occupational attainment works almost entirely through educational attainment, and we pursue this same research question using additional socioeconomic outcome measures and nationally representative data. Of course, this approach assumes a unidirectional way to specify the sequencing and results should be interpreted with this in mind. But given the status attainment and life course literatures, this appears to be the most commonsensical ordering of outcomes.

We obtained standard errors for all of our estimates by using the Fisher's z' transformation that converts correlations to the normally distributed variable z'. The formula for the transformation is $z' = .5[\ln(1 + \rho) - (1 - \rho)]$. We then calculated standard errors of z' based on the formula $\sigma_{z'} = 1/\sqrt{N-3}$. We tested differences across the life course and across resource groups using differences in the Fisher z' transformations (in almost every case, differences in transformed correlations were nearly identical to differences in raw correlations).

Findings

Differences in sibling correlations across socioeconomic outcomes

We first examine whether sibling correlations differ across socioeconomic outcomes and across socioeconomic outcomes while holding other outcomes constant. Table 2, which presents our analysis of the entire sample of PSID siblings, shows that the PSID data yield a correlation of .576 for years of schooling for all siblings. To put this in the context of other previous work, earlier studies such as Hauser and Wong (1989) have suggested that family background accounts for roughly 50 percent of the variation in educational attainment, while Kuo and Hauser (1995) put the figure closer to 60 percent. We interpret this .576 correlation as a descriptive account to which siblings' shared environment, shared genes, and effects on each other shape their educational attainment. In terms of occupational prestige, we find a correlation of .418, which is lower than the education correlation, and for earnings and income, we find correlations of .376 and .458, respectively.[3]

The second row of Table 2 reports correlations for variables purged of the effects of the socioeconomic outcome(s) that we think precede the current outcome. These correlations provide further evidence on the sequencing of social statuses. Once we account for siblings' educational attainment, we find a significantly reduced occupational prestige correlation of .09. This is in line with Hauser, Sheridan, and Warren's (1999) and Warren, Sheridan, and Hauser's (2002) findings of sibling correlations in occupations working largely through education. For earnings, however, we find that roughly 60 percent of the correlation stays intact. Finally, family income is similar to occupational prestige, in

TABLE 2
PANEL STUDY OF INCOME DYNAMICS (PSID) SIBLING CORRELATIONS: 1983-2001 WAVES (FISHER'S Z TRANSFORMATION, STANDARD ERROR OF Z, NUMBER OF PERSON-YEARS, NUMBER OF INDIVIDUALS, AND NUMBER OF FAMILIES BELOW)

	Education	Occupational Prestige (Socioeconomic Index Scores)	Ln Earnings	Ln Income
Actual value	.576***	.418***	.376***	.458***
	.657	.445	.395	.495
	.036	.036	.035	.035
	25,554	20,146	20,792	18,144
	1,777	1,859	1,876	1,871
	780	794	801	806
Residual purified of socioeconomic outcome measure(s) to the left	N/A	.091*	.229***	.061
		.091	.233	.061
		.036	.036	.037
		19,651	18,008	12,690
		1,737	1,733	1,591
		766	766	741

*$p < .05$. ***$p < .001$ (two-tailed tests).

that we find a reduction in significance once we control for earnings, occupational prestige, and education.

We explored other sensitivity tests to sibling correlations including considering only-children within the sample pool, weighting correlations by PSID sample weights, purging correlations of race and gender effects, purging sibling correlations of age and year effect, and adjusting for autocorrelation. Results for the explorations returned nearly identical sibling correlations.

Sibling convergence over the life course

We next examine whether correlations within socioeconomic outcomes shift over the life course (Table 3). We find that correlations in occupation do not converge across the life course—family background affects siblings' occupational attainments, but it does so early in life. Sibling correlations in labor market earnings and family income, however, converge across the life course. These findings run contrary to the expectation that shock and chance events increase throughout the life course and get in the way of family background effects on later-life statuses.

Siblings in their twenties (or age thirty) have a higher correlation for occupational prestige, .415, than for earnings, .289, and income, .356. This is contrasted to siblings in their thirties (or age forty), who have a higher correlation for income, .432, than for occupational prestige, .399, or earnings, .389. Finally, siblings

TABLE 3
PANEL STUDY OF INCOME DYNAMICS (PSID) SIBLING CORRELATIONS: 1983-2001 WAVES BY LIFE COURSE (FISHER'S Z TRANSFORMATION, STANDARD ERROR OF Z, NUMBER OF PERSON-YEARS, NUMBER OF INDIVIDUALS, AND NUMBER OF FAMILIES BELOW)

	Occupational Prestige (Socioeconomic Index Scores)	Ln Earnings	Ln Income
Age ≤ 30 years	.415	.289	.356
	.441	.297	.372
	.040	.039	.041
	5,223	6,013	4,177
	1,269	1,357	1,093
	627	653	590
Age 31-40 years	.399	.389	.432
	.422	.410	.463
	.037	.037	.037
	10,069	10,618	8,672
	1,664	1,694	1,593
	739	741	726
Age > 40 years	.396	.338	.503
	.419	.352	.554
	.044	.046	.043
	4,854	4,161	5,295
	998	846	1,043
	527	476	545
Difference between ≤30 and 31-40	.019	−.113°	−.091
Standard error of difference	.054	.054	.056
Difference between ≤30 and >40	.022	−.055	−.182°°
Standard error of difference	.059	.060	.060
Difference between 31-40 and >40	.003	.058	−.091
Standard error of difference	.057	.059	.057

°$p < .05$. °°$p < .01$ (two-tailed tests).

above age forty have a higher correlation for income, .503, than for occupational prestige, .396, or earnings, .338. When we test differences within socioeconomic outcomes measures and across the life course, we find that occupational attainment demonstrates early convergence, as there is no difference across the life course in sibling correlations for this measure. This can be contrasted to labor market earnings and family income where outcomes show a convergence as we move out across the life course stages. For earnings, there is a significant difference between siblings in their twenties and siblings in their thirties such that the former have a .289 correlation in earnings whereas the latter have a .389 correlation in earnings. Earnings seem to solidify in the thirties, as siblings over age forty do not differ from siblings in their thirties. Family income converges at a later stage. Sibling correlations in income are not significantly different between the first two

TABLE 4
PANEL STUDY OF INCOME DYNAMICS (PSID) SIBLING CORRELATIONS: 1983-2001 WAVES BY SUBGROUPS (FISHER'S Z TRANSFORMATION, STANDARD ERRORS OF Z, NUMBER OF PERSON-YEARS, NUMBER OF INDIVIDUALS, AND NUMBER OF FAMILIES BELOW)

	Occupational Prestige	Ln Earnings	Ln Income
Black	.566	.088	.158
	.642	.088	.159
	.130	.131	.130
	1,076	1,096	1,248
	118	117	120
	62	61	62
White	.413	.399	.525
	.439	.422	.583
	.039	.039	.039
	16,083	16,507	14,673
	1,410	1,426	1,408
	666	675	675
Difference	.203	−.334°	−.424°°
Standard error of difference	.136	.137	.136

°$p < .05$. °°$p < .01$ (two-tailed tests).

age groups, whereas correlations show a significant increase between the first and third age groups. Siblings in their twenties have a correlation of .356, whereas siblings above age forty have a correlation of .503. These findings seem indicative of volatility in earlier life course stages that get in the way of "true" family background effects. We situate our findings within stratification theories in the concluding section of this analysis.

Sibling differences between racial groups

Do African American siblings, with fewer resources and opportunities, resemble each other less than white siblings and do life course stratification dynamics vary between racial groups? Table 4 reports racial comparisons, and we find that sibling resemblance among African Americans is much lower than it is for whites in terms of labor market earnings and family income. Sibling resemblances among African Americans and whites do not differ in terms of occupational prestige.

Table 5 reports our final analysis on the interaction between racial group and stage in the life course. We report correlations in occupational prestige, earnings, and income by the three life course groups. Cell sizes are relatively small and reduce our ability to detect significant differences between whites and blacks. In Table 3 we saw that correlations in income increased across the life course, and in Table 4 we saw that black siblings have much lower correlations than white siblings. Comparing these two factors, we find that black siblings show a dramatic

TABLE 5
PANEL STUDY OF INCOME DYNAMICS (PSID) SIBLING CORRELATIONS: 1983-2001 WAVES BY LIFECOURSE AND SUBGROUPS (FISHER'S Z TRANSFORMATION, STANDARD ERROR OF Z, NUMBER OF PERSON-YEARS, NUMBER OF INDIVIDUALS, AND NUMBER OF FAMILIES BELOW)

	Occupational Prestige	Ln Earnings	Ln Income
Black			
Age ≤ 30 years	.519	.050	.181
	.575	.050	.183
	.160	.156	.160
	295	337	308
	75	82	74
	42	44	42
Age 31-40 years	.540	.246	.535
	.604	.251	.597
	.140	.140	.146
	512	538	584
	93	94	88
	54	54	50
Age > 40 years	.712	.048	.826
	.892	.048	1.174
	.167	.183	.162
	269	221	356
	65	54	68
	39	33	41
Difference between ≤30 and 31-40	−.029	−.201	−.414
Standard error of difference	.213	.210	.217
Difference between ≤30 and >40	−.316	.002	−.991°°°
Standard error of difference	.231	.240	.228
Difference between 31-40 and >40	−.288	.203	−.578°°
Standard error of difference	.218	.230	.218
White			
Age ≤ 30 years	.431	.324	.558
	.461	.336	.629
	.044	.043	.046
	3,902	4,517	3,091
	945	1,013	782
	524	546	481
Age 31-40 years	.392	.412	.337
	.414	.438	.351
	.040	.040	.041
	8,030	8,445	6,994
	1,285	1,310	1,214
	626	631	611

(continued)

TABLE 5 (CONTINUED)

	Occupational Prestige	Ln Earnings	Ln Income
Age > 40 years	.368	.348	.516
	.386	.363	.571
	.047	.050	.046
	4,151	3,545	4,588
	827	699	861
	450	407	467
Difference between ≤30 and 31-40	.047	−.102	.279°°°
Standard error of difference	.059	.059	.061
Difference between ≤30 and >40	.075	−.027	.058
Standard error of difference	.064	.066	.065
Difference between 31-40 and >40	.029	.075	−.220°°°
Standard error of difference	.062	.064	.062

°°$p < .01$. °°°$p < 001$ (two-tailed tests).

increase in correlations in income across the life course—from .181 in their twenties to .826 above age forty. The same cannot be said of whites. Here, we find that white siblings have similar correlations in income in their twenties and above age forty and lower correlations in their thirties ($\rho = .337$).

African Americans also converge in occupational prestige and in labor market earnings (toward middle age, but then away from each other post–middle age). These correlations are not significant because cell sizes are small, but they are generally indicative of a pattern of increasing similarity as African Americans age. We think that these findings represent two dynamics of racial inequality in family background effects. First, African Americans lack protective resources that help buffer socioeconomic statuses from negative chance or intervening events, especially against negative career-related events. Second, African Americans are subject to an even greater amount of earlier-life volatility than whites. These volatile earlier segments of life mask the effects of family background, and it is only later in life that African American siblings begin to move toward each other.

Discussion and Conclusions

We are not the first to use sibling correlations in socioeconomic status as a way to measure the global effects of family background and genes on socioeconomic outcomes. We build on previous analyses by reanalyzing more recent waves of PSID data—in which the siblings are on average older and more stable economically—with a substantially larger sample size of person-years and sibling sets, and we obtain similar estimates of the association between siblings on education, occupational prestige, and earnings.

There are limits on what we can infer from such correlations, and these should be mentioned. Specifically, once we open up the possibility of within-family heterogeneity in parental investment and take into account shared genetic factors, and siblings' potential effects on each other (intersibling effects), sibling correlations cannot accurately represent causal processes related to the impact of family background.

That is, while it is trivially true that if there is a zero correlation between siblings (or between parent and child), family background can be said to have no net impact, this is a descriptive account only. For example, it could be the case that family background matters enormously, but that within-family dynamics obscure this fact in sibling or parent-child associations of socioeconomic status.[4] For example, envision the case of a two-child family in which the elder child is expected to sacrifice for the benefit of the younger sibling. If such a dynamic were widespread in a given society and resulted in downward mobility for the sacrificing sibling and upward mobility for the sibling who benefited from the sacrifice, we could actually observe a negative sibling correlation and a zero parent-child correlation (since the upwardly mobile offspring would be cancelled out by the downwardly mobile offspring in a random sample of parents and children).

[W]e can read a sibling correlation as a global effect of family background . . . if we assume a model in which offspring are invested in equally . . . and in which siblings have only a mean-regressive effect on each other.

If such dynamics were systematically stratified by a measurable variable such as birth position or gender, then we could accurately describe the intrafamily dynamics by observing correlations across within-family subgroups such as latter-borns or boys. But if the way that families generated outcomes among children was based on some unobservable factor—such as parental belief in child ability—then to the researcher, the apparent result may be randomness and a potentially faulty observation that family background means little. In fact, what it would mean is that the family was acting as a primary queuing mechanism for socioeconomic opportunity.

Given the apparent difficulty in modeling the true impact of family background, in light of shared environmental *and* genetic traits and intersibling effects, what are we to make of sibling correlations? The answer is that we can read a sibling correlation as a global effect of family background—environmental and genetic factors—if we assume a model in which offspring are invested in equally (or at least that any favoritism is randomly distributed) and in which siblings have only a mean-regressive effect on each other, that is, that they tend to cause each other to be more alike than they would in each other's absence. This is not an entirely unreasonable assumption, but it is an assumption nonetheless. It is possible that in some families, sibling dynamics are polarizing, although there is little research on this.

Research in the tradition of behavioral genetics attempts to parcel out genetic and environmental components of the effect of family background on social outcomes using twin and other kin comparisons. A host of outcomes have been examined in this context, ranging from cognitive ability (Plomin 1988) to mental health (Gottesman and Shields 1982; Kendler and Robinette 1983; Reich et al. 1987) to behavioral outcomes such as delinquent behavior (Rowe 1981) to socioeconomic outcomes (Behrman et al. 1980; Behrman, Pollack, and Taubman 1995). (For a general review of this research methodology, see Plomin 1986; Plomin and Daniels 1987; or Plomin, DeFries, and Loehlin 1989.) However, these studies have been criticized for not taking account of differences in the genetic-environmental covariance among different kin and the degree of assortative mating in the population (see Goldberger 1977, 1979). And these studies have been criticized for attempting to disentangle environmental from genetic factors, when such a procedure may not be wholly possible (Feldman and Lewontin 1975; Layzer 1974). We share these concerns, and therefore, we do not attempt to unravel the knot of common genes and environment but, rather, we view correlations as descriptive of shared environment, shared genetic factors, and intersibling effects.

Building on these previous studies, we report three new findings. First, we find that family background affects different measures of socioeconomic status differently. Siblings are most similar on educational outcomes and less similar on occupational prestige, labor market earnings, and family income. Our findings are in line with stratification and status attainment models that hold that family background primarily affects educational attainment, which then affects occupational attainment and income and earnings attainment. Our finding of a .09 correlation in occupational attainment net of educational attainment bears this out precisely—family background effects on occupational attainment work largely through educational attainment. However, our findings on earnings and income indicate that family background effects are not simply confined to the educational system and instead have an independent effect on labor market and marriage dynamics. This is important, as it indicates that simply equalizing educational attainments may not go far enough to reduce the effects of family background on individuals' ultimate life chances.

Our second novel finding is that siblings converge in outcomes that take longer to stabilize (income and earnings) and remain similar across the life course in outcomes that stabilize early on (education and occupational prestige). What do these life course patterns mean? On one hand, as Jencks (1972) argued, so much of our socioeconomic fate seems determined by external chance events or "luck." Given the assumption that chance events accumulate with age, siblings might diverge from each other across the life course. On the other hand, research by economists has shown that individuals may experience much more volatility in economic outcomes, namely, in earnings and job stability, in earlier life stages and much less volatility in later life stages (Mitchell et al. 2003). Given these findings, increased volatility in youth may actually suppress the "true" effect of family background. As individuals stabilize later in adulthood, siblings should begin to resemble each other more. Siblings should return to their true family of origin effect, so to speak.

There is also a third theoretical possibility—individual parental investment behavior may shape dynamic stratification trajectories. Our findings, of course, are descriptive in nature, and we cannot offer the final word on these sets of theories. Nevertheless, our finding of sibling convergence in labor market earnings and income across the life course might indicate that parents shape their children's lives to maximize their later-life statuses. Our findings also suggest that volatility in earlier stages of the life course mask true family background effects. At the least, our descriptive evidence of sibling convergence over the life course should lead future researchers to include institutional and behavioral mechanisms in their models.

The most important finding that our analysis gives rise to is that African American siblings resemble each other less than white siblings, at least on earnings and income, but dramatically converge across the life course. In their twenties, black siblings have a .181 correlation in income, and above age forty, they have a .826 correlation in income. This suggests almost complete social reproduction in living standards by the fifth decade of life. (While statistically significant, we should keep in mind that this race-age analysis is based on a very small set of age forty or older black siblings.)

We proposed that resource-constrained parents may invest unequally in their children or in their child with the greatest chance of survival and prosperity. This behavioral dynamic may serve as one explanation for the weaker effects of family background on African Americans' socioeconomic outcomes. We think, however, that much more of the reason for these weaker effects lies in institutional constraints. African Americans have fewer resources than whites, and they have less means toward protection from negative events, which may move individuals off course from their families.

Coupled with recent findings of resource-disadvantaged and younger individuals experiencing greater fluctuations in earnings, our analysis provides some evidence in support of the contention that earlier segments of the life course are volatile and suppress an individual's "true" effect of family background. Our descriptive findings cannot provide the last word on whether institutional or individual mechanisms—or a combination of both—explain life course racial stratification dynamics. We find it most likely that African Americans' socioeconomic outcomes are affected more than whites' across the life course because African Americans lack the resources to protect themselves from the volatility of earlier, intervening chance events. But for now, our descriptive analysis is simply that. We provide new evidence on a topic central to stratification research, but we leave it to future research to test various competing mechanisms that account for differences in family background effects across the life course and across racial groups.

Notes

1. Mazumder and Levine (2003) advocated in favor of the National Longitudinal Surveys (NLS) and against the Panel Study of Income Dynamics (PSID) because "the NLS datasets allow us to construct large samples of siblings that are nationally representative in each time period and are less susceptible to sample attrition." For our purposes here, the NLS does not provide a long enough series with enough cases to explore race and life course interaction effects.

2. Indeed, this is what Mazumder and Levine (2003) found: lower correlations among high-income siblings in both the 1968 and 1979 waves of the PSID. However, when they split the sample along the median, they ended up with only a maximum of 185 multiple sibling sets in an income group (in the 1979 wave of the PSID, they had 1,086 cases from 901 families in all). Even if these were all two-sibling sets, then the maximum number of pairs for each income group would be 92—quite a small number. If siblings' mean outcome is entirely related to their background characteristics, then splitting on the mean should produce the same results as splitting on all background measures. However, such a small sample size introduces random error, and furthermore, the assumption is untestable given that many family background characteristics are unobservable. Even more important, however, is the fact that they did not split the sample based on the parental characteristics—as would be appropriate for the Becker-Tomes (1986) model—but rather by the incomes of the adult siblings themselves. This makes the sample split endogenous to their outcomes. In other words, what they may be observing could be a result of sibling decisions regarding trade-offs between equity and efficiency. If certain siblings value equality, they may sacrifice the attainment of the better-endowed sibling, bringing the overall mean down, but resulting in a higher correlation between siblings. By contrast, we split the sample by parental measures, which are at least temporally anterior to the sibling outcomes.

3. Siblings' correlation in earnings is substantially lower than their correlation in income. In analyses not shown, we found a sister correlation in earnings of .273 and a brother correlation in earnings of .498. This is on par with Solon et al.'s (1991) findings of a sister correlation of .276 and a brother correlation of .448. We attribute differences between income and earnings correlations to lower sister correlations on earnings because of two different routes to women's economic well-being through marriage and through individual earnings.

4. For a good example of how these processes can be modeled, see Behrman, Rosenzweig, and Taubman (1994).

References

Acker, Joan. 1973. Women and social stratification: A case of intellectual sexism. *American Journal of Sociology* 78:936-45.

Becker, Gary S., and Nigel Tomes. 1986. Human capital and the rise and fall of families. *Journal of Labor Economics* 4:S1-S39.

Behrman, Jere R., Zdenek Hrubec, Paul Taubman, and T. Wales. 1980. *Socioeconomic success: A study of the effects of genetic endowments, family environment, and schooling.* Amsterdam: North Holland.

Behrman, Jere R., Robert A. Pollak, and Paul Taubman. 1995. *From parent to child: Intrahousehold allocation and intergenerational relations in the United States.* Chicago: University of Chicago Press.

Behrman, Jere, Mark Rosenzweig, and Paul Taubman. 1994. Endowments and the allocation of schooling in the family and in the marriage market: The twins experiment. *Journal of Political Economy* 102:1131-74.

Behrman, Jere R., and Paul Taubman. 1990. The intergenerational correlation between children's adult earnings and their parents' income: Results from the michigan panel survey of income dynamics. *Review of Income and Wealth* 46:115-27.

Biblarz, Timothy J., Vern L. Bengston, and Alexander Bucur, 1996. Social mobility across three generations. *Journal of Marriage and the Family* 58:188-200.

Blau, Peter, and Otis D. Duncan. 1967. *The American occupational structure*. New York: Free Press.

Brown, Charles. 1996. Notes on the "SEO" or "census" component of the PSID. Panel Study of Income Dynamics working paper.

Cherlin, Andrew. 1992. *Marriage, divorce, remarriage.* Cambridge, MA: Harvard University Press.

Conley, Dalton. 2004. *The pecking order: Which siblings succeed and why.* New York: Pantheon.

Corcoran, Mary, Roger Gordon, Deborah Laren, and Gary Solon. 1990. Poverty and the underclass: Effects of family and community background on economic status. *American Economic Review* 80: 362-66.

Duncan, Greg J., and Daniel Hill. 1989. Assessing the quality of household panel survey data: The case of the PSID. *Journal of Business and Economic Statistics* 7 (4): 441-51.

Duncan, Otis Dudley. 1968. Inheritance of poverty or inheritance of race? In *On understanding poverty*, ed. Daniel P. Moynihan, 85-110. New York: Basic Books.
Featherman, David, and Robert Hauser. 1978. *Opportunity and change*. New York: Academic Press.
Feldman, M. W., and R. C. Lewontin. 1975. The heritability hangup. *Science* 190:1163-68.
Furstenberg, Frank, Jr., and Andrew Cherlin. 1991. *Divided families: What happens to children when parents part*. Cambridge, MA: Harvard University Press.
Goldberger, Arthur 1977. Twin methods: A skeptical view. In *Kinometrics: Determinants of socioeconomic success within and between families*, ed. Paul Taubman, 299-324. Amsterdam: North-Holland.
———. 1979. Heritability. *Economica* 46:327-47.
Goldthorpe, John. 1983. Women and class analysis: In defense of the conventional view. *Sociology* 17: 465-88.
Gottesman, I. I., and J. Shields. 1982. *Schizophrenia: The epigenetic puzzle*. Cambridge: Cambridge University Press.
Grusky, David B., and Thomas A. DiPrete. 1990. Recent trends in the process of stratification. *Demography* 27:617-37.
Hauser, Robert M., and David L. Featherman. 1976. Equality of schooling: Trends and prospects. *Sociology of Education* 49:99-120.
Hauser, Robert M., and P. Mossel. 1985. Fraternal resemblance in educational attainment and occupation. *American Journal of Sociology* 91:650-73.
Hauser, Robert M., and William Sewell. 1986. Family effects in simple models of education, occupational status, and earnings: Findings from the Wisconsin and Kalamazoo studies. *Journal of Labor Economics* 4:S83-S115.
Hauser, Robert M., Jennifer T. Sheridan, and John Robert Warren. 1999. Socioeconomic achievements of siblings in the life course—New findings from the Wisconsin Longitudinal Study. *Research on Aging* 21:338-78.
Hauser, Robert, and R. Wong. 1989. Sibling resemblance and intersibling effects in educational attainment. *Sociology of Education* 62:149-71.
Hill, Martha S. 1992. *The Panel Study of Income Dynamics: A user's guide*. Newbury Park, CA: Sage.
Hodge, Robert W., Paul M. Siegel, and Peter H. Rossi. 1964. Occupational prestige in the United States, 1925–1963. *American Journal of Sociology* 70:286-302.
Hout, Michael. 1988. More universalism, less structural mobility: The American occupational structure in the 1980s. *American Journal of Sociology* 93:1358-1400.
Jencks, Christopher. 1972. *Inequality: A reassessment of the effect of family and schooling in America*. New York: Basic Books.
Jencks, Christopher S., S. Bartlett, M. Corcoran, J. Crouse, D. Eaglesfield, G. Jackson, K. McClelland, P. Mueser, M. Olneck, J. Schwartz, S. Ward, and J. Williams. 1979. *Who gets ahead? The determinants of economic success in America*. New York: Basic Books.
Kendler, K. S., and C. D. Robinette. 1983. Schizophrenia in the National Academy of Sciences–National Research Council twin registry: A 16-year update. *American Journal of Psychiatry* 140:1551-63.
Kuo, H.-H. Daphne, and Robert M. Hauser. 1995. Trends in family effects on the education of black and white brothers. *Sociology of Education* 68:136-60.
Layzer, D. 1974. Heritability analyses of IQ scores: Science or numerology? *Science* 183:1259-66.
Lee, Chul-In, and Gary Solon. 2006. Trends in intergenerational income mobility. National Bureau of Economic Working Paper 12007.
Levine, David I., and Bhashkar Mazumder. 2002. Choosing the right parents: Changes in the intergenerational transmission of inequality between 1980 and the early 1990s. Working Paper Series WP-02-08, Federal Reserve Bank of Chicago.
Mayer, Susan E., and Leonard M. Lopoo. 2005. Has the intergenerational transmission of economic status changed? *Journal of Human Resources* 40:169-85.
Mazumder, Bhashkar, and David I. Levine. 2003. The growing importance of family and community: An analysis of changes in the sibling correlation in earnings. Working Paper 2003-24, Federal Reserve Bank of Chicago.
McGue, Matt, and Thomas J. Bouchard. 1998. Genetic and environmental influences on human behavioral differences. *Annual Review of Neuroscience* 21:1-24.

Mitchell, Olivia S., John W. R. Phillips, Andrew Au, and David McCarthy. 2003. Retirement wealth and lifetime earnings variability. Pension Research Council Working Paper PRC WP 2003-4, University of Pennsylvania, Wharton School, Philadelphia.

Plomin, R. 1986. *Development, genetics and psychology*. Hillsdale, NJ: Lawrence Erlbaum.

———. 1988. The nature and nurture of cognitive abilities. In *Advances in the psychology of human intelligence*, ed. R. J. Sternberg. Hillsdale, NJ: Lawrence Erlbaum.

Plomin, R., and D. Daniels. 1987. Why are children in the same family so different from each other? *Behavioral and Brain Sciences* 10:1-16.

Plomin, R., J. C. DeFries, and J. C. Loehlin. 1989. *Behavioral genetics: A primer*. 2nd ed. New York: W.H. Freeman.

Porter, James N. 1974. Race, socialization and mobility in educational and early occupational attainment. *American Sociological Review* 39:303-16.

Portes, Alejandro, and Kenneth L. Wilson. 1976. Black-white differences in educational attainment. *American Sociological Review* 41:414-31.

Reich, T., P. Van Eerdewegh, J. Rice, J. Mullaney, J. Endicott, and G. L. Klerman. 1987. The familial transmission of primary major depressive disorder. *Journal of Psychiatric Research* 21:613-24.

Rowe, D. 1981. Environmental and genetic influences on dimensions of perceived parenting: A twin study. *Developmental Psychology* 17:203-8.

Solon, Gary, Mary Corcoran, Roger Gordon, and Deborah Laren. 1991. A longitudinal analysis of sibling correlation in economic status. *Journal of Human Resources* 26:509-34.

Solon, Gary, Marianne E. Page, and Greg J. Duncan. 2000. Correlations between neighboring children in their subsequent educational attainment. *Review of Economics and Statistics* 82:383-92.

Stevens, Gillian, and David L. Featherman. 1981. A revised socioeconomic index for occupational status. *Social Science Research* 10:364-93.

Warren, John Robert, Jennifer T. Sheridan, and Robert M. Hauser. 2002. Occupational stratification across the life course: Evidence from the Wisconsin Longitudinal Study. *American Sociological Review* 67:432-55.

Wilson, George. 1999. Reaching the top: Racial differences in mobility paths to upper-tier occupations. *Work & Occupations* 26:165-86.

Wilson, George, and Debra Branch McBrier. 2005. Race and loss of privilege: African American/white differences in the determinants of job layoffs from upper-tier occupations. *Sociological Forum* 20:301-21.

What Happens to Potential Discouraged? Masculinity Norms and the Contrasting Institutional and Labor Market Experiences of Less Affluent Black and White Men

By
DEIRDRE A. ROYSTER

Though less affluent black and white boys and men adhere to similar gendered norms and aspirations and begin with similar labor market potential, they are often sorted into very different and unequal educational and labor market trajectories. Using national-level descriptive data and key qualitative studies of institutional processes, this article contrasts less affluent black and white men's educational, labor market, and criminal justice system experiences and elucidates the processes of differentiation that reproduce those unequal patterns. In each institutional arena, less affluent black males pay a disproportionate price for enacting masculinity norms in comparison to white males. White boys and men are also presented with more desirable labor market options (and second-chance opportunities when they need help) that are denied their black male counterparts. This article suggests that only a complex strategy, which requires less affluent black men to resist more constructively while citizen groups hold institutions more publicly accountable, can enhance the labor market trajectories of black men.

Keywords: masculinity; employment; networks; schoolwork; racial disparity; incarceration

Langston Hughes, in his 1951 collection of poems *Montage of a Dream Deferred*, asked the now famous question, "What Happens to a Dream Deferred?" Hughes used the poem to explore the pain and frustration blacks experienced during the pre–civil rights era as their aspirations were leveled in the face of rigid educational and occupational barriers. The

Deirdre A. Royster, director of the Center for the Study of Inequality and an associate professor, just completed a three-year term chairing the Department of Sociology at the College of William and Mary. Her book, Race and the Invisible Hand: How White Networks Exclude Black Men from Blue Collar Jobs *(University of California Press, 2003), was a finalist for the 2004 C. Wright Mills Best Book Award (Society for the Study of Social Problems) and was winner of the 2004 Oliver Cromwell Cox Best Book Award (American Sociological Association Section on Racial and Ethnic Minorities). Her research focuses on race and inequality, with a special focus on obstacles working-class and entrepreneurial African Americans have faced in the U.S. economy.*

DOI: 10.1177/0002716206296544

often-quoted poem wondered whether the deferred dreams of blacks dried up, festered, decayed, or exploded. Scholarly reports such as the 1968 National Advisory Commission Report on Civil Disorders (Kerner Commission 1968) suggested that all four of Hughes's expectations regarding blacks' deferred dreams came to pass, especially among young black men living in cities who protested the most loudly and destructively (Blauner 1969, 1972). During the civil rights and post–civil rights eras, many previously closed educational and occupational opportunities opened up and were embraced by a set of blacks who were poised to benefit from lower barriers, but another set of less affluent blacks, who were not so poised, have experienced far more difficulty in reaching their own dreams and in assisting their children, especially male children, in reaching their potential and attaining higher status (Oliver and Shapiro 1997; Wilson 1987). In this article, I analyze how less affluent black boys and men suffer more severe penalties for their performances of masculinity than white male peers and how contemporary institutional processes discourage less affluent black boys and men more than white male peers. Both of these factors, one cultural and one institutional, lead to less affluent black men experiencing severe and sometimes permanent labor market disadvantages vis-à-vis their white male peers.

Perhaps no group's labor market difficulties cause more widespread concern than those of less affluent black men (Holzer, Offner, and Sorenson 2005; Chandra 2000; Moss and Tilly 2001a, 2001b, 1996, 1991; Wilson, Tienda, and Wu 1995; Mincy 1994); for at least twenty years, scholars and others have expressed singular concern about black men's occupational prospects, especially for those living in U.S. cities that have lost many thousands of manufacturing and other solid blue-collar jobs (Glasgow 1980; Freeman and Wise 1982; Wilson 1987; Weiss 1990; Freeman 1991; Bound and Freeman 1992; Wilson 1996). Undoubtedly "work disappearing" harms black men's prospects (Holzer and Danziger 2001), but other patterns, cultural and institutional, also contribute to black men being far less able than white male peers to gain access to jobs that have not disappeared or to make gains during economic growth periods (like the late 1990s).

Less affluent black boys' and men's performances of American masculinity norms leave them especially vulnerable to sanction beyond their communities of origin (Martino 2000; Newman 1999; Morrell 1998; Kelly 1994; Kunjufu 1986). Some black men's angry, immature, and indifferent responses to public authorities, for example, earn black boys and men special scorn, even when the actions of public authorities are questionable or blatantly unfair (Mincy 1994; Majors and Bilson 1992). In addition, three institutional patterns differentiate the labor market prospects of less affluent black and white men: educational inequities that underprepare and stigmatize black boys and delay black men's transitions from school to work (Ainsworth and Roscigno 2005; Johnston and Viadero 2000); persistent employer discrimination (Mason 2005; Pager and Quillian 2005; Moss and Tilly 2001a, 2001b; Holzer 1996; Braddock and McPartland 1987) and black men's severe network disadvantages during job search, hiring, and early job-entry stages (Royster 2003; Falcon and Melendez 2001); and hypersurveillant police practices and unusually severe sentencing patterns that attach a criminal record (or the suspicion of such) to a disproportionately high number of less affluent black men (Pettit and Western 2004; Pager 2003; Mauer 1997; Tonry 1996). This syndrome of gendered patterns of resistance and alienation exhibited by black boys and men and discriminatory institutional experiences makes addressing less affluent black men's labor market difficulties especially complex (Holzer, Offner, and Sorenson 2005). Yet not examining the connections between these overlapping arenas results in a less comprehensive understanding of the dilemmas black boys and men face.

Less affluent black boys' and men's performances of American masculinity norms leave them especially vulnerable to sanction beyond their communities of origin.

My goal in this article is to explore and, whenever possible, compare and contrast cultural patterns and institutional experiences that influence the early labor market experiences of less affluent black and white boys and men. Using both national-level data and key qualitative studies of institutional processes, I elucidate how educational, labor market, and criminal justice systems sort boys and men, who exhibit similar cultural patterns and often begin with similar labor market potential, into very different and unequal trajectories during the early life course. Because I focus on *processes of differentiation*, my analysis relies heavily on a few qualitative studies that provide an in-depth examination of the lived institutional experiences of boys and young men. Enhancing the labor market trajectories of significant numbers of black men will require interventions on the cultural front as well as in the three institutional arenas. Specifically, preventing black boys and young men from becoming discouraged learners while in school would increase their chances of not becoming discouraged workers in the labor market, preventing blue-collar employers from discriminating and relying on informal recruiting and selecting mechanisms would increase black men's chances of winning a proportionate share of the remaining good blue-collar jobs, and preventing black men from being disproportionately targeted by law enforcement and sentenced to hard time would prevent black men from becoming permanently disempowered workers and citizens.

Our society's failure to date to act in each of these institutional arenas has created a set of understandably frustrated black boys and men who have not been able to reach their academic or occupational potentials and who are not fully aware of the costs they pay for assuming masculine identities that many find troubling (Mirza 1999). Moreover, this failure has vastly diminished black men's capacities for accumulating wealth (Shapiro 2004) to assist their families and political power to advance their interests through public policies (Allard and Mauer 2000). By contrast, less affluent white men pay a far lower price for adhering to American masculinity norms (Mac an Ghaill 1994) and have weathered sometimes falling behind their female peers in schools, the loss of tens of thousands of blue-collar jobs, and some of the highest incarceration rates in the world by maintaining a dominant hold on a set of highly desirable race- and gender-segregated blue-collar jobs (Hamilton 2006). Indeed, this dominant position has made it possible for less affluent white men to keep their share of those living in poverty relatively low (while their white female peers have become poorer) and to continue earning more than any other group with modest educational accomplishments (Shapiro and Kenty-Drane 2005; McElroy 2005). A rough chronology examining the institutional experiences of males from childhood to young adulthood demonstrates the contrasting cultural and institutional experiences outlined above more concretely.

When Boys Can't Be Boys: Labor Market Disadvantages That Start in Schools

In the past few years, the media have brought to light an emerging school pattern in which girls' academic accomplishments seem to be outstripping those of boys, causing some to fear that boys' academic efforts are not being adequately nurtured by teachers, most of whom happen to be women (Brooks 2006; Whitmire 2006; Gurian and Stevens 2005; Conlin 2003; Sommers 2000). As with several such anxiety-producing patterns—for example, concerns that arose over the increasing number of unsupervised "latchkey kids" associated with a rising number of working mothers—black youth were a harbinger group; they had exemplified some aspects of the pattern well before the media or public took notice. Everyone, it seems, is aware that black girls have been outperforming (graduating at higher rates, for example) their black male peers (and perhaps for many this was not surprising), but it seems that white males were not expected to fall behind their female peers. Actually, white males have not fallen behind academically; rather, white girls have begun to catch up with them, narrowing the traditional gaps substantially (Barnett and Rivers 2006). Girls' recent gains on boys have caused some optimistic speculation that women may begin to break through sex barriers in male-dominated occupations and catch up with men in terms of earnings, occupational prestige, and authority (Alperstein 2005). Certainly, for those headed for college, the pattern of unequal accomplishment has resulted in what some students call the "60/40 problem" in which the female-male ratio has become uncomfortably unequal on some campuses (Lewin 1998).

But given persistent patterns of sex segregation within many college majors, women are a long way from proportional representation in many, especially the most remunerative, occupational fields (England, Christopher, and Reid 1999). The one group for whom the dire predictions may come closest to truth, however, is black boys (Mason 2004; Hawkins 1996).

The Schott Foundation for Public Education (Holzman 2006) recently published its 2006 "State Report Card on Public Education and Black Male Students." In the exhaustive report, each state's record is reviewed, providing a glimpse of gaps across the country. The Schott Report cites a 2002 U.S. Department of Education Office of Civil Rights Survey that showed black boys were 8.7 percent of enrolled students, yet they were 23.8 percent of all recorded suspensions and 22.88 percent of all recorded expulsions. White males were 30.61 percent of enrolled students and constituted a comparable proportion of those suspended (32.48 percent) and expelled (34.32 percent) from school. In 2003-2004, the Schott Foundation claims that 55 percent of black males did not receive diplomas with their cohorts, but according to Manhattan Institute researchers Jay Greene and Marcus Winters (2006), black males are even worse off than the Schott Foundation suggests. Using a sophisticated estimation method, they convincingly demonstrated that in 2003, the national public school graduation rate differed substantially for black and white students: 78 percent of whites graduated, while only 55 percent of black students did. By gender, 73 percent of white and 59 percent of black female public school students graduated, while 67 percent of white and 48 percent of black male public school students graduated. Greene and Winters's figures show a 19 percent difference in black and white males' graduation rates, while the Schott Foundation figures are closer to a 25 percent gap with the gap ranging from a low of 7 percent to a high of 47 percent across states. In addition, the Schott Foundation report indicates that advanced placement (AP) participation among black students nationally is about half what would be predicted based on enrollments. Only 3.65 percent of those in gifted and talented programs were black males (who constitute 8.7 percent of enrolled students), while white males were slightly overrepresented among students in these programs (they constitute 35.77 percent of those in gifted and talented programs). More troubling are the low numbers of black male students achieving basic-level competencies in critical subjects. For example, the rate of black male students scoring at or above basic levels in grade 4 reading increased from 23 percent in 1992 to 36 percent in 2005, while for white males the comparable figures were 65 percent in 1992 and 72 percent in 2005. The rate of black male students scoring at or above basic levels in grade 8 reading for the same period rose from 35 percent to 43 percent; for white males the comparable figures were 69 percent to 76 percent. Black males are making progress, albeit slowly, but they remain far behind white males.

General concern about why boys are falling behind girls has opened up a critical discussion about classroom dynamics, many involving middle-class, predominantly white, female teachers and boys of different race and class backgrounds (Weaver-Hightower 2005; Delpit 1988). Some worry that school practices tend to favor girls' more docile deportment, placing boys, and perhaps especially less affluent boys of color, at risk of receiving excessive discipline (Hull 1994). Given that black boys trail behind both their female and male peers in terms of academic achievement, black boys' negative experiences in school may foreshadow their eventual labor market difficulties. A number of scholars argue, and present data to support the contention, that at least some portion of the wage and employment gap between black and white men would seem to be the direct result of unequal preparation and achievement in schools (Farkas and Vicknair 1996). But it is also important to note that the black-white test score gap, as well as several other measures of educational attainment/achievement, has narrowed during the past thirty to forty years (Jencks and Phillips 1998). In addition, after holding constant family background and school characteristics, the difference in school achievement shrinks considerably, but not completely (Roscigno, Tomaskovic-Devey, and Crowley 2006; Conley 1999). The question remains, however, why black boys, especially less affluent black boys, have had such vastly different rates of school success compared to their white male peers.

Several ethnographers have examined classroom dynamics searching for an answer to this question (Carter 2005; Lopez 2003; Fine and Weiss 1998; MacLeod 1995). One of the first to specify the ways in which less affluent black boys' institutional experiences of school differed from those of other students was sociologist Ann Ferguson. Her 2000 book *Bad Boys: Public Schools in the Making of Black Masculinity* focuses on black boys' experiences in a California school. A number of her findings have been noted in other states including Massachusetts, Michigan, Connecticut, Ohio, and Minnesota (Minnesota Department of Children, Families and Learning 1996; Hull 1994). Ferguson's intensive study of two groups of black boys, ten boys that school personnel designated as "troublemakers" and ten others identified as being good "schoolboys," sheds light on the processes that lead to the troubling statistics mentioned earlier. I focus on Ferguson's study because she has been unusually able to interrogate critically both the punishing actions of school personnel and the meaning of punishment for black boys—a meaning that is not always imbued with shame. As she explains, her study examines "how institutional norms and procedures in the field of education are used to maintain racial order, and how images and racial myths frame how we see ourselves and others in a racial hierarchy" (p. 19).

Ferguson (2000) began her project in the "Rosa Parks" elementary school by noting that while the school was fifty percent black and one-third white, the composition of the school's intervention program for "at-risk" students was 90 percent black and male, as were two rooms to which students were sent for punishment. She encountered, among white school personnel, a declaration that school policy was in practice color-blind, even though it could not claim to be so in effect. According to Ferguson, "The institutional discourse was that getting in trouble was not about race but a matter of individual choice and personal responsibility: each child made a choice to be 'good' or 'bad' " (p. 17). But Ferguson further explained that "this discourse of 'individual choice' was undercut by a more covert, secretive conversation about race"—a conversation that black school personnel, children and families sometimes engaged her in—that acknowledged the racial dimensions of an "enormous chasm of power that separated grown-ups and young people" (p. 13). Ferguson observed this chasm in the classroom when teachers, many of whom were white females, singled out (and disciplined) black boys far more frequently than any other students who demonstrated common forms of student disruption. Ferguson also astutely observed a tendency among school personnel to characterize black boys and their misbehaviors as the behavior of adults (Wright et al. 1998). That is, behaviors Ferguson observed—talking out of turn, arguing with teachers, and using profanity, for example—that she perceived as the mischievous, and not at all unusual behavior of ordinary boys, were perceived by school personnel as the cunning, dangerous, and predatory behaviors of men. As she explained, the "meaning and consequences of these acts for young black males . . . are different, highly charged with racial and gender significance with scarring effects on adult life chances" (p. 10).

Once the boys, who had been initially labeled as troublemakers, understood that their behaviors would persistently earn them extreme sanction, they began to both resist the injustice of the double standard they faced in ways consistent with black forms of protest and to simultaneously cultivate and glorify outlaw identities consistent with American masculinity norms (Donaldson 1993). But Ferguson (2000) cautioned her readers that none of the black boys escaped the school's costly system of rules, rewards, and punishments, nor the attractions of being seen as a defiant outlaw by their peers (at least some of the time). The black

> schoolboys were always on the brink of being redefined into the Troublemaker category by the school. The pressures and dilemmas this group faced around race and gender identities from adults and peers were always palpable forces working against their maintaining a commitment to the school project. (p. 10)

The parents of "schoolboys," who were slightly better off than the parents of "troublemakers," waged a constant campaign to keep their sons on the "straight and narrow." They expressed high expectations for their sons, coached them on how to manage frustrating situations, but simultaneously expressed worry that their sons were being targeted. Ferguson was eyewitness to the classroom and hallway dynamics that result in the "continual attrition" of schoolboys into the ranks of the "troublemakers" and concluded that "school labeling practices and the exercise of rules operated as part of a hidden curriculum to marginalize and isolate black male youth in disciplinary spaces and brand them as criminally inclined" (p. 2).

The emergent academic disengagement Ferguson (2000) observed among the black boys she studied was stimulated by alienation within the school. Black boys' alienation is not entirely unlike that experienced by working-class, white ethnic boys who were often disparaged in the hostile, nativist schools of the late nineteenth and early twentieth centuries (Steinberg 2001; Perlmann 1988). The difference is that the old labor market had many opportunities for modestly, and even poorly, educated men whose white skin color meant that they would not be barred from entry (Roediger 2005; Guglielmo 2003; Brodkin 2000; Steinberg 1995). But among today's less affluent students, both their lower levels of educational attainment and their skin color function to block their work opportunities. Moreover, among less affluent students who are not headed for college, it is even less likely that reduced educational inequalities between young men and women will serve as a potent force to desegregate the ubiquitously sex-segregated workspaces of the secondary labor market. That is, some less affluent men will most likely continue to avoid pink-collar ghettos as stridently as ever—further limiting their employment options. Today the labor market favors the educated, and informal recruitment and hiring practices, especially in construction and related fields, continue to favor whites and men (Sullivan 1989).

Race, Unequal Networks, and the School to Work Transition

More successful schooling experiences for black boys and adolescents would certainly help more black men to earn a solid living and to avoid unemployment, but wage and employment rate gaps within each educational level mean that white men would remain ahead. According to economist and education policy specialist Susan Williams McElroy (2005), who has summarized 2000 U.S. Census and 2001 and 2002 Bureau of Labor statistics for men aged twenty-four to sixty-four, the costs of low educational attainment are exceedingly high for black men. Examining the educational extremes, in 1999, the 11 percent of black males who failed to earn a diploma (median earnings $22,061) earned only 54 percent of the earnings of the 15 percent of black males with a college degree (median earnings $40,907). The 6 percent of white males without diplomas (median earnings $26,900), trailed behind their college-educated peers (median earnings $51,922) by 48 percent but out-earned black peers by 18 percent. Black men at each level of academic achievement were out-earned by white peers in 1999; black male high school graduates and college graduates earned 79 percent and 80 percent of white male high school and college graduates' median earnings, respectively. The 20 percent gap shows up again when we examine youth unemployment. Economist Michael Stoll (2005) documented youth employment patterns from 1985 through the economic growth period of the late 1990s, showing that black male employment among those aged sixteen to twenty-four lagged behind white male peers by at least 20 percent each and every year. But economist Robert Cherry (2001) suggested that most official figures, like these, severely underrepresent the dire state of young black men's labor market difficulties. In his 2001 book, *Who Gets the Good Jobs: Combating Race and Gender Disparities*, he explained that

> In 1999, 19% of all black men between ages sixteen and twenty-four were neither in school nor at work. . . . Only about one quarter of black teenagers are employed compared to half of white teenagers. Among those sixteen to twenty four years old, 50.7% of white students but only 28.6% of black students are employed. (p. 176)

In addition, Cherry (2001) argues that an apparent decline in black men's unemployment during the late 1990s was the result of black men's withdrawal from the labor force; he estimated that official rates typically underestimate black men's unemployment rate by about 7 to 8 percent. Finally, black men's difficulties are also exacerbated by underemployment, a persistent pattern in which they have been unable to locate full-time, year-round work at rates comparable to white peers (Cain 1986). In the aggregate, black men trail white men both in terms of educational and occupational accomplishments, making it unreasonable to hold hope for equal market outcomes at the national level (Albertson and Harris-Lacewell 2005). But the question remains whether young black and white men, just entering the labor market, and with sufficiently comparable premarket attributes, could make similar inroads in the labor market.

I sought an answer to this question when I studied a set of twenty-five black and twenty-five white males who graduated from the same vocational high school and sought work in the Baltimore area in the 1990s. The men I studied and wrote about in my 2003 book, *Race and the Invisible Hand: How White Networks Exclude Black Men from Blue-Collar Jobs*, allowed me to examine their full school records and provided detailed information about their schooling, work-study, and postsecondary work experiences. Since all were high school graduates from the same school and the black and white men did not differ statistically on standardized reading and math test scores or their grade point averages, or on a set of character, motivation, and preparedness measures I developed, both sets of men should have performed equally well in their first few years seeking work in Baltimore's regional labor market. But instead, labor market patterns for these men mirrored those of black and white men at the national level; black men earned only 73 percent of the median earnings of white men and had unemployment rates that were 10 percent higher than white peers. Moreover, the black men in my study, like those throughout the nation, experienced more and longer spells of unemployment than their white peers (Cherry 2001).

Being able to examine the process of transition for these two groups, who shared teachers in common and sought work in the same urban labor market, allowed me to compare how these similar young men tried to use school-based and personal resources to find and capture opportunities and how adults they knew helped or failed to help them. In several ways, within and beyond school, black men were at a severe disadvantage that hurt them in the labor market. At times, they faced a double standard that some teachers may have used to justify providing black males with less help. Black men wound up relying on formal, rather than more useful informal, transition strategies while in school and after graduating. Black men's personal contacts were neither as numerous nor as powerful as white men's, and black men's contacts were circumspect in ways white contacts did not appear to need to be. Young white men maintained access to important, but racially exclusive, informal recruitment spaces and enjoyed being the preferred workers for jobs in white working-class neighborhoods and in other spaces throughout the city. White men were generally unaware of their many advantages over black male peers; indeed, several claimed that black men had access to more opportunities than themselves as the result of "reverse racism," their nomenclature for affirmative action.

White male students were the beneficiaries of double or relaxed standards in at least three ways: their distinct hobbies, dress, and initiative in seeking work-study opportunities were not negatively scrutinized as were those of black males; work-study rules were bent so that they could pursue opportunities before they were officially allowed to do so; and without demonstrating a mastery of trade superior to black male peers, they were more often offered employment and other meaningful assistance, like recommendation letters, by white male teachers. Two of the black men who studied electrical construction observed that white male students frequently wore black t-shirts with "satanic looking" designs on them, yet they were not reprimanded, while black males' preferred clothing styles, certain jean brands and sweat suits, for example, were officially prohibited. Black students also implied that ambitious black students in the trades sometimes earned resentment, alongside respect, from white male shop teachers. The experience of the top black student in electrical construction, "Hank Searles," illustrates the black students' perspective well. In discussing his electrical construction teacher, "Mr. Dodd," Hank explained,

> Me and him had problems with the small stuff. What happened was, we had a new rule come into effect with the way we could dress at school. And one day we couldn't wear "Used Jeans" because there were tears in them, no cotton t-shirts with no collar, no sweat suits, but you could wear the sweatshirt. He tried to say that I couldn't wear the sweatshirt one day and we got into [it] one day and from then on we rarely had too much to say to each other. He was the teacher and I was the student and we kept it like that. (Royster 2003, 127)

Hank's experience contrasts sharply with that of white students who never discussed difficulties with teachers or school rules and saw their shop teachers as friends as well as teachers. As one white student, who had worked with Mr. Dodd on several jobs, explained, "We kept it as a teacher-student relationship in the classroom. It was more like friends outside, but he didn't treat me any better than anybody" (Royster 2003, 135).

Sometimes white teachers bent the rules to help white students. Machine shop student "Darren Zuskind" revealed this kind of help when he explained how his teacher, "Mr. Wooten," assisted him: "He's the one that got me out on work-study in the tenth grade. At Glendale they would never let you out on work-study in the tenth grade, it had to be eleventh, so Mr. Wooten let me leave school early from his class and not say anything" (Royster 2003, 137). (Mr. Wooten also arranged the job interview with someone he had worked with years before.)

Another black electrical construction student, "Craig Morning," explained that Mr. Dodd became less committed to helping him, when he revealed he hoped to pursue a rap career: "Yes, by twelfth grade, I knew that's what I wanted to be and he [Mr. Dodd] knew that and I don't think he appreciated it. So when I came up to him about certain things, he was like, he's not going to pursue this anyway, so it doesn't matter as much" (Royster 2003, 131). By contrast, Mr. Dodd was highly supportive of white student "Sean Mullino," who was pursuing a musical career in a rock band. Sean showed me a recommendation letter Mr. Dodd had written for him that ended, "Sean is an excellent student who has excelled in every phase of this course. He has an excellent attendance record and can always be trusted to work with minimum supervision. I feel given the opportunity Sean will make an excellent employee in an electrically related position" (Royster 2003, 136). I examined Craig's and Sean's grades in Mr. Dodd's classes; both boys earned Bs. Their school records differed in one relevant respect; Craig, the black student, was part of the commonwealth plus program because of his outstanding attendance, while Sean, the white student, had missed too many school days to qualify. I was curious about whether black students had been able to get recommendation letters from their white male shop teachers and discovered that some had reservations about asking. As Hank Searles explained, when I asked if the electrical construction teacher, "Mr. Hinkel," had ever written a recommendation for him, "No, I never asked him." I probed, "Would he if you had asked him?" And Hank replied, "Yes, but I don't think I would have asked him because I think he had a touch of prejudice" (Royster 2003, 128).

Comparing the actual experiences of black and white men in the same school also revealed that black men came to rely heavily on a less efficacious formal job placement system, while white men relied almost exclusively on a very efficacious informal job placement system run by white male shop teachers. While in school, white men rarely sought the help of the job placement office, while black men knew the part-time, black female job placement counselor, "Lydia Williams," well. Ms. Williams struggled to maintain the school's relationship with white employers, many of whom became associated with the school when its principals, teachers, and students were all, or nearly all, white. Unlike the black students, white male students were indifferent to Ms. Williams and the job placement office, some rarely needing to go there, even when they had work-study forms to get signed. Brick masonry student "Danny Spano's" response was not atypical. I asked Danny, who had had several work-study jobs, if he had met with Ms. Williams to arrange them. He replied, "No, I've heard of her, but I never met her." (His shop teacher had hand-delivered his paperwork and gotten the requisite signature for him.) Danny also said, when I asked whether any other school personnel, not including teachers, had helped him, "No, I never spoke to my principals. I didn't even know their names" (Royster 2003, 124).

White male shop teachers offered verbal encouragement to all of their students, but in providing more meaningful assistance to white male students, they wound up being added to the already ample personal contacts white men had. The only black male student, Hank, who had any older white male contacts in his network, established those contacts while on job sites, not in school. The vast majority of the white males I studied got several of their earliest work experiences under the supervision of their shop teachers. These early jobs enabled the men to purchase their own tools, cars, and trucks and to gain important work experiences—all of which made them more attractive to blue-collar employers who often value the possession of tools, on-site experience, and transportation more than a high school diploma alone. Again, only one black male, Hank, had worked enough to purchase his own tools and a work van. White male teachers seemed, not surprisingly, less able to relate to black male students than to white male students with whom they shared a class, race, gender, and sometimes neighborhood background. In addition, bringing young white men onto jobs in working-class white communities, where many teachers enjoyed a client base, is uncontroversial, but the same cannot be said for young black male students, who would have been far less welcome in those spaces (see Holzer and Ihlanfelt [1998] on customer preferences).

In listening to story after story, I began to detect a pattern among the white males who had worked for teachers. The teachers' small companies specialized in small residential construction and reconstruction, much of their clientele from working-class white neighborhoods in the city. During the warmer months of the year, the teachers scheduled numerous jobs including bathroom and kitchen remodeling, basement finishing, brick patio and low wall construction, decks, and landscaping. Typically, white students would be brought to the site, introduced to the property owner, and set to work, initially under the teacher's supervision, but later left on their own with their teacher only periodically checking up on the work. This seemed to suit the home owners fine, some of whom took a real liking to the students. A few white men described work they had done in the houses of older white women, who were sometimes especially solicitous.

One young man described a bathroom remodel in which he was left on his own to do tile destruction during the first few days of the job; his story illustrated a level of intimacy that only white males would be expected to establish in white working-class communities. He complained that the "lady of the house" had not turned on the air-conditioner despite what he estimated was at least 95-degree heat. Without asking her, he removed his t-shirt; she in turn offered him a cold glass of lemonade. After he "downed the lemonade," she made him stop to have a sandwich, and her "nonstop talking" prevented him from returning to work for at least a half hour. This young white man's experience was common and highlighted a sociogeographic reality many researchers overlook, namely, that bringing black male workers into certain spaces breaks serious cultural and community taboos. If teachers had brought young black male students to work on this sort of job, especially unsupervised, in neighborhoods like this one that had antiblack skinhead activity, teachers might lose work opportunities. And of course, some black students might have been reluctant to go into such neighborhoods. While it is acceptable (but not preferable) to have young black men doing short-term projects, such as cable installation or reading gas meters in white working-class neighborhoods, having them work on longer-term projects inside the *intimate* spaces of houses—kitchens, bathrooms, bedrooms, basements—breaks with white working-class cultural and community norms of keeping young black males out of private/feminized white spaces. But these are not the only spaces that are off limits to young black men.

In some of those same neighborhoods, many white men, including those with fewer familial contacts, worked in bars and taverns, public/masculinized white spaces that were also effectively closed off to black males. In these mainly male and all-white spaces, young white men worked as busboys and servers and were surrounded by older white tradesmen who acted as gatekeepers for the trades they studied and hoped to enter. Several white men described gaining entry to apprenticeships and jobs in these understudied informal job-placement centers. These spaces were particularly helpful for white men who had few older men in their networks. On average, though, white males listed seven more adult male contacts than black males, and their contacts were far more likely to include business owners, supervisors, and others in a position to hire workers in jobs they were seeking. In addition, in these spaces, older white men from multiple trade fields sometimes offered to connect the younger men to new trade fields that the young men had not trained in or to specific union-run apprentice programs. Unlike black males, who were at times told not to name their contacts, white males were expected to name their contacts, even when they were not particularly close, as a matter of routine. The assistance older white men gave younger white men represented a huge advantage over black peers who were often fending for themselves, some trying desperately not to have widespread stereotypes rule them out before they got their feet in the door (Falcon and Melendez 2001). Hank Searles is a case in point. The most successful black male I interviewed, Hank wore a suit and tie to interviews for electrical construction jobs, so concerned was he to convey a positive impression to employers who he knew might not look past the color of his skin to observe his solid trade skills.

All black men seeking employment, but especially those who are less affluent and who have lower educational preparation, must contend with enduring stereotypes that mark them all as unskilled, nonproductive, and perhaps even dangerous employees (Bobo and Massagli 2001). In *No Shame in My Game: The Working Poor in the Inner City* (1999), anthropologist Katherine Newman reported that local black youth were at a disadvantage for being hired even at their local fast-food restaurants. Employers preferred Latinos, other groups, and even persons who commuted from more distant neighborhoods. Many of the black men I studied were unable to translate their trade training into skilled jobs and instead wound up working in low-skill service sector jobs; seventeen of the twenty-five black men responded by pursuing additional training at their own cost. By contrast, nine of the twenty-five white men I studied had already received *employer-sponsored* training.

My examination of the school-work transition of young black and white men demonstrated a number of differential patterns in school, in access to useful contacts, in early work experiences, and in wage and unemployment rates. Because employers face few penalties for using informal recruiting strategies, well-connected white males routinely hear of and get the best-paying blue-collar jobs in cities like Baltimore, especially in construction (Moss and Tilly 2001b). Moreover, black men's contacts are circumspect about offering help. Some suggest that mentioning their names would not be helpful among whites who are hiring; others fear risking their reputations by suggesting a young black worker who might not work out (sociologist Sandra Smith [2005] made similar observations for poor black job seekers). Younger white men, even those who had been in legal trouble and who had demonstrated troubling workplace behavior, like arguing with the boss, managed to maintain adult contacts, who wrote their bad behavior off as "boys will be boys" shenanigans (Mills and Lingard 1997). While black boys and men who stay out of trouble and generally play by the rules, like those I studied, are still the majority of all black men (including those between the ages of sixteen and twenty-four), the disproportionate numbers of black men who have criminal records appears to create an unearned stigma for most black men that many young white men, even those with criminal records, can avoid (Western and Pettit 2005; Travis 2005; Pager 2003; Western 1998).

Stigmas Assumed, Stigmas Earned: Hidden Penalties Associated with Incarceration

One of the most significant studies published in recent years, Devah Pager's (2003) "Mark of a Criminal Record," demonstrated that even employers who do not know young white men personally are willing to read their trouble with the law as forgivable boyish behavior that does not rule them out as potential employees. Pager found in her innovative audit study that employers preferred white men with criminal records over black men without them—suggesting that black men who have played by the rules are seen as more of a risk than white men who have broken them. For a substantial number of black men, however, negative stigmas have been earned through convictions (Holzer, Raphael, and Stoll 2004; Pattillo, Weiman, and Western 2004). Sadly, many of these young men are unaware, until it is too late, of the wide range of labor market and other opportunities that can be formally foreclosed as the result of felony convictions in particular (Uggen, Manza, and Thompson 2006).

According to Andrew Barlow (2005),

> Black men have over eight times the chance to be incarcerated at some point in their lives than do white men. An estimated 12 percent of all African American Men aged twenty to thirty four are currently in jail or prison, as compared to 1.6 percent of white men in the same age group. Including men awaiting trial, on bail, on parole, or on probation, some 32 percent of all black men aged twenty to twenty nine are currently under some type of correctional control. . . . A 2003 Bureau of Justice Statistics report calculates that 28 percent of all black men in the United States will be incarcerated at some point in their lives. (p. 223)

In addition, Western, Kleykamp, and Rosenfeld (2006, 2305) documented increasing levels of incarceration since the 1980s. They showed that from 1983 to 1988, just over 7 percent of black males with less than a high school diploma annually entered prison. This number rose to 14.6 percent from 1989 to 1994 and further to 16.3 percent between 1995 and 2001. During the same periods, poorly educated white men's annual incarceration rates increased much less dramatically rising from 1.6 percent between 1983 and 1988 to 2.5 percent between 1989 and 1994 and finally to 3.3 percent between 1995 and 2001. Western, Kleykamp, and Rosenfeld asserted that one in six black male dropouts went to prison every year in the 1990s and that prison admission statistics for black males remain five to ten times higher than for white males.

Yamagata and Jones's (2000) examination of youths' self-reported behaviors and patterns in arrest and incarceration also indicate that black youth are more severely penalized than white youth for similar infractions. Their report, "And Justice for Some: Differential Treatment of Minority Youth in the Justice System," showed that while black youth are 15 percent of the entire youth population, they make up 26 percent of youth who are arrested, 44 percent of youth who are detained by police, 46 percent of youth who are judicially waived to criminal court, and 58 percent of youth admitted to state prisons. Moreover, while whites make up 79 percent of the youth population, they were only 71 percent of those arrested in 1998. Black youth are arrested at twice the rate of white youth, and disparities persist even when the self-reported behaviors of white youth should make their rates of arrest higher than those of black youth. For example, even though white youth report committing higher levels of weapons possession crimes, black youth are arrested 2.5 times more often for weapons offenses. White youth report using drugs at 6 to 7 times the rate of black youth, but black youth are arrested at higher rates than whites for drug crimes. To make matters worse, black youth are overrepresented in drug arrests (they are 33 percent of all youth drug arrests) but underrepresented for drug treatment (they are 17 percent of youth admitted to state-funded drug treatment programs). Black youth arrested for drug offenses are a third less likely than white youth to be diverted to drug treatment facilities.

George Bridges and Sara Steen (1998) compared 233 narrative reports written by juvenile probation officers to determine why black youth with similar criminal histories and identical convictions as white youth received harsher sentence recommendations than white youth. They found a conspicuous pattern in which probation officers saw the crimes of youth of color as the result of "internal forces"—inadequate moral character, personal failures, and attitudinal problems—but saw white youths' crimes as the result of "external forces"—poor home life, environment, few solid role models. Minority youth were held accountable for personal failings, while white youth were seen to be victims whose actions were mitigated by larger social forces beyond their control.

Records of arrest and even more so of conviction and incarceration prove to be additional obstacles to any worker, but for those who seek training or public sector jobs, convictions may be especially costly (Petersilla 2003). For instance, the Higher Education Act of 1998 bars inmates and ex-felons from eligibility for Pell Grants, the federal student loans, as well as other forms of grants or work assistance that are no longer limited to use at four year colleges (Legal Action Center 2004). Many students at two-year colleges and even technical training schools now use federal and state grants to make enhancing their skill sets affordable. Increasingly ex-offenders, in particular drug offenders, are prohibited from federal, state, and county jobs as well as access to public and private housing

(Rubinstein and Mukamal 2002). Given that blacks work disproportionately in the public sector and therefore have their greatest networking capacities in that sector, becoming ineligible for public sector employment is especially costly for young black workers (Steinberg 1995). In addition, the conditions of probation or parole may preclude employment in certain lower-skilled jobs located in the marginal or informal labor market, especially jobs located near legally marginal workplaces such as bars and liquor stores. Furthermore, state laws requiring bonding and occupational licenses routinely deny employment as barbers, security guards, social workers, taxi drivers, optometrists, car sellers, and locksmiths to those with a felony conviction (Legal Action Center 2004). Most of these laws stipulate that the offense that makes an ex-offender ineligible should either be directly job-related or that "hiring the ex-offender would create a threat to people or property" (Article 23A New York Corrections Law). But in practice, the very label "convict" or "ex-offender" is customarily taken as a mark of poor character, untrustworthiness, or risk (Western 2006; Wacquant 2001). In addition, President Clinton's welfare reform legislation, officially known as the Personal Responsibility and Work Opportunity Reconciliation Act of 1996, also makes any felon who is fleeing to avoid arrest or imprisonment or has violated conditions of her or his probation or parole ineligible for Supplemental Security Income (i.e., income and health care).

Educational and economic marginality are strongly associated with incarceration, which, in this era, can lead to the automatic forfeiture of political power, specifically the vote (Manza and Uggen 2006; Uggen and Manza 2002; Miller 1997). According to political scientist Dianne Pinderhughes (2005), about 13 percent of all adult black men, 1.4 million ex-felony offenders, are currently disenfranchised. Pinderhughes highlights a conclusion of a 1996 Sentencing Project briefing paper: "Given current rates of incarceration, three in ten of the next generation of black men can expect to be disenfranchised at some point in their lifetime. In states that disenfranchise ex-offenders, as many as 40 percent of black men may permanently lose the right to vote" (p. 557) and to hold public office. At the same time, while increasingly fewer black men can advance their interests through public policies, a not insubstantial number of less affluent white men have chosen to use their considerable numbers to elect conservative politicians who have aggressively pursued agendas designed to maintain, rather than disrupt, some of their historic labor market (and other) advantages vis-à-vis less powerful groups of workers (Rogers and Texeira 2000).

Rescuing Less Affluent Black Men from the Educational and Occupational Margins: Cultural Challenges and Institutional Accountability

How is it possible that in thirty years or so of intense study, black youth employment difficulties seem no closer to being effectively addressed today than they were in the late 1970s and early 1980s, when it was becoming clear that deindustrialization combined with "last hired/first fired" syndrome would make black youth, men especially, the harbinger of underemployment and unemployment realities to come (Duster 1995)? Can it be that the powerful models that were developed within sociology, labor economics, and public policy failed to specify the full dimensions of the problem as some have argued (Patterson 2006)? Might the sound prescriptions offered by researchers have lacked a social movement or organizational support to force legislators and institutions to enact policies that would have helped this group? Both problems, failures of problem explication and of political strategy and will, explain why we do not yet adequately understand nor address less affluent black men's educational and employment difficulties. To better explain black men's difficulties, I have offered an analytic synthesis of relevant research on black and white boys' and men's diverging experiences in institutions. In this section, I draw out the implications of my examination. Specifically, I discuss the multiple cultural challenges that black boys and men present, but also face in their interactions with institutions, and ways families and others could do more to assist them; and I propose ways of holding institutions, which have poorly served black boys and men, more accountable.

Today's black males, perhaps especially the young, expect to adhere to larger American male cultural norms, but many, perhaps especially less affluent black boys and adolescents, may not fully realize that they are still not welcome to do so (Young 2003). That is, the "boys will be boys" *apologia* that is often applied to the mischief and misdeeds of white boys and men will not be placed in service for black boys and men. This used to be an understood, if informal, policy that most blacks lived with, but some historical examples demonstrate that not everyone was clear about the rules. The sad case of Emmett Till is a case in point.

I sometimes try to imagine how the woman whom Emmett Till tragically whistled at in the summer of 1955 would have felt had the young man who had publicly admired her been white. I suspect she might have been embarrassed or flattered by the attention; she might have shared the episode in a humorous anecdote with girlfriends or even to highlight her alternative prospects to a neglectful husband. Or perhaps she might have scolded the young man for improper advances and warned him against similar actions. In no scenario is it likely that a white male admirer would have been viciously tortured and murdered as Emmett Till was. It was not the act of male admiration or flirtation that was prohibited; rather, it was that act when performed by a black male toward a white female. But either Emmett Till did not adequately understand the cultural norms of white manhood (and not just southern variants) that reserved the right to admire white females exclusively to white men or he chose to risk/resist it anyway, perhaps as a show of bravery for his friends (Connell 1995). Black boys' and men's performances of ordinary acts of boyhood and manhood was then, and remains now, far more institutionally controversial than white boys' and men's similar actions (Saint-Aubin 1994), but some black youth, like Emmett Till, are either not fully aware that American society is not color-blind or they are willing to risk defiance of the rules anyway.

Educator and comedian Bill Cosby and journalist Juan Williams (author of the 2006 book *Enough: The Phony Leaders, Dead-End Movements, and Culture of Failure That Are Undermining Black America—And What We Can Do about It*) are certainly not the first older black men to express consternation about black boys' and men's troubling choices. And they are motivated by a frustration about the way that some younger black men seem to cavalierly risk their lives and life chances. But they as well as some scholars misdiagnose the cultural component of black men's attitudes and behaviors as being about "blackness," when it is far more about how black boys and men play "masculinity games" (Dyson 2005). Certainly blackness can be associated with resistance and opposition to unjust and unequal treatment, but the more troubling attitudes and behaviors exhibited by black boys and men often reflect ordinary and hyper styles of masculinity (Cole and Guy-Sheftall 2003).

Recent examinations of young men of color have demonstrated that managing masculinity norms expected within home communities and "femininity" norms within schools has become especially challenging for less affluent black boys and adolescents (Lopez 2003; Carter 2005). If institutional cultures in school are coming to be seen as hostile even toward white boys, it is not hard to imagine the more unique cultural dilemma faced by boys, men, and families of color who must navigate a variety of hostile institutional cultures, often equipped with limited cultural and political resources (Cross and Fhagen-Smith 2001; Delpit 1988). But some less affluent families watch institutional practices and school personnel vigilantly, advocate for their black sons when institutions are indifferent or unfairly punitive, and strategize with sons about how to establish and manage "schoolboy" status (Thompson 2004; Comer et al. 1996). How might more families and other concerned adults become similarly invested in both helping black boys and young men to navigate institutions more effectively and in holding institutions accountable for equitable treatment for black boys and men?

Sociologist Orlando Patterson (1999) has long argued that culture is a component of the employability problems of young black men and that social scientists have expertly demonstrated the logistics of the problem, specifically the various structures that have limited the progress of black urban youth, but fail to provide similarly lucid examinations of black youth culture and its part in the difficulties. Some scholarship conforms to Patterson's contention. For example, Elijah Anderson's (1990) examination of very poor black men and the "code of the streets" they adhere to, to stave off threats and save face in the ghetto. Another example might be Sygnithia Fordham and John Ogbu's (1986) exploration of how some black youth see commitment to academic pursuits as "acting white." But I would counter that a major weakness in these approaches is that they do not compare black boys and men to similarly situated whites. When young white men face life circumstances as circumscribed as those of young black men, their responses are quite similar, as Jay MacLeod (1995) found when he examined young black and white men living in the same northeastern housing project (Willis 1981). Cosby, Williams, and Patterson are right that culture contributes to the problems that less affluent black men face today, but they identify only one culture as problematic—the culture of less affluent black families and youth. In my view, identifying and critiquing multiple cultural influences, including the cultures of powerful institutions and their agents, is critical to advancing a workable agenda for assisting black boys and men.

In essence, one form of resistance that is destructive can be replaced by another that is empowering, if schools, employers, and policing and sentencing institutions are held publicly accountable.

Any scholar entering the territory connecting structure to agency or culture risks "blaming the victim," that is, mistaking effects for causes and placing the onus for needed change solely on relatively powerless individuals, rather than powerful institutions and actors. But not entering this territory is cowardly according to scholars like Patterson (2006), who has argued that structuralists delude themselves by thinking it is easier or more politically correct to attempt to change what he perceives to be inflexible structures rather than the behaviors and beliefs, or culture, of groups. Patterson argued that changing black youth culture would be both easier and more effective in quickly enhancing the labor market prospects of black youth. Maybe, but some of the research I have discussed shows that irrespective of how young black men actually think and behave, gatekeeping teachers and employers presume them to be suspect. Nevertheless, black boys' and men's institutional vulnerability makes greater attitudinal and behavioral accommodation necessary, but such accommodation will be injurious to black boys and men if they and their allies do not wage a simultaneous campaign of resistance to business-as-usual patterns in institutions (Cross and Fhagen-Smith 2001). That is, it may be possible for many more adults to coach black boys to adopt less masculine attitudes and behaviors as many black families already do (often believing that they are coaching to de-emphasize race, rather than masculinity), but this effort will not be successful unless black boys see those same adults participate in resistance strategies that hold institutions accountable for treating black boys and men more equitably. In essence, one form of resistance that is destructive can be replaced by another that is empowering, if schools, employers, and policing and sentencing institutions are held publicly accountable. Historically, black efforts to hold American institutions accountable have been time-consuming and difficult, but such efforts have sometimes met with success (Robinson 1997).

For example, the effort to desegregate schools led by Charles Hamilton Houston involved collecting data and contrasting the public school resources that were available to black and white communities (Klinkner and Smith 1999). Houston and his colleagues also captured the disparities on film. All of Houston's strategies were aimed at delegitimizing segregated schooling systematically. Blacks made some of their most significant labor gains during the early cold war era when black leaders like A. Phillip Randolph of the Brotherhood of Sleeping Car Porters brought international shame to the U.S. government for its demonstrably racist employment practices. Randolph also threatened a huge protest march on Washington that led to the desegregation of the army and the federal government and more intense black worker recruitment in war-related industries (Klinkner and Smith 1999; Robinson 1997). (This threatened march was far more effective than the recent "Million Man March" carried out under Nation of Islam leader Louis Farrakhan, which asked nothing of the federal government despite the disproportionate suffering of black boys and men in schools, work settings, and prisons.) A second wave of gains came as the result of civil rights era protests, direct action campaigns, and inner-city rebellions that eventually brought much needed jobs and community institutions through President Johnson's "War on Poverty" (Quadagno 1994; Morris 1984). Affirmative action policies that helped to open up the trades through programs like the Philadelphia Plan, minority set-aside block grants, and other inclusive policies have come under serious attack and are likely to be dismantled under the current Supreme Court. In earlier eras, black advancement was ultimately contingent on both the weapons of the strong—holding institutions accountable through the vote, legal strategies, boycotts, organized resistance—and the weapons of the weak—selective property destruction and urban unrest. But in this era of massive black incarceration, it may be harder to marshal the weapons of the strong to effectively aid the weak.

Conclusion

Sociologist James Rosenbaum (1984) pointed out that status attainment in the United States can involve participating in increasingly high-stakes "tournaments" that begin as early as elementary school. Implicit in the model is an underlying pattern of attrition in which early losers are not eligible to compete for the more desirable opportunities attached to later tournaments. Many scholars fear that the accumulation of early schooling difficulties and failures makes a substantial number of less affluent black men (and women) unlikely to ever become competitive in the labor market—these would be early tournament losers, Ferguson's (2000) "troublemakers." In earlier sections of this article, I provided data on school failure patterns that showed that black boys are among the students most vulnerable to being labeled ineducable and incorrigible. Those early labels lead many black boys to disengage from school and too often to conform to some adults' expectations by enacting performances of "little thugs" who seem bound for adult gangster-hood. They cultivate an indifferent "cool pose" or sullen toughness—a masculine shell to hide in—because they have few, if any, powerful advocates to require more of them and the institutions that are supposed to serve them (Mirza 1999). Among less affluent black male students, only boys who enjoy the protection and advocacy of strategic-minded adults have a chance to negotiate the early educational gauntlet without earning a hyperstigmatizing disciplinary "record" (Hale 2001). And if less affluent boys manage that feat, they still are unlikely to accumulate academic accomplishments that make college attendance and professional careers possible. Instead, they are lucky to make it to a second round in which the best labor market prospects are in the blue-collar sphere.

Among less affluent black male students, only boys who enjoy the protection and advocacy of strategic-minded adults have a chance to negotiate the early educational gauntlet without earning a hyperstigmatizing disciplinary record.

In the second round, those who have "played by the rules" and earned a high school diploma can presumably, by virtue of these earlier accomplishments, make a credible claim on desirable jobs in the labor market. Unfortunately, my work suggests, like Ferguson's (2000), that black boys and men experience a differential tolerance among some teachers and employers and that they are all but excluded from the networks of older white men who remain blue-collar gatekeepers. Black adolescents and men do not get returns on their high school investments comparable to white male peers primarily because so many jobs are accessed through informal recruitment and hiring mechanisms that advantage white men. It is usually at this life stage, during the years of high school–work transition, that young men demonstrate risk-taking behaviors that, for some, lead to legal trouble. My examination of the disparate treatment that black youth, and males in particular, receive at the hands of police, probation officers, and judges makes clear that black boys and men are held to a much tougher standard than are white male peers (Tushar 2005). Black men are vulnerable to labor market exclusion without criminal records, but when they have them employers feel even more justified in not considering them for jobs.

The all too rare black men who get to third-round tournaments typically come from families whose educational and occupational exposures have enabled them to monitor and coach their sons on deportment and a host of other signals used by institutions to assess potential. These parents often advocate hard for their sons, requiring institutions and their agents to be responsive to their sons' needs (Hale 2001). Their actions are time-consuming, expensive, at times humiliating, and financially costly, but they do it because they can and it is necessary (Shapiro 2004). Less affluent parents need far more help in accomplishing these tasks, but as I have argued, the credibility of helpers is contingent upon a commitment to holding institutions accountable publicly—a strategy squarely within the civil rights, larger black resistance, and other organizing paradigms including, on occasion, labor unions (Kelly 1994).

Lani Guinier and Gerald Torres, in their 2002 book *The Miner's Canary: Enlisting Race, Resisting Power, Transforming Democracy*, discussed how the resistance traditions of people of color in the United States can be incorporated into contemporary movements to expand democracy and reduce inequality. Guinier and Torres provided examples of concrete strategies for holding institutions accountable and for resuscitating constructive forms of cultural resistance connected with black-led freedom struggles in particular. But working-class resistance strategies, such as union organizing, also provide important models of organized resistance that could be especially important for improving black men's contemporary labor market prospects. As sociologist Michelle Lamont explained in her 2000 book *The Dignity of Working Men: Morality and the Boundaries of Race, Class, and Immigration*, "Resistance is often the unintended consequence of workers defending their dignity and attempting to gain respect" (p. 245). Lamont, who studied a variety of working men, identified among her black male subjects a unique emphasis on "the caring self," a moral self that exhibits compassion and care for others. This positive moral value espoused by working-class black men is an important counterforce to dominant American masculinity norms that are destructive.

Socializing less affluent boys and men to eschew troubling masculinity norms and embrace constructive black resistance models will not work in the absence of a reinvigorated and widespread alternative justice framework that holds institutions accountable.

Given the high levels of poverty and institutional unfairness that less affluent black boys and adolescents witness and experience, they should resist institutional injustice, but resisting constructively requires guidance, discipline, and eschewing aspects of American masculinity that are incompatible with justice struggles. For example, current American masculinity norms offer an uncritical acceptance and glorification of both pimp and playboy figures that incorporate misogynist, aggressive, irresponsible, and exploitative attitudes and behaviors (Cole and Guy-Sheftall 2003). These images are ubiquitous and embraced by male youth across class, racial, and ethnic categories (Connell 1995). The aim of working collectively with black (and other) women on political struggles affecting less affluent community members, such as disenfranchisement, labor market exclusion, or HIV treatment and services, is made more difficult by masculine cultures that undermine women's dignity (Cole and Guy-Sheftall 2003). Black culture and black working men's culture in particular, however, provide a necessary alternative style of resistance and protest, predicated on a modulated masculinity norm, in which the vulnerable and the weak, rather than being denigrated and abused, are defended and valued (Kelly 1994).

Socializing less affluent boys and men to eschew troubling masculinity norms and embrace constructive black resistance models will not work in the absence of a reinvigorated and widespread alternative justice framework that holds institutions accountable. Specifically, progressive citizen groups should hold local schools accountable for educating black children (black girls trail behind their female peers too) for parity (Anyon 2005). Citizens' groups must require schools to maintain data on raced and gendered patterns of achievement but also patterns of enriched opportunity and punishment allocation. Citizens' groups can provide schools with more support financially and as tutors and mentors as a subset of a larger school reform agenda. Monitoring selection mechanisms and occupancy patterns for the jobs young workers can attain without a college degree is another key site for institutional accountability. Credibility will require a reinvigorated effort at eliminating exclusionary labor practices and a stronger effort to increase the minimum wage and provide basic health coverage for vulnerable workers as well. Finally, the figurative and literal deathblow for many less affluent black men is the American prison complex. At multiple levels, from surveillance patterns in neighborhoods to disproportionate numbers of death-penalty sentences, less affluent black men live constantly too close to the threat of incarceration. Concerned citizens have sufficient evidence to indict the justice system and to demand change, including forcing police officers to maintain records of race for police stops to requiring judges to use fair sentencing guidelines. Although blacks may need to take the lead in this renewed effort at improving less affluent black men's life chances, all Americans have a chance to participate in a revived Civil Rights Movement by demanding for black boys and men what is today so often provided to white boys and men without a struggle.

References

Ainsworth, J. W., and V. J. Roscigno. 2005. Stratification, school-work linkages and vocational education. *Social Forces* 84 (1): 257-84.
Albertson, B., and M. Harris-Lacewell. 2005. Good times? Understanding African American misperceptions of racial economic fortunes. *Journal of Black Studies* 35 (5): 650-83.

Allard, P., and M. Mauer. 2000. *Regaining the vote: An assessment of activity relating to felon disenfranchisement laws*. January. The Sentencing Project. www.sentencingproject.org.

Alperstein, J. F. 2005. Commentary on girls, boys, test scores and more. *Teachers College Record*, May 16. http://www.tcrecord.org, ID number: 11874 (accessed October 10, 2006).

Anderson, E. 1990. *Streetwise: Race, class, change in an urban community*. Chicago: University of Chicago Press.

Anyon, J. 2005. *Radical possibilities: Public policy, urban education, and a new social movement*. New York: Routledge.

Barlow, A. L. 2005. Globalization, racism, and the expansion of the American penal system. In *African Americans in the U.S. economy*, ed. C. A. Conrad, J. Whitehead, P. Mason, and J. Stewart, 223-31. Lanham, MD: Rowman & Littlefield.

Barnett, R. C., and C. Rivers. 2006. "Boy" crisis in education is nothing but hype. *Women's eNews*, March 15. http://www.womensenews.org/article.cfm/dyn/aid/2671 (accessed October 2, 2006).

Blauner, R. 1969. Internal colonialism and ghetto revolt. *Social Problems* 16 (2): 393-408.

———. 1972. *Racial oppression in America*. New York: Harper & Row.

Bobo, L. D., and M. P. Massagli. 2001. Stereotyping and urban inequality. In *Urban inequality: Evidence from four cities*, ed. A. O'Connor, C. Tilly, and L. Bobo, 89-162. New York: Russell Sage Foundation.

Bound, J., and R. Freeman. 1992. What went wrong? The erosion of the relative earnings and employment of young black men in the 1980s. *Quarterly Journal of Economics* 107 (1): 201-32.

Braddock, J. H., and J. McPartland. 1987. How minorities continue to be excluded from equal employment opportunities: Research on labor market and institutional opportunities. *Journal of Social Issues* 43 (1): 5-39.

Bridges, G. S., and S. Steen. 1998. Racial disparities in official assessments of juvenile offenders: Attributional stereotypes as mediating mechanis. *American Sociological Review* 63 (4): 554-70.

Brodkin, K. 2000. *How Jews became white folks: And what that says about race in America*. New Brunswick, NJ: Rutgers University Press.

Brooks, D. 2006. The gender gap in schools. *New York Times*, May 23.

Cain, G. 1986. The economic analysis of labor market discrimination: A survey. In *Handbook of labor economics*, vol. 1, ed. O. Aschenfelter and R. Layard. Amsterdam: Elsevier Press.

Carter, P. L. 2005. *Keepin' it real: School success beyond black and white*. New York: Oxford University Press.

Chandra, A. 2000. Labor-market dropouts and the racial wage gap: 1940-1990. *American Economic Review* 90 (2): 333-38.

Cherry, R. 2001. *Who gets the good jobs? Combating race and gender disparities*. New Brunswick, NJ: Rutgers University Press.

Cole, J. B., and B. Guy-Sheftall. 2003. *Gender talk: The struggle for women's equality in African American communities*. New York: Ballantine.

Comer, J. P., N. M. Haynes, E. T. Joyner, and M. Ben-Avie. 1996. *Rallying the whole village: The Comer process for reforming education*. New York: Teachers College Press.

Conley, D. 1999. *Being black, living in the red: Race, wealth, and social policy in America*. Berkeley: University of California Press.

Conlin, M. 2003. The new gender gap. *Business Week Online*, May 23. http://businessweek.com/magazine/content/03_21/b3834001_mz001.htm (accessed October 2, 2006).

Connell, R. W. 1995. *Masculinities*. Berkeley: University of California Press.

Cross, W. E., and P. Fhagen-Smith. 2001. Patterns of African American identity development: A life span perspective. In *New perspective on racial identity development: A theoretical and practical anthology*, ed. C. L. Wijeyesinghe and B. W. Jackson III. New York: New York University Press.

Delpit, L. 1988. The silenced dialogue: Power and pedagogy in educating other people's children. *Harvard Educational Review* 68 (3): 280-98.

Donaldson, M. 1993. What is hegemonic masculinity? *Theory and Society* 22 (5): 643-57.

Duster, T. 1995. Postindustrialization and youth unemployment: African Americans as a harbingers. In *Poverty, inequality, and the future of social policy: Western states in the new world order*, ed. K. McFate, R. Lawson, and W. J. Wilson, 461-88. New York: Russell Sage Foundation.

Dyson, M. E. 2005. *Is Bill Cosby right? Or has the black middle class lost its mind?* New York: Basic Books.

England, P., K. Christopher, and L. L. Reid. 1999. Gender, race, ethnicity, and wages. In *Latinas and African American women at work*, ed. I. Browne. New York: Russell Sage Foundation.

Falcon, L. M., and E. Melendez. 2001. Racial and ethnic differences in job searching in urban centers. In *Urban inequality: Evidence from four cities*, ed. A. O'Connor, C. Tilly, and L. Bobo, 341-71. New York: Russell Sage Foundation.

Farkas, G., and K. Vicknair. 1996. Appropriate tests of racial wage discrimination require controls for cognitive skill: Comment on Cancio, Evans, and Maume. *American Sociological Review* 61:557-60.

Ferguson, A. A. 2000. *Bad boys: Public schools in the making of black masculinity*. Ann Arbor: Michigan University Press.

Fine, M., and L. Weiss. 1998. *The unknown city: Lives of poor and working-class young adults*. Boston: Beacon.

Fordham, S., and J. Ogbu. 1986. Black students' school success: Coping with the burden of acting white. *Urban Review* 18 (3): 176-206.

Freeman, R. 1991. Employment and earnings of disadvantaged young men in a labor shortage economy. In *The urban underclass*, ed. C. Jencks and P. Peterson. Washington, DC: Brookings Institution.

Freeman, R. B., and D. A. Wise. 1982. *The youth labor market problem: Its nature, causes and consequences*. Chicago: University of Chicago Press.

Glasgow, D. 1980. *The black underclass: poverty, unemployment, and entrapment of ghetto youth*. New York: Vintage.

Greene, J. P., and M. A. Winters. 2006. Public school graduation rates in the United States. Manhattan Institute for Policy Research, Civic Report no. 31. http:/www.manhattan-institute.org/html/cr_31.htm (accessed October 2, 2006).

Guglielmo, T. A. 2003. Rethinking whiteness historiography: The case of Italians in Chicago, 1890-1945. In *White out: The continuing significance of racism*, ed. A. W. Doane and E. Bonilla-Silva, 49-62. New York: Routledge.

Guinier, L., and G. Torres. 2002. *The miner's canary: Enlisting race, resisting power, transforming democracy*. Cambridge, MA: Harvard University Press.

Gurian, M., and K. Stevens. 2005. What is happening with boys in school? *Teachers College Record*, May 2. http://wwwtcrecord.org, ID number: 11854 (accessed October 2, 2006).

Hale, J. E. 2001. *Learning while black: Creating educational excellence for African American children*. Baltimore: Johns Hopkins University Press.

Hamilton, D. 2006. The racial composition of American jobs. In *The state of black America 2006*. New York: National Urban League.

Hawkins, D. 1996. Gender gap: Black females outpace male counterparts at three degree levels. *Black Issues in Higher Education* 13:20-22.

Holzer, H. J. 1996. *What employers want: Job prospects for less educated workers*. New York: Russell Sage Foundation.

Holzer, H., and S. Danziger. 2001. Are jobs available for disadvantaged workers in urban areas? In *Urban inequality: Evidence from four cities*, ed. A. O'Connor, C. Tilly, and L. Bobo. New York: Russell Sage Foundation.

Holzer, H. J., and K. R. Ihlanfelt. 1998. Customer discrimination and employment outcomes for minority workers. *Quarterly Journal of Economics* 133 (3): 835-67.

Holzer, H. J., P. Offner, and E. Sorenson. 2005. What explains the continuing decline in labor force activity among young black men? *Labor History* 46 (1): 37-55.

Holzer, H. J., S. Raphael, and M. A. Stoll. 2004. Will employers hire former offenders? Employer preferences, background checks, and their determinants. In *Imprisoning America: The social effects of mass incarceration*, ed. M. Pattillo, D. Weiman, and B. Western, 205-46. New York: Russell Sage Foundation.

Holzman, M. 2006. *Public education and black male students: The 2006 state report card*. Schott Educational Equity Index. Cambridge, MA: The Schott Foundation for Public Education.

Hughes, L. 1951. *Montage of a dream deferred*. New York: Henry Holt.

Hull, J. 1994. Do teachers punish according to race? *Time*, April 4, pp. 30-31.

Jencks, C., and M. Phillips. 1998. *The black-white test score gap*. Washington, DC: Brookings Institution Press.

Johnston, R. C., and D. Viadero. 2000. Unmet promise: Raising minority achievement. *Education Week*, March 15, pp. 18-21.
Kelly, R. D. G. 1994. *Race rebels: Culture, politics, and the black working class*. New York: Free Press.
Kerner Commission. 1968. *Report of the National Advisory Commission on Civil Disorders*. Washington, DC: Government Printing Office.
Klinkner, P. A., and R. M. Smith. 1999. *The unsteady march: The rise and decline of racial equality in America*. Chicago: University of Chicago Press.
Kunjufu, J. 1986. *Motivating and preparing black youth for success*. Chicago: African American Images.
Lamont, M. 2000. *The dignity of working men: Morality and the boundaries of race, class, and immigration*. New York: Russell Sage Foundation.
Legal Action Center. 2004. *After prison: Roadblocks to reentry: A report on state legal barriers facing people with criminal records*. A Report by the Legal Action Center. http://www.lac.org/lac/upload/lacreport/LAC_PrintReport.pdf.
Lewin, T. 1998. American colleges begin to ask, where have all the men gone? *New York Times*, December 6, p. A1.
Lopez, N. 2003. *Hopeful girls, troubled boys: Race and gender disparity in urban education*. New York: Routledge.
MacLeod, J. 1995. *Ain't no makin' it: Leveled aspirations and attainment in a low income neighborhood*. San Francisco: Westview.
Mac an Ghaill, M. 1994. *The making of men: Masculinities, sexualities, and schooling*. Buckingham, UK: Open University Press.
Majors, R., and J. M. Billson. 1992. *Cool pose: The dilemmas of black manhood in America*. New York: Lexington Books.
Manza, J., and C. Uggen. 2006. *Locked out: Felony disenfranchisement and American democracy*. Oxford: Oxford University Press.
Martino, W. 2000. Mucking around in class, giving crap, and acting cool: Adolescent boys enacting masculinities at school. *Canadian Journal of Education* 25 (2): 102-12.
Mason, P. 2004. Understanding recent empirical evidence on race and labor market outcomes in the USA. *Review of Social Economy* 58 (3): 319-38.
———. 2005. Persistent racial discrimination in the labor market. In *African Americans in the U.S. economy*, ed. C. A. Conrad, J. Whitehead, P. Mason, and J. Stewart, 141-50. Lanham, MD: Rowman & Littlefield.
Mauer, M. 1997. *Intended and unintended consequences: State racial disparities in imprisonment*. The Sentencing Project. www.sentencingproject.org.
McElroy, S. W. 2005. Race and gender differences in the U.S. labor market: The impact of education attainment. In *African Americans in the U.S. economy*, ed. C. A. Conrad, J. Whitehead, P. Mason, and J. Stewart, 133-40. Lanham, MD: Rowman & Littlefield.
Miller, J. 1997. *Search and destroy: African American males in the criminal justice system*. New York: Cambridge University Press.
Mills, M., and B. Lingard. 1997. Masculinity politics, myths, and boys' schooling: A review essay. *British Journal of Educational Studies* 45 (3): 276-92.
Mincy, R. 1994. *Nurturing young black males: Challenges to agencies, programs, and social policy*. Washington, DC: Urban Institute Press.
Minnesota Department of Children, Families and Learning. 1996. *Student suspension and expulsion: Report to the legislature*. St. Paul: Minnesota Department of Children, Families and Learning.
Mirza, H. S. 1999. Review: Black masculinities and schools: A black feminist response. *British Journal of Sociology of Education* 20 (1): 137-47.
Morrell, R. 1998. Of boys and men: Masculinity and gender in Southern African studies. *Journal of Southern African Studies* 24 (4): 605-30.
Morris, A. D. 1984. *The origins of the civil rights movement: Black communities organizing for change*. New York: Free Press.
Moss, P., and C. Tilly. 1991. Why black men are doing worse in the labor market: A review of supply-side and demand-side explanations. Working Paper, Social Science Research Council, New York.

———. 1996. Soft skills and race: An investigation of black men's employment problems. *Work & Occupations* 23 (3): 252-76.

———. 2001a. *Stories employers tell: Race, skill, and hiring in America*. New York: Russell Sage Foundation.

———. 2001b. Why opportunity isn't knocking: Racial inequality and the demand for labor. In *Urban inequality: Evidence from four cities*, ed. A. O'Connor, C. Tilly, and L. Bobo, 444-95. New York: Russell Sage Foundation.

Oliver, M. L., and T. M. Shapiro. 1997. *Black wealth, white wealth: A new perspective on racial inequality*. New York: Routledge.

Newman, K. 1999. *No shame in my game: The working poor in the inner city*. New York: Vintage.

Pager, D. 2003. The mark of a criminal record. *American Journal of Sociology* 108:937-75.

Pager, D., and L. Quillian. 2005. Walking the talk? What employers say versus what they do. *American Sociological Review* 70 (3): 355-80.

Pattillo, M., D. Weiman, and B. Western, eds. 2004. *Imprisoning America: The social effects of mass incarceration*. New York: Russell Sage Foundation.

Patterson, O. 1999. *Rituals of blood: Consequences of slavery in two American centuries*. Washington, DC: Counterpoint/Civitas.

———. 2006. A poverty of the mind. *New York Times*, March 26.

Perlmann, J. 1988. *Ethnic differences in schooling and social stratification among Irish, Italian, Jews and blacks in an American city, 1880-1935*. Cambridge: Cambridge University Press.

Petersilla, J. 2003. *When prisoners come home: Parole and prisoner reentry*. New York: Oxford University Press.

Pettit, B., and B. Western. 2004. Mass imprisonment and the life course: Race and class inequality in U.S. incarceration. *American Sociological Review* 69:151-69.

Pinderhughes, D. 2005. The renewal of the Voting Rights Act. In *State of black America 2005*. New York: National Urban League.

Quadagno, J. 1994. *The color of welfare: How racism undermined the war on poverty*. Oxford: Oxford University Press.

Robinson, C. J. 1997. *Black movements in America*. New York: Routledge.

Roediger, D. R. 2005. *Working toward whiteness: How America's immigrants became white*. New York: Basic Books.

Rogers, J., and R. Texeira. 2000. *America's forgotten majority: Why the white working class still matters*. New York: Basic Books.

Roscigno, V. J., D. Tomaskovic-Devey, and M. Crowley. 2006. Education and the inequalities of place. *Social Forces* 84 (4): 2121-45.

Rosenbaum, J. 1984. *Career mobility in a corporate hierarchy*. New York: Academic Press.

Royster, D. A. 2003. *Race and the invisible hand: How white networks exclude black men from blue-collar jobs*. Berkeley: University of California Press.

Rubinstein, G., and D. Mukamal. 2002. Welfare and housing—Denial of benefits to drug offenders. In *Invisible punishment: The collateral consequences of mass imprisonment*, ed. M. Mauer and M. Chesney-Lind, 37-49. New York: New Press.

Saint-Aubin, A. F. 1994. Testeria: The dis-ease of black men in white supremacist, patriarchal culture. *Callaloo* 17 (4): 1054-73.

Shapiro, T. 2004. *The hidden cost of being African American: How wealth perpetuates inequality*. Oxford: Oxford University Press.

Shapiro, T., and J. Kenty-Drane. 2005. The racial wealth gap. In *African Americans in the U.S. economy*, ed. C. A. Conrad, J. Whitehead, P. Mason, and J. Stewart, 175-84. Lanham, MD: Rowman & Littlefield.

Smith, S. S. 2005. Don't put my name on it: Social capital activation and job-finding assistance among the black urban poor. *American Journal of Sociology* 111 (1): 1-57.

Sommers, C. 2000. *The war against boys: How misguided feminism is harming young men*. New York: Simon & Schuster.

Steinberg, S. 1995. *Turning back: The retreat from racial justice in American thought and policy*. Boston: Beacon.

———. 2001. *The ethnic myth: Race, ethnicity, and class in America*. Boston: Beacon.
Stoll. M. 2005. The black youth employment problem revisited. In *African Americans in the U.S. economy*, ed. C. A. Conrad, J. Whitehead, P. Mason, and J. Stewart, 294-304. Lanham, MD: Rowman & Littlefield.
Sullivan, M. 1989. *Getting paid: Youth, crime and work in the inner city*. Ithaca, NY: Cornell University Press.
Thompson, G. 2004. *Through ebony eyes: What teachers need to know but are afraid to ask about African American students*. San Francisco: Jossey-Bass.
Tonry, M. 1996. *Malign neglect: Race crime and punishment in America*. Oxford: Oxford University Press.
Travis, J. 2005. *But they all come back: Facing the challenges of prisoner reentry*. New York: Urban Institute Press.
Tushar, K. 2005. *Racial disparity in sentencing: A review of the literature*. The Sentencing Project. www.sentencingproject.org.
Uggen, C., and J. Manza. 2002. Democratic contraction? The political consequences of felon disenfranchisement laws in the United States. *American Sociological Review* 67:777-803.
Uggen, C., J. Manza, and M. Thompson. 2006. Citizenship, democracy, and the civic reintegration of criminal offenders. *Annals of the American Academy of Political and Social Science* 605 (1): 281-310.
Wacquant, L. 2001. Deadly symbiosis: When prison and ghetto meet and mesh. *Punishment and Society* 3:95-134.
Weaver-Hightower, M. 2005. Dare the school build a new education for boys? *Teachers College Record*, February 14. http://www.tcrecord.org, ID number: 11743 (accessed October 10, 2006).
Weiss, L. 1990. *Working class without work: High school students in a deindustrialized economy*. New York: Routledge.
Western, B. 1998. *Does criminal conviction affect employment?* Princeton, NJ: Princeton University.
———. 2006. *Punishment and inequality in America*. New York: Russell Sage Foundation.
Western, B., M. Kleykamp, and J. Rosenfeld. 2006. Did falling wages and employment increase U.S. imprisonment? *Social Forces* 84 (4): 2291-2311.
Western, B., and B. Pettit. 2005. Black-white wage inequality, employment rates, and incarceration. *American Journal of Sociology* 111:553-78.
Whitmire, R. 2006. Boys and books: Boy trouble. *The New Republic*, January 18. http:/www.tnr.com/doc.mhtml?i=20060123&s=whitmire012306&c=2 (accessed October 2, 2006).
Williams, J. 2006. *Enough: The phony leaders, dead-end movements, and culture of failure that are undermining black America—And what we can do about it*. New York: Crown Books.
Willis, P. 1981. *Learning to labor: How working class kids get working class jobs*. New York: Columbia University Press.
Wilson, F. D., M. Tienda, and L. Wu. 1995. Race and unemployment: Labor market experiences of black and white men 1968-1988. *Work & Occupations* 22:245-70.
Wilson, W. J. 1987. *The truly disadvantaged: The inner city, the underclass, and public policy*. Chicago: University of Chicago Press.
———. 1996. *When work disappears: The new world of the urban poor*. New York: Knopf.
Wright, C., D. Weekes, A. McGlaughlin, and D. Webb. 1998. Masculinised discourses within education and the construction of black male identities amongst African Caribbean youth. *British Journal of Sociology of Education* 19 (1): 75-87.
Yamagata, E. P., and M. A. Jones. 2000. *And justice for some: Differential treatment of minority youth in the justice system*. Washington, DC: Building Blocks for Youth.
Young, A. 2003. *The minds of marginalized black men: Making sense of mobility, opportunity and future life chances*. Princeton, NJ: Princeton University Press.

Black Underrepresentation in Management across U.S. Labor Markets

By
PHILIP N. COHEN
and
MATT L. HUFFMAN

Although many researchers have documented higher levels of black-white inequality in areas with a high concentration of blacks, the mechanisms underlying this finding have been elusive. Black underrepresentation in management may be one such mechanism. We ask whether black workers' underrepresentation in managerial jobs is especially pronounced in labor markets with a larger black population. Using a unique, two-level data set that combines a large data set of private sector firms with Census data on local labor markets, the authors' hierarchical logistic models strongly support this hypothesis. Net of establishment and labor market-level controls, the likelihood that an establishment exhibits a significant underrepresentation of blacks in management is substantially increased when it operates in a high-proportion black labor market context.

Keywords: inequality; management; labor markets; underrepresentation

Racial inequality in the labor market has been the subject of a large body of research aimed at identifying how and where such inequality is produced and reproduced. Investigators have probed a diverse set of topics, including the association between residential segregation

Philip N. Cohen is an associate professor of sociology at the University of North Carolina, Chapel Hill, and a fellow at the Carolina Population Center. His research concerns inequality in labor markets and families, including most recently patterns of inequality across U.S. labor markets, the gender division of labor across countries, and the role of disabilities in work and family outcomes for mothers and children.

Matt L. Huffman is an associate professor of sociology at the University of California, Irvine. His current research investigates inequality by gender and race in organizations and labor markets.

NOTE: The authors contributed equally to this article and list their names alphabetically. We thank Bliss Cartwright and Ronald Edwards from the U.S. Equal Employment Opportunity Commission for their assistance with the data and feedback on the entire article. We also thank Barbara Entwisle for her helpful comments and suggestions. Any remaining errors or omissions are entirely our own.

DOI: 10.1177/0002716206296734

and blacks' disadvantage (Massey and Denton 1993), job and occupational segregation (Cotter, Hermsen, and Vanneman 2003; Huffman and Cohen 2004; Reskin and Cassirer 1996; Tomaskovic-Devey 1993), and employer discrimination (see Darity and Mason 1998). Some studies document racial inequality in specific contexts or occupations, or for specific populations (Adler, Koelewijn-Strattner, and Lengermann 1995; Wilson, Sakura-Lemessy, and West 1999; Catanzarite and Aguilera 2002), while others focus on the demographic composition of contextual units—be they jobs or occupations (Huffman and Cohen 2004; Grodsky and Pager 2001; Jacobs and Blair-Loy 1996; Kmec 2003), organizations (Baron and Newman 1990; Tomaskovic-Devey 1993) or labor markets (Beggs 1995; McCall 2001; Cohen 1998; Hirsch and Schumacher 1992).

> *Net of establishment and labor market-level controls, the likelihood that an establishment exhibits a significant underrepresentation of blacks in management is substantially increased when it operates in a high proportion black labor market context.*

Much of this research operates with an implicit or explicit presumption that the mechanisms for producing inequality are to be found in relations and practices within establishments, especially the actions of managers. For example, neighborhood segregation permits employers to practice racial discrimination through geographic exclusion (Wilson 1996), and local racial composition is thought to affect white hostility, which triggers employer (manager) discrimination in hiring and wage setting (Huffman and Cohen 2004). Despite this presumption, however, access to positions of managerial authority is usually analyzed as an *outcome* for those who seek such jobs, rather than as a condition for reproducing inequality for workers in general. Furthermore, little of this research explicitly examines data at the level of the establishment (Tomaskovic-Devey et al. 2006)—a quarter century after Baron and Bielby's (1980) appeal to "bring the firms back in" to studies of inequality. And no existing large-scale studies on racial inequality link actual work establishments to their local labor market contexts.

Our investigation approaches these deficiencies in several ways. First, we focus on access to managerial jobs within work establishments, using data from all large establishments in the United States reporting to the Equal Employment

Opportunity Commission (EEOC) in 2002. Second, we study the labor markets in which establishments operate, which provide an important social context within which practices are carried out—and normalized or contested. If racial labor market inequality indeed results from the actions of managers, then black access to managerial authority may be an important mechanism for producing inequality for all workers.[1] And variation in the pattern of this access across local labor markets can help us understand the dynamics of this process. Thus, we examine whether local labor market features—in particular racial composition—condition the level of access to management for black workers.

Contextual Effects on Inequality

Many studies link population proportion black to black-white inequality in the United States across an array of labor market outcomes (e.g., Beggs 1995; Huffman and Cohen 2004; Cohen 1998, 2001; Semyonov, Hoyt, and Scott 1984; Tienda and Lii 1987). The "competition" or "visibility-discrimination" hypothesis attributes this positive association between racial concentration and inequality to a white response to the threat posed by larger minority group size (Blalock 1967; Burr, Galle, and Fossett 1991; Beggs, Villemez, and Arnold 1997). Additionally, whites have more to gain from discriminating in areas with a higher percentage black (Glenn 1963).

Research on both the behaviors and attitudes of whites supports the visibility-discrimination hypothesis (Burr, Galle, and Fossett 1991). Beyond labor market outcomes, the relationship between black representation and whites' antiblack behaviors has been shown in, for example, lynching and race riots (Reed 1972; Tolnay and Beck 1995; Olzak, Shanahan, and McEneaney 1996; Tolnay, Deane, and Beck 1996), school segregation (Pettigrew 1957), and voting for segregationist candidates (Heer 1959). These studies complement research showing a positive relationship between percentage black in the local population and whites' antiblack attitudes (Fossett and Kiecolt 1989; Taylor 1998) and evidence of greater white opposition to government policies that alleviate racial inequality, such as busing (Quillian 1996; Olzak, Shanahan, and West 1994). Because the black composition of most areas in the United States does not change dramatically from decade to decade, these effects may produce long-lasting results through the stable association between race and job composition, the legacy of political structures, corporate culture, and so on.

On the other hand, a queuing or "overflow" mechanism suggests that, where there are more black workers in the labor market, their absolute presence should increase in higher-status positions—or at least those of middling status—as positions at the bottom of the labor market hierarchy (or queue) are filled (Lieberson 1980; Tienda and Lii 1987). In fact, residential and school segregation may actually enhance opportunities for potential black managers, by creating more demand for their work. However, as Semyonov, Hoyt, and Scott (1984) demonstrated, the competition and queuing processes are not mutually exclusive, and even where a larger number of black workers occupy better jobs, this does not imply increased *odds* of attaining higher-status positions for individual black workers—they may in fact suffer greater discrimination *and* greater absolute presence in higher-status jobs. Put another way, suitable for our purposes here, underrepresentation depends on the relevant pool of available labor. For example, if the managerial workforce is 6 percent black in one city and 20 percent black in another, the latter market might in fact reflect greater underrepresentation if its relevant pool of black workers is larger.

Although research strongly suggests that the white racism associated with black population size produces and sustains labor market inequality, we do not know exactly how this translates into labor market inequality. Unfortunately, most available data sets and research designs are of little help, as they do not permit us to pinpoint the mechanisms at work (Reskin 2003). Nevertheless, there is suggestive evidence. In our earlier work (Huffman and Cohen 2004) we tested whether the positive association between black-white wage inequality and the percentage black in the local population is driven more by job segregation than by a wage penalty associated with black-dominated jobs. We found that segregation is the more likely mechanism. However, that study lacked data on actual work establishments—we constructed "jobs" from local occupation-industry cells. Even narrowing the mechanism down to either job segregation or composition penalties does not solve the question of whose action is responsible, although employers—and the managers who may act on their behalf—are the presumptive suspects. The identity of managers is thus of central importance.

Access to Managerial Authority

Compared to nonmanagers, managers typically enjoy more prestige, job autonomy, authority, and earnings (Reskin and McBrier 2000; Jacobs 1992). Inequality research has therefore treated managerial jobs as scarce resources that are unequally distributed and contested. Most of this research has centered on women's access to management, often with a focus on organizational demography (Blau 1977; Kanter 1977; Pfeffer 1983), and the positive effect of female representation in lower levels of the hierarchy on the representation of women in management (Blum, Fields, and Goodman 1994; Huffman 1999; Reskin and McBrier 2000).

Research on race/ethnic inequality in management is less common, but such bottom-up pressure has been found with regard to race/ethnicity as well (Elliott and Smith 2001; Shenhav and Haberfeld 1992; Stainback and Tomaskovic-Devey 2006). On the other hand, increasing representation among subordinate groups may heighten majority resistance and the tendency to discriminate (Jacobs 1992; Pfeffer and Davis-Blake 1987). Previous research also suggests management is better integrated in larger establishments, either because of the need for legitimacy associated with greater visibility (Scott 1992; Stainback and Tomaskovic-Devey 2006; Tomaskovic-Devey 1993), or as a result of formalized personnel decisions (Reskin and McBrier 2000; Szafran 1982). Finally, some industrial niches also are more integrated (Baron, Jennings, and Dobbin 1988).

Recent research has begun to address more systematically the access by women and race/ethnic minority group members to managerial positions, using data now available from the EEOC, and we benefit from this development (Tomaskovic-Devey et al. 2006). However, studies have not yet fully taken advantage of the geographic variation in patterns of underrepresentation apparent in the data. Thus, for example, although Stainback and Tomaskovic-Devey (2006) found minority managerial representation is greater in establishments with more minority workers, they did not control for local population composition, which might drive this association. We address that question in this article. On the other hand, existing research using EEOC data, as well as this article, are limited by the inability to distinguish between levels of managerial authority or rewards to managers. For example, we cannot test whether it is beneficial to have black managers in higher-level management positions, as has been postulated for women (Cohen and Huffman 2006).

Research Agenda

We investigate the long-standing finding of greater inequality in high percentage black labor markets by testing the relationship between black underrepresentation in managerial jobs and local population percentage black. The direct examination of managerial jobs is a significant innovation in this area of research. Although previous research has examined overall job segregation (e.g., Huffman and Cohen 2004), and relative access to broad occupational categories (e.g., Semyonov, Hoyt, and Scott 1984), there is no test of this association that measures black representation in managerial jobs at the level of actual work establishments.

We also benefit from research on methods for measuring discrimination and underrepresentation that have been developed for employment discrimination litigation (Bendick 2000; Gastwirth 1984, 1992). Although we are not engaged in identifying discrimination in a legal sense, or directly analyzing the hiring or promotion practices of establishments, we are able to take advantage of several innovations from that research to refine our questions here. First, rather than simply measuring the proportionate representation of black managers, we pay careful attention to the relevant labor pool to construct measures of underrepresentation. Second, we measure underrepresentation using a statistical test of the difference between establishments' managerial composition and that of the relevant labor pool. We describe each of these innovations in turn.

Labor pools

We explore large establishments' black managerial composition in the private sector workforce relative to four populations or labor pools. First, we compare managerial representation to the composition of the *entire local workforce*.[2] This is the broadest measure and represents the endpoint of many processes, including local access to education, work experience, and access to other kinds of jobs. Previous research has shown that the black population composition effect is substantially mediated by such premarket factors (Cohen 1998). This measure is thus the least directly linked to the concept of employer discrimination but rather simply identifies workplaces in which the authority structure is out of balance with the racial composition of the local workforce, which may be an important determinant of managerial decision making.[3] Using our measure, 19 percent of establishments—employing 32 percent of black workers—have an underrepresentation of blacks in management relative to this pool.

Second, we compare managerial representation to the composition of *managers in the local workforce*. For managerial positions that require skills that are broadly applicable across industrial settings, such as human resource managers, establishments may hire from a pool of all local workers with managerial experience. Even if they hire instead from a pool of workers just entering management, they presumably compete with local companies hiring similarly qualified managers. In either case a lower proportion black among managers in the establishment might reflect hiring discrimination. We find that 4 percent of establishments with 6 percent of black workers have black underrepresentation based on this availability pool.

Other managerial positions demand more specialized skills or experience, such as engineering managers. For such jobs the relevant pool of available workers is narrower than the entire population of local managers. Thus, our third measure compares managerial representation to the composition of *managers in the same industry of the local workforce*—which we refer to as the local industry. Because our indicator of management jobs is very broad, we cannot distinguish between types of manager or levels of authority, as is possible with more detailed occupational data (Cohen and Huffman 2006). We believe detailed industrial identification will help differentiate these cases. Based on this pool, approximately 3 percent of establishments with 4 percent of all black workers have an underrepresentation of black workers in management jobs.

Finally, we compare managerial representation to the composition of *all workers within the establishment*. Clearly, some managerial positions cannot be filled from the lower ranks within an organization. For example, accounting managers are not likely to be hired from among the pool of mechanics in an auto dealership. However, consistent evidence shows that the composition of the nonmanagerial workforce is associated with both the race/ethnicity and gender of those in positions of authority (Smith 2002; Stainback and Tomaskovic-Devey 2006). We note that similar to our first indicator, this measure is not directly linked to the concept of employer discrimination. Regardless of whether the outcome represents discrimination in the hiring of managers, however, this indicator of racial disparity in internal authority structure—with managers who are not black managing black workers—might be a mechanism for the production of racial wage gaps. We find that approximately 13 percent of the establishments in our data set have a significant deficiency of black workers in management using this pool for comparison. However, because of interfirm segregation, these establishments employ more than half—53 percent—of all black workers.

We are particularly interested in whether these outcomes vary across labor markets as a function of population racial composition. If establishments in labor markets with greater black concentration are more likely to exhibit black underrepresentation in management—at any of these levels—that may help explain the persistent finding that racial wage disparities are greater in such labor markets. This finding would complement those we previsouly reported (Huffman and Cohen 2004) by demonstrating another mechanism through which black population concentration magnifies labor market inequality.

Underrepresentation

Our second innovation is to use measures of underrepresentation drawn from discrimination litigation analysis. We determine whether each establishment has significantly fewer black managers than would be reasonably expected given their availability in the relevant labor pool and the number of managers in the firm. We use a binomial test common in statistical approaches to employment discrimination to classify each establishment in terms of how its employment of black managers compares to the racial composition of the establishment's availability pool (see Bendick 2000; Gastwirth 1984; Finkelstein and Levin 2001). The test statistic is based on the discrepancy between the number of managers in an establishment who are black and the expected number given random selection and the racial composition of the available labor pool. This discrepancy, when divided by the standard deviation of the expected number of black managers, approximates a standard normal random variable. Therefore, it can be assigned a p-value that can be used to determine whether an establishment's representation of black managers is below what one would reasonably expect to occur by chance (Bendick 2000; Gastwirth 1984). We use a 5 percent cutoff (one-tailed) to identify which establishments have a statistically significant underrepresentation of black workers in managerial positions.[4] Establishments are assigned scores on a dichotomous indicator for each of the four labor pools if they surpass the cutoff point. These indicators are the dependent variables in our multivariate models.[5]

Data and Method

Data

Our analyses are based on establishment-level data on U.S. private sector firms from the EEOC for the year 2002. As part of its efforts to gauge compliance with equal employment legislation, the EEOC has collected data on the sex and racial/ethnic composition of private sector employment since the mid-1960s. These data include employment counts by race and sex across nine occupational categories: officials and managers, professionals, technicians, sales workers, office and clerical workers, craft workers, operatives, laborers, and service workers.[6] The EEOC data also include geographic identifiers, allowing us to link establishments to U.S. metropolitan areas (MAs) using data from the U.S. Census Bureau's Summary Files, which we use to define local labor markets.[7] Other strengths and weakness of using the EEO reports to study race and gender segregation are discussed in Robinson et al. (2005) and Tomaskovic-Devey et al. (2006). We include only those establishments with ten or more workers in our analysis.[8] This restriction leaves 171,780 establishments with complete information.[9]

Measures

Our variables are measured at two levels: establishments and MAs. At the establishment level, dependent variables are dummy variable indicators of statistically significant ($p < .05$) black managerial underrepresentation relative to the four labor pools discussed above.[10] At the MA level, our primary independent variable is the adult population proportion black.

Control variables at the establishment level include the natural logarithm of the *total establishment size*, the *proportion female* and *proportion black* in each establishment, and the *proportion of workers in establishment who are managers*. The proportion of workers in management has been used to measure the demand for managers in other research predicting the demographic composition of management positions (see Reskin and McBrier 2000). Finally, we control for systematic differences across broad industry categories by using nineteen dummy variables, each corresponding to a two-digit North American Industrial Classification (NAICS) industry category.[11]

At the MA level, we include several key control variables in addition to our key independent variable, percentage black. These controls include *percentage Latino*, the *log of population size*, the *unemployment rate*, the *percentage of workers employed in public sector*, the *percentage in-migration*, and the *percentage in manufacturing*. These are similar to those used in other research on labor market variation in black-white inequality (Huffman and Cohen 2004). Descriptive statistics for all variables appear in Table 1.

Statistical models

Our data comprise establishments nested within local labor markets; as such, establishments in our data set share values on all local labor market variables. Because of this nested structure, we estimate two-level hierarchical logistic models (Guo and Zhao 2000; Raudenbush and Bryk 2002; DiPrete and Forristal 1994).[12] Hierarchical models allow simultaneous estimation of micro- and macro-level equations. In our analysis, the micro-level model is estimated at the establishment level, while the macro-level model is estimated at the level of the labor market. Because our outcome variables are dichotomous (coded 1 if the establishment has an underrepresentation of blacks in management), we model them as probabilities using a logit link function (Raudenbush and Bryk 2002, 294-301; Guo and Zhao 2000).[13]

TABLE 1
DESCRIPTIVE STATISTICS FOR VARIABLES USED IN THE ANALYSIS

	Mean	SD	Range
Establishment-level variables ($N = 171{,}780$)			
Underrepresentation: All workers in metropolitan area (MA)	0.19	0.39	0.00-1.00
Underrepresentation: All managers in MA	0.04	0.20	0.00-1.00
Underrepresentation: All managers in MA industry	0.03	0.17	0.00-1.00
Underrepresentation: All workers in establishment	0.13	0.34	0.00-1.00
Proportion managers in establishment	0.12	0.11	0.00-1.00
Proportion black in establishment	0.14	0.17	0.00-1.00
Proportion female in establishment	0.46	0.24	0.00-1.00
Log of establishment size	4.86	0.86	2.30-10.39
MA-level variables ($N = 275$)			
Percentage black (18+)	10.03	10.31	0.20-47.73
Percentage Latino (18+)	8.12	13.65	0.44-93.60
Log of population size	12.75	1.12	10.97-16.87
Unemployment rate	5.87	1.76	2.64-13.09
Percentage in public sector	15.64	4.98	6.60-36.10
Percentage in-migration	27.90	3.44	16.99-35.62
Percentage in manufacturing	13.98	6.75	2.02-42.56

Specifically, if p_{ij} is the probability that establishment i in labor market j has a statistically significant ($p < .05$) underrepresentation of blacks in management, our establishment-level model can be expressed as

$$\text{Log}[p_{ij}/(1 - p_{ij})] = \beta_{0j} + \beta_{10}X_{1ij} + \beta_{20}X_{2ij} + \ldots + \beta_{k0}X_{kij},$$

where β_{0j} is the intercept of the establishment-level model, and the coefficients β_{10} through β_{k0} represent the net effects of the k establishment-level predictors (which include eighteen industry dummy variables). All of our establishment-level predictors except for proportion black are centered around their grand means (see Raudenbush and Bryk 2002).

Thus, the intercept (β_0) can be interpreted as the predicted log odds that an establishment with average characteristics on the establishment-level variables exhibits black managerial underrepresentation. At the labor market level, then, we are interested in predicting variation in the intercept of the establishment-level model: whether local labor market black population composition is associated with the odds of statistically significant black managerial underrepresentation. Here, our key independent variable is the proportion black in the local labor market. Our MA-level model is

$$\beta_{0j} = \gamma_{00} + \gamma_{01}W_{1j} + \ldots + \gamma_{0q}W_{qj} + u_{0j},$$

TABLE 2
CORRELATION BETWEEN UNDERREPRESENTATION INDICATORS

Indicator of Underrepresentation	1	2	3
1. Relative to all workers in metropolitan area (MA)	—		
2. Relative to all managers in MA	.07	—	
3. Relative to all managers in MA-industry	.05	.46	—
4. Relative to all workers in establishment	.31	.05	.04

NOTE: All correlations significant at $p < .001$ (two-tailed tests).

where γ_{00} is the intercept of the MA-level model, and γ_{01} through γ_{0q} are the net effects of the q MA-level variables. At the MA level, proportion black is our key predictor. If the coefficient for this variable is significant and positive, it suggests that net of our establishment and labor-market controls, establishments operating in labor markets with higher proportion black populations have a higher likelihood of an underrepresentation of blacks in management than those in other comparable labor markets with lower black population concentrations. The final term in our MA-level model (u_{0j}) is assumed to be a normally distributed random variable with mean 0 and variance τ_{00}. All MA-level variables are centered at their grand means except population percentage black.

Results

As noted above, underrepresentation relative to the pool of nonmanagerial workers is much more common than that relative to the pool of managers. In other words, black workers are underrepresented in management *generally* relative to their numbers in the workforce, whether measured at the establishment or labor market levels. Significant underrepresentation relative to the pool of managers in the local industry or local labor market is less common, because underrepresentation is systematic rather than concentrated among a few establishments. This pattern is further seen in Table 2, which shows the correlations between establishments on the underrepresentation variables. Here we see high correlations between the worker-pool indicators (.31) and between the manager-pool indicators (.46), but lower correlations across these levels of comparison (all are highly significant).

The EEOC data set represents individual establishments as data points regardless of their size. Thus, large corporations and small establishments count equally toward the means in Table 1, the bivariate correlations in Table 2, and the regression results to follow. This is appropriate if one considers each establishment a site for decision making. Nevertheless, because of the counts of workers provided in the data, it is possible to determine how many workers are found in establishments with various qualities. As noted above, interfirm segregation

TABLE 3
BLACK UNDERREPRESENTATION IN MANAGEMENT:
HIERARCHICAL LINEAR REGRESSION RESULTS

Dependent Variable	Y_1 Coefficient	Y_2 Coefficient	Y_3 Coefficient	Y_4 Coefficient
Metropolitan area (MA) variables				
Intercept	−6.476°°°	−5.817°°°	−6.383°°°	−5.344°°°
MA proportion black	0.332°°°	0.111°°°	0.112°°°	0.078°°°
MA proportion Latino	−0.011	−0.002	−0.011	−0.013°
Log of population size	0.324°°	0.329°°°	0.453°°°	0.207°°°
Unemployment rate	−0.118	−0.044	−0.016	−0.099°
Percentage manufacturing	−0.033°	−0.011	−0.022	−0.003
Percentage public sector	−0.047°	−0.030°	−0.030	−0.022
Establishment variables				
Proportion black	−9.766°°°	0.095	−0.066	7.177°°°
Proportion female	−0.214°°°	0.021	0.085	−0.099
Proportion managers	12.520°°°	0.248°	0.200	5.500°°°
Log of establishment size	2.077°°°	0.026	0.003	1.430°°°
Variance components				
Intercept (τ_{00})	1.579°°°	0.270°°°	0.517°°°	0.401°°°
Chi-square (267 df)	10,950	930	1,235	3,532

NOTE: All models include controls for industry (eighteen dummy variables—see text for industry definitions). Dependent variable definitions: Y_1 = underrepresentation relative to all workers in MA. Y_2 = underrepresentation relative to all managers in MA. Y_3 = underrepresentation relative to all managers in MA industry. Y_4 = underrepresentation relative to all workers in the establishment.
°$p < .05$. °°$p < .01$. °°°$p < .001$ (two-tailed tests).

means that black workers are concentrated in a disproportionately small number of firms—the average black worker in the data works at an establishment that is 33 percent black, even though the average establishment is only 14 percent black. This distinction is most significant with regard to underrepresentation relative to the worker pools. We will return to this issue later in the discussion.

What kinds of firms exhibit underrepresentation?

The hierarchical logistic regression models for our underrepresentation outcomes are shown in Table 3. The top part of the upper panel shows effects of labor market (MA) characteristics on the log odds of black managerial underrepresentation, and the bottom part shows the establishment-level effects. The lower panel shows variance components for the intercepts, which are the only coefficients in the models permitted to vary across labor markets. Overall, the establishment-level model appears to explain underrepresentation for the worker pools (first and fourth models) better than it does for the manager pools (second and third models).

Establishments with more black workers are less likely to show managerial underrepresentation relative to all workers in the labor market, reflecting the tendency of black managers to lead black workers; but these firms are more likely to show underrepresentation relative to their own workforces, reflecting racial hierarchies within the firms. This is consistent with previous findings that black workers are concentrated under black managers (Stainback and Tomaskovic-Devey 2006) but further shows that even this concentration of managers is more likely to reflect underrepresentation *relative to the pool of workers below*. Surprisingly, establishments with more managers and larger establishments are more likely to show significant managerial underrepresentation. This differs from the findings of Stainback and Tomaskovic-Devey (2006), because they analyzed percentage-minority as their outcome, while we measure statistical underrepresentation—which is mathematically more likely to occur in larger establishments. None of the establishment-level variables are significantly associated with underrepresentation relative to the managerial pool in the local industry (Y_3), which is commonly used as the benchmark in antidiscrimination lawsuits (Bendick 2000).

Our principal concern is the association of MA population proportion black and managerial underrepresentation, and here the regression results in Table 2 are clear: on all four measures, black managerial underrepresentation is predicted to be more likely in local labor markets with a greater concentration of black residents. The size of the net effect of black labor market concentration is substantial in all four models. In an odds ratio metric, the coefficients on MA proportion black range from 1.08 ($e^{0.078} = 1.08$) in the model predicting Y_4, to 1.39 ($e^{0.332} = 1.39$) in the model predicting Y_1. In percentage terms, establishments at the mean of all firm and labor market characteristics are predicted to show underrepresentation relative to managers in the local industry in just 0.5 percent of cases in labor markets that are 10 percent black. But in markets that are 30 percent black that prediction is more than nine times greater, 4.7 percent. At the high end of the range, more than 45 percent black, predicted probabilities of underrepresentation are greater than 50 percent for all indicators except that for establishment workforce composition.

Taken together, our results are consistent with an interpretation of black-white wage inequality in which inequality results from the actions of managers and black managers are less likely to contribute to such inequality. If that is the case, the patterns uncovered here would reflect an important mechanism for the common finding that greater wage inequality is observed where black population concentration is higher.[14]

Discussion and Conclusion

Our primary goal in this article was to investigate the long-standing finding of greater inequality in high proportion black labor markets by subjecting the relationship between black representation in managerial jobs and local population composition to close empirical scrutiny. In doing so, we explore possible mechanisms underlying this relationship. Although a large body of previous research documents the overall relationship, virtually none of that research uncovers the mechanisms that may account for it. We consider our research an important step in that direction.

As such, the current research complements our earlier work (Huffman and Cohen 2004), which found that local black population concentration was positively associated with black-white job-level segregation. Our main substantive conclusion—that proportion black in the local labor market significantly increases the odds that black workers will be underrepresented in managerial roles—is consistent with the presumption that managerial action contributes to racial inequality, and that access to management may affect the patterns of such action across labor markets.

Our main substantive conclusion is that proportion black in the local labor market significantly increases the odds that black workers will be underrepresented in managerial roles.

We stress that this conclusion is important even if population composition is not in fact the causal variable driving managerial underrepresentation. Whatever the reason for the association, it may be responsible for the population composition effect on wage inequality and job segregation that has so often been observed (Tienda and Lii 1987; Cohen 1998; Huffman and Cohen 2004). We illustrate this point with Figure 1, which shows the proportion of black *workers* found in establishments with black underrepresentation in management on each of the four measures, across the thirty-nine metropolitan areas that have one thousand establishments or more in the data set, with no statistical controls. Clearly, black workers are more likely to find themselves concentrated under the authority of nonrepresentative management structures in labor markets with larger black populations. If such manager pools are more likely to make hiring, promotion, firing, and wage decisions that disadvantage black workers, then we would expect more black-white inequality in these markets. The association between managerial composition and wage inequality at the labor market level remains to be examined in future work.

FIGURE 1
METROPOLITAN AREA (MA) POPULATION PERCENTAGE BLACK AND PROPORTION OF BLACK WORKERS IN UNDERREPRESENTED ESTABLISHMENTS

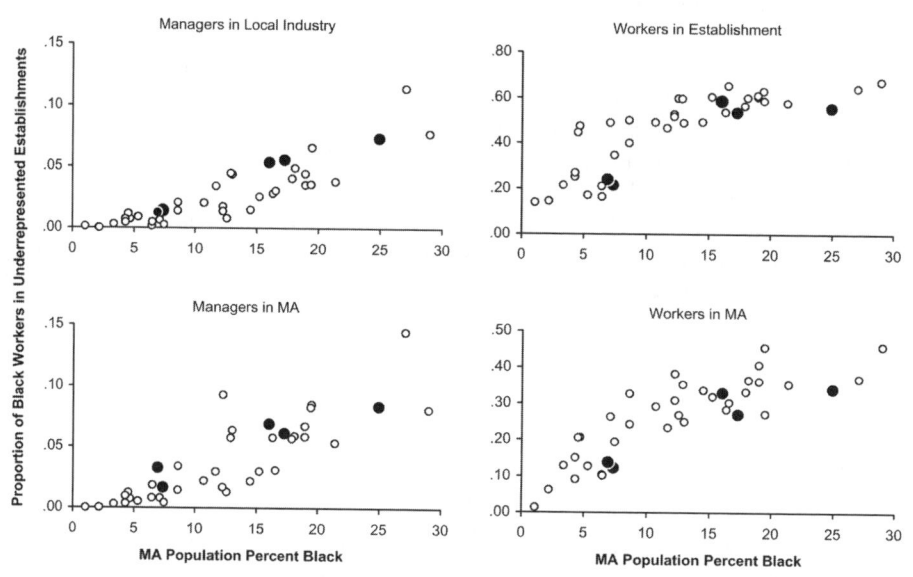

NOTE: Thirty-nine MAs with one thousand or more establishments. The five largest MAs are highlighted: New York, Los Angeles, Chicago, Washington, D.C., and San Francisco.

This finding also is important for other theoretical questions. For example, a queuing perspective, which predicts an increase in blacks' presence in higher-status positions when there are more black workers in the labor market, is unsupported by our findings. Even if there are more black managers where their population is relatively large, we find strong evidence that the *odds* of their underrepresentation are much higher when local proportion black is higher. Thus, even though black workers may have a greater absolute presence in higher-status jobs in high proportion black areas, they may in fact be subject to increased discrimination in such a context, resulting in stronger race-based social closure processes (Tomaskovic-Devey 1993) and overall lower odds of attaining managerial positions. This is where our explicit focus on the available labor pool—largely unique to this research—becomes critical.

We also note several provocative findings regarding the relationship between establishment characteristics and the likelihood of observing an underrepresentation of black workers in management. For example, establishments with a larger percentage of black workers are more likely to exhibit managerial representation that approximates the pool of all workers in the local labor market. This could result from "bottom up ascription," the tendency for black managers to manage black workers (Stainback and Tomaskovic-Devey 2006). At the same time, these establishments are more likely to show underrepresentation relative to their own workforces, reflecting greater internal racial hierarchies, the nature or causes of which we are not able to ascertain from this analysis. Additionally, large establishments, and those with a larger percentage of managers, are more likely to show managerial underrepresentation on three of our four measures. Although they were not our central focus, these establishment-level effects clearly beg for more theoretical and empirical attention—we hope that our results spur future research in those directions.

> *Clearly, black workers are more likely to find themselves concentrated under the authority of nonrepresentative management structures in labor markets with larger black populations.*

Although we make important substantive, theoretical, and methodological contributions to the literature, our analysis is not without limitations. First, although the EEOC data are exceptional in terms of sample size and coverage of the U.S. private sector work force, they do not provide all relevant establishment-level information. For example, we have no information about establishments' personnel practices, recruitment methods, or level of formalization, all of which could be important for predicting the composition of an establishment's managerial workforce (e.g., Huffman 1999; Reskin and McBrier 2000). In addition, the EEOC data do not allow us to distinguish between levels of managerial authority or the rewards that may accrue to managers (Cohen and Huffman 2006). However, it should be noted that EEOC definition of managers includes low-level managers; as such, our results regarding the relationship between local proportion black and underrepresentation might be even stronger if the definition included only upper-level managers.

Notes

1. This assumes black managers have both the motivation and the power to discriminate less against black workers than do other managers, which also has been the subject of a very limited collection of studies (Elliott and Smith 2004; Shenhav and Haberfeld 1992; Smith 2002).

2. We use the term "local workforce" to refer to workers in large private sector establishments, those required to report the race/ethnic and gender composition of their employees to the Equal Employment Opportunity Commission (EEOC). In contrast, we measure the local population using Census data, which include all people in the metropolitan area.

3. Note that in the case of race, much more than in the case of gender (e.g., Stainback and Tomaskovic-Devey 2006) the composition of the local labor market is a more relevant benchmark than that of the national population. Overall, of course, we expect there to be greater representation of black workers among managers in labor markets with higher concentrations of black population.

4. The one-tailed test is suitable because we are only testing for black underrepresentation, not overrepresentation; our concern is with the probability that a *lower* than expected number of black managers is likely to have occurred by chance.

5. The applicability of such indicators in employment discrimination litigation hinges crucially on the identification of the relevant labor pool from which employers are determined to be hiring or promoting. Thus, all workers in the labor market or establishment are unlikely to be used as benchmarks in legal cases. However, from the point of view of social inequality—not limited to the question of discriminatory culpability on the part of particular managers—these indicators clearly are important. An alternative approach is to count the workers in a given reference pool (e.g., the establishment, industry, or local industry) who are and are not in management positions, and calculate the relative odds that black versus white workers hold management positions. These odds ratios can be compared across firms or industries to identify those with greater or lesser racial inequalities (see U.S. EEOC 2006).

6. One shortcoming of the EEOC data is that they include race-sex distributions for specific workplaces at the aggregate level of major occupational groups (e.g., managers, professionals, technicians, etc.). However, Robinson et al. (2005) have shown that estimates based on the EEOC data are generally reliable and valid.

7. We use CMSAs (consolidated metropolitan statistical areas). Where applicable, we use NECMAs (New England consolidated metropolitan areas).

8. Of the establishments included in our analysis, approximately 3 percent have fewer than fifty employees. Because the EEO-1 reporting requirements apply to establishments with fifty or more employees, the 3 percent with fewer than fifty are normally headquarters facilities. Because these facilities also employ managers, we include them.

9. The original 2002 EEO file contains 225,541 records. Of the cases not used in our analysis, approximately 96 percent were excluded because they were either outside metropolitan areas (MAs) or aggregate reports for multiestablishment companies. The remaining 4 percent comprised establishments with fewer than ten employees and six establishments we deleted that were coded as pubic sector.

10. We note that our use of dichotomous variable indicators increases interpretability of the outcome at the expense of lost details on the extent of underrepresentation, which could be the subject of additional analysis (see Gastwirth and Greenhouse 1987).

11. The industries are (1) Agriculture, Forestry, Fishing and Hunting; (2) Mining; (3) Utilities; (4) Construction; (5) Manufacturing; (6) Wholesale Trade; (7) Retail Trade; (8) Transportation and Warehousing; (9) Information; (10) Finance and Insurance; (11) Real Estate and Rental and Leasing; (12) Professional, Scientific, and Technical Services; (13) Management of Companies and Enterprises; (14) Administrative and Support and Waste Management and Remediation Services; (15) Educational Services; (16) Health Care and Social Assistance; (17) Arts, Entertainment, and Recreation; (18) Accommodation and Food Services; and (19) Other Services (except Public Administration).

12. The models were estimated using the HLM software package (v. 6.0).

13. For reasons outlined by Raudenbush and Bryk (2002, 303-4), we report results from unit-specific models rather than population-average models. In our case, the two sets of results are substantively similar.

14. Because of how our measures of underrepresentation are constructed, some establishments with very few managers have no chance of showing underrepresentation. To address this, we reestimated our models including only those establishments ($N = 88,525$) with ten or more managers. The results—especially our key finding regarding the effect of labor market percentage black—are substantively similar to the results we present here.

References

Adler, Marina A., Gijsberta J. Koelewijn-Strattner, and Joseph J. Lengermann. 1995. The intersection of race and gender among chemists: Assessing the impact of double minority status on income. *Sociological Focus* 28 (3): 245-59.

Baron, James N., and William T. Bielby. 1980. Bringing the firms back in: Stratification, segmentation, and the organization of work. *American Sociological Review* 45:737-65.

Baron, James N., P. D. Jennings, and Frank R. Dobbin. 1988. Mission control? The development of personnel systems in U.S. industry. *American Sociological Review* 53:497-514.

Baron, James N., and Andrew E. Newman. 1990. For what it's worth—Organizations, occupations, and the value of work done by women and nonwhites. *American Sociological Review* 55 (2): 155-75.

Beggs, John J. 1995. The institutional environment: Implications for race and gender inequality in the U.S. labor market. *American Sociological Review* 60:612-33.

Beggs, John J., Wayne J. Villemez, and Ruth Arnold. 1997. Black population concentration and black-white inequality: Expanding the consideration of place and space effects. *Social Forces* 76:65-91.

Bendick, Marc, Jr. 2000. Using EEO-1 data to investigate claims of employment discrimination. Paper Presented to the American Bar Association, July 10, New York.

Blalock, Hubert M. 1967. *Toward a theory of minority group relations*. New York: Wiley.

Blau, Peter M. 1977. *Inequality and heterogeneity*. New York: Free Press.

Blum, Terry C., Dail L. Fields, and Jodi S. Goodman. 1994. Organization-level determinants of women in management. *Academy of Management Journal* 37 (2): 241-68.

Burr, Jeffery A., Omer R. Galle, and Mark A. Fossett. 1991. Racial occupational inequality in southern metropolitan areas: 1940-1980: Revisiting the visibility-discrimination hypothesis. *Social Forces* 69:831-50.

Catanzarite, Lisa, and Michael B. Aguilera. 2002. Working with co-ethnics: Earnings penalties for Latino immigrants at Latino jobsites. *Social Problems* 49 (1): 101-27.

Cohen, Philip N. 1998. Black concentration effects on black-white and gender inequality: Multilevel analysis for U.S. metropolitan areas. *Social Forces* 77 (1): 207-29.

———. 2001. Race, class, and labor markets: The white working class and racial composition of U.S. metropolitan areas. *Social Science Research* 30:146-69.

Cohen, Philip N., and Matt L. Huffman. 2006. Working for the woman? Female managers and the gender wage gap. Manuscript, University of North Carolina, Chapel Hill; and University of California, Irvine.

Cotter, David A., Joan M. Hermsen, and Reeve Vanneman. 2003. The effects of occupational segregation across race. *Sociological Quarterly* 44:17-36.

Darity, William A., and Patrick L. Mason. 1998. Evidence on discrimination in employment: Codes of color, codes of gender. *Journal of Economic Perspectives* 12 (2): 63-90.

DiPrete, Thomas A., and Jerry D. Forristal. 1994. Multilevel models: Methods and substance. *Annual Review of Sociology* 20:331-57.

Elliott, James R., and Ryan A. Smith. 2001. Ethnic matching of supervisors to subordinate work groups: Findings on "bottom-up" ascription and social closure. *Social Problems* 48:258-76.

———. 2004. Race, gender, and workplace power. *American Sociological Review* 69:365-86.

Finkelstein, Michael O., and Bruce Levin. 2001. *Statistics for lawyers*. New York: Springer.

Fossett, Mark A., and K. Jill Kiecolt. 1989. The relative size of minority populations and white racial attitudes. *Social Science Quarterly* 70:820-35.

Gastwirth, Joseph L. 1984. Statistical methods for analyzing claims of employment discrimination. *Industrial and Labor Relations Review* 38:75-86.

———. 1992. Statistical reasoning in the legal setting. *American Statistician* 46 (1): 55-69.

Gastwirth, Joseph L., and Samuel W. Greenhouse. 1987. Estimating a common relative risk: Applications in equal employment. *Journal of the American Statistical Association* 82:38-45.

Glenn, Norval D. 1963. Occupational benefits to whites from the subordination of Negroes. *American Sociological Review* 28:443-48.

Grodsky, Eric, and Devah Pager. 2001. The structure of disadvantage: Individual and occupational determinants of the black-white wage gap. *American Sociological Review* 66:542-67.

Guo, Guang, and Hongxin Zhao. 2000. Multilevel modeling for binary data. *Annual Review of Sociology* 26:441-62.

Heer, David M. 1959. The sentiment of white supremacy: An ecological study. *American Journal of Sociology* 64 (6): 592-98.

Hirsch, Barry T., and Edward J. Schumacher. 1992. Labor earnings, discrimination, and the racial composition of jobs. *Journal of Human Resources* 27:602-28.

Huffman, Matt L. 1999. Who's in charge? Organizational influences on women's representation in managerial positions. *Social Science Quarterly* 80 (4): 738-56.
Huffman, Matt L., and Philip N. Cohen. 2004. Racial wage inequality: Job segregation and devaluation across U.S. labor markets. *American Journal of Sociology* 109 (4): 902-36.
Jacobs, Jerry A. 1992. Women's entry into management—Trends in earnings, authority and values among salaried managers. *Administrative Science Quarterly* 37 (2): 282-301.
Jacobs, Jerry A., and Mary Blair-Loy. 1996. Race, gender, local labor markets and occupational devaluation. *Sociological Focus* 29:209-30.
Kanter, Rosabeth M. 1977. *Men and women of the corporation*. New York: Basic Books.
Kmec, Julie A. 2003. Minority job composition and wages. *Social Problems* 50 (1): 38-59.
Lieberson, Stanley. 1980. *A piece of the pie: Blacks and white immigrants since 1880*. Berkeley: University of California Press.
Massey, Douglas S., and Nancy A. Denton. 1993. *American apartheid: Segregation and the making of the underclass*. Cambridge, MA: Harvard University Press.
McCall, Leslie. 2001. Sources of racial wage inequality in metropolitan labor markets: Racial, ethnic, and gender differences. *American Sociological Review* 66 (4): 520-41.
Olzak, Susan, Suzanne Shanahan, and Elizabeth H. McEneaney. 1996. Poverty, segregation, and race riots: 1960 to 1993. *American Sociological Review* 61 (4): 590-613.
Olzak, Susan, Suzanne Shanahan, and Elizabeth West. 1994. School desegregation, interracial exposure, and antibusing activity in contemporary urban America. *American Journal of Sociology* 100:196-241.
Pettigrew, Thomas F. 1957. Demographic correlates of border-state desegregation. *American Sociological Review* 22 (6): 683-89.
Pfeffer, Jeffery. 1983. Organizational demography. In *Research in organizational behavior*, ed. Larry L. Cummings and Barry M. Staw, 299-359. Greenwich, CT: JAI.
Pfeffer, Jeffery, and Alison Davis-Blake. 1987. The effect of the proportion of women on salaries: The case of college administrators. *Administrative Science Quarterly* 32:1-24.
Quillian, Lincoln. 1996. Group threat and regional change in attitudes toward African Americans. *American Journal of Sociology* 102:816-60.
Raudenbush, Stephen W., and Anthony S. Bryk. 2002. *Hierarchical linear models: Applications and data analysis methods*. 2nd ed. Thousand Oaks, CA: Sage.
Reed, John S. 1972. Percent black and lynching: A test of Blalock's theory. *Social Forces* 50 (3): 356-60.
Reskin, Barbara F. 2003. Including mechanisms in our models of ascriptive inequality. *American Sociological Review* 68 (1): 1-21.
Reskin, Barbara, and Naomi Cassirer. 1996. Occupational segregation by gender, race and ethnicity. *Sociological Focus* 29 (3): 231-43.
Reskin, Barbara F., and Debra B. McBrier. 2000. Why not ascription? Organizations' employment of male and female managers. *American Sociological Review* 65 (2): 210-33.
Robinson, Corre L., Tiffany Taylor, Donald Tomaskovic-Devey, Catherine Zimmer, and Matthew W. Irvin. 2005. Studying race or ethnic and sex segregation at the establishment level: Methodological issues and substantive opportunities using EEO-1 reports. *Work & Occupations* 32 (1): 5-38.
Scott, Richard W. 1992. *Organizations: Rational, natural, and open systems*. Englewood Cliffs, NJ: Prentice Hall.
Semyonov, Moshe, Danny R. Hoyt, and Richard I. Scott. 1984. Place, race, and differential occupational opportunities. *Demography* 21:259-70.
Shenhav, Yehouda, and Yitchak Haberfeld. 1992. Organizational demography and inequality. *Social Forces* 71 (1): 123-43.
Smith, Ryan A. 2002. Race, gender, and authority in the workplace: Theory and research. *Annual Review of Sociology* 28:509-42.
Stainback, Kevin, and Donald Tomaskovic-Devey. 2006. Managing privilege: The stable advantage of white males in U.S. labor markets, 1966-2000. Manuscript, University of Massachusetts, Amherst.
Szafran, Robert F. 1982. What kinds of firms hire and promote women and blacks? A review of the literature. *Sociological Quarterly* 23:171-90.
Taylor, Marylee C. 1998. How white attitudes vary with the racial composition of local populations: Numbers count. *American Sociological Review* 63 (4): 512-35.

Tienda, Marta, and Ding-Tzann Lii. 1987. Minority concentration and earnings inequality: Blacks, Hispanics, and Asians compared. *American Journal of Sociology* 93:141-65.

Tolnay, Stewart E., and E. M. Beck. 1995. *A festival of violence: An analysis of southern lynchings, 1882-1930*. Urbana: University of Illinois Press.

Tolnay, Stewart E., Glenn Deane, and E. M. Beck. 1996. Vicarious violence: Spatial effects on southern lynchings, 1890-1919. *American Journal of Sociology* 3:788-815.

Tomaskovic-Devey, Donald. 1993. *Gender and racial inequality at work: The sources and consequences of job segregation*. New York: ILR Press.

Tomaskovic-Devey, Donald, Catherine Zimmer, Kevin Stainback, Corre Robinson, Tiffany Taylor, and Tricia McTague. 2006. Documenting desegregation: Segregation in American workplaces by race, ethnicity, and sex, 1966-2003. *American Sociological Review* 71:565-88.

U.S. Equal Employment Opportunity Commission. 2006. *Diversity in the finance industry*. Washington, DC: EEOC Office of Research, Information and Planning. http://www.eeoc.gov/stats/reports/finance/index.html (accessed October 19, 2006).

Wilson, George, Ian Sakura-Lemessy, and Jonathan P. West. 1999. Reaching the top: Racial differences in mobility paths to upper-tier occupations. *Work & Occupations* 26 (2): 165-86.

Wilson, William J. 1996. *When work disappears: The world of the new urban poor*. New York: Vintage Books.

Demobilization of the Individualistic Bias: Housing Market Discrimination as a Contributor to Labor Market and Economic Inequality

By
GREGORY D. SQUIRES

Racial discrimination in the nation's housing markets and patterns of residential segregation have contributed to labor market inequalities and economic disparities generally. Housing values are suppressed in minority communities, undercutting wealth accumulation by nonwhite families. Job growth in suburban communities coupled with the concentration of public housing in central city communities restricts minority access to jobs. A range of institutionalized practices by housing providers and public policies by government agencies at all levels have nurtured and exacerbated racial inequalities grounded in traditional stereotypes. But a number of policy options are available to ameliorate these inequities. Eschewing individualistic explanations of racial inequality that point to personal deficiencies and cultural characteristics of minority communities, these policy recommendations—premised on a structural perspective—offer promise for reducing racial inequities in housing and related economic disparities.

Keywords: segregation; steering; exclusionary zoning; discrimination

The sociological imagination enables us to grasp history and biography and the relations between the two within society. That is its task and its promise.... It is a quality of mind that seems most dramatically to promise an understanding of the intimate realities of ourselves in connection with larger social realities.
—Mills (1968, 6, 15)

A cult of individualism has long dominated life in the United States. This has been most evident in popular explanations for who gets what and why in American society as socioeconomic success and failure have long been explained in terms of voluntary decisions that individuals make. Those who are successful tell themselves (and are often told by others) that their fortune is due to their intelligence, hard work, self-reliance, and related entrepreneurial attributes. Meanwhile, poverty and other measures of socioeconomic failure are explained

DOI: 10.1177/0002716206294953

away in terms of the absence of these same characteristics. Those who are not succeeding, we are told, lack the skill, experience, initiative, and other qualities necessary to meet the test of the competitive system (Gilder 1981; Murray 1984; Thernstrom and Thernstrom 1997; McWhorter 2000).

A cult of individualism has long dominated life in the United States. This has been most evident in popular explanations for who gets what and why in American society.

This worldview is perhaps most explicitly (and problematically) offered to account for persisting patterns of racial inequality. As Patrick Buchanan offered in a particularly colorful statement, but one expressing a sentiment hardly unique to him alone,

> What the black poor need more than anything today is a dose of the truth. Slums are the products of the people who live there. Dignity and respect are not handed out like food stamps; they are earned and won. . . . The first step to progress, for any group, lies in the admission that its failures are, by and large, its own fault, that success can come only through its own efforts, that, while the well-intentioned outsider may help, he or she is no substitute for personal sacrifice. (Patrick J. Buchanan, in *The Arizona Republic*, May 24, 1990, as cited in Edsall and Edsall 1991)

At the height of the civil rights movement during the 1960s, there was some recognition that extraindividualistic factors contributed to racial inequality. But with the passing of that era, victory has been declared and the prevailing conventional wisdom is that a color-blind society has, basically, been achieved, at least

Gregory D. Squires is a professor of sociology and chair of the Department of Sociology at George Washington University. He has served as a consultant and expert witness for fair housing groups and civil rights organizations around the country including HUD, the National Fair Housing Alliance, the National Community Reinvestment Coalition, and many others. He also served a three-year term as a member of the Consumer Advisory Council of the Federal Reserve Board. He has written for several academic journals and general interest publications including Social Problems, Social Science Quarterly, Urban Affairs Review, Journal of Urban Affairs, The Nation, The American Prospect, *the* New York Times, *and the* Washington Post. *Prior to joining the faculty at George Washington, he taught at the University of Wisconsin–Milwaukee and served as a research analyst for the U.S. Commission on Civil Rights.*

to the extent that is humanly possible. Racial inequalities persist, to be sure, but they are accounted for by the personal failings or cultural limitations among nonwhites themselves (for discussion of this dynamic, see DeMott 1990, 1995; Brown et al. 2003; and Bonilla-Silva 2003).

The individualistic bias pervades dominant explanations of inequality in two primary mechanisms for the allocation of privilege, labor markets and housing markets. The following pages

- examine racial inequalities in housing and how they influence inequalities in the labor market and economy generally;
- explore the individualistic bias that shapes these understandings and alternative approaches that yield a better understanding of, and greater hope for ameliorating, those inequalities; and
- identify policies, based on a different set of premises, that can yield more equitable outcomes in the allocation of housing and related economic rewards.

Mobilization of the Individualistic Bias

Political scientists have long written about a mobilization of bias, a process whereby some issues are organized into politics while others are organized out. That is, some issues are placed on the agenda for discussion while others are kept off. But this is not a neutral process. The mobilization of bias generally reinforces myths, rituals, and institutions that reflect dominant values and interests of powerful groups (Schattschneider 1960; Bacharach and Baratz 1962).

The individualistic bias referred to in the following pages is a similar but broader ideological phenomenon that pervades American society and is not simply a characteristic of particular organizations, though it is that as well. This worldview ignores the role of race, ethnicity, gender, and other ascriptive characteristics that still count. It ignores the role of unearned advantages (and disadvantages) of class like the uneven effects of inheritance. (Twenty-eight percent of whites receive an inheritance averaging $52,430 compared to 7.7 percent of blacks with an average bequest of $21,796, and these figures do not reflect gifts given while parents are still alive [Shapiro 2004, 67-72]). And it ignores the role of government policy and a range of other nonindividualistic factors that shape socioeconomic success and failure. By rejecting such explanations for privilege (and particularly white privilege), a number of myths, rituals, and institutions are reinforced that perpetuate unearned advantages. Perhaps more important, this process suppresses efforts to ameliorate them. Powerful interests convince themselves that their privileged positions reflect their own hard work, thus justifying their rewards. The other side of this coin, of course, is the belief that those who receive fewer rewards are themselves responsible for their plights. And many who are in fact victims of broader social forces internalize this belief, failing, as C. Wright Mills (1968) warned, to understand their personal troubles as reflections of the public issues that constitute the fundamental problem. Whitewashing race and related unearned advantages dispels any need to alter current distributive patterns along with any personal or institutional responsibility for pursuing any policies other than the status quo.

The limitations of this perspective are perhaps clearest in the labor market, where human capital theory remains the dominant explanation for who gets what and why. Human capital theory, and the neoclassical paradigm in which it is rooted, emphasize the role of voluntary choices made freely by individual "buyers" (employers) and "sellers" (employees) in unfettered labor markets. Employees with more education, skills, experiences, and other attributes that employers demand will be able to attract higher wages and better working conditions generally than those with less "human capital." Perhaps more important, those who forgo the opportunity to maximize current consumption (by getting a job today) in favor of making further investments in their own human capital (by staying in school) are voluntarily making an individual choice that will lead to even greater rewards in the future. Those who do not exercise such judgment will earn less (Becker 1964). Racial disparities in the labor market, consequently, reflect the different choices that whites and nonwhites have made. The solution, from this perspective, is basically to enhance the human capital of those entering the labor market. A key to accomplishing this objective is to convince those near the lower end of the labor queue of the values of deferred gratification and a longer-term "future orientation" (Banfield 1968; Sowell 1981, 1984; Williams 1982; McWhorter 2000).

Whitewashing race and related unearned advantages dispels any need to alter current distributive patterns along with any personal or institutional responsibility for pursuing any policies other than the status quo.

But this perspective is as flawed as it is dominant. Several structural factors intervene to shape wages and other labor market outcomes (Friedman 1984). The quality and, consequently, prestige, of schooling institutions, for example, vary dramatically by race and class for reasons that have virtually nothing to do with the academic potential of students who attend those schools (Anyon 2005; Kozol 2005). Wages and other benefits associated with jobs often depend more on whether they are in primary or secondary occupations and industries than the qualifications of employees who occupy these positions (Averitt 1968; Gordon, Edwards, and Reich 1982; Holzer and Danziger 2001). Government policies (e.g., levels of minimum wage requirements, presence of living wage laws, enforcement of labor laws) affect earnings, as does the presence or absence of union representation (Mishel, Bernstein, and Allegretto 2005; Freeman and Medoff 1984; LeRoy 2005; Pollin and Luce 1998). "Statistical discrimination" where employers use race as a proxy for various human capital variables has long perpetuated racial inequalities despite the illegalities of such selection mechanisms (Arrow 1972). Old-fashioned racial stereotyping and intentional discrimination also persist. For example, recent research has shown that African Americans without a criminal record are less likely to be called back for interviews or offered jobs than even less qualified whites with a record (Pager 2003). Just knowing an applicant's name is often sufficient to trigger discrimination whereby those with white-sounding names are treated more favorably than comparable or better-qualified applicants with black-sounding names (Bertrand and Mullainathan 2004).

Similar distortions occur in representations of housing markets. Racial segregation and its many costs (discussed below) have long been explained away in terms of voluntary individual choice. In his classic essay, Charles Tiebout (1956) claimed that where families live reflects choices they make, limited by their financial capacity, to pursue the bundle of services for which they are willing to pay. In essence, they "vote with their feet" in selecting from the options that are available in different municipalities and communities. From this perspective, individual buyers (families and others seeking housing) and sellers (municipalities seeking to grow their populations) meet in unfettered markets. Racial segregation in particular is often accounted for in these terms. As Nathan Glazer (1975, 134, 158-59) argued, "We deal with a market of millions of individual purchasers and hundreds of thousands of individual suppliers. . . . Housing is still for the most part a matter of free choice, limited by economic capacity and tastes." In making that choice, it is argued, racial and ethnic groups often choose to live in homogeneous neighborhoods, again reflecting voluntary choices among individual households (Thernstrom and Thernstrom 1997).

No doubt preferences do matter and financial capacity does limit housing options. And evidence shows that some minority households place less value on integration today than a decade or two past. Such "integration fatigue" may well explain the choices of some. But the available social science evidence clearly demonstrates that, once again, extraindividualistic forces are the primary factors that account for inequality in housing markets in general and patterns of segregation in particular, contrary to popular explanations (Massey and Denton 1993; Cashin 2004).

A range of institutionalized private practices and public policies have directly led to a national housing pattern in which the typical black resident lives in a neighborhood that is 51 percent black while the typical white resident lives in a neighborhood that is 80 percent white and just 7 percent black. Hispanics and Asians are also segregated, though at lower levels. However, segregation from whites has increased in the past ten years for these groups while leveling off if not declining slightly for blacks (Lewis Mumford Center 2001a, 2001b).

Overt violence, intimidation, and explicit legal segregation began a continuing process of segregation at the turn of the twentieth century. In some neighborhoods local laws prohibited selected racial, ethnic, and religious groups from living in those areas (Massey and Denton 1993; Loewen 2005). Often these groups were physically intimidated from moving into a community, or encouraged to immediately move out, by such tactics. The name of the town Anna, Illinois, stands for "Ain't No Niggers Allowed," and few blacks have ever lived there. Following a series of lynchings in 1909, Anna expelled all African American residents, and the town has been all white ever since (Loewen 2005, 3). The film *Rosewood* illustrated just one of at least thirty cases where black residents were killed or forced from their homes and their entire neighborhoods were destroyed (Loewen 2005).

But most of the policies and practices that give rise to segregation are more subtle. They include ongoing racial steering and discrimination by real estate rental and sales agents. In a 2000 nationwide study of housing discrimination, the Urban Institute found that racial minorities encountered unlawful discrimination in approximately one out of every five visits to a sales or rental agent (Turner et al. 2002; Turner and Ross 2005). In that study, whites were often steered as well as blacks. Among the advice offered white testers were the following comments: "It is not the neighborhood in which to buy a home; too many Hispanics living there"; "That area is full of Hispanics and Blacks that don't know how to keep clean"; and "There are lots of Latinos living there. . . . I'm not supposed to be telling you that, but you have a daughter and I like you" (Galster and Godfrey 2005).

Redlining and racial discrimination on the part of mortgage lenders and property insurers have long limited opportunities for racial minorities and residents of minority neighborhoods. If financial services are more readily available today than in the past this reflects, in part, the growth of predatory lending whereby residents of traditionally underserved neighborhoods are offered products at prices far exceeding the risk they pose, often leading to foreclosure and the loss of a home in the process (Munnell et al. 1996; Ross and Yinger 2002; Immergluck 2004; Squires 2003a, 2005).

Arbitrary and discriminatory appraisal practices contribute to such inequities. Often properties are underappraised in minority neighborhoods (due to unfair stereotyping and the racial discrimination that follows), resulting in the denial of a mortgage loan, which means that at least some voluntary transactions that have been negotiated by individual buyers and sellers fall through. Real estate agents lose the deal, sellers fail to sell their homes, and buyers are unable to become home owners (Schwemm 1996). More recently, the problem is inflated appraisals (whereby appraisers fear the loss of business if they do not come in with the number that the lender wants), which lead to home sales for families that, in fact, cannot afford the mortgage payments and general upkeep of the home. This, again, leads to foreclosure and the loss of a home, along with the household's life savings in some cases (National Community Reinvestment Coalition 2005b).

Public policies have also contributed to housing inequalities. In the 1930s the Federal Housing Administration warned of "inharmonious racial groups" in its underwriting guidelines and insured few mortgage loans in central-city neighborhoods until the 1960s, effectively providing official sanction for the redlining of those neighborhoods (Jackson 1985). Exclusionary zoning laws (e.g., maximum density and minimum lot size rules) in most suburbs reduce the supply of affordable housing, exercising an adverse disparate impact on racial minorities (Massey and Denton 1993). The tax deduction for mortgage interest and property taxes coupled with federally funded highways fueled suburban development in racially exclusive communities (M. Orfield 2002; Rusk 2001). And the concentration of public housing in predominantly black inner-city neighborhoods locked poor blacks in those communities (Hirsch 1983; Fullilove 2004).

Underlying and contributing to these policies and practices have been traditional racial stereotyping and discrimination. African Americans have been particularly affected as several studies have found them to be the most disfavored minority group by whites as well as other racial and ethnic groups (Charles 2005). Evidence indicates that it is the presence of blacks, and not just neighborhood conditions often associated with black neighborhoods (e.g., bad schools, high crime) that accounts for white aversion to such areas. In one survey, whites reported that they would be unlikely to purchase a home that met their requirements in terms of price, number of rooms, and other housing characteristics in a neighborhood with good schools and low crime rates if there was a substantial representation of African Americans. The presence of Hispanics or Asians had no such effect (Emerson, Chai, and Yancey 2001).

Clearly, more than voluntary choices by individual actors in free markets shape the opportunity structure in the United States.

The role of discrimination is evident to most racial minorities, but whites simply do not see it. In a survey of Washington, D.C., area residents, 58 percent of whites said that blacks and whites have the same choices and opportunities in the local housing market. Just 16 percent of blacks offered this same assessment. This same survey showed that white home owners were twice as likely as blacks to secure their first choice of housing when they moved into their current home (Squires, Friedman, and Saidat 2002). These findings are consistent with previous research demonstrating that whites and nonwhites have very different beliefs about the housing opportunities available to different groups and the extent to which voluntary, individual choice determines who lives where (Kluegel and Smith 1986; Sigelman and Welch 1994).

Clearly, more than voluntary choices by individual actors in free markets shape the opportunity structure in the United States. The housing patterns and practices noted here contribute to disparities in housing consumption and broader economic inequalities generally. Where different groups of people live and the homes in which they live are not simply neutral or random demographic phenomena. They profoundly influence the allocation of rewards in the United States.

Costs and Consequences of Housing Inequality

If segregated living patterns reflected little more than a random or neutral allocation of where people live, or truly resulted simply from voluntary choice, they would constitute little more than a statistical curiosity. But segregation, housing inequalities generally, and the underlying causes yield dramatic differences in the quality of life of various groups, providing unearned privileges for some and unwarranted punishments for others. Serious life consequences flow from these inequities, which are not primarily reflections of voluntary individual choice, culture characteristics of diverse groups, or neutral market forces. People do make decisions. There are cultural differences. Market forces exist to be sure. But these social realities are contextualized. They reflect and reinforce privileges grounded in race and class standing, which in turn are reflected and reinforced by conscious policy decisions (Wilson 1996). The upside is that if policy played a significant role in getting us where we are today, it can help us get somewhere else in the future.

Housing inequalities are quite concrete, but they embody much more than simply differences in the types of structures where people live. Those inequalities include, of course, the market value of homes. But they also include neighborhood amenities (or lack thereof) depending on where a home is located. Among those amenities are the local public schools and job networks, along with various opportunities to accumulate wealth and other socioeconomic benefits.

Perhaps the most explicit signals of housing inequality are home ownership rates and the value of homes families own. Home ownership for virtually all groups has increased in recent years, but significant racial and ethnic gaps persist. From 1993 to 2004, home ownership among African Americans grew from 42.3 to 48.8 percent and for Hispanics from 41.2 to 49.7 percent. But whites exhibited a much higher rate in both years: 70.0 and 76.0 percent (U.S. Census Bureau 2004; National Association of Realtors 2005). And the values of homes owned by different groups varied dramatically. The median value of homes owned by whites in 2000 was $123,400 compared to $80,600 for blacks and $105,600 for Latinos (Bennefield 2003, 3). Racial disparities are also reflected in who owns the highest-priced homes. In 2000, 1 out of every 72 white homeowners had a home worth $1 million or more compared to 1 out of every 762 minority homeowners (Di 2005, 289). Perhaps more telling is the fact that appreciation in home values is undercut by the presence of other minorities, and particularly African Americans, even after taking into consideration characteristics of the homes (e.g., number of rooms), socioeconomic status of homeowners, region of the country, and other nonracial factors (Flippen 2004).

These housing inequities constitute major contributors to wealth inequalities generally. While blacks earn about 60 percent of what whites earn, the typical black family has about one-tenth the wealth of a typical white family (Conley 1999; Shapiro 2004). The fact that for blacks home equity accounts for two-thirds of assets compared to two-fifths for whites make these housing inequities even more problematic (Oliver and Shapiro 1995). Overall, disparities in the nation's housing and home finance market have cost the current generation of blacks about $82 billion, with the disparity in home equity averaging $20,000 for those with mortgages (Oliver and Shapiro 1995, 151, 171).

The disparate financial capacities created by these housing disparities are severe costs in and of themselves. These inequities are dramatically compounded by the segregated housing patterns characteristic of most metropolitan areas. In addition to the impact on home values, segregation also adversely affects access to a host of other amenities.

They start right at birth and continue throughout the life cycle. As of 1995, the black infant mortality rate was 14.3 per 1,000 live births compared to 6.3 for whites and Latinos. And the black/white ratio actually increased between 1950 and 1990 from 1.6 to 2.4 (Kington and Nickens 2001, 264-65). This pattern no doubt reflects, at least in part, the uneven distribution of health services. For example, in the affluent Washington, D.C., suburb of Bethesda, Maryland, there is one pediatrician for every 400 children while in the poor black neighborhoods in the District's southeast side there is one for every 3,700 (Dreier, Mollenkopf, and Swanstrom 2001, 68).

Educational resources reflect the same inequities. Public schools have become even more segregated in recent years, after two decades of progress on this front. For example, in 2000, 40 percent of black students attended schools that were 90 to 100 percent black compared to 32 percent of black students who attended such schools in 1988 (G. Orfield and Eaton 2003). The percentage of white students in the schools of the typical black student declined from more than 36 to less than 31 during these years. And the share of Latino students attending schools that were 90 to 100 percent minority grew from 23 percent during the late 1960s to 37 percent in 2000 (Frankenberg, Lee, and Orfield 2003, 30, 33). Given the reliance on property taxes to fund public education, residential segregation leads to large disparities in the resources for schools in white and nonwhite communities. For example, per pupil expenditures in the New York City public schools in 2002-2003 were $11,627 compared to $22,311 in suburban Manhasset. A similar pattern prevails in Chicago, Detroit, Milwaukee, Boston, and most other metropolitan areas (Kozol 2005, 324). Money alone, of course, does not account for educational inequalities, and money alone may not resolve them. But when coupled with school tracking systems, unfair stereotyping of students, and lower expectations (by teachers and other students) for minority academic performance, it is evident that public education is not the "balance wheel of the social machinery" that Horace Mann envisioned over 150 years ago (Bowles and Gintis 1976; Anyon 2005).

The most immediate determinant of the quality of life in the United States—economic and otherwise—is probably one's location in the labor market. Spatial mismatch theory has provided an important part of the explanation for racial economic inequality and particularly the contribution of segregation to that disparity (Kain 1968, 2004; Brueckner and Zenou 2003). Racial minorities, and particularly African Americans, have long been concentrated in economically declining central-city neighborhoods while the fastest job growth has been in predominantly white suburban communities. Consequently, minorities are less likely to hear about job openings, it is more difficult for them to get to interviews since they are far less likely to own cars and public transportation does not serve urban-to-suburban commuters well, and it is more costly for them to take such jobs if they are offered because of the lengthy and often automobile-dependent commute. These problems are exacerbated for welfare recipients, who have been under increasing pressure to find jobs in recent years (Allard and Danziger 2002). Negative stereotypes many employers associate with race and ethnicity, as well as street addresses where these groups tend to reside, compound these problems for nonwhites (Tilly et al. 2001; Wilson 1996).

Housing segregation also undercuts opportunities for minorities to informally demonstrate to potential employers both "hard" and "soft" skills that are frequently quite job-related. Just as job discrimination blocks the opportunity for minorities to interact informally with employers and accumulate valuable social capital (Wilson, Sakura-Lemessy, and West 1999), housing segregation limits opportunities for informal social interaction between whites and nonwhites. With relatively few white neighbors (and with whites still controlling a disproportionate share of work-related organizations), minorities have fewer opportunities to demonstrate to potential employers and business partners the job-related skills neighbors often display to each other. They are less able, for example, to demonstrate technical skills like auto mechanics or plumbing by tuning up a neighbor's car or fixing a leaky faucet. There are fewer opportunities to reveal perhaps even more important noncognitive attributes like leadership and collegiality by directing a community organization or Boy Scout troop or just being a gregarious neighbor.

In many ways, racial discrimination and segregation in the nation's housing markets undercut the ability of, and opportunity for, racial and ethnic minorities to compete in the labor market, accumulate economic and other assets, and access virtually all of the rewards presumably available to those individuals who "play by the rules." As Douglas Massey and Nancy Denton (1993, 14) put it, "Barriers to spatial mobility are barriers to social mobility." But once again, if these social realities reflect intentional public policies and private practices, and not simply the choices, values, cultures, or other characteristics of particular individuals, then different policy can alter those practices and change the opportunity structure.

Policy Options

A starting point is traditional law enforcement. Far more could be accomplished by government agencies to enforce Title VII of the Civil Rights Act of 1964 banning employment discrimination and Title VIII of the Civil Rights Act of 1968 (better known as the Federal Fair Housing Act) prohibiting discrimination in all housing-related services. State and local agencies with similar authority could also be more proactive. But often the enforcement and regulatory agencies are as much of a problem as the industries they regulate. Particularly in the area of housing and housing-related financial services, community-based organizations have been the most proactive forces (Massey and Denton 1993; Immergluck 2004; Squires 2003b).

For example, using leverage provided by the Fair Housing Act, the National Fair Housing Alliance and its member organizations generated more than $225,000,000 for plaintiffs in fair housing cases since 1990. Among the defendants who have paid substantial fines and have changed the way they do business are large real estate companies, rental agents, mortgage lenders, insurance companies, and other providers of housing and housing-related services (National Fair Housing Alliance 2006). Using leverage provided by the Community Reinvestment Act, which bans redlining by banks and thrift institutions, community-based organizations have generated more than $4 trillion for investments in previously underserved communities. These investments include home mortgage loans, small business loans, new branch banks, financial literacy programs, and other initiatives (National Community Reinvestment Coalition 2005a).

Mobility programs that have enabled poor black families to move to integrated settings have demonstrated positive results. In Chicago, the Gautreaux Program (named after a civil rights activist who filed a lawsuit challenging the U.S. Department of Housing and Urban Development [HUD] and the Chicago Housing Authority for intentionally segregating public housing in that city) helped more than seven thousand families move from public housing to other locations in the metropolitan area between 1976 and 1998. Under that program, 75 percent of participants were to move to the suburbs. Compared to those who stayed in the city, suburban movers fared better in several ways. The children were more likely to go to college, and among those who did so, a higher percentage of suburban movers went to four-year schools rather than junior colleges. Suburban movers were less likely to encounter problems with law enforcement authorities. They were also more likely to find jobs and to earn higher wages and receive more benefits than those who remained in the city (Rubinowitz and Rosenbaum 2000).

HUD followed the Gatreaux Program with its Moving to Opportunity (MTO) experiment in five cities including Baltimore, Boston, Chicago, Los Angeles, and New York. MTO, launched in 1994, focused on poverty status rather than race. That is, selected families in high-poverty neighborhoods were given the opportunity to move to low-poverty communities. Research to date has not found the educational or employment benefits of Gautreaux, but participants report finding much safer communities and have fewer physical and mental health problems (Goering and Feins 2003).

In a related initiative, HUD launched its Hope VI project in 1992 with the following objectives: (1) improving the living environment of residents of severely distressed public housing through demolition, repair, and replacement of those projects; (2) improving neighborhoods around public housing sites; (3) decreasing the concentration of poverty; and (4) building sustainable communities. Preliminary research indicates that Hope VI has successfully demolished many of the nation's most problematic public housing complexes and replaced some of them with higher-quality housing, often in mixed-income communities. Many former residents of the razed projects have been rehoused in their former neighborhoods or provided with housing vouchers that enabled them to find better, safer housing in other communities (Popkin et al. 2004).

If exclusionary zoning laws have been central for perpetuating racial segregation, inclusionary laws constitute a critical remedy. In fact, today literally hundreds of municipalities have implemented some form of this approach. Some are mandatory and some are voluntary. Basically, inclusionary zoning calls for communities or developers to produce a certain percentage of affordable housing units in new developments. Sometimes developers can receive bonuses or exclusions from local zoning laws to build more units than are normally permitted if they include greater numbers of units for low-income households (M. Orfield 2002; Rusk 2001).

These examples are meant to be illustrative, not exhaustive. And they are meant to complement rather than replace other individualistic approaches. For example, financial literacy programs (and other efforts to enhance the education and increase the human capital of lower-income households) can turn residents of traditionally underserved communities into more informed housing consumers, more attractive employees, and generally more efficacious citizens who can better serve their own economic interests. But if the cult of individualism is not challenged, barriers to spatial mobility will persist, and they will continue to deny social mobility as well.

Collective problems require collective responses. The personal troubles many families experience in segregated communities in fact reflect public issues rather than individual failings. It is time to demobilize the individualistic bias that has long framed popular understandings of the opportunity structure in the United States, and particularly conventional explanations of racial inequality.

References

Allard, Scott W., and Sheldon Danziger. 2002. Proximity and opportunity: How residence and race affect the employment of welfare recipients. *Housing Policy Debate* 13 (4): 675-700.

Anyon, Jean. 2005. *Radical possibilities: Public policy, urban education, and a new social movement.* New York: Routledge.

Arrow, Kenneth. 1972. Some mathematical models of race discrimination in the labor market. In *Racial discrimination in economic life*, ed. Anthony Pascal. Lexington, MA: D.C. Heath.

Averitt, Robert T. 1968. *The dual economy: The dynamics of American industry structure.* New York: Horton.

Bacharach, Peter, and Morton Baratz. 1962. The two faces of power. *American Political Science Review* 56:947-52.

Banfield, Edward C. 1968. *The unheavenly city revisited.* Boston: Little, Brown.

Becker, Gary S. 1964. *Human capital: A theoretical and empirical analysis with special reference to education.* New York: Columbia University Press.

Bennefield, Robert L. 2003. *Home values: 2000.* Washington, DC: U.S. Census Bureau.

Bertrand, Marianne, and Sendhil Mullainathan. 2004. Are Emily and Greg more employable than Lakisha and Jamal? A field experiment on labor market discrimination. *American Economic Review* 94 (4): 991-1013.

Bonilla-Silva, Eduardo. 2003. *Racism without racists: Color-blind racism and the persistence of racial inequality in the United States*. New York: Rowman & Littlefield.

Bowles, Samuel, and Herbert Gintis. 1976. *Schooling in capitalist America: Educational reform and the contradictions of economic life*. New York: Basic Books.

Brown, Michael K., Martin Carnoy, Elliott Currie, Troy Duster, David B. Oppenheimer, Marjorie M. Shultz, and David Wellman. 2003. *White-washing race: The myth of a color-blind society*. Berkeley: University of California Press.

Brueckner, Jan K., and Yves Zenou. 2003. Space and unemployment: The labor-market effects of spatial mismatch. *Journal of Labor Economics* 21 (1): 242-66.

Cashin, Cheryll. 2004. *The failures of integration: How race and class are undermining the American dream*. New York: Public Affairs.

Charles, Camille Zubrinsky. 2005. Can we live together? Racial preferences and neighborhood outcomes. In *The geography of opportunity: Race and housing choice in metropolitan America*, ed. Xavier de Sousa Briggs. Washington, DC: Brookings Institution.

Conley, Dalton. 1999. *Being black, living in the red: Race, wealth, and social policy in America*. Berkeley: University of California Press.

DeMott, Benjamin. 1990. *The imperial middle: Why Americans can't think straight about class*. New York: William Morrow.

———. 1995. *The trouble with friendship: Why Americans can't think straight about race*. New York: Atlantic Monthly Press.

Di, Zhu Xiao. 2005. Does housing wealth contribute to or temper the widening wealth gap in America? *Housing Policy Debate* 16 (2): 281-96.

Dreier, Peter, John Mollenkopf, and Todd Swanstrom. 2001. *Place matters: Metropolitics for the twenty-first century*. Lawrence: University Press of Kansas.

Edsall, Thomas Byrne, and Mary D. Edsall. 1991. *Chain reaction: The impact of race, rights, and taxes on American politics*. New York: Norton.

Emerson, Michael O., Karen J. Chai, and George Yancey. 2001. Does race matter in residential segregation? Exploring the preferences of white Americans. *American Sociological Review* 66 (6): 922-35.

Flippen, Chenoa. 2004. Unequal returns to housing investments? A study of real housing appreciation among black, white, and Hispanic households. *Social Forces* 82 (4): 1523-51.

Frankenberg, Erica, Chungmei Lee, and Gary Orfield. 2003. *A multiracial society with segregated schools: Are we losing the dream?* Cambridge, MA: The Civil Rights Project, Harvard University.

Freeman, Richard B., and James L. Medoff. 1984. *What do unions do?* New York: Basic Books.

Friedman, Samuel R. 1984. Structure, process, and the labor market. In *Labor economics: Modern views*, ed. William Darity Jr. Boston: Kluwer-Nijhoff.

Fullilove, Mindy Thompson. 2004. *Root shock*. New York: Ballantine.

Galster, George, and Erin Godfrey. 2005. By words and deeds: Racial steering by real estate agents in the U.S. in 2000. *Journal of the American Planning Association* 71 (3): 251-68.

Gilder, George. 1981. *Wealth and poverty*. New York: Basic Books.

Glazer, Nathan. 1975. *Affirmative discrimination: Ethnic inequality and public policy*. New York: Basic Books.

Goering, John, and Judith D. Feins. 2003. *Choosing a better life: Evaluating the moving to opportunity social experiment*. Washington, DC: Urban Institute Press.

Gordon, David M., Richard C. Edwards, and Michael Reich. 1982. *Segmented work, divided workers: The historical transformation of labor in the United States*. New York: Cambridge University Press.

Hirsch, Arnold R. 1983. *Making the second ghetto: Race & housing in Chicago 1940-1960*. New York: Cambridge University Press.

Holzer, Harry J., and Sheldon Danziger. 2001. Are jobs available for disadvantaged workers in urban areas? In *Urban inequality: Evidence from four cities*, ed. Alice O'Connor, Chris Tilly, and Lawrence D. Bobo. New York: Russell Sage Foundation.

Immergluck, Dan. 2004. *Credit to the community: Community reinvestment and fair lending policy in the United States*. Armonk, NY: M. E. Sharpe.

Jackson, Kenneth T. 1985. *Crabgrass frontier: The suburbanization of the United States*. New York: Oxford University Press.

Kain, John. 1968. Housing segregation, Negro employment and metropolitan decentralization. *Quarterly Journal of Economics* 82 (2): 175-97.

———. 2004. A pioneer's perspective on the spatial mismatch literature. *Urban Studies* 41 (1): 7-32.

Kington, Raynard S., and Herbert W. Nickens. 2001. Racial and ethnic differences in health: Recent trends, current patterns, future directions. In *America becoming: Racial trends and their consequences*, vol. II, ed. Neil J. Smelser, William Julius Wilson, and Faith Mitchell. Washington, DC: National Academy Press.

Kluegel, James R., and Eliot R. Smith. 1986. *Beliefs about inequality: Americans' views of what is and what ought to be*. New York: Aldine de Gruyter.

Kozol, Jonathan. 2005. *The shame of the nation: The restoration of apartheid schooling in America*. New York: Crown.

LeRoy, Greg. 2005. *The great American jobs scam: Corporate tax dodging and the myth of job creation*. San Francisco: Berrett-Koehler Publishers Inc.

Lewis Mumford Center. 2001a. Ethnic diversity grows, neighborhood integration lags behind. http://mumford1.dyndns.org/cen2000/WholePop/WPreport/page1.html (accessed September 18, 2002).

———. 2001b. *Metropolitan racial and ethnic change—Census 2000*. Albany, NY: Lewis Mumford Center.

Loewen, James W. 2005. *Sundown towns: A hidden dimension of American racism*. New York: New Press.

Massey, Douglas S., and Nancy Denton. 1993. *American apartheid: Segregation and the making of the underclass*. Cambridge, MA: Harvard University Press.

McWhorter, John. 2000. *Losing the race: Self-sabotage in black America*. New York: Free Press.

Mills, C. Wright. 1968. *The sociological imagination*. Oxford: Oxford University Press.

Mishel, Lawrence, Jared Bernstein, and Sylvia Allegretto. 2005. *The state of working America 2004/2005*. Ithaca, NY: ILR.

Munnell, Alicia, Geoffrey M. B. Tootell, Lynn E. Browne, and James McEneaney. 1996. Mortgage lending in Boston: Interpreting HMDA data. *American Economic Review* 86 (1): 25-53.

Murray, Charles. 1984. *Losing ground: American social policy 1950-1980*. New York: Basic Books.

National Association of Realtors. 2005. *Homeownership*. April 27. Washington, DC: National Association of Realtors.

National Community Reinvestment Coalition. 2005a. *CRA commitments*. Washington, DC: National Community Reinvestment Coalition.

———. 2005b. *Predatory appraisals: $tealing the American dream*. Washington, DC: National Community Reinvestment Coalition.

National Fair Housing Alliance. 2006. *$190,000,000 and counting*. Washington, DC: National Fair Housing Alliance.

Oliver, Melvin L., and Thomas M. Shapiro. 1995. *Black wealth/white wealth: A new perspective on racial inequality*. New York: Routledge.

Orfield, Gary, and Susan E. Eaton. 2003. Back to segregation. *The Nation* 276 (8): 5.

Orfield, Myron. 2002. *American metropolitics: The new suburban reality*. Washington, DC: Brookings Institution.

Pager, Devah. 2003. The mark of a criminal record. *American Journal of Sociology* 108:937-75.

Pollin, Robert, and Stephanie Luce. 1998. *The living wage: Building a fair economy*. New York: New Press.

Popkin, Susan J., Bruce Katz, Mary K. Cunningham, Karen D. Brown, Jeremy Gustafson, and Margery Austin Turner. 2004. *A decade of Hope VI: Research findings and policy challenges*. Washington, DC: Urban Institute and Brookings Institution.

Ross, Stephen L., and John Yinger. 2002. *The color of credit: Mortgage discrimination, research methodology, and fair-lending enforcement*. Cambridge, MA: MIT Press.

Rubinowitz, Leonard S., and James E. Rosenbaum. 2000. *Crossing the class and color lines: From public housing to white suburbia*. Chicago: University of Chicago Press.

Rusk, David. 2001. *The "segregation tax": The cost of racial segregation to black homeowners*. Washington, DC: Brookings Institution

Schattschneider, E. E. 1960. *The semisovereign people: A realist's view of democracy in America*. New York: Holt, Rinehart and Winston.

Schwemm, Robert G. 1996. Housing discrimination and the appraisal industry. In *Mortgage lending, racial discrimination, and federal policy*, ed. John Goering and Ron Wienk. Washington, DC: Urban Institute.

Shapiro, Thomas M. 2004. *The hidden cost of being African American: How wealth perpetuates inequality*. New York: Oxford University Press.

Sigelman, Lee, and Susan Welch. 1994. *Black Americans' views of racial inequality: The dream deferred*. Cambridge: Cambridge University Press.

Sowell, Thomas. 1981. *Markets and minorities*. New York: Basic Books.

———. 1984. *Civil rights: Rhetoric or reality?* New York: William Morrow.

Squires, Gregory D. 2003a. Racial profiling, insurance style: Insurance redlining and the uneven development of metropolitan America. *Journal of Urban Affairs* 25 (4): 391-410.

———, ed. 2003b. *Organizing access to capital: Advocacy and the democratization of financial institutions*. Philadelphia: Temple University Press.

———, ed. 2005. *Why the poor pay more: How to stop predatory lending*. Westport, CT: Praeger.

Squires, Gregory D., Samantha Friedman, and Catherine E. Saidat. 2002. Experiencing residential segregation: A contemporary study of Washington, D.C. *Urban Affairs Review* 38 (2): 155-83.

Thernstrom, Stephan, and Abigail Thernstrom. 1997. *America in black and white: One nation, indivisible*. New York: Simon & Schuster.

Tiebout, Charles. 1956. A pure theory of local expenditures. *Journal of Political Economy* 64:416-24.

Tilly, Chris, Philip Moss, Joleen Kirschenman, and Ivy Kennelly. 2001. Space as a signal: How employers perceive neighborhoods in four metropolitan labor markets. In *Urban inequality: Evidence from four cities*, ed. Alice O'Connor, Chris Tilly, and Lawrence D. Bobo. New York: Russell Sage Foundation.

Turner, Margery, and Stephen L. Ross. 2005. How racial discrimination affects the search for housing. In *The geography of opportunity: Race and housing choice in metropolitan America*, ed. Xavier de Souza Briggs. Washington, DC: Brookings Institution Press.

Turner, Margery Austin, Stephen L. Ross, George C. Galster, and John Yinger. 2002. *Discrimination in metropolitan housing markets: National results from phase I HDS 2000*. Washington, DC: Urban Institute.

U.S. Census Bureau. 2004. *Housing vacancies and homeownership: Annual statistics 2001*. December 2. Washington, DC: U.S. Census Bureau.

Williams, Walter. 1982. *The state against blacks*. New York: McGraw-Hill.

Wilson, George, Ian Sakura-Lemessy, and Jonathan P. West. 1999. Reaching the top: Racial differences in mobility paths to upper-tier occupations. *Work and Occupations* 26 (2): 165-86.

Wilson, William J. 1996. *When work disappears: The world of the new urban poor*. New York: Knopf.

Racialized Life-Chance Opportunities across the Class Structure: The Case of African Americans

By
GEORGE WILSON

Considerations of how socioeconomic outcomes are racialized within discrete class categories have been neglected in assessing the race/class determinants of life-chance opportunities of African Americans. This article addresses this shortcoming. Specifically, it synthesizes findings from recent sociological research concerning how segregation in two institutional spheres, residence and employment, produce racialization at two class levels—among the impoverished and the middle class. The article documents that segregation plays a significant role in producing racial inequality at both class levels, though it exerts different influences across class categories: at the impoverished level, segregation in the residential sphere, and at the middle-class level, segregation in the employment sphere, emerge as critical underpinnings of African Americans' inferior life-chance opportunities. The implications of the findings for using traditional Weberian and Marxist modes of class analyses in assessing the life-chance opportunities for African Americans as well as how the findings contribute to the resolution of the race/class debate are discussed.

Keywords: race; segregation; residence; employment; African Americans

Sociologists generally agree that in the post-1965 "civil rights" era the African American population has become increasingly differentiated across the American class structure (for reviews, see Jaynes and Williams 1989). In fact, the increasing class differentiation is the basis for the broadening of stratification analyses. Those analyses have increasingly spanned a wide spectrum of the class structure from the impoverished, who are marginally attached to the labor force, to the relatively privileged "middle class," who occupy professional and managerial/executive and highly skilled positions.

George Wilson is an associate professor of sociology at the University of Miami. His research interests focus on the institutional production of racial and ethnic inequality in the workplace and the social structural determinants of beliefs about the causes of racial and economic inequality.

DOI: 10.1177/0002716206295331

Significantly, the rise of a differentiated African American population in recent decades is related to the interpretation by sociologists that social class constitutes the fundamental determinant of life-chance opportunities. In this vein, the "new class bifurcation" (Farley 1996) among the African American population is a product of a combination of macroeconomic and sociopolitical factors. These factors range from the shift from a manufacturing to a service-based economy, the "severed bridge" (Wilson 1996) between low-wage and high-wage labor markets, the movement of industries out of central cities, and the effect of a range of affirmative action policies (Wilson 1978; Hout 1984; Featherman and Hauser 1978). Overall, the logic of this class-based interpretation of life-chance opportunities culminates in a powerful conclusion: in the civil rights era, the gap in economic opportunities has widened across social class lines so that it operates irrespective of social class. Therefore, the socioeconomic standing and trajectory of African Americans more closely resemble those of white class peers than African Americans at other levels of the class structure (Wilson 1978; Farley 1996; Hout 1984; Pomer 1986).

At the impoverished level, segregation in the residential sphere, and at the middle-class level, segregation in the employment sphere, are particularly crucial in explaining the inferior life-chance opportunities of African Americans.

In fact, sociologists have marshaled considerable empirical support for the notion that in recent decades the effects of social class have increased in accounting for the life-chance opportunities of African Americans (see Hout 1984; Pomer 1986; Wilson 1997; Wilson and Royster 1995). Specifically, among African Americans in the post-1965 "civil rights era," the effects of social class account for socioeconomic attainments on both an intragenerational and intergenerational basis. For example, the effect of socioeconomic origins on destinations among African Americans has increased since the early 1970s: African Americans who moved up in socioeconomic status in the 1970s and 1980s compared to the 1960s were drawn disproportionately from relatively advantaged socioeconomic origins (Pomer 1986; Hout 1984). Furthermore, by the late 1970s, the occupational standing of African Americans depended on socioeconomic criteria to a greater extent than was true two decades earlier: those who beat the odds and attained a level of occupational success were able to hold on to those positions to a greater extent than in the past (Wilson 1997; Hout 1984).

These findings, however, should not preclude documenting the multitude of ways in which life-chance opportunities are simultaneously "racialized" (O'Connor 2001), that is, situations in which race operates as a basis for their distribution. In this vein, one rapidly accumulating body of research in recent decades has examined how discrimination across two stratification-relevant institutional spheres in daily life, employment and residence, explain life-chance opportunities at a nuanced level among those who, by conventional measures—such as income and occupation—are similarly situated in the American class structure (Collins 1997; Maume 2004; Corcoran 2001; Landry 1987). This body of research, which has played the crucial role of enhancing our understanding of the importance of spatial dynamics in structuring racial stratification, examines the impact of race primarily at two diametrically opposite locations of the American class structure—at the impoverished and the middle-class levels. To date, literally hundreds of studies from sociologists have now been published analyzing the dynamics of racial stratification across the employment and residential spheres at each of these class levels (for reviews see Wilson 1997; Royster 2003; Zubrinski 2001).

Nevertheless, this research has not been adequately integrated. For example, sociologists have failed to synthesize findings regarding (1) how dynamics across the spheres of residence and employment explain racialized socioeconomic outcomes and (2) the extent to which dynamics in the spheres of residence and employment operate uniformly to account for racialized outcomes at discrete levels of the class structure. In fact, the failure to do so has impeded progress along a relatively new and important area of research in racial stratification—namely, documenting the causes of racial inequality among incumbents who occupy similar positions—at least in title—in the American class structure. This synthesis forms part of the foundation of a more mature understanding of the dynamics of inequality on a within-class basis, which will, in turn, move us closer to arriving at a more informed determination of the roles played by race and class in structuring life-chance opportunities for African Americans.

This article examines the manner in which spheres of employment and residence help to explain the racialization of life-chance opportunities at both the impoverished and the middle-class levels. In particular, it is a critical review and synthesis of the sociological literature at these two levels of the class structure. Overall, this examination produces a two-pronged thesis. First, a common set of causal underpinnings account for racialization at both the impoverished and middle-class levels: segregation by race in the employment and residential spheres is a crucial source of the inferior life-chance opportunities of African Americans, relative to white class peers. Nevertheless, sociological research to date suggests these causal underpinnings exert different influences across class categories. At the impoverished level, segregation in the residential sphere, and at the middle-class level, segregation in the employment sphere, are particularly crucial in explaining the inferior life-chance opportunities of African Americans. Second, the manner in which segregation accounts for racialization of socioeconomic outcomes has implications regarding how to theorize about racial stratification. Specifically, the dynamics of racialization suggest that it is necessary to modify the use of social class—at least in classic Marxian and Weberian formulations—in assessing stratification dynamics of African Americans. At the impoverished and middle-class levels, the combined effect of inferior socioeconomic attainments and a disproportionate reliance, particularly in the employment sphere, on politically mediated sources of economic opportunities, vis-à-vis the private labor market upon which whites rely, creates a virtual caste system that links the life-chance opportunities of African Americans across class categories.

Racialization across the Class Structure

Background

Causal dynamics in the area of racial stratification have traditionally focused on explaining the unequal representation of groups across social class categories (McKee 1992; Collins 1997). In this vein, causal mechanisms associated with a range of traditional theoretical perspectives such as internal colonialism (Hechtor 1972), split-labor market (Bonacich 1973), and competition theory (Lieberson 1980) have been used to explain how "the forces of racism and prejudice endemic to American society" (McKee 1992, 36) lead to the overrepresentation of African Americans at low levels of the American class structure and their underrepresentation at higher levels.

Significantly, variation in life-chance opportunities among African American and white class peers has, for at least two reasons, received far less attention. First, the sheer magnitude of positional differences between African Americans and whites has placed a premium on producing theories of racial stratification to explain it (McKee 1992). Second, prominent theories of social stratification have not provided an impetus for sociologists to explore the possibility of race-based differences among incumbents in a similar class position (Wilson, Sakura-Lemessy, and West 1999). In this vein, "supply-side" conceptions such as "human capital" theory (Becker 1957; Arrow 1972) assume that African Americans and whites who share a similar class position receive similar "returns" in the form of both workplace-based rewards and investments in real estate to human capital credentials such as levels of educational attainment and experience in the workforce (Featherman and Hauser 1978); similarly, the "status attainment tradition" (Blau and Duncan 1967) maintains that background socioeconomic status acts in an identical fashion across racial groups to structure levels of peer- and parent-driven aspirations for success and the subsequent attainment of socioeconomic rewards (Featherman and Hauser 1978). Finally, in terms of "demand-side" conceptions, "dual labor market theory" (Hodson and Kaufman 1982; Kaufman 1983) maintains there are similar consequences for whites and African Americans when slotted in the resource-poor and heavily nonunionized "peripheral sector," as well as when allocated in the core sector where firms tend to be resource-rich and contain unionized positions as well as internal labor markets so that meaningful career status is normative.

Racialization among the poor

In the past several decades, sociologists have amassed a considerable amount of evidence that theories of racial and social stratification have been deficient because they have not accounted for findings from empirical research that life-chance opportunities among incumbents at discrete class levels are racialized. A first body of research challenges the notion that African Americans and whites in poverty face a similar set of socioeconomic prospects. In particular, research conducted in the post-1980 period, when poverty was "rediscovered" as a social problem, documents systematic variation in life-chance opportunities along racial lines at the low end of the American class structure. Relevant in this regard are studies that use a variety of methodological strategies including treatises and case studies (Wilson 1996, 1987; Massey and Denton 1993; Gans 1995; Ellwood 1988), ethnographies (Royster 2003; Edin 1993; Anderson 1990; Dunier 1992; Newman 1999), as well as survey-based analyses (Hernandez 2001; Freeman 1991; Duncan and Brooks-Gunn 2001; Danziger and Weinberg 1994; Zubrinski 2001; Jencks and Mayer 1990; Krysan and Farley 2002; Farley and Frey 1994; Johnson and Oliver 1991; Kasarda 1990, 1983; Kirschenman and Neckerman 1991; Bane and Ellwood 1986; Blank 1989, 1993; Gottschalk, Mclanahan, and Sandefur 1994; Corcoran 2001; Newman 1999; Corcoran and Adams 1997) and typically delineate poverty from nonimpoverished status on the basis of income or labor market status (i.e., employed full-time or not).

Overall, these studies, when distilled, demonstrate that African Americans tend to experience both longer spells of poverty than whites and suffer from more extreme economic deprivation in poverty than whites. For example, African Americans are more likely than whites to experience "permanent poverty" (Gottschalk 1994; Corcoran and Adams 1997), that is, impoverishment that is of relatively long and uninterrupted duration. In particular, permanent poverty has pronounced intergenerational and intragenerational consequences: impoverished status persists across the individual life course and is also likely to be transmitted from parents to children (Bane and Ellwood 1986; Blank 1993, 1989). Conversely, poverty experienced by whites is more likely to be "temporary" (Gottschalk 1994); that is, it is relatively finite in duration over the individual life course and is not as likely to be transmitted across generations (Gottschalk 1994; Corcoran 2001; Corcoran and Adams 1997). In addition, African Americans are more likely than whites to experience "dire" (Danziger and Weinberg 1994) poverty, that is, a socioeconomic status characterized by extreme marginality. Specifically, empirical studies have established that after introducing statistical controls for family size and family composition, the average household income of impoverished African American families in the past decade or so was approximately

30 percent below the federally mandated poverty line. In contrast, the household income for the average poor white family during the same time span fell about 10 percent below the poverty line (Jargowsky 1997; Corcoran 2001; Freeman 1991).

In addition, studies have identified crucial sources of the unique form of deprivation that African Americans experience, relative to whites, a hallmark of which is its spatial concentration (Massey and Denton 1993, 1987; Jargowsky 1997). Specifically, studies of trends in residential segregation by social class among African Americans and whites have consistently found the African American poor are, on average, approximately one-half as likely as impoverished whites to live in neighborhoods that have at least a moderate nonpoor presence (that is, in neighborhoods in which the nonpoor exceeds 20 percent of the population (Zubrinski 2001; Massey and Denton 1993). These findings, in fact, are relatively consistent across the past two decades in both central-city and suburban areas of virtually all major metropolitan areas and in both older housing stocks constructed before the passing of federal antidiscrimination laws in housing in the 1960s and 1970s as well as for housing stocks constructed after the advent of the antidiscrimination laws (Krysan and Farley 2002; Farley and Frey 1994; Johnson and Oliver 1991).

Significantly, these studies have also demonstrated that, as poverty increases in concentration, a wide range of disadvantageous demographic and economically driven "neighborhood effects" (Sampson, Morenoff, and Gannon-Rowley 2002; Jencks and Mayer 1990) are triggered that negatively impact on the life-chance opportunities of the neighborhood's residents. The studies find that concentrated poverty is associated with inferior local/neighborhood opportunity structures. Firms and businesses in those neighborhoods provide only limited prospects for stable and remunerative long-term employment. At the same time, only inferior mobility-related institutions, such as schools and training/vocational facilities, provide opportunities to become competitive in the labor market—a labor market increasingly predicated on acquiring skills at an early career stage to achieve favorable career trajectories (Johnson and Oliver 1991; Duncan and Brooks-Gunn 2001). In addition, concentrated poverty limits the access of the African American poor to the racially integrated and "socioeconomically viable" (Massey and Denton 1993) informational networks that lead to awareness of favorable employment opportunities (Johnson and Oliver 1991; Kirschenman and Neckerman 1991). It also precludes opportunities to demonstrate qualities of workers to employers in such a way as to combat invidious stereotypes regarding lack of productivity and fitness for work that impede opportunities in the labor market (Neckerman and Kirschenman 1991; Wilson 1996). In addition, concentrated poverty is related to the rise of injurious social psychological states such as dampened career aspirations, the formation of counterproductive values such as fatalism and resignation, and finally, the development of the seeds of an "oppositional culture" (Ainsworth-Darnell and Downey 1998; Downey and Ainsworth-Darnell 2002) that represents a strategy for coping with limited prospects for socioeconomic advancement (Wilson 1996; Anderson 1990).

Finally, studies of racial stratification among the poor document that prospects for achieving mobility out of impoverished status differ among African Americans and whites. African Americans in poverty, largely by virtue of residing in neighborhoods with disadvantaged neighborhood effects, face an inferior set of opportunities in the private labor market (Corcoran 1992). Accordingly, they are reliant disproportionately upon one source—government-sponsored programs—to provide training to acquire labor market skills (Freeman 1991). Conversely, the route to social mobility is broader for impoverished whites. In addition to government intervention, whites are able to rely upon an additional source—the private labor market—as a means of attaining social mobility (Corcoran 1992; Freeman 1991).[1] Geographic proximity to firms/businesses with internal labor markets and career ladders that are part of either the manufacturing sector or the burgeoning service-based sector of the American economy provides training opportunities, relatively favorable returns to human capital investments, and ultimately, social mobility through placement in positions that afford career status (Johnson and Oliver 1991; Newman 1999).

Racialization among the middle class

In the past several decades, sociological research has also documented race-based differences in life-chance opportunities at the relatively privileged middle-class level. This research has been eclectic methodologically, encompassing both survey-based analyses (Wilson 1997; Wilson, Sakura-Lemessy, and West 1999; McBrier and Wilson 2004; Kluegel 1978; Thomas 1995; Wilson and McBrier 2005; Smith 2001; Smith and Elliott 2002) and case studies (Collins 1997, 1993; Fernandez 1982, 1975; Pattillo-McCoy 1999; Landry 1987; Brown and Erie 1981). A further hallmark of this research has been its timeliness: it uncovers race-specific dynamics several decades into the post-1965 civil rights era as African Americans have increased their representation in occupationally based positions typically used to define the middle class—specifically, professionals, managers, and administrators—at a more rapid rate than whites (Farley 1996; Farley and Allen 1987).[2]

A synthesis of existing studies at the middle-class level documents that a parallel set of dynamics across the same institutional spheres identified in studies of the poor are responsible for the racialization of socioeconomic rewards among African Americans and white class peers. However, here the dynamics in the employment sphere rather than the residential sphere emerge as particularly important. The politically mediated nature of the rise of African Americans into, and placement within, the middle class is implicated as a source of racial inequality: to combat discrimination in the private sector, the government has historically provided a "niche" for African Americans within the middle class job structure (Collins 1997; Wilson 1997). Indeed, several studies document that the majority of the African American middle class spend the majority of their careers in the public sector (Patillo-McCoy 1999; Brown and Erie 1981). Nevertheless, the public sector as the locus of privilege for African Americans has had detrimental socioeconomic consequences. For example, the public sector offers progressively lesser economic returns relative to the private sector as work careers unfold

(Brown and Erie 1981; Wilson 1997). Furthermore, job responsibilities in the public sector tend to focus on providing services to the poor and, therefore, do not provide contact with the kind of customers/clients, namely, the nonpoor, that allow them to be perceived by prospective employers in the private sector as potentially attractive recruits (Collins 1997, 1993).

> *[T]he constraints on residential options among the African American middle class that result in living in close proximity to other African Americans are associated with inferior residential investments.*

However, not to be overlooked is that relatively privileged African Americans—for a set of reasons that differ from those that operate in the public sector—suffer from inequities, relative to whites, when working in the private sector. Specifically, African Americans in the private sector tend to perform politically induced "racialized labor" (Collins 1993), that is, engaging in job functions that are "directed at, used by, or concerned with, minority group members" (Collins 1997, 54). In predominantly white-owned and -managed firms in the private sector, African Americans perform work-based functions that are tied into satisfying the consumer needs of minority customers/clients as well as in community/equal employment opportunity capacities (Collins 1997, 1993). Significantly, racialized labor places African Americans on inferior-rewarded, "peripheral" (Collins 1997) mobility tracts vis-à-vis performing "mainstream labor" (Collins 1997), that is, servicing the needs of a relatively lucrative, predominantly white client base (Collins 1993; Brown and Erie 1981). To date, performing racialized labor, relative to mainstream labor, has been found to translate into many negative consequences: (1) inferior earnings "returns" for investments in human capital credentials; (2) restriction to internal career ladders that impose "glass ceilings" limiting upward mobility trajectories; (3) positions with circumscribed reward-relevant job characteristics, such as limited span and scope of supervisory responsibility and job autonomy; and (4) high rates of downward occupational mobility out of the middle class (Maume 2004; Collins 1997, 1993; McBrier and Wilson 2004; Farley and Allen 1989; Wilson 1997; Smith 2005).

Finally, studies also document that irrespective of allocation into the public or private sectors, African American incumbents in middle-class occupations are disadvantaged because of reliance on racially segregated job networks (Wilson

1997; Collins 1993; Moore 1981). In particular, restricted access to integrated job networks precludes African Americans from demonstrating to employers the informal, "particularistic" (Kluegel 1978; Smith 2001) criteria such as loyalty, trustworthiness, and leadership potential that are important in structuring employment evaluations (Kluegel 1978; Fernandez 1975; Wilson 1997). Accordingly, the lack of opportunities for African Americans to demonstrate requisite informal criteria creates obstacles that keep them from overcoming deep-rooted stereotypes regarding suitability for, and productivity at, work. The result limits their mobility opportunities relative to white incumbents (Wilson, Sakura-Lemessy, and West 1999; Kluegel 1978; Pettigrew 1985).

Segregation in the residential sphere also helps to account for racialization of socioeconomic outcomes at the middle-class level. A line of studies document that the African American middle class tends to reside in neighborhoods composed of higher proportions of the poor than neighborhoods in which white class peers reside (Denton and Massey 1987; Squires and Kubrin 2006). Accordingly, African Americans have limited ability to translate "socioeconomic assimilation" (Denton and Massey 1987), that is, substantial financial resources, into "spatial assimilation (Denton and Massey 1987), that is, neighborhoods with significant proportions of middle-class residents. Significantly, the constraints on residential options among the African American middle class that result in living in close proximity to other African Americans are associated with inferior residential investments. These consumers end up both "buying high" as an initial financial outlay and, as a long-term investment, receiving low levels of appreciated value in real estate (Galster 1990; Massey and Denton 1993; Squires and Kubrin 2006). However, middle-class African Americans' accumulation of human capital and financial resources, relative to the African American poor, is able to partially overcome the deleterious consequences associated with residing in neighborhoods that contain disadvantaged neighborhood effects. Perhaps most important, relatively privileged African Americans—unlike the African American poor—are not restricted exclusively to the "neighborhood/local opportunity structure" (Anderson 1990, 145) that contains a disproportionate number of low-level service sector firms (see Patillo-McCoy 1999; Anderson 1990; Dunier 1992).

The dynamics by which segregation in the employment and residential spheres at both the impoverished and middle-class levels helps to produce racialization are summarized in Table 1.

Discussion

Racialization and segregation in employment and residence at the impoverished and the middle-class levels

Assessing the "racialization" of socioeconomic attainment within discrete categories of the American class structure contributes toward our understanding of the race/class determinants of life-chance opportunities for African Americans. This article has integrated findings concerning how segregation across the spheres of

TABLE 1
SUMMARY OF DYNAMICS OF RACIALIZATION AMONG
THE POOR AND MIDDLE CLASS

Institutional Sphere	Poor		Middle Class	
	African American	White	African American	White
1. Residence				
A. Class/race neighborhood composition	All poor/African American	Poor and nonpoor/African American and white	Poor and nonpoor/African American and white	Nonpoor/white
B. Value of real estate investment	Extremely inferior	Moderately inferior	Moderately inferior	Extremely good
C. Neighborhood conditions	Deleterious neighborhood effects	Nondeleterious neighborhood effects	Deleterious neighborhood effects	Nondeleterious neighborhood effects
2. Employment				
A. Employment status	Chronic unemployment; chronic underemployment	Marginal unemployment; marginal underemployment	Career instability	Career stability
B. Income level	Extremely low	Marginally low	Moderate High	
C. Mobility rates and trajectory	Poor: Employment in service sector with no career ladders	Moderate: Employment in service and manufacturing sectors with career ladders	Moderate: Racialized jobs and segregated network	Good: Mainstream jobs and integrated networks
D. Source of mobility	Politically mediated in public sector	Nonpolitically mediated in public and private sectors	Politically mediated in public and private sectors	Nonpolitically mediated in public and private sectors
3. Life-chance consequences (combination of 1 and 2)	Permanent poverty; extreme marginality	Temporary poverty; nonextreme marginality	Moderate rewards across work career	High rewards across work career

employment and residence helps to explain the racialization of life-chance opportunities for African Americans at the impoverished and middle-class levels. The synthesis reveals that segregation in these two spheres constitutes common causal underpinnings of the racialization of rewards at both class levels. Nevertheless, the causal underpinnings appear to exert different influences across class categories: at the impoverished level, segregation in the residential sphere, and at the middle-class level, segregation in the employment sphere, emerge as particularly critical underpinnings of African Americans' inferior life-chance opportunities.

Significantly, the grounding of racialized socioeconomic outcomes in segregation at the impoverished and middle-class levels makes it important to identify the sources of segregation. In this vein, the persistence of segregation in the residential and employment spheres should be seen as intimately related to the subtle, institutional, and ostensibly nonracial dynamics that characterize "modern racial discrimination" (Pettigrew 1985; Pettigrew and Martin 1987) rather than as a product of the ill will and intentionality associated with traditional "Jim Crow" racism (Bobo, Kluegel, and Smith 1997). Above all, modern discrimination is characterized by its indirect character. It encompasses institutionally based and facially neutral practices that are rooted in such phenomena as "business necessity" (Pettigrew and Martin 1987) and forms of "self-interest" (Bobo and Kluegel 1993) that when applied in a uniform manner capture the legacy of discrimination and produce results that have a disproportionately negative impact on African Americans (Pettigrew 1985; Bobo, Kluegel, and Smith 1997). Overall, when prejudice underlies these practices, a relatively modern and benign constellation of stereotypes regarding the culture/motivational deficiencies of African Americans is implicated (Pettigrew 1985; Bobo, Kluegel, and Smith 1997; Wilson, Sakura-Lemessy, and West 1999).

In the sphere of employment, a similar set of dynamics associated with modern racial discrimination account for the restriction of the African American poor to the low-end service sector economy as well the African American middle class in public sector jobs and marginalized slots in the private sector. For example, "business necessity" associated with the perceived need to ensure continued loyalty of valued white clients/customers (Wilson 1997; Fernandez 1981) as well as statistical discrimination emanating from stereotypes about the work ethic of minority group workers (Tomaskovic-Devey and Skaggs 1999; Pettigrew 1985) put a premium on allocating both the African American poor and middle class into marginal slots relative to White class peers (Collins 1997; Wilson 1997). The one conspicuous difference in determinants of racial segregation in the employment sphere across class categories derives from the effects of segregation in the residential sphere: impoverished African Americans have experienced particularly limited economic opportunities by virtue of their residential concentration in neighborhoods that have experienced the greatest ravages of deindustrialization (Anderson 1990).

The roots of segregation in the residential sphere at both the impoverished and middle-class levels also lie in the subtle dynamics associated with the modern form of discrimination. For example, the legacy of racial inequality manifested in differences in accumulated wealth across racial groups who occupy similar class positions results in a wider residential labor market for whites than African Americans (Conley 1999; Oliver and Shapiro 1995).[3] Furthermore, forms of "self-interest" such as the perceived need to maintain the value of real estate investments among white home owners (Galster and Keeney 1988) and the desire of brokers/realtors to maximize economic returns in real estate transactions (Galster and Keeney 1988) result in discriminatory practices—triggered primarily by real estate agents—that restrict African Americans to a relatively limited range of residential options (Galster, Freiberg, and Houk 1987). These practices include "racial steering" (Galster 1990), in which African Americans and whites are directed toward separate housing stocks that are unequal in terms of the value of their financial investment and "blockbusting" (Galster 1990), in which realtors sell previously white-owned property to African Americans at inflated prices pursuant to targeting a transformation in neighborhood composition from predominantly white to African American (Massey and Denton 1993).

Racialization and social class analysis

An additional issue that logically follows from the analysis of racialization at discrete levels of the American class structure concerns the propriety of using the term "social class" in assessing the life-chance opportunities of African Americans. Traditional conceptualizations of social class in sociology, namely, those in the Marxian and Weberian traditions, posit that class position is based on two criteria: level of socioeconomic rewards and a source of the rewards (Giddens 1970). Specifically, studies in the Weberian tradition maintain that a "set of shared life-chance opportunities" (Giddens 1970, 209) constitute the essence of class position. Life-chance opportunities refer to "a market situation in the private labor market" (Giddens 1970, 210) that is "separate and apart from members of other class groupings" (Giddens 1970, 211). Similarly, studies in the Marxian tradition maintain that class position designates accumulated resources associated with level of ownership and control of capital and the expropriation of labor in business and industry (Wright 1997; Robinson and Kelley 1979).

Significantly, the twofold criteria that constitute defining characteristics of social class in the Marxist and Weberian conceptualizations offer a basis for concluding that social class captures the dynamics of stratification of whites but not African Americans. First, sociological research has established that African Americans receive an inferior level of rewards relative to whites, at both the impoverished and middle-class levels. Second, the socioeconomic standing and trajectories for African Americans, at both the impoverished and middle class levels, relative to whites, is premised on a "politically driven interventionist economy" (Brown and Erie 1981, 313) designed to overcome discrimination in the private labor market. Specifically, the African American poor tend to suffer from an economic plight that requires "radical state-based intervention to ensure subsistence and impart skills necessary to become meaningfully integrated into the labor market" (Anderson 1990, 84). For the African American middle class, politically induced dynamics "are indispensable to the creation of a relatively hospitable niche within the middle class job structure that drives careers and economic trajectories" (Collins 1997, 116). Conversely, for whites, at both the impoverished and middle-class levels, life-chance opportunities are dependent upon a source that is in line with the tenets of traditional Marxian and Weberian conceptions of social class, namely, the dynamics of the private labor market.

Overall, to resolve the issue of the propriety of using class analysis in explaining life-chance opportunities of African Americans in the civil rights era, sociologists need to address several fundamental concerns. First, class, at least when its defining characteristics in the Marxian and Weberian traditions are strictly construed, appears to have limited heuristic value in explaining the life-chance opportunities of African Americans. Accordingly, how is it reconciled with findings that structural location, often referred to as "class position," has produced a fundamental bifurcation in the socioeconomic standing and trajectories between the African American poor and middle class? In terms of using class, in the context of analyses of African Americans, it may be able to be retained, but at a minimum, there should be a call to reconceptualize class in a formal manner that incorporates a broader range of defining characteristics than levels of rewards and source of rewards. Second, how is class analysis to be salvaged in view of the racial link in life-chance opportunities that exists across structural locations among the African American population? It appears that class may be retained but its reconceptualization on broader grounds should acknowledge theoretically what role E. Franklin Frazier's (1957) notion of "quasi-caste dynamics" played in determining the life-chance opportunities for African Americans. Frazier, nearly five decades ago, recognized that the newly emerging population of African American professionals and successful businessmen had dissimilar socioeconomic trajectories from the African American poor, yet were linked with them in facing exclusion from participation in the mainstream labor market, namely, the private sector where the most favorable socioeconomic rewards and trajectories lay; this link among incumbents across social class categories, according to Frazier, is a product of one of the central tenets of caste, a shared restriction in mobility opportunities that operates on an ascriptive basis—namely, race.

Conclusion

A review and synthesis of the dynamics of racialization in this article contributes to the ongoing debate about the relative effects of race and social class in explaining life-chance opportunities among African Americans in the post-1965 civil rights era. This debate has been contentious and highly politicized as manifested in scholars having tended to argue that the influence of one dominates the other (Niemonen 2002; Wilson and Royster 1995). In fact, the contentiousness has precluded adopting a broader, more inclusive posture that, based on the totality of evidence from sociological research, assigns an important role to both as causal factors in determining life-chance opportunities in the post-1965 civil rights era (Pettigrew 1985). Accordingly, the findings that emerge from the review and synthesis in this article build on previous sociological research and suggest one way in which both can be assigned an important causal role. Specifically, social class tends to play a crucial role in structuring the basic parameters of socioeconomic standing and trajectories. Simultaneously, however, one way in which race operates—as documented in this article—is that it restricts attainments among African Americans, relative to whites, within these parameters, thereby establishing a link in life-chance opportunities with other African Americans, irrespective of class status.

> *[S]egregation in the employment and residential spheres shows little signs of abating . . . [and] the detrimental consequences of segregation appear to be increasing.*

Furthermore, one point concerning the implications of these findings bears mentioning: there is not a strong basis for concluding that the racialized outcomes at the impoverished and middle-class levels will be reduced any time soon. First, segregation in the employment and residential spheres shows little signs of abating. For example, in the residential sphere, discriminatory real estate practices that contribute to residential segregation have proven to be resistant to change. The continuing viability of practices such as racial steering and blockbusting is a product of forms of economic self-interest as well as notorious lax enforcement of antidiscrimination laws in housing (see Galster 1990). In the employment sphere, dynamics that underlie the placement of the African Americans in marginalized slots relative to white class peers also persist: social psychologists have struggled to identify how to reduce the prevalence of invidious racial stereotypes (Pettigrew 1985). Judicial rulings by a majority of federal district courts have made it increasingly unlikely that segregation as an unintended consequence of practices that constitute, for example, "business necessity" will be deemed to violate equal employment opportunity law (Fernandez 1982). Second, the detrimental consequences of segregation appear to be increasing. For example, the acceleration of a phenomenon such as deindustrialization is producing a growing spatial concentration of firms at the low end of the new service sector economy in metropolitan areas, where African Americans reside, thereby exacerbating negative stratification-based trajectories, particularly for the African American poor (Newman 1999; Johnson and Oliver 1991). Third, political intervention, which has played a disproportionate role in providing opportunity for African Americans, relative to whites, across the American class structure is waning. In recent decades, the cumulative effect of growing insensitivity toward the plight of the poor, fiscal crisis in government funding, and perceptions that government has become too large and intrusive is serving to constrict the already relatively marginal life-chance opportunities for both the African American poor and middle class (Quadagno 1994; Edsall and Edsall 1991).

Finally, it is important to point out that more research is needed to fill out our understanding of the extent to which patterns of segregation in both the residential and employment spheres explain racialization of socioeconomic outcomes across the American class structure. Researchers need to undertake analyses at additional levels of the class structure such as the working class, that is, manual workers, who occupy a position between the impoverished and the middle class. Systematic analyses of racial stratification dynamics among the working class continue to be rare compared to other class categories (Royster 2003; Horton et al. 2000). Furthermore, research is needed to assess dynamics for other minorities such as Latino and sub-Latino groups as well as Asian and sub-Asian groups. In recent decades, these populations have come to more directly compete with other groups as they have increasingly abandoned residential and occupational enclaves in pursuing expanded occupational and housing options (Zubrinski 2001; O'Connor 2001). Finally, temporal analyses, that is, longitudinal and trend designs, are needed to assess the extent to which racialization is a product of period effects and exerts variation across stages of the work career as there is documented variation in levels of segregation across institutional spheres and the stratification-relevant importance of segregation on these bases (Farley 1996; Krysan and Farley 2002; O'Connor 2001). Overall, when this research is undertaken, it promises to shed light on one of the most important issues in the sociological analysis of racial stratification—the extent to which ascription operates as a cleavage that defines inequality in contemporary American society.

Notes

1. The majority of government-sponsored programs continue to be income- rather than race-targeted (see O'Connor 2001).

2. This is the most widely used conceptualization of the middle class in the racial context (see Patillo-McCoy 1999; Wilson, Sakura-Lemessey, and West 1999).

3. It is recognized that racial differences in wealth accumulation are a fundamental determinant of intraclass differences in life-chance opportunities across racial groups. The wealth gap, which captures the legacy of racial discrimination, has created large differences in financial resources that have widespread consequences. In this article, wealth differences are considered only to the extent they help to account for segregation in the institutional spheres under consideration—employment and residence.

References

Ainsworth-Darnell, James, and Douglas Downey. 1998. Assessing the oppositional culture explanation for racial/ethnic differences in school performance. *American Sociological Review* 63:536-553.

Anderson, Elijah. 1990. *Streetwise*. Chicago: University of Chicago Press.

Arrow, Kenneth. 1972. Models of job discrimination. In *Racial discrimination in economic life*, ed. A. H. Pascal, 83-102. Lexington, MA: Lexington Books.

Bane, Mary Jo, and David Ellwood. 1986. Slipping into and out of poverty: The dynamics of spells. *Journal of Human Resources* 21:1-23.
Becker, George. 1957. *Human capital: A theoretical and empirical analysis with special reference to education*. New York: Praeger.
Blank, Rebecca. 1989. Analyzing the length of welfare spells. *Journal of Public Economics* 39:245-73.
―――. 1993. Why were poverty rates so high in the 1980's. In *Poverty and prosperity in the USA in the late twentieth century*, ed. Dimitri Papadimitriou and Edward Wolff, 15-53. New York: Macmillan.
Blau, Peter, and Otis Duncan. 1967. *The American occupational structure*. New York: John Wiley.
Bobo, Lawrence, and James Kluegel. 1993. Opposition to race-targeting: Self-interest, stratification ideology, or racial attitudes. *American Sociological Review* 58:443-64.
Bobo, Lawrence, James Kluegel, and Ryan Smith. 1997. Laissez-Faire racism: The cystallization of a kinder, gentler, antiblack ideology. In *Racial attitudes in the 1990's*, ed. Steven Tuch and Jack Martin, 15-44. Westport, CT: Praeger.
Bonacich, Edna. 1973. The split-labor market: A theory of ethnic antagonism. *American Sociological Review* 38:212-31.
Brown, Michael, and Steven Erie. 1981. Blacks and the legacy of the Great Society: The economic and political impact of federal social policy. *Public Policy* 29:299-330.
Collins, Sharon. 1993. Blacks on the bubble: the vulnerability of black executives in a white corporation. *Sociological Quarterly* 34:429-47.
―――. 1997. *Black corporate executives: The making and breaking of a black middle class*. Philadelphia: Temple University Press.
Conley, Dalton. 1999. *Being black but living in the red*. Berkeley: University of California Press.
Corcoran, Mary. 1992. Rags to rags: Poverty and mobility in the United States. *Annual Review of Sociology* 13:13-41.
―――. 2001. Mobility, persistence, and consequences of poverty for children. In *Understanding poverty*, ed. Sheldon Danziger and Robert Haveman, 58-83. New York: Russell Sage Foundation.
Corcoran, Mary, and Terry Adams. 1997. Race, sex, and the intergenerational transmission of poverty. In *Consequences of growing up poor*, ed. Greg Duncan and Jeanne Brooks-Gunn, 461-518. New York: Russell Sage Foundation.
Danziger, Sheldon, and Daniel Weinberg. 1994. The historic record: Trends in family income, inequality, and poverty. In *Confronting poverty*, ed. Sheldon Danziger, Gary Sandefur, and Daniel Weinberg, 18-50. New York: Russell Sage Foundation Press.
Denton, Nancy, and Douglas Massey. 1987. Residential segregation of blacks, Hispanics, and Asians by socioeconomic status and generation. *Social Science Quarterly* 43:197-211.
Downey, Douglas, and James Ainsworth-Darnell. 2002. The search for oppositional culture among black students. *American Sociological Review* 67:156-64.
Duncan, Greg, and Jeanne Brooks-Gunn. 2001. Income effects across the life span: Integration and interpretation. In *Consequences of growing up poor*, ed. Greg Duncan and Jeanne Brooks-Gunn, 596-610. New York: Russell Sage Foundation.
Dunier, Mitchell. 1992. *Slim's table*. Chicago: University of Chicago Press.
Edin, Kathryn. 1993. *There's a lot of money left at the end of the month: How AFDC recipients make ends meet in Chicago*. New York: Garland Press.
Edsall, Thomas, and Mary Edsall. 1991. *Chain reaction: The impact of race, rights, and taxes on American politics*. New York: Norton.
Ellwood, David. 1988. *Poor support: Poverty in the American family*. New York: Basic Books.
Farley, Reynolds. 1996. *The new American reality*. New York: Russell Sage Foundation.
Farley, Reynolds, and Walter Allen. 1987. *The quality of life and the color line in America*. New York: Russell Sage Foundation.
Farley, Reynolds, and William Frey. 1994. Changes in the segregation of whites from blacks in the 1980's. *American Sociological Review* 59:23-45.
Featherman, David, and Philip Hauser. 1978. *Opportunity and change*. New York: Academic Press.
Fernandez, James. 1975. *Black managers in white corporations*. Lexington, MA: Lexington Books.
―――. 1982. *Racism and sexism in white corporations*. New York: Wiley.
Frazier, E. Franklin. 1957. *The black bourgeosie*. Chicago: University of Chicago Press.

Freeman, Richard. 1991. Employment and earnings of disadvantaged young men in a labor shortage economy. In *The urban underclass*, ed. Christopher Jencks and Paul Peterson, 45-72. Washington, DC: Brookings Institution.
Galster, George. 1990. Racial steering by real estate agents: Mechanisms and motives. *Review of Black Political Economy* 19:39-63.
Galster, George, Fred Freiberg, and Diane Houk. 1987. Racial differentials in real estate advertising practices. *Journal of Urban Affairs* 9:199-215.
Galster, George, and William Keeney. 1988. Race, residence discrimination, and economic opportunity. *Urban Affairs Quarterly* 24:87-117.
Gans, Herbert. 1995. *The war against the poor*. New York: Basic Books.
Giddens, Anthony. 1970. *Capitalism and modern social theory*. London: Cambridge University Press.
Gottschalk, Peter. 1994. The dynamics of intergenerational poverty and welfare participation. In *Confronting poverty*, ed. Sheldon Danziger, Gary Sandefur, and Daniel Weinberg, 85-108. Cambridge, MA: Harvard University Press.
Gottschalk, Peter, Sara Mclanahan, and Gary Sandefur. 1994. Dynamics and intergenerational transmission of poverty and welfare participation. In *Confronting poverty*, ed. Sheldon Danziger, Gary Sandefur, and Daniel Weinberg, 85-108. New York: Russell Sage Foundation Press.
Hechtor, Michael. 1972. *Internal colonialism*. New Haven, CT: Yale University Press.
Hernandez, Donald. 2001. Poverty trends. In *Consequences of growing up poor*, ed. James Duncan and Jeanne Brooks-Gunn, 18-34. New York: Russell Sage Foundation.
Hodson, Randy, and Robert Kaufman. 1982. Economic dualism: A critical review. *American Sociological Review* 47:727-39.
Horton, Hayward Derrick, Beverly Allen, Cedric Herring, and Melvin Thomas. 2000. Lost in the storm: The sociology of the black working class, 1850-1990. *American Sociological Review* 65:128-37.
Hout, Michael. 1984. Occupational mobility of black men: 1962-1973. *American Sociological Review* 98:575-92.
Jargowsky, Paul. 1997. *Poverty and place*. New York: Russell Sage Foundation.
Jaynes, David, and Robin Williams. 1989. *A common destiny: Blacks and American institutions*. Washington, DC: National Academy Press.
Jencks, Christopher, and Susan Mayer. 1990. The social consequences of growing up in a poor neighborhood. In *Inner-city poverty in the U.S.*, ed. Lawrence Geary, 38-71. Washington, DC: National Academy Press.
Johnson, James, and Melvin Oliver. 1991. Economic restructuring and black male joblessness in U.S. metropolitan areas. *Urban Geography* 12:542-62.
Kasarda, John. 1983. Entry-level jobs, mobility, and urban minority unemployment. *Urban Affairs Quarterly* 19:21-40.
———. 1990. Structural factors affecting the location and timing of urban underclass growth. *Urban Geography* 11:234-64.
Kaufman, Robert. 1983. A structural decomposition of black-white earnings. *American Sociological Review* 43:585-611.
Kirschenman, Joleen, and Kathryn Neckerman. 1991. We'd love to hire them, but; the meaning of race for employers. In *The urban underclass*, ed. Christopher Jencks and Paul Peterson, 26-61. Washington, DC: Brookings Institution.
Kluegel, James. 1978. The causes and consequences of racial exclusion from job authority. *American Sociological Review* 43:285-301.
Krysan, Marie, and Reynolds Farley. 2002. The residential preference for blacks: Do they explain persistent segregation? *Social Forces* 80:937-80.
Landry, Bart. 1987. *The new black middle class*. Berkeley: University of California Press.
Lieberson, Stanley. 1980. *A piece of the pie*. Cambridge, MA: Harvard University Press.
Massey, Douglas, and Nancy Denton. 1987. Residential segregation of blacks, Hispanics, and Asians by socioeconomic status and generation. *Social Science Quarterly* 43:796-817.
———. 1993. *American apartheid*. Cambridge, MA: Harvard University Press.
Maume, David. 2004. Is the glass ceiling a unique form of inequality? Evidence from a random effects model of managerial attainment. *Work & Occupations* 31:255-83.

McBrier, Debra, and George Wilson. 2004. Going down: Race and downward mobility for white-collar workers in the 1990's. *Work & Occupations* 31:283-322.
McKee, James. 1992. *Sociology and the race problem*. Philadelphia: Temple University Press.
Moore, Joan. 1981. Minorities in the American class system. *Daedalus* 110:275-99.
Newman, Katherine. 1999. *No shame in my game*. New York: Russell Sage Foundation.
Niemonen, Jack. 2002. *Race, class, and the state in contemporary sociology*. Boulder, CO: Lynne Rienner.
O'Connor, Alice. 2001. Understanding inequality in the late twentieth century metropolis: New perspectives on the enduring racial divide. In *Urban inequality; evidence from four cities*, ed. Alice O'Connor, Chris Tilly, and Lawrence Bobo, 1-33. New York: Russell Sage Foundation.
Oliver, Melvin, and Thomas Shapiro. 1995. *Black wealth—White wealth*. Urbana: University of Illinois Press.
Patillo-McCoy, Mary. 1999. *Black picket fences: Privilege and peril among the black middle class*. Chicago: University of Chicago Press.
Pettigrew, Thomas. 1985. New black-white patterns: How best to conceptualize them. *Annual Review of Sociology* 11:329-46.
Pettigrew, Thomas, and Joanne Martin. 1987. Shaping the organizational context for African American inclusion. *Journal of Social Issues* 43:41-78.
Pomer, Marshall. 1986. Labor market structure, intragenerational mobility, and discrimination: Black male advancement out of low-paying occupations. *American Sociological Review* 51:650-59.
Quadagno, Jill. 1994. *The color of welfare: How racism undermined the war on poverty*. New York: Oxford University Press.
Robinson, Robert, and Jonathon Kelley. 1979. Class as conceived By Marx and Dahrendorf: Effects on income inequality and politics in the U.S. and Great Britain. *American Sociological Review* 44:38-55.
Royster, Deirdre. 2003. *Race and the invisible hand*. Berkeley: University of California Press.
Sampson, Robert, Jeffrey Morenoff, and Thomas Gannon-Rowley. 2002. Assessing neighborhood effects: Social processes and new directions for research. *Annual Review of Sociology* 28:443-78.
Smith, Ryan. 2001. Particularism in control over monetary resources at work: An analysis of racioethnic differences in the authority outcomes of black, white, and Latino men. *Work & Occupations* 28:15-33.
———. 2005. Do the determinants of promotion differ for white men versus women and minorities? An exploration of intersectionalism through sponsored and contest mobility processes. *American Behavioral Scientist* 48:1167-81.
Smith, Ryan, and James Elliott. 2002. Does ethnic concentration influence employees' access to authority? An examination of contemporary urban labor markets. *Social Forces* 81:255-79.
Squires, Greg, and Charis Kubrin. 2006. *Privileged places: Race, residence, and the structure of opportunity*. Boulder, CO: Lynne Rienner.
Thomas, Melvin. 1995. Race, class, and occupation: An analysis of black and white earnings for professional and non-professional males, 1940-1990. *Research in Race and Ethnic Relations* 8:139-46.
Tomaskovic-Devey, Donald, and Sheryl Skaggs. 1999. An establishment-level test of the statistical discrimination hypothesis. *Work & Occupations* 26:422-45.
Wilson, George. 1997. Pathways to power: Racial differences in the determinants of job authority. *Social Problems* 43:38-54.
Wilson, George, Ian Sakura-Lemessy, and John West. 1999. Reaching the top: Racial differences in mobility paths to upper-tier occupations. *Work & Occupations* 26:165-87.
Wilson, George, and Debra McBrier. 2005. Race and loss of privilege: African American/white differences in the determinants of layoffs from upper-tier occupations. *Sociological Forum* 20:301-21.
Wilson, George, and Deirdre Royster. 1995. Critiquing Wilson's critics: The declining significance of race thesis and the black middle class. *Research in Race and Ethnic Relations* 8:57-75.
Wilson, William. 1978. *The declining significance of race*. Chicago: University of Chicago Press.
———. 1987. *The truly disadvantaged*. Chicago: University of Chicago Press.
———. 1996. *When work disappears*. Cambridge, MA: Harvard University Press.
Wright, Eric Olin. 1997. *Class counts: Class studies in comparative perspective*. New York: Cambridge University Press.
Zubrinski, Camille. 2001. Process of residential segregation and its consequences. In *Urban inequality: Evidence from four cities*, ed. Alice O'Connor, Chris Tilly, and Lawrence Bobo, 217-72. New York: Russell Sage Foundation.

QUICK READ SYNOPSIS

Race, Ethnicity, and Inequality in the U.S. Labor Market: Critical Issues in the New Millennium

Special Editor: GEORGE WILSON
University of Miami

Volume 609, January 2007

Prepared by Herb Fayer, Jerry Lee Foundation

DOI: 10.1177/0002716206297018

Social Closure and Processes of Race/Sex Employment Discrimination

Vincent J. Roscigno, Lisette M. Garcia,
and Donna Bobbitt-Zeher, Ohio State University

Background
While analyses of variations in levels of inequality provide understanding of macro-level sociological outcomes and relations with, for instance, racial competition across neighborhoods or gender segregation at work, they tend to offer less insight into micro-interactional processes that most assuredly play a role in social closure.
- Gaps in wages, organizational power, and employment opportunities have narrowed somewhat, but disparities remain.
- Traditionally, neoeconomic theorizing and status research identify differences in human capital as the principal cause of labor market disadvantages.
  - The assumption is that one's investments, such as education, can increase productive capability and, thus, worth and compensation.
  - A solitary focus on human capital simply overlooks the role of inequality in institutional processes generally, and closure enacted by institutional and dominant group actors that reifies existing stratification hierarchies.
- Sex and race segregation at occupational and workplace levels may be even more influential—the key may be that employers and coworkers may make arbitrary and subjective decisions in hiring, promotion, and firing.

Social Closure	Social closure reflects the process by which collectivities seek to maximize advantage by restricting access and privileges to others. • It often occurs through institutional exclusion and dominant group positioning. • It also exists in everyday interactions through language, supervisory acts, or force, and shows in differential treatment and harassment once employed. • Social closure directs us to an in-depth understanding of the processes through which stratification hierarchies are both defined and maintained.

Racial Discrimination	Racial discrimination and closure processes have multiple costs and can include exclusion, inequalities in material rewards, or potential blocks to mobility.
	• Three elements shape outcomes:
	  ◦ disparate policing of minority workers on the job,
	  ◦ managerial use of particularistic or "soft skill" criteria in employee or prospective employee evaluation, and
	  ◦ ongoing racial hierarchy maintenance in the course of everyday workplace interactions.
	• Harassment isolates minority employees in their workplaces, undermines their capacity to perform their jobs properly, and impacts their sense of dignity in quite meaningful ways.
	  ◦ It may take the form of general taunting, systematic isolation on the job, or neglect of employee needs.

Sex Discrimination	Similar to racial patterns are the how and why women are not hired, are disparately fired, stagnate in terms of mobility, and are harassed with three themes: • gender appropriateness: assumptions built into the organization of work contribute to women's marginalization as well as sex segregation; • dependability, often tied to pregnancy and maternity or the belief that women will put family before work; and • harassment, including that which is explicitly sexual in character.
Conclusion	Social stratification is more than simply a remnant of historical exclusion played out through slowly declining intergenerational disadvantages in, for instance, education, skills, job experience, or wealth. • By virtue of the data that have been employed in this article, it is obvious that human action and agency are part and parcel of social closure and stratification maintenance, creation, and challenge. By default, this implicates organizations and institutions themselves in the inequalities. • As the qualitative materials suggest, human beings actively engage in reifying inequality within organizational environments, and victims of inequality are much more than mere recipients of differential treatment. • Victims, instead, often go through a series of steps to try to counter the inequality they are experiencing, including negotiation, avoidance, confrontation and politically and legally fighting what is unjust. NOTE: There is no reason to believe that the differential treatment we have uncovered does not apply equally to other institutional domains including,

for instance, education, politics, medical care, housing, and legal-judicial processes. The implication of this is that all social interaction—formal and informal, context-specific or not—has the potential to recreate status hierarchies whether or not the parties involved are aware of it.

Discrimination and Desegregation: Equal Opportunity Progress in U.S. Private Sector Workplaces since the Civil Rights Act

Donald Tomaskovic-Devey and Kevin Stainback,
University of Massachusetts–Amherst

Background   This article seeks to evaluate the impact of the extension of the Civil Rights Act to equal opportunity in employment is the central goal:
- the enactment of the equal employment opportunity (EEO) law should not be expected to automatically produce EEO progress by design;
- progress made within private sector employment since 1966; and
- trends in race/ethnic segregation and access to quality employment to illustrate the unevenness of progress toward equal opportunity.

NOTE: Eliminating discrimination will not simply follow from legal change. Organizations are conservative in the sense that they tend to reproduce past behaviors irrespective of the personalities or preferences of their employees.

Employment Segregation   Employment segregation is the product of a series of micro-level mechanisms—prejudice, cognitive bias, statistical discrimination, social closure around desirable employment opportunities, and network-based recruitment.
- While some decisions may be explicitly bigoted in justification, many are the result of more subtle social psychological processes of cognitive bias, stereotyping, and in-group preferences.
- Cultural prejudice as well as the more subtle processes of cognitive bias against minority group members and in favor of whites remain culturally widespread and active at the societal level.

Statistical Discrimination   Statistical discrimination refers to employers using known average differences in competencies between groups to discriminate.
- The employer relies on stereotypes about status group productivity to justify making discriminatory hiring decisions against individuals.

Social Closure   Social closure occurs when opportunities are closed to outsiders and reserved only for members of one's own group.
- Dominant groups keep their monopoly over the most desirable jobs.
- Evidence shows that when women or minorities gain access to managerial jobs it is often supervising other women or minorities.
- Status groups dynamically attempt to preserve their advantages by limiting access to others outside of the status group.

EEO	EEO change is likely to arise when there are significant coercive or normative pressures for change in the workplaces. • Change can be driven by prominent firms changing, coercion by powerful actors, government support, and internal company pressures. • It is fairly clear that EEO law has encouraged the adoption of formalized human resource practices to demonstrate compliance.
Minorities' Limited Gains	Minority employment has made strong gains in the regulated private sector but most of those gains came immediately after the 1964 Civil Rights Act. • Today, more than 50 percent of workers would have to exchange jobs to produce workplaces in which white men were integrated with minority workers and white women. • White women and black women are as segregated as they were in 1966. NOTE: We see a substantial slowdown in the rate of integration of minority men with white men. Among males, Hispanic-white segregation essentially plateaued after 1973. Black-white workplace segregation among males continued to drop, although at a slower rate, through the early 1980s. Among males, Asians remained the most segregated from white males.
Occupational Trends	In occupation employment trends, craft production jobs stand out as highly rewarded, relatively autonomous, and clearly desirable positions. • White males were far and away the most advantaged in access to the most desirable working-class jobs. • White males' access to managerial jobs was uniformly high across the entire post–Civil Rights Act period and has not declined appreciably. • Professional jobs are obvious targets for social closure attempts with black males and females making gains and Hispanic males not gaining, while Asians, especially Asian women, made good gains. NOTE: With the exception of white men, all status groups are most likely to become managers in workplaces when a large population of similar people is employed among nonmanagers.
Findings	The general expectation is that EEO progress will be difficult and uneven. • African American and Hispanic employees are still grossly underrepresented among managerial and professional workers. • Hispanic and black men have achieved better representation among the most desirable blue-collar jobs. • White male privilege still exists in access to desirable blue-collar jobs. • Among professional jobs, we see the promise of the Civil Rights Act realized, with all groups making strong gains. The greatest gains have come in professional employment, in which white women are now overrepresented relative to their overall employment. • White women have made uninterrupted progress except in access to craft production jobs, but white women have become increasingly segregated from black and Hispanic women in the private sector.

Racial Composition of Workgroups and Job Satisfaction among Whites

David J. Maume and Rachel Sebastian,
University of Cincinnati

Background Segregation is a pervasive feature of the labor market, yet more attention is paid to gender than racial segregation. Yet it is at the workplace where intergroup contact is likely to be highest, since whites and minorities are *unlikely* to interact in other settings like neighborhoods, churches, and schools. Furthermore, managing diversity will become increasingly challenging as the workforce becomes more diverse.
- Despite the importance of this relationship, there have been few studies directly testing the effect of workgroup integration on the job attitudes of whites. This study attempts to address this deficiency in the existing literature by using more recent data and estimating a model with a full set of controls.

Organizational Demography The organizational demography perspective posits that workgroup integration negatively affects individual job attitudes, either because whites are biased against minorities or whites perceive minorities to be a threat to their jobs. Some studies showed that attitudes toward coworkers mediate this relationship, however.
- Yet the existing literature relies on older and/or unique samples that may not characterize the typical white worker today, and existing studies often fail to control for important determinants of job attitudes.

Status Composition The status composition perspective also identifies bias as the mechanism by which workgroup heterogeneity affects individual job rewards, although here the bias is located in organizations rather than in individuals.
- When jobs are increasingly held by minorities, the organization *devalues* those jobs in its pay and promotion policies.
- Studies showed that workers in jobs dominated by blacks were less likely to be promoted and had higher turnover rates. Thus, whites in integrated jobs may increasingly believe that they had been placed in jobs that were devalued by their employers, which could account for their dissatisfaction with their jobs.

Controlled Variables The authors make several observations on the effects of the control variables.
- Age and tenure have positive effects on job satisfaction.
- More educated workers have higher standards in what they expect from a job; their current jobs often fail to meet those standards, producing lower levels of job satisfaction.
- Men are less satisfied with their jobs than women.
- Job satisfaction tends to be lower in larger, impersonal, bureaucratic firms.

	NOTE: Those in jobs requiring creativity are more satisfied, as are those who exercise autonomy in deciding what tasks to perform and when to do them. Job satisfaction rises when respondents perceive that their jobs are secure and/or they have a chance to advance in their firms. Workers are less satisfied when they are in high-pressure jobs and/or ones that are physically demanding.
Findings	An important finding is that the size of the minority presence in the workgroup no longer significantly predicts job satisfaction when job characteristics are controlled. • If whites are reluctant to work with minorities, this may not be because of overt racial prejudice, but rather reflects a concern that one is located in a job that is devalued in the eyes of one's employer. • The number of problems with coworkers is the second strongest predictor (negative) of maximum job satisfaction.

Future Studies	One limitation of this study is that it takes into account the *number* of problems with coworkers, but not the *content* of those problems.
	• It is entirely possible that as workgroups become more racially diverse, racial tensions and misunderstandings increase, which produces more conflict with coworkers.
	• To fully investigate, it is necessary to inquire whether race-related conflict increases with minority representation in the workgroup and how this impacts on white attitudes and performance.
	  • If this is the case, it suggests that white prejudice against minority coworkers is persistent and contradicts the notion of a declining significance of race.
	  • If this is *not* the case, however, it suggests that employers need to pay attention to other factors that might affect coworker relations and, by extension, job satisfaction.
	• A priority of future research should be to examine the determinants of managerial decisions to eschew an adversarial stance toward workers in favor of policies that treat them as valued partners in the production process.
	  • Hodson (2004) found that when management treats all workers with dignity and respect, workers are more satisfied with their jobs irrespective of the racial composition of workgroups.

The Use of Field Experiments for Studies of Employment Discrimination: Contributions, Critiques, and Directions for the Future

Devah Pager, Princeton University

Background	Have we solved the problems of racial discrimination or have these acts become too subtle and covert for detection? In this article the author • considers the arguments from recent debates over the contemporary relevance of labor market discrimination,

- provides an introduction to field methods for studying discrimination,
- addresses the primary critiques of the audit methodology and the potential threats to the validity of studies of this kind, and
- considers how we might reconcile evidence from field experiments with the different conclusions from analyses of large-scale survey data.

Debates about Discrimination

The Civil Rights movement brought with it a wave of reform, spurring an unprecedented growth of black upward mobility. These improvements have led some to conclude that discrimination represents merely "the problem of an earlier era." But:
- contemporary forms of discrimination may be subtle and covert, leading to less frequent detection and awareness by the general public;
- debates about the relevance of discrimination have been difficult to resolve, in part because of the challenges in identifying, measuring, and documenting its presence or absence in all but extreme cases; and
- field experiments offer the opportunity to observe discrimination directly.

Conflicting Research

Audit studies, in which equally qualified pairs of job applicants apply to real job openings, provide an opportunity to observe employers' hiring decisions directly.
- Across a range of audit studies, employers show a strong preference for whites over equally qualified minority applicants.
- These results stand in stark contrast to recent research, using statistical techniques, which finds that the majority of the black-white wage gap can be explained by skill differences or other individual deficiencies.

Audit Method Results

How can we account for the substantial evidence of discrimination indicated by the audit results?
- First, the employment relationship is characterized by a number of discrete decisions: hiring, wage setting, promotion, and termination—discrimination may affect all, none, or some of these decisions.
- Discrimination is likely to be most pronounced at early stages of the employment relationship (hiring), when information about the applicant is at a minimum and when the chances of being caught are low.
- It is likewise important also to consider the interdependence between hiring discrimination and wage disparities:
  - Discrimination at the point of hire may lead blacks to spend more time unemployed (excluded from wage estimates).
  - Rejection and hostility in the job search process may lead to discouragement among all but the most motivated and able black workers.
  - If discrimination at the point of hire leads to higher rates of unemployment or nonparticipation among blacks, estimates of racial wage disparities will be biased by the more "select" sample of blacks included among wage earners.

The Future

The author considers several directions for future research.
- First, it would be useful for future research to develop a standardized audit framework that could be replicated across testing sites and over time, similar to the model pursued in recent housing audits.

- Second, the introduction of additional experimental variables (e.g., skill, education, criminal record, etc.) would allow researchers to calibrate the effects of race against other key labor market determinants.
- Finally, additional research should make efforts to empirically map the findings from audit studies onto population surveys of job search and employment patterns.

Conclusion Research on discrimination poses numerous complications, with issues of measurement of central concern.
- Active comparisons across studies can help to shed light on the relative strengths and weaknesses of existing approaches.
- The audit design can provide strong and direct measures of discrimination at the point of hire, a powerful mechanism regulating the wider array of labor market opportunities.
- Future research should extend this focus to include a broader perspective on the employment process, from search decisions to hiring behavior to wages, tenure, and promotion, comparing findings across studies for a more complete picture of discrimination.

Family Background, Race, and Labor Market Inequality

Dalton Conley and Rebecca Glauber,
New York University

Background African American siblings and white siblings look similar in terms of occupational prestige correlations, but African American siblings have much lower correlations in labor market earnings and family income.
- The effect of global family background on African Americans' labor market and socioeconomic outcomes is much weaker than the effect of global family background on whites' outcomes.
- The early stages of careers are characterized by volatility and chance events that suppress the "true" effect of family background on labor market and socioeconomic outcomes.
  - This dynamic is especially pronounced for African Americans, as they lack the necessary resources to insulate themselves from intervening chance events.
- Two questions remain relatively unexplored:
  - Do siblings converge or diverge in labor market and socioeconomic outcomes over the life course?
  - Do siblings from racial groups that putatively differ on the degree of opportunity they enjoy and the level of resources at their command vary with respect to how similar they turn out?

NOTE: The current study makes several important contributions to the literature, specifically by examining life course and race differences in the strength of global family background on socioeconomic outcomes. The study benefits from its use of the Panel Study of Income Dynamics (PSID), in that

QUICK READ SYNOPSIS: RACE, ETHNICITY, AND INEQUALITY 241

	it both allows for the inclusion of sisters and avoids the limitations inherent in a sample that is not nationally representative or includes only young adults. And most important, with the nationally representative PSID, we can examine racial differences in stratification dynamics across the life course.
Sibling Correlations	Given the apparent difficulty in modeling the true impact of family background, in light of shared environmental *and* genetic traits and intersibling effects, what are we to make of sibling correlations? • We can read a sibling correlation as a global effect of family background—environmental and genetic factors—if we assume a model in which offspring are invested in equally (or at least that any favoritism is randomly distributed) and in which siblings have only a mean-regressive effect on each other. 　• We see that they tend to cause each other to be more alike than they would in each other's absence.
New Findings	Building on previous studies, this study reports three new findings. • Family background affects different measures of socioeconomic status differently—siblings are most similar on educational outcomes and less similar on occupational prestige, labor market earnings, and family income. • Siblings converge in outcomes that take longer to stabilize (income and earnings) and remain similar across the life course in outcomes that stabilize early on (education and occupational prestige). • Individual parental investment behavior may shape dynamic stratification trajectories. NOTE: The most important finding this analysis gives rise to is that African American siblings resemble each other less than white siblings, at least on earnings and income, but dramatically converge across the life course.
Other Effects	The authors propose that resource constrained parents may invest unequally in their children, or in a child with the greatest chance of survival and prosperity. • This dynamic may serve as one explanation for the weaker effects of family background on African Americans' socioeconomic outcomes. • The authors think, however, that much more of the reason for these weaker effects lies in institutional constraints: African Americans have fewer resources than whites and they have less means toward protection from negative events that may move individuals off course from their families. • Coupled with recent findings of resource-disadvantaged and younger individuals experiencing greater fluctuations in earnings, this analysis provides some evidence in support of the contention that earlier segments of the life course are volatile and suppress an individual's "true" effect of family background. • The descriptive findings cannot provide the last word on whether institutional or individual mechanisms—or a combination of both—explain life course racial stratification dynamics. • The authors find it most likely that African Americans' socioeconomic outcomes are affected more than whites' across the life course because African Americans lack the resources to protect themselves from the volatility of earlier, intervening chance events.

What Happens to Potential Discouraged? Masculinity Norms and the Contrasting Institutional and Labor Market Experiences of Less Affluent Black and White Men

Deirdre A. Royster, College of William and Mary

Background

This article contrasts less affluent black and white men's educational, labor market, and criminal justice system experiences and elucidates the processes of differentiation that reproduce unequal patterns.
- Less affluent black males pay a disproportionate price for enacting masculinity norms in comparison to white males.
- White boys and men are also presented with more desirable labor market options that are denied their black male counterparts.
- Some black men's angry, immature, and indifferent responses to public authorities earn black boys and men special scorn.
- Black boys' negative experiences in school may foreshadow their eventual labor market difficulties.
- This article suggests that only a complex strategy that requires less affluent black men to resist more constructively, while citizen groups hold institutions more publicly accountable, can enhance the labor market trajectories of black men.

NOTE: In this article, the author analyzes how less affluent black boys and men suffer more severe penalties for their performances of masculinity than white male peers and how contemporary institutional processes discourage less affluent black boys and men more than white male peers.

Institutional Patterns

Three institutional patterns differentiate the labor market prospects of less affluent black and white men:
- educational inequities that underprepare and stigmatize black boys and delay black men's transitions from school to work;
- persistent employer discrimination and black men's severe network disadvantages during job search, hiring, and early job-entry stages; and
- hypersurveillant police practices and unusually severe sentencing patterns that attach a criminal record (or the suspicion of such) to a disproportionately high number of less affluent black men.

NOTE: Preventing black boys and young men from becoming discouraged learners while in school would decrease their chances of becoming discouraged workers in the labor market. Holding employers and police accountable for black men's fair treatment is equally important.

Schooling, Networks, Stigma, and Employment

More successful schooling experiences for black boys and adolescents would help more black men to earn a solid living, but wage and employment rate gaps within each educational level mean that white men would remain ahead.
- Black male students are disproportionately punished in schools, resulting in their being labeled as "troublemakers" and becoming academically disengaged even before reaching high school.

- Even when black male high school students played by the rules, white male students were the beneficiaries of double or relaxed standards in at least three ways:
  - Their distinct hobbies, dress, and initiative in seeking work-study opportunities were not negatively scrutinized as were those of black males.
  - Work-study rules were bent so that they could pursue opportunities before they were officially allowed to do so.
  - Whites were more often offered employment and other meaningful assistance by white male teachers.
- White males are embedded in powerful networks of older white men who are still the primary gatekeepers in blue-collar trades.
- All black men seeking employment, but especially those who are less affluent and who have lower educational preparation, must contend with enduring stereotypes that mark them all as unskilled, nonproductive, and perhaps even dangerous employees.
- As the result of disproportionate surveillance and disparate sentencing patterns, many black men have criminal records, or are suspected of having them, thereby increasing black men's employment difficulties.

NOTE: Identifying and critiquing multiple cultural influences, including the cultures of powerful institutions and their agents, is critical to advancing a workable agenda for assisting black boys and men who experience a differential tolerance among some teachers and employers.

Conclusion Given the high levels of poverty and institutional unfairness that less affluent black boys and adolescents witness and experience, they should resist institutional injustice, but resisting constructively requires guidance, discipline, and eschewing aspects of American masculinity that are incompatible with justice struggles.
- Black working men's culture provides a necessary alternative style of resistance and protest, predicated on a modulated masculinity norm, in which the vulnerable and the weak, rather than being denigrated and abused, are defended and valued.
- Socializing less affluent boys and men to eschew troubling masculinity norms and embrace constructive black resistance models will not work in the absence of a reinvigorated and widespread alternative justice framework that holds institutions accountable.
- Progressive citizen groups should hold local schools accountable for educating black children. (Black girls trail behind their female peers, too.) For parity, they must require schools to maintain data on raced and gendered patterns of achievement, but also patterns of enriched opportunity and punishment allocation.
- Monitoring selection mechanisms and occupancy patterns for the jobs young workers can attain without a college degree is another key site for institutional accountability.
- The figurative and literal deathblow for many less affluent black men is the American prison complex—at multiple levels, from surveillance patterns in neighborhoods to disproportionate numbers of death-penalty sentences, less affluent black men live constantly too close to the devastating threat of incarceration.

Black Underrepresentation in Management across U.S. Labor Markets

Philip N. Cohen, University of North Carolina at Chapel Hill;
and Matt L. Huffman, University of California, Irvine

Background   The primary goal of this article was to investigate the long-standing finding of greater inequality in high-proportion-black labor markets.
- Black underrepresentation in management may be one mechanism underlying the findings.
- The investigation approach has the following features:
  - measuring access to managerial jobs within work establishments, using data from large establishments from the Equal Employment Opportunity Commission;
  - situating establishments in the labor markets in which they operate, with data from the 2000 U.S. Census; and
  - examining whether the racial composition of local labor markets conditions the level of access to management for black workers.

Labor Pools   The study explores large establishments' black managerial composition in the private sector workforce relative to four populations or labor pools.
- It compares managerial representation to the composition of the *entire local workforce*.
- It compares managerial representation to the composition of *managers in the local workforce*.
- A third measure compares managerial representation to the composition of *managers in the same industry of the local workforce*.
- Finally, it compares managerial representation to the composition of *all workers within the establishment*.

Results   Of particular interest is whether these outcomes vary across labor markets as a function of population racial composition. If establishments in labor markets with greater black concentration are more likely to exhibit black underrepresentation in management, that may help explain the persistent finding that racial wage disparities are greater in such labor markets.
- More than half (53 percent) of black workers are found in establishments with significantly lower proportion black managers than workers. About one-third of black workers work in establishments with fewer black managers than would be expected according to the composition of the total local workforce. Six percent of black workers work for establishments with black managerial underrepresentation relative to the pool of all local managers; 4 percent work for establishments with underrepresentation relative to managers in the local industry.
- Our central finding is that black workers are more likely to be underrepresented in management—according to all four measures of underrepresentation—in labor markets with greater proportion black populations.

Conclusion   Taken together, the results are consistent with an interpretation of black-white wage inequality in which inequality results from the actions of managers, and

black managers are less likely to contribute to such inequality. Thus, black underrepresentation in management could be an important mechanism for the pattern of greater inequality found in places with larger black populations.
- Black workers are more likely to find themselves concentrated under the authority of nonrepresentative management structures in labor markets with larger black populations.
- Even though black workers may have a greater absolute presence in higher-status jobs in high-proportion-black areas, they may in fact be subject to increased discrimination in such a context, resulting in stronger race-based social closure processes, and overall lower odds of attaining managerial positions.

Demobilization of the Individualistic Bias: Housing Market Discrimination as a Contributor to Labor Market and Economic Inequality

Gregory D. Squires, George Washington University

Background
Discrimination in the nation's housing markets and residential segregation have contributed to labor market inequalities and economic disparities.
- Housing values are suppressed in minority communities undercutting wealth accumulation by nonwhite families.
- Job growth in the suburbs coupled with the concentration of public housing in central city communities restricts minority access to jobs.
- A range of institutionalized practices by housing providers and public policies by government agencies at all levels have nurtured and exacerbated racial inequalities grounded in traditional stereotypes.
- Powerful interests convince themselves that their privileged positions reflect their own hard work, thus justifying their rewards.
- In this article, a number of policy options offer promise for reducing racial inequities in housing and related economic disparities.

Individualism
A cult of individualism has long dominated life in the United States.
- Successful people credit hard work, self reliance, and intelligence.
- Failures are explained in terms of the absence of these attributes.

NOTE: The individualistic bias pervades explanations of inequality in two mechanisms for the allocation of privilege—labor and housing markets.

Structural Factors
Several structural factors intervene to shape wages and other labor market outcomes.
- The quality and, consequently, prestige, of schooling institutions.
- Wages often depend more on whether jobs are in primary or secondary occupations and industries than employee qualifications.
- Government policies affect earnings as does the presence or absence of union representation.
- Racial stereotyping and intentional discrimination also persist.

	NOTE: The housing patterns and practices noted here contribute to disparities in housing consumption and broader economic inequalities generally. Where different groups of people live, and the homes in which they live, profoundly influence the allocation of rewards in the United States.
House Values	Perhaps the most explicit signals of housing inequality are homeownership rates and the value of homes families own. • The values of homes owned by different groups varies dramatically. • Disparities are also reflected in who owns the highest-priced homes. • More telling is the fact that appreciation in home values is undercut by the presence of other minorities, and particularly African Americans. • Housing inequities are major contributors to general wealth inequalities.
Education	Educational resources reflect the same inequities. • Public schools have become even more segregated in recent years. • Given the reliance on property taxes to fund public education, residential segregation leads to large disparities in the resources for schools in white and nonwhite communities.
Employment	The most immediate determinant of the quality of life in the United States—economic and otherwise—is probably one's location in the labor market. • Racial minorities, and particularly African Americans, have long been concentrated in economically declining city neighborhoods while the fastest job growth has been in mostly white suburban communities. • Consequently, minorities are less likely to hear about job openings, are far less likely to own cars. Public transportation does not serve urban to suburban commuters well for interviews and commuting.
Housing Segregation	Housing segregation limits opportunities for informal social interaction between whites and nonwhites—with relatively few white neighbors, minorities have fewer opportunities to demonstrate to potential employers and business partners the job-related skills neighbors often display to each other. • In many ways, racial discrimination and segregation in the nation's housing markets undercut the ability of, and opportunity for, racial and ethnic minorities to compete in the labor market, accumulate economic and other assets, and access virtually all of the rewards presumably available to those individuals who "play by the rules."
Policy Options	Below is a list of recommended policy options. • A starting point is traditional law enforcement of Civil Rights Acts prohibiting discrimination in all housing related services. • Government can use leverage provided by the Fair Housing Act. • Mobility programs that have enabled poor black families to move to integrated settings have demonstrated positive results. • If exclusionary zoning laws have been central for perpetuating racial segregation, inclusionary laws constitute a critical remedy. • Financial literacy programs can turn residents of underserved communities into informed housing consumers, attractive employees, and citizens who can better serve their own economic interests.

Racialized Life-Chance Opportunities across the Class Structure: The Case of African Americans

George Wilson, University of Miami

Background
Considerations of how socioeconomic outcomes are racialized within discrete class categories have been neglected in assessing the race/class determinants of life-chance opportunities of African Americans.
- This article synthesizes findings from recent sociological research concerning how segregation in two institutional spheres, residence and employment, produce racialization at two class levels: among the impoverished and the middle class.
- It shows that segregation plays a significant role in producing racial inequality at both class levels, though it exerts different influences across class categories that emerge as critical underpinnings of African Americans' inferior life-chance opportunities,
  - at the impoverished level, in residential segregation; and
  - at the middle-class level, in employment segregation.
- Sociologists have marshaled considerable empirical support for the notion that in recent decades the effects of social class have increased in accounting for the life-chance opportunities of African Americans.
  - These findings, however, should not preclude documenting the multitude of ways in which life-chance opportunities are simultaneously "racialized."
  - We need to document the causes of racial inequality among incumbents who occupy similar positions—at least in title—in the American class structure.

Two-Pronged Thesis
Overall, this examination produces a two-pronged thesis.
- First, a common set of causal underpinnings accounts for racialization at both the impoverished and middle-class levels: segregation by race in the these spheres is a crucial source of the inferior life-chance opportunities of African Americans, relative to white class peers.
- The manner in which segregation accounts for racialization of socioeconomic outcomes has implications regarding how to theorize about racial stratification.

Class Structure
Variation in life-chance opportunities among African American and white class peers has, for at least two reasons, received far less attention.
- First, the sheer magnitude of positional differences between African Americans and whites has placed a premium on producing theories of racial stratification to explain it.
- Second, prominent theories of social stratification have not provided an impetus for sociologists to explore the possibility of race-based differences among incumbents in a similar class position.

The Poor	A first body of research challenges the notion that African Americans and whites in poverty face a similar set of socioeconomic prospects.
• Research documents systematic variation in life-chance opportunities along racial lines at the low end of the American class structure.
• Relevant are studies that typically delineate poverty from nonimpoverished status on the basis of income or labor market status.
Middle Class	Sociological research has also documented race-based differences in life-chance opportunities at the relatively privileged middle-class level.
• African Americans have increased representation in occupationally based positions typically used to define the middle class, professionals, managers, and administrators, at a more rapid rate than whites.
• To combat discrimination in the private sector, the government has historically provided a "niche" for African Americans within the middle-class job structure.
• In predominantly white-owned and -managed firms in the private sector, African Americans perform work-based functions that are tied into satisfying the consumer needs of minority customers/clients.
• Restricted access to integrated job networks precludes African Americans from demonstrating to employers the informal criteria such as loyalty, trustworthiness, and leadership potential that are important in structuring employment evaluations.
• Segregation in the residential sphere also helps to account for racialization of socioeconomic outcomes at the middle class level.
Conclusion	A review of the dynamics of racialization in this article contributes to the debate about the relative effects of race and social class in explaining life-chance opportunities among African Americans in the post–civil rights era.
• Social class tends to play a crucial role in structuring the basic parameters of socioeconomic standing and trajectories.
• Race restricts attainments among African Americans, relative to whites, thereby establishing a link in life-chance opportunities with other African Americans, irrespective of class status.
• There is not a strong basis for concluding that the racialized outcomes at the impoverished and middle-class levels will be reduced soon.
• More research is needed to fill out our understanding of the extent to which patterns of segregation in both the residential and employment spheres explain racialization of socioeconomic outcomes across the American class structure.

Weeks-Townsend Memorial Library
Union College
Barbourville, KY 40906